The Blackface Minstrel
Show in Mass Media

The Blackface Minstrel Show in Mass Media

20th Century Performances on Radio, Records, Film and Television

TIM BROOKS

McFarland & Company, Inc., Publishers
Jefferson, North Carolina

This book has undergone peer review.

ISBN (print) 978-1-4766-7676-0
ISBN (ebook) 978-1-4766-3730-3

LIBRARY OF CONGRESS AND BRITISH LIBRARY
CATALOGUING DATA ARE AVAILABLE

© 2020 Tim Brooks. All rights reserved

No part of this book may be reproduced or transmitted in any form or by any means, electronic or mechanical, including photocopying or recording, or by any information storage and retrieval system, without permission in writing from the publisher.

Front cover: Al Jolson in the 1927 film *The Jazz Singer*
(Warner Bros. Pictures/Photofest)

Printed in the United States of America

*McFarland & Company, Inc., Publishers
Box 611, Jefferson, North Carolina 28640
www.mcfarlandpub.com*

Acknowledgments

Researching a sprawling historical subject such as this (especially the parts that have not previously been explored) is a long and winding road. Along the way, one is helped by many friends and strangers. This has been a fascinating journey for me, and I would be remiss if I did not express my great appreciation to the friends, strangers, and strangers-who-have-become-friends who contributed so willingly over the past few years to the book you are holding. They helped in many ways to flesh out my (and hopefully your) understanding of that strange American phenomenon known as the minstrel show, sharing documents, recordings, films, broadcasts and other materials, as well as offering advice.

A number of institutions opened their collections to me, and a number of individuals proved helpful in navigating the wealth of material available. At the Library of Congress, there were George Willeman, Karen Fishman, Matt Barton, and Gregory Lukow; at the New York Public Library for the Performing Arts, Jonathan Hiam and Danielle Cordovez; at the Paley Center for Media, Ron Simon; at the Thomas Edison National Historic Park, Gerald Fabris; and at CBS-TV, the ever helpful and much-missed John Behrens.

Among the fellow scholars and collectors who offered a helping hand were Frank Andrews, Bob Brimson, Sam Brylawski, Paul Charosh, Bill Dean-Myatt, Allen Debus, Michael Devecka, Patrick Feaster, Paul Gambaccini, David Giovannoni, J. David Goldin, John Graziano, Ron Hutchinson, Peter T. Kiefer, Bill Klinger, Allen Koenigsberg, Richard Markow, Rich Martin and Meagan Hennessey, Jack Raymond, Deane Root, Morton J. Savada, Anthony Slide, Merle Sprinzen, and Jonas Westover. During my many years of assembling an extensive collection of original minstrel recordings on 78-rpm discs and cylinders (since no one else had one), I have met many fine collectors and dealers, and I regret that I don't now have the names of them all. Finally, comments by the anonymous manuscript readers were helpful.

To the Association for Recorded Sound Collections and the Society for American Music, which allowed me to give presentations at their conferences on this subject and benefit from knowledgeable audience reactions, I tender my thanks.

At McFarland, Senior Acquisitions Editor Gary Mitchem expertly shepherded this book into print.

To everyone mentioned here (and all those whom I cannot recall), a sincere thank you. And now the curtain rises.

Table of Contents

Acknowledgments v

Preface 1

1. The Origins of Blackface Minstrelsy 7
2. The Minstrel Show on Records 32
3. The Minstrel Show on Radio 95
4. The Minstrel Show in Motion Pictures 138
5. The Minstrel Show on Television 178
6. Epilogue and Conclusions 197

Appendix 1. Prominent Minstrel Troupes Active after 1890 207
Appendix 2. Discography of Minstrel Recordings 214
Appendix 3. Early Recording Artists with Minstrel Experience 250
Chapter Notes 255
Bibliography 265
Index 269

Preface

Understanding the Minstrel Show

Much has been written about the origins of the minstrel show. There has also been much written about what it meant, and how minstrelsy, which began in the 1840s, reflected the state of American race relations at the time. These studies assume, and in some cases explicitly state, that the minstrel show died out as professional entertainment by the end of the 19th century, surviving only in local amateur productions for a number of years thereafter. In other words, it was part of another era, not our own.

But it did not die. This book explores the largely untold story of the *second* 50-plus years of the minstrel show, years that brought it into media that we know today—radio, records, motion pictures and television. It will explore how minstrelsy changed, how it was able to not only survive but also thrive for so long in a more modern America, and what finally brought about its sudden banishment. What turned it, abruptly, from a beloved part of American history into the bête noire that it is today, and when did that happen?

I worked for many years in the television industry and have long been interested in its history (and that of modern media generally). I became curious about the subject of minstrelsy while working on an earlier book, *Lost Sounds: Blacks and the Birth of the Recording Industry*, which focused on pioneering black artists during the period from 1890 to 1919. Poring through original newspapers (both white and African American) and other resources of the time, I noticed many references to the minstrel show as a living, contemporary form of professional entertainment. As a longtime researcher of mass media, I was aware that minstrel shows turned up in television, records, radio and motion pictures as well. While researching additional books about the history of the recording industry, I assembled a large, unique collection of "minstrel first part" recordings, which are audio recreations of the opening of a minstrel show, a type of recording that was very popular from the 1890s to the 1910s, though very little has been written about them. I also tracked down many films, TV kinescopes and recordings of radio shows.

Films, and especially sound recordings, have been virtually ignored by print-oriented scholars in studies of minstrelsy, and one goal of this book is to show why they are important. Reference to aural resources can lead, I believe, to a deeper understanding of what a minstrel show was and why, for better or worse, the genre had such appeal.

I wanted to know how all these pieces fit together. Judging from the evidence of contemporary sources, the professional minstrel show was anything but dead in the early

1900s. Further research revealed that it was even more prevalent during the first half of the 20th century than I had imagined. The purpose of this book is not to endorse the minstrel show but to understand it—and why it lasted so long.

The Peculiar Entertainment

Unfortunately, the overwhelming academic focus on minstrelsy's origins freezes our understanding of what a minstrel show was. It limits that understanding to the era of slavery and the years that immediately followed.

It may be uncomfortable to admit, but the minstrel show clearly evolved over time. It was not in 1943 what it had been in 1843. While the structure was familiar, the content was not, and that is the first clue to its surprising longevity. Some—though certainly not all—of the aspects that we find offensive today, such as dialect and blackface, were toned down or eliminated over time, as were the racially disparaging songs and jokes of earlier years. In later years, the minstrel tradition represented both an exercise in nostalgia and contemporary entertainment. Tradition was represented by the minstrel show structure, an old and honored form of entertainment that had been enjoyed by multiple generations. Yet the songs that were sung and the jokes that were told were often very up to date. Many were about human foibles to which anyone could relate.

Another dynamic, one that we can recognize from our own time, helped sustain the professional minstrel show's mass popularity. There is a synergy between what we are exposed to every day in the media and what is considered acceptable. If the media tell us something is OK, it must be OK. During the 1920s, 1930s, and 1940s, minstrel shows were commonplace in mass media, and there was no widespread objection to them, not even from African Americans or leadership groups such as the National Association for the Advancement of Colored People (NAACP). As long as the more egregious aspects of earlier years were downplayed, the shows were portrayed as unobjectionable. Just as important, even in this relatively progressive era, social and political leaders accepted minstrel shows. For example, President Franklin D. Roosevelt apparently saw no problem in attending a minstrel show put on by the children of Warm Springs, Georgia.

This fact, incidentally, should be a warning regarding what is considered acceptable in our own time. If the media, and social leaders, tell us that something is acceptable (or unacceptable), does that mean that it is? How do we avoid groupthink?

Considering the minstrel show's widespread endorsement and one-hundred-plus-year history, the end came quite suddenly during just a few years in the late 1940s and early 1950s. Social attitudes were changing. The loyalty of African American soldiers in World War II, as well as other factors, had begun to awaken many white Americans to the injustices of the Jim Crow system, and even though minstrel shows were not as explicitly demeaning as they had once been, they still mocked a vulnerable minority and were a reminder of an earlier, crueler time.

In addition, control of the media, particularly the broadcast media, had become very concentrated. The networks, dependent on the support of advertisers, were highly sensitive to advertiser pressure, and advertisers, in turn, wanted to avoid anything controversial. The NAACP and other organizations, with the backing of the liberal Truman administration, became active in their opposition to the minstrel show format, and once they realized that they could maximize their effectiveness by concentrating their fire on the limited number of targets in the broadcast media, and scaring off their advertisers, the war was over.[1]

The old-fashioned American minstrel show, which was widely considered acceptable just 10 years earlier, was suddenly and permanently driven from the air.

How It Began

From its beginnings, the minstrel show was a distinctively American form of entertainment. Many authors have reflected on its seminal importance to the country's emerging culture, and how it influenced so much that would come later.

"Blackface minstrelsy is now recognized as America's first original contribution to world theatre.... America's first popular mass entertainment" (Annemarie Bean et al., *Inside the Minstrel Mask*)

"The first formal public acknowledgment by whites of black culture" (Eric Lott, *Love & Theft*)

"Minstrelsy was the first commercially successful synthesis of the disparate cultural elements in the history of 'American' popular culture" (William Mahar, *Behind the Burnt Cork Mask*)

"For the first time in the United States, a national art culture, a frame of reference that everyone understood" (Greil Marcus in *Love & Theft*)

"America's first cultural export" (Nick Tosches, *Where Dead Voices Gather*)

"The first truly American form of mass entertainment" (John Strausbaugh, *Black Like You*)[2]

This book describes how minstrelsy evolved over the years, and particularly how it moved into (and, in fact, thrived in) 20th-century mass media. This propagation into the new media began with sound recordings in the 1890s and continued during the massive spread of radio in the 1920s, sound motion pictures in the 1930s, and ultimately television in the late 1940s. Each of these media will receive its own chapter. Minstrelsy in Britain is covered at the end of each chapter, because Britain is the only other country in the world that had its own long and vibrant history with professional minstrelsy, both on stage and in media. The reasons behind this phenomenon are fascinating.

Some of the performers involved are famous. They include Judy Garland and Mickey Rooney singing and mugging their way through a big-screen minstrel show, Bing Crosby crooning a love ballad in blackface, Ed Sullivan staging a full-scale minstrel show on CBS-TV, Elvis Presley performing in a high school minstrel show, and, of course, Al Jolson. Some figures, though once well known, are forgotten today. Have you ever heard of young Len Spencer, who brought minstrelsy into the first modern mass medium—namely, recording? Or young Dailey Paskman, who planted it firmly in broadcasting?

First, let's get some terms straight. *Minstrelsy*, as used in this book, refers to a style of entertainment originating in the United States in the 19th century. Obviously there were minstrels in medieval times, who were generally solo court entertainers, and the term was no doubt borrowed from them, but here we are concerned with the "modern" type.[3] The *minstrel show* was a structured entertainment, first performed in the United States in the 1840s, bringing together groups of these entertainers. Blackface (or, more broadly, racial imitation) is a much larger subject that overlaps with the minstrel show but is not the same thing. Radio's *Amos 'n' Andy*, for example, represented racial imitation but was not a minstrel show.[4] The broader subject of blackface will be dealt with tangentially, as appropriate.

Blackface minstrelsy was minstrelsy performed by white performers in black makeup, usually burnt cork. *Black minstrelsy*, as used in this book, was performed by African Americans, who might or might not apply blackface to heighten or exaggerate their natural skin tones. African American (and mixed-race) troupes became popular after the Civil War and endured until the end of the minstrel show form itself. These troupes provided the first important entree for blacks into show business and, while never as widespread as white troupes, were accepted alongside their white contemporaries.

I will not use the contemporary term *nigger minstrel*—which usually meant whites in blackface—as it is offensive and unnecessary today.

Given its standardized opening, the minstrel show might appear to have a rather rigid format, but there was in fact a good deal of variation over its long history. All of the participants might wear blackface, or only some of them might (usually the endmen). In some late cases, nobody did. Black dialect was also a defining characteristic of minstrelsy, although that, too, was jettisoned in some late cases.

Although minstrelsy is considered racist today—and indeed it was—the minstrel show was not only about race. It was a very lively and irreverent form of comic entertainment that mocked practically everyone, including ethnic and immigrant groups, the ruling elite, politicians, social climbers, urban and rural folks, northerners, southerners and westerners. In a very un–politically correct era, it was the *Saturday Night Live* of its time. Like all comedy, it singled out and amplified the most extreme characteristics (whether true or false) of each group. The idea that it (or *Saturday Night Live*, for that matter) might provide a "dignified, respectful" portrait of any of its targets, as some modern critics seem to demand, was of course preposterous, the opposite of comedy.

That said, the principal comedians in a minstrel show posed as lower-class African Americans, using blackface and dialect. Therein lies the reason for its eventual banishment from popular culture, a long and contentious process that will be explored in the following pages.

A great deal of academic literature has been published during the past 50 years about minstrelsy, some of it descriptive but much of it interpretive. Scholars are constantly arguing with each other about "what it all meant"—and, believe me, there are lots of opinions on that. Virtually all of this literature deals with the early days of minstrelsy, in the 1840s and 1850s, or even periods before that. Some of the scholarship acknowledges the enormous growth in the minstrel field during the immediate post–Civil War period, but few seem to be interested in what happened after that, in the late 19th and 20th centuries. In addition, an inordinate amount of study has focused on black minstrelsy, as opposed to blackface (white) minstrelsy, which was a much larger field. It has been surprisingly difficult to gather accurate information about white minstrels and their shows in the later years of minstrelsy. The best book on white performers of these later years is still Edward L. Rice's *Monarchs of Minstrelsy*, published more than one hundred years ago in 1911. Where are the modern scholars of this field?

Although this book focuses more on description than interpretation, a word should be said about the latter. Any interpretation of the past must confront the conflict between what might be called *presentism* and *historicism*. Do we judge the actions of those in the past according to our values and conventions (presentism) or in the context of their own time (historicism)? Every era has its progressives and regressives, along with its mainstream, but all work within the morals and values of their time. An excessive reliance on presentism distorts history. If we are to understand the minstrel show, I believe, we must take both of these viewpoints into account.

For those who are interested in learning more about minstrelsy as it emerged in the 19th century, the foundational text is Robert C. Toll's *Blacking Up: The Minstrel Show in Nineteenth Century America* (1974). Other recommended books on this era include Annemarie Bean et al., *Inside the Minstrel Mask* (1996); W.T. Lhamon, Jr., *Raising Cain* (1998); William J. Mahar, *Behind the Burnt Cork Mask* (1999); and Hans Nathan, *Dan Emmett and the Rise of Early Negro Minstrelsy* (1962). Dale Cockrell's well-regarded *Demons of Disorder* (1997) deals with the period leading up to the introduction of the minstrel show in 1843. Eric Lott's frequently cited *Love & Theft* (1993) is a highly opinionated interpretation of the meaning of the minstrel show, as is Katrina Dyonne Thompson's more recent *Ring Shout, Wheel About: The Racial Politics of Music and Dance in North American Slavery* (2014). For those interested in the evolution of minstrelsy in Britain, the basic text is Michael Pickering's *Blackface Minstrelsy in Britain* (2008).

Details on all of these books, and many more, may be found in the bibliography of this volume. An even more extensive bibliography may be found online at http://burntcorkthebook.com/further-research/basic-minstrel-bibliography/.

One thing missing from nearly all of these books is any sense of minstrel routines as *humor*. Some read like they were written by dour academics picking apart the corpse of a joke, looking for Deep Meaning. Missing from the printed page is the entire aural experience—the laughter, the upbeat music, the big grins, and the raucous camaraderie that characterized virtually every minstrel performance. Unfortunately, I cannot provide a soundtrack for this book, but I have transcribed many of the jokes and routines and hope that while reading them you can imagine the noisy, comic environment in which they were delivered. Humor in the 19th and early 20th centuries was, of course, different from what it is now—full of "corny" puns, wordplay, and mockery that today seems cruel, as well as references that modern readers might not understand—and that has to be taken into account. But I hope you can put yourself into your own little time machine and try to "hear" these routines. If you seek out films or recordings, listen to a whole performance—not someone's carefully edited clips.

Why weren't these shows more widely recognized as offensive at the time? In part, it may have been because, surprisingly, even the African American community was deeply divided on the subject. Blacks had their own minstrel shows starting in the late 19th century, and in the 20th, every time there were complaints about a show, other members of the black community would defend it. Examples included radio's *Amos 'n' Andy* in 1931, as well as TV's *American Minstrels* in 1949 and *The Ed Sullivan Show* in 1953. I will explore those controversies (and others) in subsequent chapters.

In summary, it is not true, as some have maintained, that minstrelsy died out as professional entertainment in the first half of the 20th century. I hope to show that during that entire period the minstrel show was prominent in mass media and professional performance, granting it a stamp of respectability that made it an acceptable form of entertainment for amateurs to perform as well. I will also explore how it was finally driven out of the mass media halfway through the 20th century, as well as how we see its echoes right up to the present day.

1

The Origins of Blackface Minstrelsy

Before we explore minstrelsy in the 20th century, we need to briefly sketch how it developed in the previous century. In 1820, if a middle-class American decided to step out on a pleasant evening and seek some entertainment, most of the choices would probably have come from Britain. The United States in its early years remained closely tied to Britain, in culture as well as in trade and customs. High culture was Shakespeare; low culture was English drinking songs. Even the song that would eventually become the national anthem, "The Star-Spangled Banner," borrowed its melody from an English drinking song: "To Anacreon in Heaven."

After the War of 1812, in which the new nation fought the mighty British Empire to a stalemate, there was surge in patriotism in the United States and an increasing desire on the part of ordinary Americans to develop a culture of their own. They wanted it to reflect American values of independence and individualism, as opposed to the rigid social hierarchies of Europe. It would also need to embody the boundless optimism of a people eager to expand across a vast, underpopulated continent. Concurrently, there was a rise in political populism, bringing Tennesseean Andrew Jackson to the presidency in 1829 and ending the dominance of that office by the eastern elite. Jackson, known as "the people's president," celebrated his election by opening the Executive Mansion to the public, with ordinary people invading the grounds, trampling on the fine carpets and breaking dishes and crockery. Eight years later, Jackson was succeeded by his ally Martin Van Buren.

Distinctively American heroes began to emerge in story and song. Among them were frontiersman Natty Bumppo (1820s), rough-hewn river boatman Mike Fink (1820s), and soldier/adventurer Davy Crockett (1830s). In 1826, James Hackett promoted the crafty Yankee character, Brother Jonathan.

A distinctive part of the American social fabric, of course, was the African American population—some slave, some free. White actors appearing in blackface became relatively common in the 1820s and 1830s. Chris Matthews, an Englishman visiting America, observed African Americans and incorporated his characterizations of them into plays. His use of the song "Possum Up a Gum Tree" has been cited as the first certain example of a white man using black material in a blackface act.[1] In 1828, Thomas "Daddy" Rice introduced his song and dance "Jump Jim Crow," which became a sensation.

> Wheel about and turn about and do jis so,
> Eb'ry time I wheel about I jump Jim Crow.

Soon after that, George Dixon introduced a song about a free black dandy, "Zip Coon," which rivaled Rice's work in popularity. The tune is known today as "Turkey in the Straw."[2]

The "Big Bang" of Minstrelsy

Rice, Dixon and others like them were individual acts. By the early 1840s, audiences were ready for a full evening's entertainment reflecting black culture—or at least black culture as whites imagined it. The country had been through a punishing economic depression in the late 1830s and early 1840s (largely the result of Jackson's misguided policies), and it needed some cheering up.

The origin of the minstrel show—the "Big Bang" of minstrelsy, as it were—is often dated rather precisely to the evening of February 6, 1843, at the Bowery Amphitheatre in New York City. On that night, four out-of-work blackface performers (Dan Emmett, Billy Whitlock, Dick Pelham and Frank Brower) took the stage as a group, calling themselves "The Virginia Minstrels," and sat in a semi-circle trading jokes and songs. Emmett played the fiddle, Whitlock the banjo, Pelham the tambourine, and Brower bones played like castanets. In their repertoire was "Old Dan Tucker" and two sketches: "Dan Tucker on Horseback" and a mock love scene called "The Serenade."[3]

The Virginia Minstrels did not last long, breaking up in less than a year, but their sensational success lead to a huge wave of imitators. Chief among these were the Christy Minstrels, who started in upstate New York, reached New York City in 1846, and played there to great success for 10 years. The leader of the troupe was Edwin P. Christy, but the acknowledged star was Christy's stepson, dancer and principal comedian George Harrington, who adopted the stage name "George Christy."

Edwin Christy (1815–1862) was instrumental in developing the basic structure of the classical minstrel show.[4] Christy was a Barnum-like showman, and he relentlessly promoted the new form of entertainment. There were three acts. In the first act, called "Minstrel First Part," the entire cast appeared on stage, standing in a semi-circle with a

The first minstrel troupes were small and did not have interlocutors. The endmen (Tambo and Bones) seem to have been present from the start, however.

Advertising often depicted exaggerated poses, to capture the energy of a minstrel show, and also stereotypical facial characteristics. *Source: Harvard Theatre Collection*

master of ceremonies (or "interlocutor") in the middle. Following a lively introductory overture, the interlocutor would call out, "Gentlemen, be seated!" The principal comedians (or endmen), typically called Tambo and Bones after their instruments (tambourine and castanet bones), were seated on the ends and traded jokes and puns with each other and with the pompous interlocutor. Others could join in or be called on by the interlocutor to come forward to present songs and dances. Tambo and Bones, and often all the participants (except perhaps the interlocutor), were white men in blackface. In the early years, the performers were usually dressed in rough, lower-class clothing, though soon, in a play for respectability, a kind of exaggerated tuxedo-like minstrel costume evolved.

Act 2 was called the olio and consisted of a series of standalone acts, similar to the later vaudeville show, permitting a great deal of variety to be incorporated into the performance. These acts could be singers, dancers, comedians, acrobats, instrumentalists, or virtually any other specialty (and not necessarily in blackface). Act 3, the "End Piece," was an extended sketch or parody of a popular play or event.

Although Edwin Christy died in 1862, his name lived on as synonymous with minstrelsy. Many later troupes styled themselves as "Christy Minstrels," especially in England (which Christy himself never visited). Some recording groups from the early 1900s called themselves Christy Minstrels, and Christy was portrayed several times in motion pictures,

Christy's Minstrels set the early standard. Note that minstrel clothing was already becoming more respectable by 1847.

usually interacting with Stephen Foster. In the 1960s, a new and quite popular folk vocal group paid tribute to him with the name "The New Christy Minstrels."

Prior to the Civil War, minstrel troupes were small, white, and all male (the women who appeared in sketches—typically mammies or wenches—were played by men in drag). Typically there were four to eight performers, sometimes with a separate band.[5]

The content of minstrel shows is much misunderstood. The principal jokesters in a minstrel show wore blackface, spoke in fractured English, and presented a picture of African Americans that is understandably considered offensive today. However, there were also jokes at the expense of virtually every other group—country hicks, city swells, various immigrant/ethnic groups, politicians, and aristocrats. The minstrel show was middle- and lower-class America making fun of pretension and cultural differences no matter where they appeared in society. Minstrels were equal opportunity offenders. If you lived in America in the 1840s, you needed to have a thick skin, regardless of your station in life.

Blackface is sometimes referred to as "the minstrel mask." It was indeed a mask, much like that of a clown (clowns in circus makeup sometimes appeared in minstrel shows as well). Often exaggerated, with white or red around the lips and eyes, and dark black elsewhere on the face and neck, the makeup signaled to the audience that this was a cartoon, not a real person on the stage doing and saying silly things. It also provided a shield for some performers, emboldening them to do or say otherwise unacceptable things, because it "wasn't really them." Blackface was sometimes used as a plot device in sketches and stories to hide the identity of a performer, so that an audience member would not realize that a person they saw later (without makeup) was in fact the same person who had been on stage earlier in makeup.

Some later writers speculated that audiences might not have realized that the performers were not real African Americans, but this theory seems unlikely. Sheet music and programs often showed the stars without makeup (or with *and* without makeup) to reassure the audience. One minstrel joke ran as follows:

> ENDMAN: "Why am I like a young widow?"
> INTERLOCUTOR: "Why are you like a young widow?"
> ENDMAN: "Because I do not stay long in black!"[6]

Music was a big part of the minstrel show, and from the very beginning the shows emphasized current popular songs. An analysis of more than 150 playbills from the first 10 years of the minstrel stage reveals that the most performed songs were all hits of the day, now mostly forgotten, especially the lively "Miss Lucy Long," "Old Dan Tucker," "Stop Dat Knocking," and "Railroad Overture" (railroads were relatively new at the time).[7]

Christy's longevity stemmed in part from his alliance with popular songwriter Stephen Foster, with whom he signed an exclusive deal (in 1851) to feature Foster's songs. Christy even paid Foster to let him take credit for composing "Old Folks at Home." Other Foster hits featured in Christy's shows included "Oh! Susanna" (1848), "Nelly Was a Lady" (1849), "Camptown Races" (1850), "Ring de Banjo" (1851), "Massa's in the Cold, Cold Ground" (1852), "My Old Kentucky Home" (1853), "Old Dog Tray" (1853), "Jeanie with the Light Brown Hair" (1854), "Hard Times Come Again No More" (1855), and "Old Black Joe" (1860). Curiously, although Foster's songs are now the best-remembered songs of this era, they turn up infrequently in minstrel show programs or songbooks of the period.[8]

The minstrel show, as originated by Dan Emmett's Virginia Minstrels and codified by Christy and others, did not remain static but evolved over time. As the national debate over slavery intensified in the 1850s, minstrel portrayals of blacks, which had been nuanced and often ambivalent toward slavery (recognizing its cruelty), became much more pro-slavery. Portrayals coalesced into two stereotypes: the contented slave enjoying happy times down on the old plantation, and the unhappiness of slaves who had become free but longed to go home to their benevolent "massa." In addition, there was mockery of the northern free black, who was usually portrayed as a dandy.

If anything, these attitudes hardened following the publication of Harriet Beecher Stowe's sensational anti-slavery novel *Uncle Tom's Cabin* in 1852. The book was a runaway best seller, possibly the second-best-selling book of the entire 19th century (after the Bible). It was also furiously controversial, with theatrical versions that were both pro- and anti-slavery and at least 14 rebuttal novels. Minstrels generally mocked the novel, as well as Mrs. Stowe herself. The novel's subtitle, "Life Among the Lowly," became "Life Among the Happy" in a Christy sketch. Sanford's New Orleans Minstrels called their version "Happy Uncle Tom's Cabin."[9]

Civil War and the Postwar Boom

When the Civil War broke out in 1861, war-related songs and sketches dominated the minstrel shows. Most minstrel troupes were based in the North, and at first the

African American minstrels entertaining Union soldiers during the Civil War.

attitude was flag-waving support of the Union, which later turned to sorrow over the extensive loss of life (e.g., "When This Cruel War Is Over"). This change did not represent a basic shift in position on slavery, however. Abolitionists were lambasted for "causing" the war, and black troops were mocked.

Bear in mind, however, that no matter how serious we may be about the "meaning" of minstrelsy, or its racial or political dimensions, to audiences at the time the lively, raucous shows were never about seriously discussing anything. Their appeal lay in a perceived image of "good, clean entertainment, music, and fun."

Major changes took place in the structure and tone of minstrel shows after the war. Before the war, most troupes had been relatively small and geographically limited. Many, like Christy in New York and Carncross in Philadelphia, stayed put in one city—even in one theater—for years, constantly changing their material to remain fresh. After the war, however, touring became the norm, with troupes appearing from coast to coast, emphasizing stars and unique productions.

Facing competition from spectacular stage productions such as the sprawling musical comedy *The Black Crook*, which revolutionized stage entertainment in 1866–1867,

After the Civil War, troupes became much larger and their shows more elaborate. Here Haverly's Minstrels (in whiteface) march up the steps of the Capitol for the inauguration of President James A. Garfield in 1881.

minstrel shows introduced their own "big productions," with 20–40 performers on stage and elaborate third-act afterpieces. They often traveled in custom railroad cars, not so much for luxury as for practicality with their large casts and considerable stage equipment.

Pioneers of the big minstrel show wave of the 1870s–1880s were J.H. Haverly ("40—Count 'Em—40!") and Primrose and West. Some entrepreneurs emphasized this new type of show with extravagant names like Mastodon Minstrels, Mammoth Minstrels, Megetharians, and Giganteans. Songs continued to be current popular hits (Stephen Foster was phased out), and sketches were often about contemporary events.[10]

In 1891, the theatrical newspaper the *Clipper* commented on how the portrayal of blacks was changing as well:

> The Southern darkey of ten years ago is a thing of the past. It is common nowadays for a minstrel soloist to sing an Irish ballad, while the genuine colored man's dialect is very seldom heard. A careful perusal of the past few years' records of minstrelsy will show that class of entertainment is changing. Today thousands of dollars are spent on gorgeous stage settings and costumes. The performers appear in spangles and tights, court wigs and gowns.[11]

There were attempts to broaden the minstrel show in other ways. Women had never been part of the casts in the pre-war years, but in the 1870s female troupes began to test the waters, though not too successfully. One of the principal female companies was

This 1877 poster shows all the principal elements of a minstrel extravaganza, with the (white) proprietor prominently featured at the bottom.

Madame Rentz's Female Minstrels, which emphasized pulchritude and soon morphed into a burlesque company (traditional minstrelsy had always been "clean").

Far more dramatic was the spread of black troupes, whose African American performers emphasized that they were the "real thing," offering more authentic portrayals of the Old South. These early black troupes generally did not use blackface, except for the endmen, who retained it as a mask. Most of the black troupes were run by white managers (with a few exceptions), and they still traded in darky stereotypes that are offensive to modern eyes and ears. But they toned down the overt racism of earlier all-white troupes and, more important, provided the first major entree into show business for large numbers of African Americans. Some became major stars and were paid commensurately. This development would have been virtually impossible before the Civil War. It was the first major step toward integrating African Americans into American cultural life, a process that would continue during the years to come.[12]

Although there were earlier attempts, the first widely popular black minstrel troupe appears to have been Brooker & Clayton's Georgia Minstrels, which launched in 1865 and toured the Northeast with a cast of 18, none of whom wore cork. Billed as "simon pure negroes" who had previously been slaves in Macon, Georgia, the troupe was co-managed by black entrepreneur Charles B. Hicks, although it was owned by whites (Clayton, Thomas & Co.). J.A. Brooker was the musical director. As the season progressed,

Top: Some troupes were integrated. Primrose and West advertised "40 whites and 30 blacks," though the white endmen were still in blackface. *Bottom*: Audiences could be enormous.

the performers were sometimes billed simply as "Slave Troupe" or "Georgia Minstrels." After the first season, Hicks left to form his own Georgia Minstrels troupe and became one of the most successful black minstrel managers. The term *Georgia Minstrels* subsequently became a generic name for black troupes.[13]

While black minstrel troupes traded largely on portrayals of the Old South, the new, large white troupes began to focus more on national developments and humorous social commentary about cities, industrialization, and other minority groups, including American Indians and Chinese Americans. In the 1870s, minstrelsy was also influenced by the knockabout, character-driven Irish comedy of Ned Harrigan and Tony Hart, pioneers of musical comedy and famous for their "Mulligan Guard." The spectacular success in the 1870s of the touring Fisk Jubilee Singers and similar groups, which introduced America to the spiritual, was also reflected in the minstrel shows, albeit usually in a comic way (minstrel shows were, after all, comedies). A body of long-lived minstrel songs was created—mostly in the 1870s and 1880s—that reflected these themes, including "Hear Dem Bells," "Dese Bones Gwine to Rise Again," "Play on the Golden Harp," "Upon the Golden Shore," "Climbing Up the Golden Stairs" and "Buckle on de Golden Sword."

Decline?

Most existing literature on minstrelsy focuses on its early years and suggests that the genre had gone into steep decline—or even extinction—by the 1890s. The original American entertainment form did indeed face a growing array of competitors for public attention by then. Vaudeville, which was a succession of independent acts (much like the minstrel show's olio), began to take off in the 1880s, particularly under the stewardship of impresario Tony Pastor. He offered "clean" shows that were acceptable to women and families, broadening the vaudeville audience considerably. On top of that development, interest in African Americans was now addressed by traveling spectacles such as *South Before the War*, a massive collection of set-pieces that toured the country from 1892 to 1901. Similar shows included *Black America, Darkest America,* and *Slavery Days. Black America* was like a traveling theme park; originating in Ambrose Park, Brooklyn, New York, in the summer of 1895, it featured cabins, faux cotton fields, and a cast of 500. This experience later went on tour.

As for the minstrel show, Robert Toll comments that "minstrelsy lost its dominance of the entertainment business in the 1890s."[14] Other latter-day historians are even faster to put minstrelsy in its grave. According to one, "After 1870, the popularity of the minstrel show declined rapidly, and in 1919 only three troupes remained in the U.S." Others say, "By 1890 American minstrelsy became a primarily amateur activity on the popular stage, though vestiges of minstrelsy can be easily identified in vaudeville, musical revues, and American musical theater"; "The traditional minstrel show all but died at the end of the 19th century"; and "By the start of the Civil War minstrel shows were on the decline. By the 1870s they had been surpassed in popularity by vaudeville shows, and by the 1890s they were all but extinct."[15] These statements are simply wrong.

In the 1890s, the first decade of the new mass media (including the commercial recording industry and the beginnings of motion pictures), professional stage minstrelsy was still going strong. It might be more accurate to say that it "shared the stage" with other forms of entertainment—notably vaudeville and musical theater, which were on the rise—but it was far from extinct and, in fact, continued to be alive and kicking well into the 20th century. Minstrelsy also shared many elements with vaudeville and the rather loosely structured musical theater of the time, including music and standalone acts.[16] But contemporary audiences would never mistake one type of show for the other. The party atmosphere of a minstrel show and the distinctive opening "first part" ("Gentlemen, be seated!") set it apart.

I have traced dozens of major troupes that were active in the 1890s and beyond. Of the following, notice how many were active after 1890.

One of the most important white troupes was Haverly's Minstrels (active c. 1873–1898). J.H. "Colonel Jack" Haverly (1837–1901) began in the business in 1864 and managed numerous troupes, including his own "Mastodons" in the 1870s. His name was one of the best known in minstrelsy, and he continued to tour until the late 1890s. Equally famous were Primrose and West (active c. 1877–1910s). Dancer George Primrose (1852–1919) appeared with Haverly and others in the 1860s, formed a duo with Billy West in 1871, and launched his own "big" troupe in 1877. Primrose toured under various names (including Barlow, Wilson, Primrose and West; Thatcher, Primrose and West; Primrose and West; Primrose and Dockstader; and then his own name) until well into the 1910s. Primrose and West celebrated their 25th anniversary with an all-star performance at Madison Square Garden in New York on March 9, 1896. Comedian George Thatcher had his own troupe (active c. 1880–1897) after splitting from Primrose.[17]

To these old-timers were added new white troupes, many originating in the 1880s. These included Al G. Field's Greater Minstrels (active c. 1886–1927), Lew Dockstader's

The minstrel parade preceding a show was a long-standing tradition, and these continued past 1900.

The fact that blackface entertainers were actually white men was sometimes emphasized by juxtaposing pictures of them with and without burnt cork.

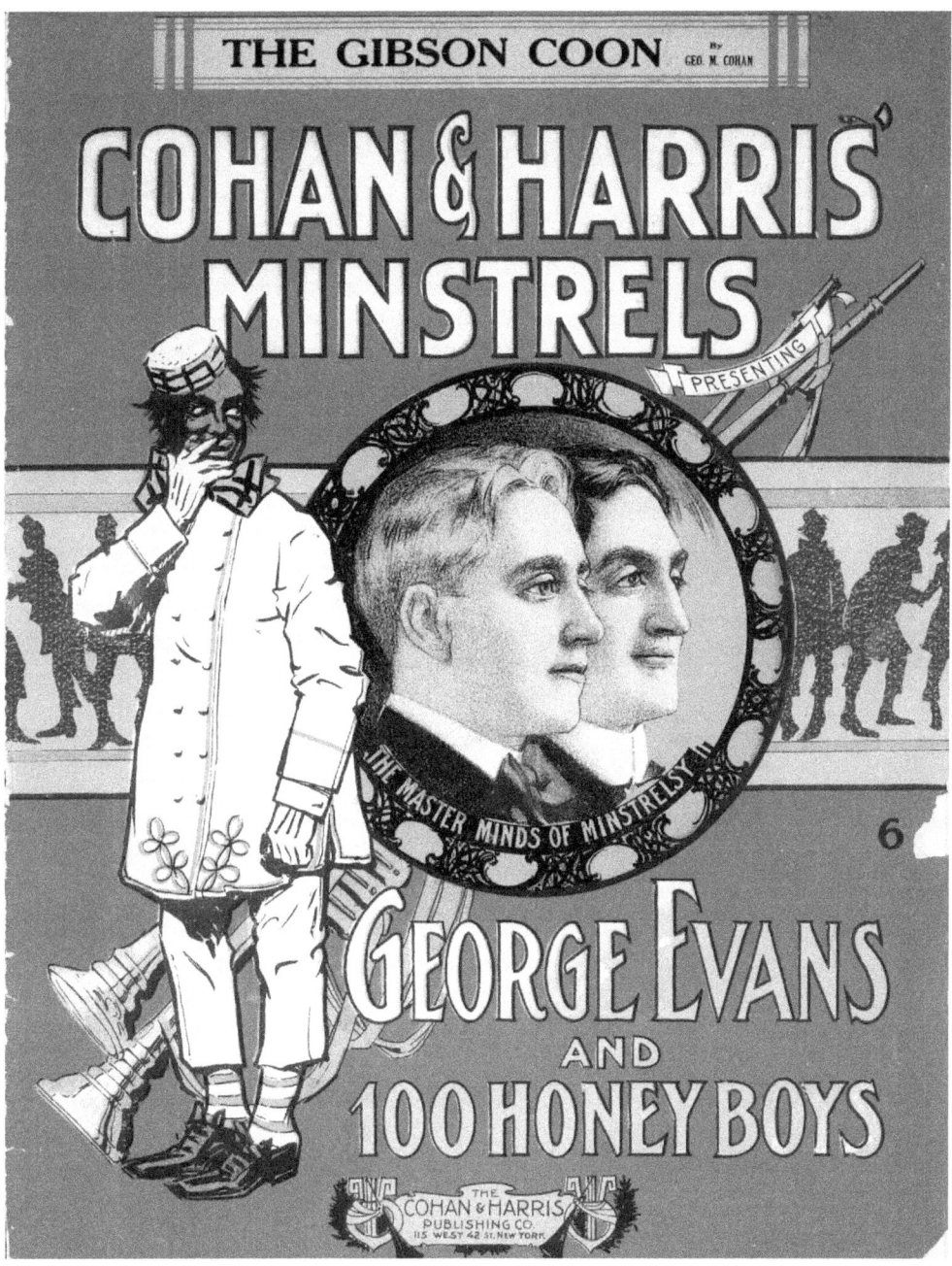

Even George M. Cohan ran a minstrel show. It starred "Honey Boy" Evans, who eventually took over the troupe and whose name lived on long after his death.

Minstrels (c. 1886–1910s), Carncross' Minstrels (c. 1860–1896), Barlow Brothers' Minstrels (c. 1877–1895), W.S. Cleveland's Minstrels (c. 1888–1901), Martin and Selig's Mastodon Minstrels (1890s), Al Reeves' Big Black and White Company (1890s), and George "Honey Boy" Evans' Minstrels (c. 1910–1915).

One of the most interesting of the "late" minstrel troupes was the Cohan and Harris

Minstrels, formed in 1908 by Broadway star George M. Cohan and his partner Sam Harris, and which included major talent, particularly singer/songwriter George "Honey Boy" Evans (who, among other things, wrote "In the Good Old Summertime"). In 1910, Evans bought out Cohan and Harris and continued the troupe under his own name. Although Evans died in 1915, his name lived on in "Honey Boy" troupes managed by John W. Vogel and others until the mid-1930s and in amateur and small-time professional troupes after that, right up to the early 1960s.[18]

These were white (or, in some cases, mixed-race) troupes. There were also black troupes crisscrossing the country. Among them were Richards and Pringle's Georgia Minstrels (c. 1883–early 1910s); Kersands' Colored Minstrels, headed by black star Billy Kersands (c. 1885–1907); Sam T. Jack's Creole (Burlesque) Company (c. 1890–1899); Hicks and Sawyer's Colored Minstrels (c. 1886–1891); Dan McCabe and Billy Young's Minstrels (c. late 1870s–1907); Rusco and Swift's Minstrels, which also appeared as Rusco and Holland and as Rusco and Hockwald (c. 1890–1927); Al G. Field's Colored Minstrels (c. 1895–1898); the Mallory Brothers' Minstrels (1890s); and Mahara's Mammoth Colored Minstrels (c. 1892–1909). The Mahara troupe included W.C. Handy as its bandmaster for several years.

Many smaller troupes were also active in the 1890s and 1900s (see appendix 1). Every trade paper contained stories from the minstrel field and traced the troupes' routes.

One of the reasons why some modern scholars have tended to exaggerate the "death" of minstrelsy is that, from time to time, stories did appear in the contemporary press lamenting the passing of the "good old days" of minstrel shows. As early as the 1870s, articles would occasionally comment about how minstrelsy was in decline—but then it would get bigger than ever. More such stories popped up in the 1880s and again in the 1890s, even as minstrel troupes continued to thrive. Some of the older *names*, of course, passed from the scene, but, as noted above, new ones arose to replace them. To paraphrase Mark Twain, contemporary reports of minstrelsy's death were greatly exaggerated.

Stage minstrelsy endured in part because its content changed continuously, to keep up with the times. Terms like *modern minstrels*

BILLY KERSANDS.
CALLENDER'S (GEORGIA) MINSTRELS.

One of the biggest black stars of the minstrel stage was Billy Kersands, who also headlined his own troupe.

Minstrel shows tried to stay contemporary, as in this one trumpeting "Remember the *Maine*" (the American battleship sunk in Havana harbor in 1898).

and *up-to-date minstrels* were used to assure theatergoers that this was not their grandfather's minstrel show. Featured songs were usually current popular hits or songs written specifically for the shows. Typical was an 1891 Primrose and West show, in which six out of seven identified songs had been published within the past three years (the one oldie was "Annie Laurie"). There was also a sketch called "Fun-o-Graph," parodying Thomas Edison's recently introduced phonograph. An examination of a dozen Primrose and West and Primrose and Dockstader playbills and reviews, dated 1891–1912, in the Harvard Theatre Collection reveals the same thing. More than 90 percent of the datable songs were contemporary. Stephen Foster–era material was rare. Sketches likewise played on contemporary events. By 1912, Dockstader's audiences were being regaled with a Teddy Roosevelt political satire called "The Bull Moose Dream."[19]

Most of the songs had nothing to do with African Americans. What could possibly be considered racial about "In the Garden of My Heart" or "Where Love Is King"? However, from the mid–1880s until the early 1900s, there was an unfortunate national craze for "coon songs," songs that specifically mocked blacks and dealt in exaggerated stereotypes. These appeared in sheet music, in vaudeville, on Broadway—and in minstrel shows. In the latter part of this period many of these songs were paired with catchy ragtime melodies (ragtime became popular in the mid–1890s), which made them a perfect fit for the mostly upbeat minstrel show. Minstrel shows featured many of these songs (e.g., "All Coons Look Alike to Me," "Darktown Is Out Tonight") because they were the popular

Minstrel shows featured many kinds of acts, including circus clowns.

songs of the day. When "coon songs" passed from public favor in the 1910s, they passed from the minstrel shows as well.

Minstrel shows' depiction of blacks also changed. As early as 1882, an influential guide to staging a minstrel show commented, "In [the early days of minstrelsy] the Ethiopian entertainments were confined to mere representations of the plantation boor. In the march of time there has been a marked improvement both in the Negro and the character of the entertainment designed to portray his peculiarities."[20] There was still, of course, the use of the blackface mask, although this practice was often confined to the endmen, with the rest of the cast in normal whiteface. The ragged clothes of the early minstrels were replaced by resplendent outfits, long-tail coats, top hats and white gloves. The endmen usually wore exaggerated collars, large bowties and striped pants (like a clown's costume), but other cast members might appear in 18th-century English court attire or formal dress. Sometimes there were white-faced circus clowns. The one thing a study of late 19th-century minstrel iconography suggests is that, apart from the endmen, there was no standardization in appearance for the performers.

Another aspect of minstrelsy considered demeaning is the use of dialect, fractured English and nonsensical stump speeches. This usage was controversial. It should be remembered that dialect was not then necessarily perceived as demeaning and was used even by respectable African American authors. Defenders could say that it replicated how many African Americans actually spoke (other minority groups, including rural whites, were also represented as speaking non-standard English). Critics said that it made blacks seem uneducated or even unintelligent.

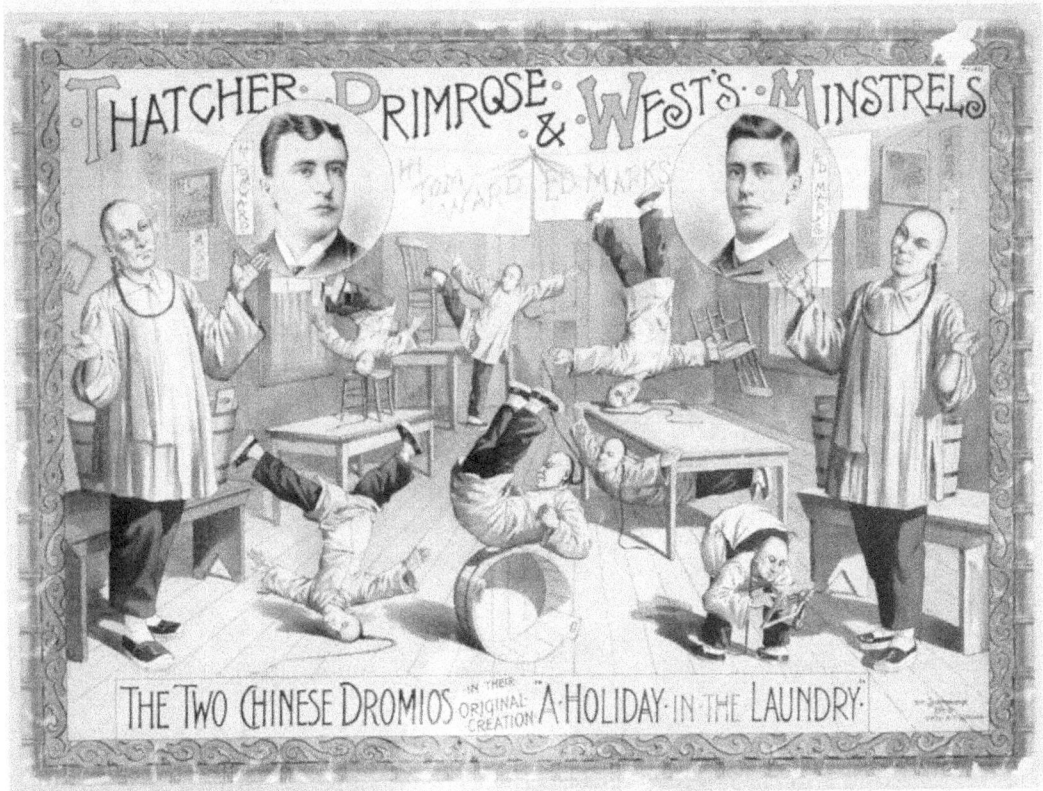

White actors lampooned many ethnic groups besides African Americans, including Chinese.

So what was the appeal of minstrel shows? What kept them going for so long? They were equally popular in all parts of the country, both the liberal North and the conservative South. African Americans attended in large numbers, especially those shows performed by black troupes, proud to see "their own" on stage at last, whatever the setting.[21] The minstrel show was considered "good, clean fun." The word *clean* is important, because much of the entertainment world of that era catered to sex and smut, while minstrel shows (and, later, vaudeville) studiously avoided that tendency. Viewers would rarely see anything off-color in a minstrel show. You could take your wife and kids.

A night with the minstrels also promised a lot of cheerful, upbeat music, interspersed with the occasional ballad from a "sweet-voiced tenor" to pull at one's heartstrings. Tap dances and sand dances (a kind of soft shoe, with a light coating of sand on the stage to amplify the sound) were popular. The jokes, laden with puns, conundrums and misunderstandings, may sound corny to modern ears, but they came fast and furious, rat-tat-tat, and with such good humor that it would have been hard for audiences not to laugh along with the minstrels.

Finally, the very staging of the first part—with the entire cast seated on stage in ascending rows, surrounding, reacting to, and sometimes participating in the routines—communicated the feeling that audiences were guests at a party along with the minstrels on stage. This signaling of inclusion was quite different from the opposition of audience versus performers customary in plays or concerts.

A major feature of minstrel shows was dancing, including the cakewalk (1900).

Observe the sheer joy radiating from one white observer's reaction to a small, early Christy performance in 1843, even as he acknowledged its "counterfeit" nature. (Note that in 1843 "nigger minstrels" meant white minstrels in blackface):

> So droll was the action, so admirable the singing, so clever the instrumentation, and so genuine was the fun of these three nigger minstrels, that I not only laughed till my sides fairly ached, but that I never left an entertainment with a more keen desire to witness it again than I did the first Christy Minstrel concert I had the pleasure of [seeing].... The staple of E.P. Christy's entertainment was fun—mind, genuine negro fun ... the counterfeit presentment of the southern darkies [whom] they personally wished to illustrate, and whose dance and songs, as such darkies, they endeavored to reproduce.[22]

It would also be a mistake to assume that minstrelsy was the exclusive province of lower, uneducated classes of society. Black leader Frederick Douglass' thundering 1848 denunciation of minstrelsy is often quoted: "[Minstrelsy is] the filthy scum of white society, who have stolen from us a complexion denied to them by nature, in which to make money, and pander to the corrupt taste of their fellow white citizens." But Douglass was in the minority, even among the elite. Walt Whitman was a fan of minstrelsy, and he said of one troupe, "Indeed, their Negro singing altogether proves how shiningly golden talent can be spread over a subject generally considered 'low.'" Mark Twain later wrote, "If I could have the nigger show back again in its pristine purity, I should have little use for opera.... The genuine nigger show [was] the show which to me had no peer ... a thoroughly delightful thing." Other fans included Charles Dickens, William Thackeray and Abraham Lincoln.[23] Even Douglass himself, after attending a performance by a troupe of black minstrels in 1849, offered a more nuanced view, saying "it is something gained

Dancing for the cake.

when the colored man in any form can appear before a white audience; and we think that even this company, with industry, application, and a proper cultivation of their taste, may yet be instrumental in removing the prejudice against our race."[24] Most objections to the minstrel show revolved around the assertion that it was crude and "low class," rather than that it was racist.

There are few contemporary reflections on the minstrel show by black writers, who were generally concerned with more pressing matters such as lynching and the color line. When black intellectual James Monroe Trotter published an influential book called *Music and Some Highly Musical People* in 1878, celebrating the achievements of African Americans in the higher arts of classical and concert music, he literally had to "force himself" to attend a performance of the Georgia Minstrels (a black troupe) to see whether his life-long prejudice against the genre would be confirmed. To his obvious surprise, he found that musically, at least, they were of a very high order: "Minstrelsy has of late been divested of much of its former coarseness; that its entertainments have become so much diversified and elevated in character—the musical portions of which at times so nearly approach the classical—as to render the same entirely different from the minstrel performances so common a few years ago ... freed from the influences of an unreasoning and cruel race-hatred." Trotter apologized to his fellow black intellectuals for coming to this conclusion but suggested that perhaps they ought to see a performance before dismissing the genre.[25]

As the 20th century unfolded, and movies became big business (challenging vaudeville as well as the minstrels), *stage* minstrelsy finally began to decline. It never went away, as we will see in later chapters. But it thrived mainly in smaller venues and local productions.

One place where the stage minstrel show lived on was the circus, albeit as a sideshow. These were usually small troupes (eight to 10 men, often black), but almost every major touring circus had one. As Lynn Abbott and Doug Seroff describe it, "Within the sideshow annex, the colored company presented a minstrel show, typically consisting of an old-time 'first part' and an 'olio,' incorporating singers, dancers, comedians, and specialty acts, accompanied by a small orchestra of seldom more than ten pieces." Bandmaster P.G. Lowery was a central figure in this world in the early 1900s. The Forepaugh-Sells Brothers, Barnum and Bailey, and Sparks circuses all included minstrel troupes, as did many others.[26]

Independent black minstrel tent shows also toured the South and the West, coming into their own around 1900, prospering through the 1920s, surviving the Great Depression, and lasting until the late 1950s. Some historians maintain that these groups arose when white theater owners shut black companies out of regular theaters because they were outdrawing white companies. However that may be, the tent shows attracted both black and white audiences, depending on the town. Their turf was rural America. For example, the tent shows would descend on the Mississippi delta at fall harvest time, sometimes with several setting up in a single town. A number of these shows originally traveled in special railroad cars, although by the 1930s most had switched to trucks. During the 1910s, minstrel tent shows were an important venue for blues singers.[27]

By the 1920s and 1930s, professional stage minstrelsy—as opposed to minstrelsy in general, which, as we shall see, continued to thrive—was crumbling. However, it did not go easily. Theatrical producers tried incorporating minstrel sequences into contemporary musicals, though without much success. The 1926 Broadway revue *Rufus LeMaire's Affairs* ended its first act with an elaborate minstrel parade and first part, involving the whole cast, but the show closed after a couple of months. In 1928, the Shuberts mounted an even bigger show starring old-time blackface legends McIntyre and Heath, called *Headin' South*. It included a minstrel first part with more than one hundred actors and singers furiously dancing and singing. In the end, the show closed out of town.

In 1928, veteran minstrel Lee Roy "Lasses" White wrote in *Billboard* that minstrelsy was not dying; it was just "taking a nap." This assessment was optimistic, and White soon turned to radio and film work. Some remaining troupes tried to sound contemporary by using advertising phrases like "bring on the jazz" (Al G. Field, 1926) and "jazz style" (Rusco and Hockwald, 1927). A National Minstrel Players and Fans Association was formed in 1930 to support the field and hold conventions, but it expired after a few years. As a professional stage entertainment, the gig was up.[28]

Local Minstrelsy

Local amateur productions, which were popular almost from the beginning of the genre, continued unabated until the 1950s, and some lasted much longer than that. I believe that the prominence of blackface minstrelsy in major media (which will be discussed in subsequent chapters) did much to promote the acceptability of such shows. They were also supported by a thriving market in instruction books on "how to put on a minstrel show."

The most popular instruction book for putting on an amateur show (1880s).

Enterprising New York publishers unleashed an avalanche of minstrel-related song and joke books. Best known in the late 19th century were *Henry De Marsan's Sentimental Singer and Singers' Journal* (1868–1882), *Wehman's Minstrel Sketches, Conundrums and Jokes* (1884–1899), *Delaney's Song Books* (1892–1922), and *Madison's Budget* (1898–1922), an annual compilation of gags, routines, and monologues.[29] Wehman's little 25-cent booklet was possibly the most popular single minstrel guide sold, based on its longevity and the frequency with which it turns up today. This source contains explicit step-by-step instructions on how to mount a show, apply burnt cork blackface, and so forth.[30] Famous minstrel troupes also leveraged their brands by publishing their own guides—for example, *Haverly Negro Minstrels: Burnt Cork Specialties* (1902).

In later years, there were popular titles such as *Funny Jokes for End Men* by Arthur Leroy Kaser (1927), *The Utopia Minstrels: A Complete Minstrel Show* by Harry Grant (1938), *Bing Crosby's Minstrel Song Folio* (1943), and *Al Jolson's Old-Time Minstrel Show* (1952), the latter including music, production tips and scripts. Radio minstrel stars also published booklets, such as *Lasses White's Book of Humor and Song* (1935). One of the sources most frequently found today is *Tip Top Entertainment and Minstrel Album* (1936), compiled and edited by New York publisher Joe Davis. Billed as containing "songs and stories made famous by outstanding radio and record artists," it had 66 pages of gags and songs that have little to do with race. Samples include the following:

> BOY: "Do you know the difference between a taxi and a subway car?"
> GIRL: "No."
> BOY: "Fine, we'll take the subway."
>
> INTERLOCUTOR: "Sambo, how can I make anti freeze?"
> ENDMAN: "Hide her woolen pajamas!"[31]

Many of these publishers put out multiple showbiz-oriented booklets. For the real old-timers, Delaney even had *George Christy's Old Time Ethiopian Joker*, harking back to one of the founders of minstrelsy. Scores of these inexpensive pamphlets can be found today in archives and for sale on the Internet.

A business grew up around advising local groups on how to mount a show. Companies would send a team of advisors to a town for a week to help the local amateurs with all the myriad details involved in putting on a "professional-looking" show. The Joe Bren company was prominent in this field during the early 1900s.

Even the U.S. government pitched in. During the 1930s, the Works Progress Administration (WPA) published guides to putting on a minstrel show. Its *56 Minstrels* guide for youth groups included arrangements such as "The Coon-Town Thirteen Club," "The Darktown Follies," "Watermelon Minstrel," and "Plantation Days with the Snowflake Family." There were also instructions for a puppet minstrel show and even a script for "The Chain Gang Minstrels" in which the endmen parts were taken by convicts imprisoned for various offenses (asked whether he's having a good time, one responds, "*Havin'* a good time? Man, I'se *doin'* a good time!").[32]

Later, during World War II, the U.S.O. published similar materials advising soldiers (white soldiers, presumably) on how to mount a show. These were produced by a Writers War Board, headed by producer John Shubert and including radio comedy writer Mort Lewis. Hundreds of minstrel and comedy scripts were distributed, with the note that using blackface was not entirely necessary but was recommended for the endmen in order "to give the traditional atmosphere of the minstrel show."[33]

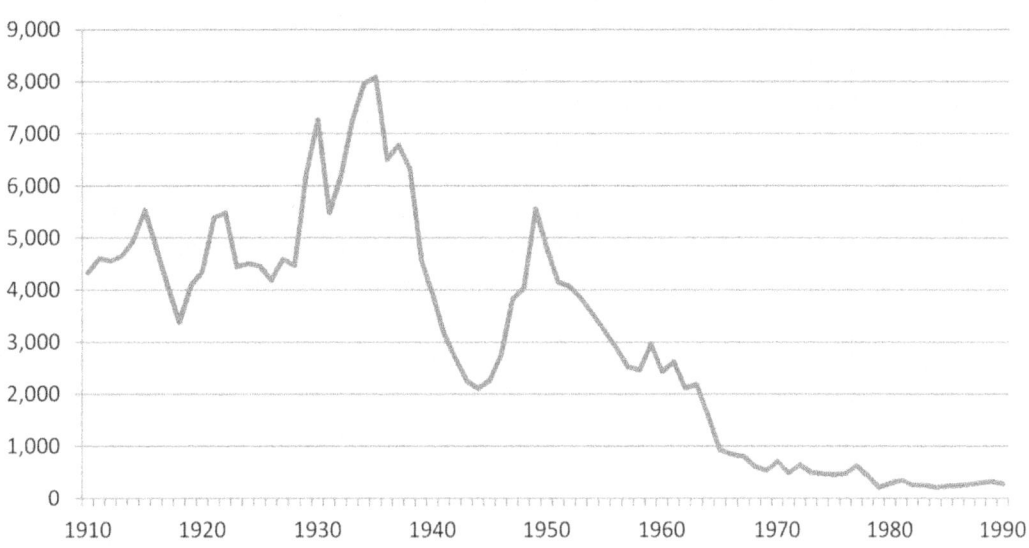

Mentions of "minstrel show" in general circulation newspapers, organized by year. *Source: Author*

How many minstrel shows were staged in the United States in the early 20th century, and when exactly did they start to disappear? A lot of vague generalities have been advanced on this subject, but one way to get actual data—imperfect, but at least indicative of trends—is to search a very large database of newspapers for the term *minstrel show* and see how often it appears each year. Some of these mentions are nostalgic references to "the old days," but close inspection suggests that most, especially prior to the 1950s, referred to current shows being staged by local clubs or broadcast on radio (see chart).[34]

Note the trends. The number is relatively stable between 1910 and 1930, at around 5,000 citations per year, except for a short dip during World War I. But during the 1930s the number unexpectedly surges. I interpret this development as reflecting the prominence of minstrelsy on radio, and thus in newspaper schedule listings. The number of references subsequently declines during World War II, logically enough, and then rebounds during the late 1940s, peaking in 1949 at more than 5,000. Only in the 1950s do the numbers start to permanently drop off. After leveling out a bit from 1957 to 1963, mentions of minstrel shows drop precipitously in 1964 and 1965, never to return. In fact, many of the references from that era are negative, about protests and excoriation of "the bad old days."

Minstrelsy in Britain

The only other country in the world that had a robust minstrel tradition was Britain. Stage minstrelsy enjoyed a parallel vogue in Britain and, in fact, lasted even longer there than it did in the United States. This may seem odd since there were few blacks in Britain at the time (and obviously no nostalgia for the American South). However, the basic elements of the minstrel show—upbeat music, jokes and skits, irreverence toward conventional mores, inclusive staging, and overall "good clean fun"—appealed to the British as much as they did to their American cousins. The exoticism of blackface probably contributed as well. As in the United States, the "clean" aspect was important, setting minstrelsy apart from what was at the time the rather disreputable British music hall.

Barely two months after their triumphant debut in New York City in February 1843, the original American minstrel troupe, the Virginia Minstrels, embarked on a tour of England.[35] Individual blackface performers had been appearing in Britain during the 1830s, as they had in America, so the British were ready for this new format, and they reacted to it as enthusiastically as the Americans. In the years that followed, numerous troupes sprang up, some of them local, some imported (or touring) from America. The Ethiopian Serenaders hit the jackpot early, appearing before the U.S. president at the White House in 1844 and in a command performance for Queen Victoria at Arundel Castle in 1846.[36] Buckley's Serenaders (active c. 1843–1876) was another important touring group from the United States, both before and after the Civil War.

The two largest British companies in the late 1800s were the Moore and Burgess Minstrels (c. 1870s–1904) and the Mohawk Minstrels (c. 1867–1904), which merged in their final years. Moore and Burgess was founded by American-born George "Pony" Moore (1820–1909), who began in blackface in 1841 and moved to Britain in 1859. Originally, like most British troupes, this group was known as "Christy Minstrels." Moore was a veteran endman and stump speaker who partnered with canny businessman Fred Burgess to build a highly successful troupe. Key to the longevity of the Mohawk Minstrels was genial interlocutor Harry Hunter, who was also a talented and prolific writer of songs and sketches.

A prominent integrated company was Sam Hague's British Minstrels (c. 1870–1888, with brief tours thereafter). Hague was originally a clog dancer who was born in England but appeared on both sides of the Atlantic, although his principal success was in Britain.

As in America, the appeal of minstrelsy reached across class lines. According to one scholar, in fact, blackface minstrelsy in Britain "reached its apogee in 1882 when the Prince of Wales took banjo lessons from James Bohee, an African-American performer."[37]

The structure of the British minstrel shows was similar to the format in America, although the endmen were known in Britain as "cornermen," while the interlocutor became the "middleman." However, the content was distinctively British. British minstrelsy quickly moved away from the somewhat raucous American version to a kind of "refined sentimentalism," with a strong emphasis on music and dance. The latter aspect was exemplified by the Ethiopian Serenaders' Master Juba (William Henry Lane), an energetic and very talented young black dancer about whom newspapers (and Charles Dickens) raved in the 1840s.

Harry Hunter was especially prolific and versatile when it came to creating new material that spanned the gamut from sentimental to comic. Some of his songs were parodies of imports such as "Grandfather's Clock" ("Grandmother's Cat"), "Just Before the Battle, Mother" ("Just Behind the Battle, Mother") and that favorite target of parodists, the pretentious "I Dreamt I Dwelt in Marble Halls" ("I Dreamt That I Dwelt on the Top of St. Paul's"). But many were indistinguishable from music hall material ("Mother, I've Called to See You," "Betsy, the Butterman's Daughter"), were "motto" songs ("Do Not Nurse Your Anger," "There's Danger in Delay"), or were nationalistic flag wavers. Sometimes Hunter would even turn out coon songs with titles like "Massa's Sent a Jellygram" or "Coon! Coon! Git Out of This Saloon." None of these pieces were ever heard in America.

American-born blackface performer Eugene Stratton (1861–1918) began his career with Haverly and later worked with the Moore and Burgess Minstrels in Britain; still later, he switched to the British music hall. Stratton introduced Sam Devere's "The Whistling Coon" to Britain and later championed the songs of British composer Leslie Stuart ("Lily of Laguna," "Little Dolly Daydream").[38]

There were plenty of amateur minstrels in Britain as well, along with street entertainers and buskers who were particularly prevalent at seaside resorts. The latter were vividly portrayed in the 1934 movie *Kentucky Minstrels*, which will be discussed in chapter 4.[39]

Michael Pickering, who has written the most detailed history of British minstrelsy, speculates that its popularity in that country rested on its reinforcement of white racial superiority during the period in which the British Empire was expanding worldwide, as well as minstrelsy's irreverence for the rigid class consciousness and straitlaced nature of the Victorian era. According to Pickering, "Minstrelsy was just as much about social relations in Britain as it was about a scantily known African-American population."[40]

American minstrel companies also toured other parts of the world, especially English-speaking countries. Most of the major white troupes visited Europe at one time or another, as did many black companies. Corbyn's Georgia Minstrels (c. 1876–1877) toured Australia in the 1870s, followed by the Hicks-Sawyer Minstrels (1888–1890). More successful was McAdoo's Minstrel and Vaudeville Company (and McAdoo's Georgia Minstrels), which toured South Africa and Australia between 1897 and 1900. The M.B. Curtis Afro-American Minstrel Company brought black American stars Billy McClain and Ernest Hogan to Australia and New Zealand in the late 1890s.

In 1854, on the eve of the signing of the historic treaty opening Japan to Western trade, Commodore Matthew Perry had his sailors stage a shipboard minstrel show for the Japanese representatives. The guests were said to have "laughed heartily at the costumes and antics of the performers." While the Japanese may not have understood the banter and the meaning of blackface, a member of the delegation sketched the affair, and "Sambo" became part of Japanese language and customs, appearing on supermarket products one hundred years later.[41]

In both Britain and America, minstrelsy moved seamlessly into each new mass medium as it emerged. First was the phonograph record in the 1890s.

2

The Minstrel Show on Records

The first of the modern mass media—namely, recorded sound—emerged in the early 1890s, at a time when minstrelsy was still a very successful form of stage entertainment. Audio recreations of minstrel shows were a popular type of recording during the early years of the industry. From the mid-1890s to the mid-1910s, hundreds of these audio vignettes were made, and they were offered by almost every record company. These products are commonly found today and tell us a lot about what a minstrel show sounded like then, though they have been almost universally overlooked by scholars. I have not been able to find a discussion of recordings in any broader minstrelsy studies.[1]

Thomas A. Edison invented the phonograph (i.e., a machine capable of recording and playing back sound) in 1877, but it took another dozen years to develop a model that was practical for everyday use. The original version recorded on strips of tinfoil, which quickly disintegrated and could not be removed from the machine without destroying them. The "improved" version recorded on wax cylinders, which, while primitive by later standards, could at least be played repeatedly and could be removed and stored for future use. In the mid-1890s, German American inventor Emile Berliner began to market an alternative type of recording device—the flat disc record—and the first "war of the formats" was on.

Edison had originally conceived the phonograph as primarily an office dictation device, although he did acknowledge other uses, including entertainment. But when the earliest regional companies attempted to market the phonograph, they became painfully aware that the office market was severely limited due to the difficulty of operating the machine, and their best chance to stay afloat was to sell prerecorded musical cylinders. This practice began in earnest in 1889–1890. The principal buyers of these cylinders, initially, were not home consumers but entrepreneurs who bought or leased the expensive phonographs and exhibited them around the country, charging audiences for the experience of hearing the new and seemingly magical machine. Some entrepreneurs deployed phonographs that were activated by inserting a coin—an early form of jukebox.

The repertoire of available recordings consisted largely of solo singers and instrumentalists, since they were most easily recorded and could be heard clearly on the primitive, all-acoustical equipment. Bands were popular due to the novelty of hearing a famous band coming out of this wondrous new machine. One ad read, "You and President Harrison may enjoy together the world-renowned United States Marine Band if you have a phonograph."[2] Recordings also memorialized bits and pieces of real life, such as speeches and stage routines, much as early movie clips often showed street scenes and public events.

One idea was to record a snippet of a minstrel show. Virtually everyone knew what a minstrel show sounded like, and they were invariably upbeat and entertaining. How novel it must have been to hear one coming out of an inert box like this newfangled phonograph.

These recordings were not actual stage shows—recording in a live venue was virtually impossible in the late 1800s—but recreations by professional recording artists. The format was typically a short but realistic recreation of the minstrel show's first part, beginning with the traditional "Gentlemen, be seated!" followed by a lively (if short) overture, a spoken introduction by the interlocutor, a couple of jokes between him and an endman, and a short vocal solo, ending with cheering and laughter. This all had to be accomplished within the two-to-three-minute playing time of a typical cylinder or disc, although individual examples over the years ranged from a minute and a half (on the small size Little Wonder discs) to a full 30 minutes (on a multi-disc set). Typically only four or five performers were needed, which was fortunate since that was the maximum number that could fit in front of the recording horn used in these pre-microphone days. Even so, the sound of so many performers, plus the small band accompanying them, could be rather faint and dispersed. Several catalogs recommended that these recordings be listened to not through an open horn but through acoustical ear tubes, which brought the listener much closer to the sound. (This is good advice for listening to them even today. Headphones provide much more sonic detail than an open speaker.)

It is uncertain who recorded the first audio representation of a minstrel show. One candidate is the Manhansset (or Manhasset) Quartet, a professional group that recorded at the Edison laboratories in the early 1890s. The cylinder has never been found, but its existence is inferred from a "title slip" (a small piece of paper that was inserted into the box with each cylinder, so as to identify the contents) reading "Minstrel 1st part: High Old Time." According to the studio log book, the quartet recorded this title and 19 others on September 27, 1891, although there is no indication of whether it was done as a song or as a full minstrel first part routine.[3] The quartet's membership varied over time, with tenor George J. Gaskin being a regular member.

The first confirmed recording of a minstrel first part is found in a catalog supplement for December 1, 1893, issued by the North American Phonograph Co., which sold Edison-branded cylinders. This source lists cylinder no. 848 as "Minstrel 1st Part, No. 1" and no. 883 as "Minstrel 1st Part, No. 2," explicitly describing them as "Minstrel 1st parts, introducing middle and end men, gags and songs, accompanied by Banta's Parlor Orchestra." Frank P. Banta (1870–1903) was a young ragtime pianist and arranger who did much recording for Edison. His "parlor orchestra" probably consisted of only three or four instruments. Banta worked in vaudeville and occasionally with minstrel shows in the New York area and knew many artists, and it is logical that he would have organized a session such as this one. Again, unfortunately, no copies are known to survive.[4]

Few stage stars recorded in the early years. For one thing, the fledgling recording companies couldn't afford them, and for another, stars simply didn't have the time. Recording was an arduous process. Prior to 1902, there was no means of mass duplicating cylinders, so an artist had to stand in front of a bank of acoustic recording machines, each with its horn pointed toward him, and sing or play his selection over and over again in order to build up enough stock to sell. Perhaps five or six good copies could be made with each rendition. A few additional copies might be dubbed from these, but the sound quality deteriorated rapidly with each dubbing. Moreover, the performance style was unique—loud, steady volume, and very distinct, without the modulation and theatrics that went into a stage performance. As a result, most recording was done by studio regulars who had mastered these unique demands and worked more or less full time at it.

Nevertheless, an occasional "name" artist was captured on wax. According to press reports, as early as September 1888, tenor Frederick Oakland of the Thatcher, Primrose and West Minstrels visited the Edison Laboratory and made experimental recordings of a number of songs. The 1892 New Jersey Phonograph Co. catalog listed 14 vocal solos by "The English minstrel vocalist, Mr. Will White," including "The Four Jolly Smiths (With Anvils)" and "The Dago's Grudge," which were subsequently sold—at least in small quantities. White was touring the United States in vaudeville at the time, though not as a headliner.[5]

Len Spencer Launches the Minstrel Record Boom

The boom in minstrel recordings got under way in 1894, due to the efforts of one young man—an ambitious performer/producer named Leonard Garfield Spencer. Spencer (1867–1914) was the son of a prominent Washington, D.C., family that operated the Spencerian Business College in that city. His grandfather was the originator of the Spencerian style of penmanship that was widely used in the United States in the late 19th century and early 20th century. His mother, Sara Andrews Spencer, was a remarkable individual—a businesswoman, notable feminist, and staunch advocate of women's rights. Spencer's middle name, Garfield, was in honor of his godfather, James A. Garfield (who later became president of the United States).

Young Len was introduced to the phonograph at the family's business college, and he became fascinated with its potential as an entertainment device. A talented amateur musician, he soon got a job singing for local phonograph companies, first Washington's Columbia Phonograph Co. (c. 1889) and then New Jersey Phonograph Co. (c. 1890). Spencer's repertoire was broad, but he specialized in coon songs and black dialect material. He then branched out into writing scripts for sketches and producing recordings. He was, in effect, one of the first record producers. In early 1894, Spencer decided to try his hand at producing recreations of the minstrel first part on a much grander scale than the tentative Edison efforts. For this task, he organized a carefully chosen recording troupe dubbed "The Spencer, Williams and Quinn Minstrels," soon renamed "The

Len Spencer, early record producer and artist.

The U.S. Phonograph Co. announced Len Spencer's minstrels in 1894 with a typical graphic.

Spencer, Williams and Quinn Imperial Minstrels," and then just "The Imperial Minstrels." It was the first of three principal minstrel recording troupes that would dominate the field over the next 20 years.

Some might question whether the studio artists who made early minstrel first part recordings were "real" minstrels and could authentically represent the genre. It is therefore worth looking at the backgrounds of the members of Spencer's little troupe.

News items indicated that Spencer was involved with local minstrel stage productions at least as early as 1891, both in Washington and in New York, as a performer, writer, and sometimes organizer. In 1896, he appeared with the nationally known Cleveland and Haverly Minstrels. In late 1898, he organized his own 25-man touring troupe called "Len Spencer's Greater New York Minstrels," which performed for the 1898–1899 season throughout the New York–New Jersey region. Judging from press accounts, the tour was a success both artistically and financially, but the group was disbanded in 1899, most likely due to the difficulty of juggling schedules for the New York–based recording talent that made up most of the cast. Among those in the ever-changing touring cast were such familiar recording names as Billy Golden, George Graham, Cal Stewart, Roger Harding, Steve Porter, Albert Campbell, Charles P. Lowe, Vess L. Ossman, and Russell Hunting. Included as a novelty act was bugler Emil Cassi, who had sounded the call for Teddy Roosevelt's charge up San Juan Hill during the Spanish-American War. Spencer served as interlocutor.[6]

"Aged-Negro delineator" and comedian Billy Williams (real name Carmody; 1854–1910) joined Spencer as endman in the recording troupe. Williams was a stage veteran who had toured with Billy Manning's Minstrels, the Original New Orleans Minstrels,

Haverly and other troupes in the 1870s, and he was known particularly for his "wench impersonations." He was also part of a blackface song-and-dance act known as Williams & Sully from 1876 to 1887. Williams left the Spencer troupe around 1897 and was for a time a "temperance evangelist." He should not be confused with the Australian music hall artist Billy Williams ("The Man in the Velvet Suit"), who recorded somewhat later. Obituaries in 1910 called the American Billy "an old-time minstrel man of considerable fame."[7]

Tenor Dan W. Quinn (1860–1938) was a prolific recording artist from about 1892 to 1906. Born in New York in 1860, he spent the 1880s as an ironworker who moonlighted as a singer at local functions in the New York area. It was at one of these, in 1892, that Quinn was discovered by a phonograph exhibitor and recruited to make some trial cylinders for the New York and New Jersey phonograph companies. His voice recorded quite well on the primitive equipment, and he became very successful. He soon met Len Spencer, who was one of the busiest employees of the New Jersey company. Thus Quinn had no known minstrel background (at least professionally); however, his role in Spencer's troupe was to sing a featured ballad (e.g., "Two Little Girls in Blue" or "Sweet Marie") or perhaps simply supply "backup singing and clapping, whistling, bones playing, and other sound effects."[8] For this task, he was admirably equipped.

Perhaps the most interesting member of Spencer's troupe was George W. Johnson (1846–1914), an African American singer and whistler whose presence made this an integrated troupe (and about whom I have written extensively). Johnson was born a slave in Virginia in 1846 and came to New York after the Civil War to eke out a living as a street singer and occasional performer at local parties. According to one account, he toured with the Georgia Minstrels in the 1870s. He became the most popular African American recording artist of the 1890s, and his two specialties—"The Whistling Coon" and "The Laughing Song"— were enormous sellers for the time. Spencer had Johnson sing the latter as the featured song on one of his

George Johnson was the first widely popular black recording artist and a member of Spencer's troupe.

minstrel records, but he prized Johnson's hearty laughter as a means of enlivening the proceedings.[9]

Thus three of the four principals of the Imperial Minstrels had professional minstrel experience. But does that really matter? They were skilled performers, and at this time virtually everyone in the entertainment field (and almost everybody in the general population as well) was familiar with, and had probably attended, a minstrel show. These shows, which ranged from multitudes of local amateur productions to large touring troupes who traveled across the nation, were ubiquitous. Listeners of the recorded vignettes would immediately recognize the familiar language of the minstrel first part.

The format that Spencer used would serve as the template for nearly all minstrel records for the next 20 years. It was, of course, not possible to reproduce an entire minstrel first part, which on stage might run from 45 to 60 minutes, in the confines of a three-minute cylinder. So Spencer presented each of the characteristic elements, in order, in an abbreviated (but realistic) form. Based on guidebooks and reviews of the period,[10] a typical minstrel first part on stage might be organized as follows:

Curtain rises, revealing entire company standing and singing the opening chorus.
Interlocutor announces, "Gentlemen, be seated!" Orchestra strikes a chord. Interlocutor then announces the opening overture.
Fast and snappy overture by the orchestra; minstrels, seated, wave tambourines.
Interlocutor addresses endmen (for example, "How are you this evening, Mr. Bones?"). They respond with jokes and witty rejoinders.
Interlocutor announces the first song by a troupe member.
The remainder of the first part then alternates between jokes and stories (between interlocutor and endmen, or between endmen) and comic and ballad songs.

In comparing this sequence to recorded recreations, it is important to note that there was some variation in the details. For example, the opening might be in a different order. The comic interludes might be simple verbal exchanges, but they might also involve props and expand into small sketches acted out in front of the assembled company. More elaborate sketches were commonly reserved for the olio or afterpiece.

Spencer's three-minute distillation might unfold as follows:

0:00—Interlocutor announces, "Spencer, Williams and Quinn's Imperial Minstrels, introducing their original minstrel first part. Gentlemen, be seated!" Orchestra strikes a chord.
0:15—Interlocutor announces, "Introductory overture."
Fast and snappy overture by the orchestra, ending with applause and tambourines.
0:32—Interlocutor addresses an endman, who responds. Laughter at punchlines. There might be two or three exchanges.
1:30—Interlocutor: "Mr. George W. Johnson in his great 'Laughing Song,'" followed by the song. Minstrels sometimes join in.
3:00—Ends with clapping, cheering, whistling.

The first six Spencer, Williams and Quinn minstrel cylinders appeared in the New Jersey release list of March 1, 1894, and were repeated in the April 1 list. The name of the company had by this time been changed to the United States Phonograph Company, although its products were still called "New Jersey cylinders." The company was proud of its achievement and introduced the cylinders with fulsome praise, under a caricature drawing of a line of minstrel "darkies" on a musical staff.

The first commercial recordings were on fragile, brown wax cylinders.

> These gentlemen have together produced a most decided novelty in their new minstrel records. Spencer and Quinn are well known to all users of the Phonograph, and comment on their work is unnecessary. They are ably assisted by Mr. Billy Williams, the aged-negro delineator and comedian, as well as by Geo. W. Johnson in his inimitable laughing specialty. Each record contains a complete minstrel first part, embracing overture with bones and tambourine accompaniment, several jokes and witty sayings, interspersed with laughter and applause by the audience, and finishing either with some comic negro song or story by Spencer, or a pathetic song by Quinn or Williams. Wherever reproduced these records have made an instantaneous hit.[11]

The reference to "wherever reproduced" is interesting, as it suggests that the cylinders may have been available before the March 1 catalog date; if so, however, it was most likely not much earlier. They are presented as new and are not mentioned in any prior New Jersey literature or ads.[12]

Each record was then given an individual description, beginning with number 1 (the cylinders themselves bore no catalog numbers):

> No. 1. "Be seated, gentlemen." Introductory Overture; the Black Serenaders, followed by applause; the Interlocutor ventures to ask Bones "How he finds things?" to which Bones replies, "Oh, I look for 'em." This strikes the audience as being a witty sally, and they applaud and laugh vociferously, Mr. Geo. W. Johnson's hearty laugh particularly being heard above the din and confusion. "How is business down at the tailor shop, Billy?" "Oh, sew sew," which reply also invokes the risibilities of the audience. "How do you feel tonight, Dan?" "Kind of Chicago." "Why, how is that?" "Oh, fair." The Interlocutor then announces that Mr. Spencer will sing "A High Old Time," all joining heartily in the chorus, at the conclusion of which the audience show their approval by round after round of applause, laughter, whistling, etc., etc.

The phrase "Be seated, gentlemen" is unusual, the normal introduction being "Gentlemen, be seated!" Researcher Patrick Feaster has pointed out that "Be seated, gentlemen" was occasionally used on stage, though it was not standard.[13] On recordings, it is unique to the New Jersey company and is in fact a way of identifying cylinders made by that entity, since the company was not otherwise identified on the cylinder. The jokes quoted are the typical puns and double meanings beloved of minstrels, though with a contemporary twist. ("Kind of Chicago.... Oh, fair" refers to the highly publicized World's Fair held in Chicago during 1893.)

The featured song from this cylinder, the fast-paced "A High Old Time," was recent, written by Harry C. Talbert of the Thatcher, Primrose and West Minstrels and published in 1888. It quickly became a favorite of Spencer's minstrels, embodying the high spirits and lively music of the show.

> Oh, my, don't you hear me humming?
> We'll have a high old time.
> Join in the ranks, everybody's coming,
> We'll have a high old time.
> Gwine to be a dance match, give away a goose.
> We'll have a high old time.
> Clear away the table, gwine to cut her loose,
> We'll have a high old time.
>
> *Chorus:*
> Won't we have a high old time, won't those wenches shine?
> Come before you're late, pull out your pencil and your slate,
> And make a note of the high old time![14]

The other five original cylinders were known by their featured songs, which were "Hear Dem Bells" (sung by Spencer), "Two Little Girls in Blue" (Quinn), "Buckle on de Golden Sword" (Spencer), "The Old Log Cabin in the Dell" (Williams), and "The Laughing Song" (Johnson). Most of these were composed by white songwriters in the 1880s or early 1890s. The participants addressed each other by their real names. Len Spencer generally played the interlocutor, although in a loose and informal manner that sometimes made him sound like "one of the boys." Billy Williams and sometimes Dan Quinn were the endmen.

Judging from the catalog descriptions, these routines were initially accompanied only by piano, tambourine and bones, but by early 1895 the series was being remade with a small orchestra. The New Jersey company made a point of noting that all of its products were original recordings and not inferior dubbed copies. Normally only four or five good copies could be obtained from a single performance by a group such as this one, and it is amazing that Spencer's troupe was able to keep repeating these performances enough to build up stock to meet what was apparently a very strong demand. They must have gotten very sick of the jokes!

No copies of the 1894 non-orchestra versions have been located, but judging from early orchestra versions (first announced in the February 1, 1895, catalog), the delivery could be very conversational, with pronounced black dialect and a fast, slangy tone. This is quite interesting, as later minstrel recordings tended to take on a more formal, theatrical tone, possibly to satisfy white buyers who wanted something they could play in their parlors or simply better understand. The atmosphere here was loose and raucous, as one might expect in an intimate setting. Here, for example, is a transcription of the "Laughing Song" cylinder, from a slightly later version (c. 1895):

> ANNOUNCER: The Imperial Minstrels, introducing their original minstrel first part. Be seated, gentlemen! (Music)
> ANNOUNCER: Introductory overture. (Orchestra plays, followed by enthusiastic clapping and whistling. The following is in broad, "darky" dialect.)
> LEN: Well, Billy ...
> BILLY: What issit, Leonard?
> LEN: Thas'a, thas'a very ferocious necktie that yo' got on there.
> BILLY: Tha's one hand ...
> LEN: I, I, I bet I know where you got it ...
> BILLY: Come on, where, where?
> LEN: 'Round your neck! (Great laughter) Hey, Billy ...
> BILLY: What issit, Leonard?
> LEN: You'se very much intellectuality, can you tell me what it is that makes a coon dog spotted?

BILLY: No, Leonard, I say, what is it that makes a coon dog spotted?
LEN: Why, his spots! (Great laughter)
BILLY: Hey, Leonard …
LEN: What is it, Billy?
BILLY: How far this 'lectuality must go on.… Did you ever notice down in a yard they's certain dogs that run around in the street?
LEN: Yeah.
BILLY: Did you ever notice how fast dey run when dey go 'cross?
LEN: I do, certainly.
BILLY: What makes dem do that?
LEN: 'Deed I don't know, Billy, what makes dem dere dogs go so fast?
BILLY: Why, dey's in a hurry to get on the other side! (Laughter)
ANNOUNCER: Mr. George W. Johnson in his great "Laughing Song" …

The success of Spencer's minstrel series led the New Jersey company to commission another five titles in late 1894 or very early 1895. Featured songs were "Upon the Golden Shore," "Dese Bones Shall Rise Again," "Rock Dat Ship," and "Play on the Golden Harp" by Spencer, as well as "Sweet Marie" by Quinn. These numbers accompanied jokes about lawyers, gambling, girlfriends, matrimony, and mothers-in-law ("no minstrel show would be complete without an elaborate mother-in-law joke").[15]

> The success of our first minstrel records has induced us to prepare a second series. All the old favorites are engaged—Spencer, Williams, Quinn, Johnson—and more besides, who were not cast for the first performance; some honestly black men, some black for revenue only, some yellow, some white, but all funny. These Ethiopian carnivals are arranged in five numbers, from seven to eleven, to avoid confusion with those first made. This is no amateur entertainment. Gentlemen, be seated.

Note the mention of the fact that the troupe was integrated, a way of emphasizing its authenticity. "Black men" presumably referred to George W. Johnson, as no other black artists are known to have been recording for New Jersey at this time.

The catalog then added an interesting admonition:

> Note—The Minstrel First Parts are made for tube use. Though all are loud and clear, it has been found impossible to preserve the various shades of comedy if made extremely loud to carry through a horn. We have preferred to keep the merit in the records, and therefore do not recommend them for horn.

"Tube use" referred to listening through acoustical ear tubes (similar to a stethoscope), rather than through an open horn. The recording and reproducing process at this time was entirely mechanical, with no amplification possible, and it must have been hard to get much volume out of these sonically complex early recordings, with their multiple voices, cross talk, and other sound effects. This statement serves as evidence that the New Jersey company was striving for realism in its early minstrel vignettes (at least to the degree possible).

The popularity of the minstrel cylinders caused New Jersey to broaden its line with four "Negro Talking Records" by "the well-known minstrel" Billy Williams ("Christmas Party," "Sermon on the Little Moses," "Sermon on de Flood and de Ark," and "Sparking in Darktown"). These could easily have been stump speeches in a minstrel show. In addition, Spencer and Williams enacted two minstrel-style sketches:

> Thompson Street Poker Club. Describing a game of poker in which Brer Spencer and Brer Williams take the leading parts. Williams is called, with two squeens and a deep-cutting razor, and Spencer lays down two two-speckers and a quick-shooting gun, and during the row the "joint is pinched."

People first heard the phonograph at traveling exhibitions, where they listened through acoustical ear tubes.

> The Crap Game. Here is the first realistic attempt to reproduce the familiar scenes of everyday gambling in darky circles. Introduces three characters, including an amusing onlooker who encourages one of the players by making bets on the side. This record depends not at all on outside effects, but is an honest representation of the droll and original scenes that attend upon the "Come seven, come eleven" hazard.[16]

The success of New Jersey's minstrel line attracted the attention of other companies. In 1895, the Chicago Talking Machine Company listed its own set of nine minstrel first part cylinders, five of which were likely made for it by the New Jersey company (including "A High Old Time"). However, four titles were not duplicated in the New Jersey catalog and may have been originals ("Standing on the Corner," "Pretty Mamie Casey," "Uncle Eph's Return," and "Pussy Green"). No artists were listed, and no copies have been found.

Much of New Jersey's business consisted of wholesaling its products to other companies for resale, and in late 1895 or early 1896 Columbia, the largest record maker, began carrying the Spencer cylinders (by now called simply the Imperial Minstrels), giving them its own catalog numbers. New Jersey continued to sell them as well, and in an early 1897 catalog it commented,

End-man's Joke: There Are Other Brands, but Not So Warm

> During the past month a new stock of the famous minstrel first parts has been prepared, employing full orchestra for every selection, six vocal soloists, with bones, tambourine and chorus, in every sketch. The services of twenty performers are required to make this series. The laugh of George W. Johnson is heard in each record.[17]

However, storm clouds were gathering over the United States Phonograph Co., maker of the New Jersey cylinders. In 1896, its chief recording engineer (a key position), Victor Emerson, defected to rival Columbia. In June 1897, Emerson lured Spencer's popular minstrels—and the energetic Spencer himself—to Columbia, and for the next few years they became one of the label's principal acts. Said Columbia,

> Spencer and Williams' Minstrels have been reorganized and engaged exclusively to entertain Columbia patrons. They bring their entire orchestra and a full complement of endmen, comedians and vocalists. The records embrace bones and tambourine overtures, jokes, negro shouts and songs, interspersed with the hearty laughter and tumultuous applause of the delighted audience. A veritable carnival of melody and good cheer.[18]

Columbia immediately began expanding the Imperial Minstrels' repertoire with new titles and changing its tone, making the songs more contemporary. Whereas the featured songs on the original list were mostly minstrel standards from the 1870s and 1880s like "A High Old Time" and "Hear Dem Bells," Columbia began to feature current hits such as "Mamie Reilly" (1897), "Hello! Ma Baby" (1899) and "I'd Leave My Happy Home for You" (1899). At this time, stage minstrelsy was striving to present itself as modern and up to date, and it seems that Columbia wanted its records to sound contemporary as well. The cast was also changing, with Billy Williams departing and Len Spencer taking the role of principal endman. There was a more formal-sounding interlocutor (at first Steve C. Porter, and later Spencer's brother Harry) and a greater variety of featured vocalists, among them Porter, Roger Harding, George J. Gaskin, and Frank C. Stanley.

The dialogue in the Columbia recordings was more theatrical than it had been in the New Jersey productions, with the stereotypical pompous interlocutor playing straight man to the irreverent black endman. Sometimes there was no black dialect at all. Minstrel stage guides were discouraging the use of dialect by this time, ostensibly for reasons of intelligibility.[19]

Compare this circa 1902 version of the "Laughing Song" routine, with its vaudeville joke and flag-waving finale, all delivered in proper English, with the loose, conversational routine from the mid-1890s cited earlier:

> INTERLOCUTOR (HARRY SPENCER): Gentlemen, be seated!
> (overture)
> LEN: I say, Mr. Henry, money is mighty cheap nowadays.
> HARRY: Money cheap, Leonard? Ha! I fail to get any of it.
> LEN: Why, you can get silver dollars for forty five and fifty five cents.
> HARRY: Why, that's absurd, nonsense.
> LEN: Everybody knows that forty five cents and fifty five cents makes a hundred cents, and you can get a dollar anywhere for that!
> (great laughter, whistles)
> LEN: Tell me, sir, why are the stars and stripes like the stars in the heavens?
> HARRY: Well, Leonard, why *are* the stars and stripes like the stars in the heavens?
> LEN (with great drama): Because, sir, it's beyond the power of any nation on earth to ever pull them down!
> (cheers)
> LEN: George W. Johnson in his great "Laughing Song"[20]

The jokes were often topical. This example is from 1898, during the Spanish-American War, when Admiral Dewey was a national hero:

> INTERLOCUTOR (STEVE PORTER): Well, Len, how do you feel?
> LEN: Well, Porter, I feel just like a pretty little flower early in the mornin'.

PORTER: A pretty little flower early in the morning? Why, how's that?
LEN: Dew-y!
(laughter)
PORTER: Say, Len, they tell me you're a hard drinker. Is that so?
LEN: A hard drinker? Why, no, Porter, that's the easiest thing I do!
(laughter)[21]

In late 1901, Columbia began selling disc records in addition to cylinders. The initial releases were on the Climax label, which for legal reasons was technically owned by a separate company (Columbia was then involved in a patent fight with the Berliner interests over the right to make disc records). Climax used a different cast (which will be discussed later), but as soon as the legal problems were resolved and Columbia was able to release discs under its own name, in mid-1902, it had Spencer's Imperial Minstrels re-record their repertoire for that medium. These discs are more frequently found today than the fragile cylinders.[22]

Columbia had the Imperial Minstrels remake the Climax titles, which largely featured minstrel standards from the 1870s and 1880s, and then a new group of eight, nearly all of which were built around current (or recent) popular hits. These included "My Wild Irish Rose" (1899), "I've a Longing in My Heart for You, Louise" (1900) and "When the Autumn Leaves Are Falling" (1900). Only two were older numbers—interestingly, they were Stephen Foster songs ("Old Folks at Home" and "My Old Kentucky Home"), which rarely seemed to turn up in minstrel shows at that time. Once again Columbia seemed to be emphasizing minstrelsy as current, not nostalgic, entertainment.

From 1897 to 1903, the Imperial Minstrels were exclusive to Columbia, but in 1903 the troupe began to make disc records for other labels as well. First came 16 sides for Zonophone, a formerly independent label that became a subsidiary of Victor Talking Machine Co. in 1903. Most of the songs featured in these recordings were older minstrel classics (there's "A High Old Time" again!). The principal jokesters were Len and Harry Spencer, with Len, Albert Campbell and Frank C. Stanley among the featured vocalists. These were followed around 1904 by at least eight sides for Leeds, one of several rogue labels that were operating in defiance of the Columbia/Victor patent monopoly. The featured songs were an odd mix of old and probably forgotten tunes ("Till the Snow Flakes Come Again" [1837], "Mother's Watch by the Sea" [1883]) and more current numbers ("Down in Mobile Long Ago" [1903]). Harry Spencer seems to have been the interlocutor, with Len as the joking endman.

After that, Len Spencer discontinued the Imperial Minstrels; in fact, the Leeds discs were labeled not as by the Imperial Minstrels but by the "Spencer Minstrels" or "Len Spencer Quintet." During 1902–1906, Spencer participated in other minstrel troupes organized by Columbia, Victor and Edison, but he increasingly concentrated on duets with newcomer Ada Jones. By 1910, he was scaling back his recording activity in general to focus on his new career as a booking agent. He was fairly successful in this endeavor, with a bustling office that he operated until the time of his sudden death in 1914.

Other Minstrel Records in the Late 1890s and Early 1900s

Once Len Spencer had shown how successful minstrel first part recordings could be, other companies quickly jumped on the bandwagon. Some, like the Chicago Talking

Machine Co. and Columbia (at first), resold New Jersey's products or bought masters from New Jersey and dubbed copies from them. The United States Phonograph Co. (New Jersey) was happy to supply the trade in this manner—for a price. However, there wasn't much of a margin in this kind of sale, and naturally some companies wanted to make their own products. Every company, it seemed, wanted minstrel records on its list. Lower-cost phonographs for home use were coming on the market, and consumers wanted to buy these records, as well as hear them at exhibitions in public spaces.

In 1896, Walcutt & Leeds, maker of "New York" cylinders, produced a series of dated minstrel performances by the Dixie Minstrel Troupe ("Engagement of March 15th, '96," "Engagement of April 1st, '96," etc.), but none of these recordings have been located. Another small company, the Excelsior Phonograph Co. of New York, produced an undetermined number by its Excelsior Minstrel Company in 1898, and at least one of those has turned up. It is a spare production, with Steve Porter as interlocutor, Roger Harding as vocalist, two unidentified others, and thin piano accompaniment. The featured song is "A Hot Time in the Old Town" (1896), a big hit at the time.

The Edison Company had discontinued cylinder production in 1894 but reentered the field in 1896, and at first, like others, it sold cylinders apparently produced for it by the New Jersey company. By late 1897, the company was ramping up production and produced two minstrel titles by Billy Golden and Dick Chalfant. Golden (1858–1926) had been in show business for nearly a quarter century by this time, specializing in blackface vaudeville routines, both solo and in various combinations. Among his best-known numbers were "Turkey in the Straw," "Roll on the Ground," and "Bye Bye Ma Honey." Golden had begun recording in the early 1890s, and it was said that he sounded so convincingly black that record companies had to periodically print a picture of him to prove that he was a white man. In the 1890s, he toured first with his wife May and later with stepdaughter Daisy (both dancers), as well as tenor Dick Chalfant, in the comedy act known as "Golden, Chalfant and Golden."[23]

In 1899, Edison released another batch of six minstrel cylinders, this time by Billy Heins and the Ancient City Quartet. Heins (1874–c. 1971) was a somewhat obscure singer and comedian who appeared in vaudeville and occasionally in minstrel troupes such as Gus Hill's Ideal Minstrels. The featured songs were rather obscure current pop tunes, including "How I Love My Lou," "Remus Takes the Cake," and, oddly, the English music hall tune "Elsie from Chelsea."

Recent research indicates that the Ancient City Quartet was African-American, which makes their cylinders significant as racially integrated performances. Edison made no mention of race in its sales literature for the half dozen minstrel recordings on which they appear, however the quartet appeared on the vaudeville stage in 1898 where it was described as "composed entirely of colored men." On the cylinders they sing in straight quartet harmony, however the quartet also recorded the faux spiritual "Big Bell," for Berliner, in a characteristic, call-and-response arrangement. On stage the Ancient City Quartette appeared with Callender's Original Georgia Minstrels (colored) and with Primrose and West.[24]

These first two groups of Edison minstrel cylinders are quite rare and apparently did not sell well. The next set, by Arthur Collins, S.H. Dudley and the Ancient City Quartette (released between 1899 and 1901), did better. The featured songs were nearly all current hits, including "Just One Girl," "Goodbye Dolly Gray," the war hit "Break the News to Mother," and the lively "Darktown Is Out Tonight." One cylinder opened with the famous cakewalk "Smoky Mokes." Another cylinder, designated "Old Time Songs," was specifically reserved for oldies—namely, "Old Black Joe" and "Massa's in the Cold, Cold Ground."

Dudley served as the pompous interlocutor, while Collins was usually the drawling endman. Both took vocals. Also taking part was "Billy," but it is unclear whether this individual was Billy Heins or Billy Williams, who apparently recorded a few more cylinders after leaving the Imperial Minstrels in 1897. The banter between the three principals was fast and snappy. Here's a typical example, based on wordplay:

> SAM: Say, Billy, when my father died he left everyone in the family fifteen thousand dollars.
> BILLY: Why, that's nothing remarkable, with my dad he left the earth.
> (laughter, rattling of bones)
> SAM: Yes, before he died he was a fireman.
> BILLY: Well, one thing is sure, he won't be out of work now.
> SAM (irritated): Oh, you go to blazes!
> BILLY: Why, that's where your father went!
> (laughter, rattling of bones)
> SAM: Arthur Collins sings "The Laughing Song"[25]

The United States Phonograph Co. of New Jersey, smarting from the loss of its best-selling Imperial Minstrels to Columbia in mid–1897, listed a new set of minstrel cylinders under the Consolidated label around 1899. The troupe was not identified by name, and this may have been a ruse to allow the company to keep selling Imperial Minstrels products after they had become exclusive to the competition. The repertoire was exactly the same as that of the Imperial Minstrels ("A High Old Time," etc.). These cylinders have not been heard and would probably be hard to identify if they were discovered, since New Jersey did not customarily identify its products.[26]

The company made one last attempt to market its once-famous minstrel cylinders in 1900, using an ad hoc group called the Alabama Troubadours. More than a dozen titles were issued, with a mix of old and new songs featured. On most of those heard by the author, New Jersey's unique introduction ("Be seated, gentlemen") is used, identifying them as almost certainly products of the U.S. Phonograph Co. According to the catalog:

> The "Alabama Troubadours" who achieved such great success in producing loud, clear and desirable records, have been re-engaged to provide our patrons with an entire new list of selections. The records listed embrace the combined efforts of such well known phonograph artists as Messrs. Dan Quinn, S.H. Dudley, Jere Mahoney, William F. Hooley, John Bieling, assisted by the "Old Homestead Quartette" and Mr. Edward Issler's incomparable orchestra. They are replete with jolly gags, sparkling wit and negro humor.[27]

In this minstrel setting, "negro humor" did not mean that the jokes were about African Americans, but rather they were told by blacks (or whites imitating them).

Billy Williams is also heard on some of these cylinders, and Williams, Dudley, Quinn and Hooley all crack jokes and address each other by name. Dudley is the interlocutor, although on many cylinders of this period he comes across less as a stuffy leader and more as "one of the gang." In fact, these studio regulars were so comfortable working with each other that the interplay sounds very natural and conversational. As we've seen in other examples, most of the jokes are not about race, although there are a few, including a mild "Jew" joke:

> DAN: I, I say, Mr. Dudley.
> SAM: Well, Daniel, what is it this time?

DAN: Can you tell me what is the scarcest thing in the world?
SAM: Well ... I don't know, Daniel. What is it?
DAN: Well, I, I'll tell ya. A ham sandwich at a Jew picnic!
(laughter, clapping, whistling)
DAN: Mr. Billy Williams sings "Old Black Joe."

There were also attempts to get well-known stage minstrels into the studio, although, due to their busy schedules (and often high salaries), this was difficult. In January 1895, Columbia proudly announced that it had obtained a few cylinders from the Manhattan Quartette of Dockstader's Minstrels, one of the major troupes in the United States. During the first week of December 1894, the troupe appeared at the Academy of Music in Washington, Columbia's home city, and it was probably then that these cylinders were recorded. The catalog indicated that there were volume problems with the recording, saying, "These records are good for tube use, but not loud enough for reproduction through the horn. We obtained only a few and patrons wishing good quartette music, free from harshness or blast, should order at once." The titles offered were "Plantation Medley," "Calliope Medley," "Southern Medley," "Sunshine Will Come Again," and "A Negro's Holiday."[28]

Not to be outdone, the New Jersey company announced in February 1895 that it had obtained a few titles from English tenor Harry Leighton, one of Dockstader's stars. The announcement read, "Clear, loud records by this popular soloist, whose singular voice is here well exemplified. We list five of his specialties sung in a very sentimental strain. Mr. Leighton was the leading soloist of Dockstader's Minstrels during the past season. They are novelties of merit."[29]

Dockstader was playing in and around the New York area during the fall of 1894, and the New Jersey company was probably able to get Leighton into its Newark laboratory for a day or two. The titles listed, which he was no doubt singing in the show, were "Give My Love to Nellie," "Venus, My Shining Star," "Waiting for Nell," "An Old-Fashioned Valentine," and "Take Back the Engagement Ring." Alas, none of these cylinders by Dockstader stars appear to have survived.

Cylinders still outsold disc records by a considerable margin at this time; discs would not surpass cylinders in overall sales until 1910. However, discs were already mounting a serious challenge to the older format, and early disc companies were anxious to cash in on the minstrel record boom. The principal disc label was Berliner Gram-o-Phone, founded by the format's inventor, Emile Berliner, and headquartered in Washington, D.C. Berliner's first minstrel discs were recorded around June 1898 and identified simply by the names of the principal performers—Parkham and Terrell on the first two, and Graham and Terrell on the third.

George Graham and John Terrell were minor Washington performers who did quite a bit of recording for Berliner at his laboratory in the city in the late 1890s. (Berliner was known for recruiting obscure local talent; he even recorded himself at times.) Graham was a monologist who was reputedly a street corner patent medicine salesman who brought his fast-talking routines to the studio. Terrell was a tenor who appeared at Walsh's Music Hall and other local venues. "Parkham" is believed to have been an eccentric Washington city guide, performer and "hackman poet" named Meigs Parham.[30] The routines were necessarily fast, as the little seven-inch discs could only hold about two minutes' worth of material. They open with the interlocutor introducing the "orchestra," which turns out to be only a piano. This piece is followed by some rapid-fire jokes (hard to understand on the crudely recorded discs) and the featured songs, which on these three discs are "Up Dar in de Sky," "Sally Warner" and "Get Your Money's Worth." The songs were all recent publications, but almost as obscure as the performers ("Sally Warner" was written by George Graham's brother Charles, a songwriter of some note).

Berliner brought in better-known recording talent for its next three releases in April 1899. Baritone S.H. Dudley (1864–1947) was a former mid-level opera singer who had toured with several companies. He began recording in the mid–1890s as a member of the Edison Quartet, specializing in popular material, and quickly became one of the most familiar names on record, including as interlocutor on numerous minstrel records. Reminiscing in later years, he referred to himself as "the Bing Crosby of 1900," although this may be a bit of an exaggeration. Dudley scaled back on his recording activities after 1904 and became a Victor executive, responsible for, among other things, *The Victor Book of the Opera*.[31]

Assisting Dudley was the Haydn Quartet, of which he and basso William F. Hooley were regular members. There was considerable turnover in tenors, with Roger Harding and "Leigh" replaced during 1899 by Jere Mahoney, Fred Rycroft and John Bieling. All of these men had extensive experience in recording, but apparently only Harding had a background in professional minstrelsy (with the Sam Devere Company). For some reason, Berliner called them "The Imperial Minstrels" on these records, even though that name was simultaneously being used by Len Spencer's more famous troupe on the Columbia label.

In the recordings, Hooley was the interlocutor and Dudley played the endman, with the inevitable chicken-stealing joke, a familiar African American reference:

> HOOLEY: Well, Sam, I'm afraid you've been up to your old tricks again.
> DUDLEY: Well, what tricks, Mr. Hooley?
> HOOLEY: Stealing chickens.
> DUDLEY: Why, I'm astonished that you're saying that, Mr. Hooley. Why, I've a system now, I'm proper living.
> HOOLEY: Then where'd you get that nice fat chicken you had yesterday?
> DUDLEY: Why, I got that chicken by weight.
> HOOLEY: By weight?
> DUDLEY: Yessir, I waited 'til I was sure the owner was asleep.
> (laughter, whistles)

Featured songs were the current hits "A Hot Time in the Old Town" and "My Coal Black Lady," as well as that traditional favorite of barbershop quartets, "Sally in Our Alley," harmonized in fine style by Mahoney and the Haydn Quartet.

Berliner brought out a final batch of minstrel records in early 1900, this time calling them the Gramophone Minstrels (perhaps Spencer had complained?). Once again Dudley and Hooley anchored the proceedings, assisted by tenor Harry Macdonough and pianist Frank P. Banta. The featured songs were a mixture of old ("Old Folks at Home") and new ("Darktown Is Out Tonight").

Despite the fact that he had invented the disc phonograph, Emile Berliner was forced out of the business in the United States in mid–1900 due to a series of negative court decisions. Disc record manufacture was carried on by his associate Eldridge R. Johnson under a different corporate structure and using an improved recording method of Johnson's design. Johnson launched his own label, at first called Improved Gram-O-Phone, then Improved Record, and finally (in 1901) Victor Talking Machine Co.

Johnson immediately had Dudley, Hooley and Macdonough return to the studio in November 1900 to re-record the same titles they had recorded for Berliner earlier in the year, now using his new process. For the new records, they were called the Georgia Minstrels, an odd choice since "Georgia Minstrels" generally designated a black minstrel troupe. Perhaps this change represented a little misleading marketing to make them appear more authentic to buyers?

The new records were so successful that the Georgia Minstrels returned in January 1901 for a set of six new titles, this time issued on Johnson's newly introduced "Monarch" 10-inch records. This format gave them a full three minutes of playing time (rather than the two minutes on seven-inch discs and most cylinders), allowing an overture and an opening chorus, jokes, and a fuller rendition of the featured song at the end. The songs were a mix of old and new, and in fact, with the additional time, it was now possible to have both on the same record—perhaps a few bars of an old favorite at the open (e.g., "In the Evening by the Moonlight" from 1880) and a new song at the end (e.g., "The Blue and the Gray," 1900). The records were beginning to sound even more like a real minstrel stage show, reflecting its variety.

Even as Victor was staking its claim to the growing disc market, Columbia—the major cylinder producer of the 1890s—was finding a way to get around the Berliner patents and begin selling discs as well as cylinders. After a few tentative forays with "toy" records and carrying other companies' products, Columbia began selling Climax disc records in the fall of 1901 (made "for" Columbia but, for legal reasons, technically the products of another company). Since Columbia couldn't use its exclusive Imperial Minstrels on these discs, it assembled another, somewhat odd troupe called, logically enough, the Climax Minstrels. These records were only on sale for a few months in 1902, and they are quite rare today.

The interlocutor was addressed as "Mr. Fairchild," an otherwise unknown name on early recordings. Nor does he sound like anyone else on record at that time. There were two actors named Fairchild active on the New York stage—Robert Fairchild and Roy Fairchild—and it may have been one of them. Whoever Fairchild was, he introduced these records in a bombastic fashion, almost shouting the words.

> FAIRCHILD (slowly and loudly): Climax Record. Minstrel First Part, introducing "My Wild Irish Rose." Gentlemen, be seated. (Orchestra strikes a chord)
> FAIRCHILD: We will commence the evening's entertainment with a grand introductory overture by our symphony orchestra. (Small orchestra plays, followed by laugh.)[32]

Fairchild was assisted by studio regulars George J. Gaskin, Albert Campbell, and possibly others. The featured songs were mostly recent hits (e.g., "My Wild Irish Rose," 1899), and those heard were sung as duets by Gaskin and Campbell—an unusual combination. The discs were available in both seven-inch and 10-inch sizes, which allowed for additional jokes, including one about the Irish:

> ENDMAN #1: Say, Mr. Fairchild, I'd like to recite a piece of poetry.
> ENDMAN #2 (WITH HEAVY BROGUE): Look here, Mr. Fairchild, that nigger don't know anything about poetry. Here's a bit of Irish poetry for ya "Fire, fire, says Mrs. Maguire. Where, where, says Mrs. O'Hare. Downtown, says Mrs. Brown. Oh run, bless us and save us, says Mrs. Davis. We'll all be burned, says Mrs. Burns."
> (great laughter)
> FAIRCHILD: Mr. Campbell and Gaskin will sing "My Wild Irish Rose."

There are a number of interesting aspects to these discs that shed light on the performance practices of minstrels during this period. The pompous introduction of "our symphony orchestra," followed by the thin sounds of an obviously tiny ensemble, could well be a joke. Featuring a song like "My Wild Irish Rose" (sung straight) is about as far from an African American focus as one can get. So is the "bit of Irish poetry," although the performer throws in the term *nigger* almost casually in setting up the joke. As for the poem, it is actually a well-known children's rhyme, showing how widely minstrels cast their nets for material—or perhaps it's just mockery of the Irish? It is probably not meant to be a mockery of blacks, since the speaker evinces a broad brogue, suggesting that he's Irish. These are aural factors discerned only by listening to a performance, rather than relying on written sources.

Dudley, Hooley and Macdonough (effectively, with one other man, the Haydn Quartet) turned up again on the Zonophone disc label in late 1901, on seven- and nine-inch discs. Hooley was again the interlocutor and Dudley the principal endman. The four seven-inch pressings featured two current songs ("Coon, Coon, Coon" and "Goodbye Dolly Gray") and two old standards ("Old Folks at Home" and "My Old Kentucky Home"). The eight longer nine-inch discs were likewise a mix of old and new, with an emphasis on the latter, including the huge ragtime hit "Just Because She Made Dem Goo-Goo Eyes" (1900). There were a few "coon songs" explicitly demeaning blacks (e.g., "My Rainbow Coon," 1900); however, these were pop hits of the day, not specific to minstrel shows.

The choice of "Coon, Coon, Coon" is interesting, as it might seem from the title to be just another of these derogatory songs. Popularized by minstrel star Lew Dockstader, and a major hit, it is in fact a lament from the black man's perspective about how he was treated in Jim Crow America.[33] This song was featured in the controversial 1977 Glynn Turman film *Minstrel Man*, a protest against discrimination.

Although it's not my color,
I'm feeling mighty blue;
I've got a lot of trouble,
I'll tell it all to you:
I'm cert'nly clean disgusted
With life, and that's a fact
Because my hair is wooly
And because my color's black.

Just as I was a-thinkin'
I had things fixed up right,
I passed a tree where two doves
Sat making love at night;
They stopped and looked me over,
I saw my finish soon.
When both those birds said good and loud,
"Look at the coon! Look at the coon! Look at the coon!"

REFRAIN [sung twice after verse]
Coon! Coon! Coon!
I wish my color would fade.
Coon! Coon! Coon!
I'd like a different shade.
Coon! Coon! Coon!
Morning, night and noon.
I wish I was a white man
'stead of a Coon! Coon! Coon![34]

The Zonophone Minstrels joked about current events, too. In the early 1900s, Carrie Nation, the fearsome anti-alcohol crusader, had just begun her campaign of marching into bars and smashing them up with a hatchet. An imposing woman who stood at six feet, 175 pounds, she was often accompanied by other temperance advocates and gave fiery lectures about the evils of alcohol, which had taken her first husband's life.

DUDLEY: Ohhh, this is a great country we live in, Mr. Hooley.
HOOLEY: Yes, it is, Sam, a glorious country. And we have never been defeated!
DUDLEY: Ah, but there was one nation that drubbed us.
HOOLEY: Impossible! What nation was that?
DUDLEY: Why, Carrie Nation!
(Great laughter, clapping, whistling)[35]

In 1903, Zonophone switched to Len Spencer's Imperial Minstrels.

The High Point of Recorded Minstrelsy?

Recorded minstrelsy reached an apex in 1903 with the release of a full half-hour show—in fact, two half-hour shows—in competing multi-disc sets issued by Victor and Columbia.

Despite the offensive title and graphics, this Lew Dockstader song is actually a lament about the unfair treatment of blacks.

From the start, the Victor Talking Machine Company wanted to be known for a quality product offered at commensurate prices, and it hired talented musicians and orchestra leaders to create its recordings. Victor heavily advertised its classical recordings, such as those by the phenomenal new tenor Enrico Caruso, to gain prestige, but its bread-and-butter popular recordings were well made too, both technically and creatively.

Thus, when in late 1902 Victor decided to produce a full minstrel show set, it was an elaborate, carefully scripted production in which the performance flowed naturally from disc to disc without being interrupted by opening announcements or "Gentlemen, be seated" at the beginning of each disc. Disc number 8 took the listener all the way to the "Grand Afterpiece," a sketch. The discs could be bought individually, but they were intended to be played in sequence. They were issued in both 10-inch and 12-inch sizes, allowing plenty of time to develop the material. (Oddly, the 12-inch discs, recorded in 1903, used the same scripts as the 10-inch versions with no additional material, just delivered a little more slowly.)

Victor was proud of the results, introducing them as follows:

An Evening with the Minstrels

A Genuine Old Time Minstrel Show

An absolute novelty in Minstrel Records—a complete performance of old-fashioned Minstrelsy, a form of entertainment of which the public never tires. This series consists of eight Monarch Records and lasts from twenty-five to thirty minutes, with not one dull moment. Bright jokes, brilliant orchestra bits, plantation songs, and novel effects come in rapid succession.

In the making of these records we have enlisted the largest company of Comedians, Singers and Musicians which have ever been used for Talking Machine Records, and no expense has been spared in their production. Although primarily intended for use in a series, each record is complete in itself, as the description indicates.[36]

Part of Victor's groundbreaking "Evening with the Minstrels" set (1903).

The artists were not identified, but heard on the discs are Len Spencer as the principal endman, S.H. Dudley or William F. Hooley as the pompous interlocutor, tenor Harry Macdonough, baritone Steve Porter, Dan W. Quinn, and numerous others. It is likely that Spencer was the producer (and perhaps writer) of this set. He recorded regularly for Victor and was the most experienced minstrel record producer in the business.

The catalog contained detailed descriptions of each of the eight discs. Number 1 ("Ethiopian Carnival of Melody") opened with a bugle call, followed by the interlocutor announcing, "Gentlemen, be seated! Medley overture by the entire company." Then came a long medley by the quartet of snippets of "Darktown Is Out Tonight," "Old Folks at Home," "Carry Me Back to Old Virginny," "Patrol Comique," "Massa's in de Cold, Cold Ground," a reprise of "Darktown Is Out Tonight," and a fast chorus of "Dixie" by the orchestra, followed by applause, whistling, and cheering, which ended the disc.

Number 2 ("My Creole Sue") is a funny routine with a surprise ending. In one version Spencer, as endman, repeatedly interrupts the increasingly irate interlocutor (Dudley) as the latter tries to begin his big song. The orchestra stops, and starts, and stops again. Finally, Spencer reveals that he once had an old mule and "whenever you open your mouth to sing you remind me of that old jackass!"—causing the company to erupt in great hilarity. Dudley, now thoroughly disgusted, fires back, "Very well, then, Mr. Macdonough will sing the song," and walks off, resulting in cheers from "the boys." This kind of extended back-and-forth routine, building up to a payoff in which the supposedly subservient endman gets the better of his stuffy boss, was a staple of stage minstrelsy but impossible to include as a short gag on a normal record.[37]

Number 3 is a long sketch, full of fast-paced wordplay and misunderstandings, in which Spencer tells Dudley how he got doused in paint by the father of his girlfriend when he crawled in her back window "to play a little penny-ante." A quartet ends the record with "Chimes of the Golden Bells."

Number 4 is another Spencer-Dudley routine in which Dudley plays an orchestra leader who needs an assistant, and Spencer is a seemingly incompetent drifter who wanders in, banters with the leader, and eventually gets the job. The dialogue plays on short and snappy back-and-forth repartee between the two, as well as a certain amount of stage business, which they both carry off like pros.

(Knock on door)
DUDLEY: Come in.
(More knocks on door.)
DUDLEY: Come in!
(More knocks on door.)
DUDLEY (NOW SHOUTING): COME IN!!
LEN: Eh?
DUDLEY: I said "come in."
LEN: Well, I am in.
DUDLEY: Well, now you're in, what can I do for you?
LEN: Huh?
DUDLEY: What do you want?
LEN: Why, I'm lookin' for somethin'.
DUDLEY: Looking for what?
LEN: Oh, almost anything will suit me.
DUDLEY: Are you seeking a position?
LEN: Huh?
DUDLEY: Are you looking for work?
LEN: Well, not if I can find anything else to do.
(Laughter)

Number 5 ("Having Fun with the Orchestra") involves Spencer doing a sketch with Porter, who frequently did comedy routines in various dialects. Here Porter plays a frustrated German bandleader whose predecessor skipped out with the band's money, and who is trying to get the discordant players back in shape. Spencer arrives and fires off a steady stream of jokes and putdowns, but eventually the band outwits him and drives him off the stage.

Number 6 ("The Cakewalk in Coontown") is perhaps the most fascinating disc of all, as it recreates, rather realistically, the sound of a cakewalk competition. These were frequently staged within the setting of a minstrel show, either as a sketch in the olio or, more likely, as the extended afterpiece. Cakewalks (and the high-stepping music that went with them) had been introduced to the public fairly recently, in the late 1880s, and they were all the rage in theaters of the time. The premise, supposedly based on antebellum slave customs, was that a man and a woman (or a man in drag) would circle around the floor, high stepping and throwing their heads back, in an exaggerated parody of the formal dances done by "the white folks" at their soirees. Judges would determine who was the best, with the prize being a cake (which was sometimes placed in the middle of the floor for the contestants to dance around). The songs written for these cakewalk exhibitions in the 1890s were lively, syncopated two-steps and rags like "Rastus on Parade" or "At a Georgia Camp Meeting."

In the Victor recreation, which unfortunately contains some offensive racial imagery, Spencer is the master of ceremonies. Some of Spencer's lines appear to come directly from *The Witmark Amateur Minstrel Guide*, published in 1899.[38] As this is a rare period audio representation of a cakewalk competition, it is worth citing in full:

(Crowd noises)

Len: Now, coons, this am to be the cream event of the season. And nobody but the blue-blooded aristocracy of Darktown's 400 will be allowed on the floor. Now I don't s'pose for a minute that any of you coons has got a razor?

Crowd (shouting back): No!

Len: Well, that's right, because you won't need 'em where I'm at. I'm just as good as a regiment of razors, and when I step in the middle of the floor it means, gimme room! Now you all know me, and you know you can't walk on the floor all covered with blood.

(Crowd chatters)

Len: Now-a I'm the judge and the jury, and if any of you bad coons tries to butt in and pester me, I'll cut you down in the flower of your youth, ya heah me?

(Crowd chatters)

Len: Take your partners for the cakewalk!

(Orchestra strikes up a lively refrain as Len shouts encouragement)

Len: "Couples, promenade!" "Cross over!" "Come down!"

(Quartet comes in, singing a special chorus: "Swing round, and show your toes my lady. Don't ... you ... take ... your ... peepers off that cake, we'll make all those other coons look shady, don't ... make ... no ... mistake!")

(Applause)

Len: Couple number two. Promenade!

(Orchestra launches into "At a Georgia Camp Meeting" while Len calls out)

Len: "Hold your head up, lady!" "Ain't no cake on the floor," "Yeah, yeah, lift your hat, coon," "Yeah, hold your face 'fore your head falls in, you gather?"

(Quartet joins in, sings a chorus of "Happy Days in Dixieland")

(Applause)

Len: Couple number *three*. Promenade!

(Orchestra resumes "At a Georgia Camp Meeting" while Len calls out)

Len: "Ah ha, look at number three," "Ah, boy, you'll walk that cake home for dinner," "Show your feet lady," "Give 'em room, give 'em room," "You're walkin' right into that cake."

(Quartet chimes in with rousing chorus of the 1896 cakewalk song, "Remus Takes the Cake!")

(Cheers, applause)

Len: Ladies and gentlemen, I desire to announce that the cake and the wallet, they come to number three!

(More cheers, applause)

(Voice during fade-out): I told ya.... I told ya so...[39]

The performance sounds remarkably "live" and realistic. The orchestra and quartet come in with split-second timing, Spencer is quite natural as the emcee, and the crowd noises add to the atmosphere. It is an unusual recording for the period, and the only extended audio recreation of a cakewalk that I have ever heard from this era. The transcription from a different take shows slight differences in wording, indicating that while the performers "followed the script" in different takes, they did not do so exactly. These variations contribute to the looseness and naturalness of the performance.[40]

Disc number 7, "Sidewalk Conversation, Funny Things You See in the Papers," is a talking sketch featuring Spencer and Dudley, in which they comment on nonsensical news stories and current events (Dudley works at Carrie Nation's newspaper, *The Daily Hatchet*—another topical reference).

The final disc, number 8, is appropriately called "Grand Afterpiece: Scenes on the Levee." It recreates, with sound effects, African Americans loading cotton on a riverboat, then breaking into song under the leadership of straw boss Spencer. This disc even includes a specially written piece by the orchestra incorporating blasts from the ship's horn as a musical counterpoint.

The "Evening with the Minstrels" set essentially consists of two discs setting up the familiar minstrel first part, followed by five discs with dialogues or sketches that could have been performed either during the first part in front of the minstrel company or during the olio in front of the lowered curtain. Number 8 is clearly labeled "Afterpiece" and meant to evoke a full stage production with crowd noises and sound effects. This setup is similar to the structure presented in Paskman and Spaeth's 1928 *Gentlemen, Be Seated!* and visualized in several movie recreations.[41] There are also spatial indicators suggesting that listeners were supposed to envision a theater setting—for example, Spencer (in number 5) referring to the orchestra "down there" (i.e., in the orchestra pit), the laughing and clapping heard after punchlines, and the reference in the catalog to "the curtain falls" after number 4.

Victor's "An Evening with the Minstrels" set was released in January 1903, and it was quite successful. Individual discs were rerecorded several times, as late as 1909 (a sure sign of continuing sales), with some discs remaining in the catalog until 1923. The cast varied over time, later including John Bieling, Edward Meeker and Billy Murray. Steve Porter was the interlocutor on some of the later takes.

Hearing about the Victor set, major competitor Columbia almost immediately rushed to release its own set on both discs and cylinders, using the same overall name: "An Evening with the Minstrels." Recording ledgers for Columbia do not survive, so we don't know for certain whether these were recorded before or after the Victor sessions, which were held in mid–December 1902. However, the Columbia set was announced in a supplement dated February 1, 1903, a month after Victor, and a dealer advertising card announcing the set as forthcoming was dated February 14, 1903, so it was probably slightly later.[42]

The Columbia set bears all the hallmarks of a rush job. There were 12 parts, lettered "A" through "L," available as seven-inch or 10-inch discs, and also as 12 cylinders similarly lettered. This was more than the Victor set, but most of them were simply complete renditions of a song, much like a regular song release. Only four contained dialogue, and those were mostly collections of random minstrel stories and jokes rather than the clever, custom-written sketches offered by Victor. There was no duplication with the Victor material. There was also no "audience" to provide laughter, nor any elaborate "Cakewalk in Coontown"–style recreations.

The principal talent was uncredited but sometimes named within the recordings; they included recording veterans Len and Harry Spencer, Arthur Collins, J.W. Myers, George J. Gaskin, Billy Golden, and George Graham. Len Spencer was most likely the producer and writer. The 12 parts were as follows (numbers are for the discs):

1109A: Introductory overture; medley of operatic airs by entire company
1109B: Song, "Our Land of Dreams" by J.W. Myers
1109C: Talking, endman stories by Len and Harry Spencer
1109D: Song, "I'm a Nigger That's Living High" by Len Spencer
1109E: Talking, jokes between interlocutor (Harry Spencer) and endmen (Len Spencer and Arthur Collins)
1109F: Song, "I'm Wearing My Heart Away for You" by George J. Gaskin
1109G: Talking, jokes between interlocutor (H. Spencer) and endman (Collins)
1109H: Song, "My Friend from My Home" by Len Spencer
1109I: Song, "Black Hussar's March" by Myers and company
1109J: Olio, trumpet specialty by Albert Bode

1109K: Olio, talking, monologue by George Graham
1109L: Olio, banjo solo, "Yankee Doodle," by Vess L. Ossman

Curiously, part "A" does not open with "Gentlemen, be seated," but launches right into a medley of familiar operatic snippets, ending with "The Anvil Chorus" from *Il Trovatore*. The featured songs were mostly contemporary (published 1901–1903), but the stories and jokes on the spoken records sound like those on a hundred other minstrel records of the period.

> INTERLOCUTOR: Now tell me, Arthur, is your wife a blonde or a brunette?
> COLLINS: Well, she's not exactly a brunette, but she's *dye-ing* to be a blonde!

The last three parts are identified as the olio, acknowledging the second act of a traditional minstrel show. Perhaps the most interesting is Part "K." Here, George Graham, an experienced raconteur, addresses the audience directly (as from the stage), cracks a few jokes, and then tells a funny story about a dream he had while sleeping in a park in Washington.

> Well, good evening, audience, I am glad to see so many friends here this evening. And before proceeding with my portion of the entertainment, I'd like to make a few explanatory remarks. I know there's a good many people see me come out on stage think that I'm going to sing some tender or sentimental song. That, I assure you, is not the case. I am supposed to be funny. Therefore I will request the audience to kindly laugh whether it is funny or not. (pause) And I'm glad to see the audience laughing, there's one man applaudin' over there. Well, brother, you are in the hopeless minority, but I sympathize with you. Well, I do declare. There's a lady with spectacles on over there laughin' too. Well, I do declare. Yes. (pause) Well, I want to tell you my experience. I was in the city of Washington last summer…

Despite the less polished production, the Columbia set was successful as well, with many of the sides remade (sometimes with different talent). It remained in the catalog until 1907 but was not reissued in double-faced form in later years.

Every Label's Got to Have a Minstrel Record!

During the years that followed the release of the Victor and Columbia minstrel records, it seemed that every label, no matter how small, wanted to have one or more minstrel records on its list. Many of these records survive today (especially the discs), and it is testimony to just how popular minstrelsy remained with record buyers as phonographs became widely available.

After Len Spencer discontinued the Imperial Minstrels in 1904, two other minstrel recording troupes sprang up to fill the void. A majority of the minstrel records made during the latter half of the first period of minstrel recording (roughly 1904–1915) were by one of these two groups. The advantage of having a troupe with continuing, stable leadership and membership was that the members learned to work closely together within the minstrel framework, often had defined roles, and could come up with new material on their own. In addition, since four persons was an ideal number to execute a minstrel performance (balancing the need for a variety of voices and the limitations of the recording technology of the time), such a troupe could double as a regular quartet on other popular recordings, as both of these new troupes did.

The Rambler Minstrels

The first troupe was the Rambler Minstrels, organized in 1906 and featuring comic singer Billy Murray. The other members were baritone and "black delineator" Arthur Collins, baritone Steve Porter, and tenor Byron G. Harlan, all recording veterans. "Mr. Porter" served as the interlocutor, while Murray, Collins, and sometimes Harlan delivered the jokes.

Billy Murray (1877–1954), one of the most famous and prolific artists of the acoustic recording era, had experience in professional minstrelsy. Born in Philadelphia and raised in Denver, at the age of 16 he joined a small theatrical troupe that was passing through town. When that opportunity didn't pan out, he teamed up with fellow troupe member Matt Keefe and made his way to the West Coast, where he (and they) sang in honky-tonks, medicine shows and small-time vaudeville. In 1897, Murray got his first taste of recording, making cylinders for the local Edison dealer, the Bacigalupi Brothers. A few years later, around 1900, he and Keefe landed positions with the Al G. Field Greater Minstrels, one of the biggest and most successful traveling minstrel shows in the nation. None of Murray's biographers seem to know exactly when that took place, but by 1902 Murray had become one of the blackface endmen and was being noticed by the press. During the fall of 1902, he opened the show with an enthusiastic version of "Bill Bailey, Won't You Please Come Home," which drew rave reviews and numerous encores. Murray remained with Field for two more years (1902–1904), a graduate education in minstrelsy.

Meanwhile, in mid-1903, while the troupe was playing in the greater New York area, Murray landed work for the national recording companies headquartered there, first Edison and then Victor and Columbia. His sharp, rather nasal voice recorded extremely well, and he could put over a comic song with brio. His records sold well, and he was soon getting more recording work than he could handle, for all companies, causing him to quit the Field troupe in 1904.[43] Thus the experience that Murray brought to the Rambler Minstrels in 1906, both in minstrelsy and in recording, was considerable.

Incidentally, anyone who thinks big-time stage minstrelsy was dead by 1900 should read the reviews for the Field troupe, which crisscrossed the country playing mid-size cities (Buffalo, Indianapolis, Minneapolis, etc.). In the afternoon they would march through town in a traditional minstrel parade and then, in the evening, perform in a large, packed theater, drawing rave reviews even from normally skeptical reviewers. Field kept his material fresh, and

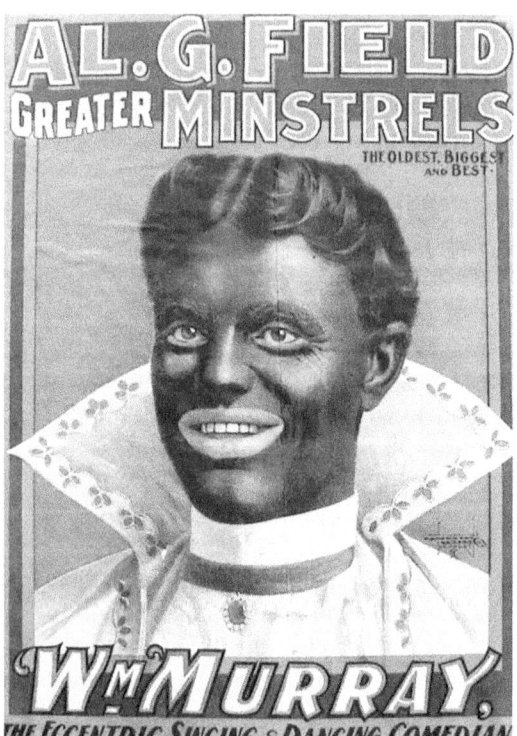

Prolific recording artist Billy Murray in his minstrel days.

his ever-changing cast was top notch. In 1901, the *Rochester (NY) Democrat and Chronicle* commented on his endmen, "They get off a lot of jokes and stories that are mostly new and all exceedingly funny. And in most minstrel shows new jokes are almost unknown."[44]

The Ramblers, as organized by Murray, recorded most heavily for Columbia, with a total of 18 minstrel routines between 1906 and 1909. Eight of these were cylinders and 10 were discs, with a good deal of overlap in repertoire. Every one of the featured songs was a current pop tune, many with no apparent relationship to minstrelsy or blacks (e.g., "Waltz Me Around Again, Willie," "San Antonio," "Crocodile Isle"). The production adhered to a very rigid, tightly scripted formula: the quartet did a fast introductory chorus; Porter announced "Gentlemen, be seated"; the four of them traded four or five quick jokes; and either Collins or Murray (usually) sang the featured number, ending with cheers and clapping. The jokes were often about marriage or served as "insult" humor directed at other cast members, particularly the stuffy interlocutor.

> PORTER: By the way, Arthur, you've known me for fifteen years, haven't you?
> COLLINS: Yes, suh … just about fifteen.
> PORTER: Well, ah, I don't like to ask it, but, ah, will you lend me five dollars?
> COLLINS: No, suh, I refuse ab-so-lutely.
> PORTER: Refuse? Why?
> COLLINS: Well, just 'cause I've known yuh for fifteen years!
> (laughter, clapping)[45]

The tight, formulaic production, emphasizing current songs and the close harmony of the quartet, gave these records a sameness that was in contrast with the loose and "live" feeling of some other minstrel records. Nevertheless, they were quite successful, all of them reissued in double-faced versions in 1908 and several remaining in the Columbia catalog until 1914. They are likewise found on many smaller labels to which Columbia provided masters, including Harmony, Oxford, Silvertone and Standard.

The Ramblers also recorded in 1906 for the Imperial label (of the Leeds and Catlin Co.), an independent label that was fighting the Victor/Columbia patent monopoly. The troupe recorded at least three routines for Imperial, using scripts and songs identical to those on the Columbia records. The quartet also duplicated six of its routines for the American label, another independent entity.

Columbia's longtime studio orchestra leader Charles A. Prince was intimately involved in the production of the label's minstrel records.

Beginning in 1907, the Ramblers developed some new material for the Zonophone label, a subsidiary of Victor. Over the next two years, they recorded a total of 13 routines for this label, some using Columbia scripts but most new. They retained their formula of tight quartet harmony, short, fast-paced jokes, and a current pop tune to finish off the record. Some of the jokes were real groaners, such as the "Venetian blind" joke that is still used today.

PORTER: I say, Arthur, what business are you in now?
COLLINS: Oh, I, I, I'm a carpenter.
PORTER: Ah ha, then perhaps you can tell me how to make a Venetian blind?
COLLINS: Um hum, I'd give him a punch in the eye!
(laughter, whistling)[46]

The quartet recorded approximately eight routines for Victor, calling itself the Christy Minstrels (1908) and the Victor Minstrels (1908–1909). The material largely duplicated the scripts being used on Zonophone and other labels. The quartet introduced one of the Victor and Zonophone routines with a very fast chorus of George M. Cohan's "Make a Lot of Noise," a song that so perfectly embodied the party atmosphere of a minstrel show that it became a favorite of the genre in years to come.

> Hey, hey, hey-hey-hey!
> I want everyone to make a lot of noise,
> I want every boy to be one of the boys,
> I want every girl to wear a Sunday gown,
> Let's have some fun in a wide open town.
> I want every day to be a holiday,
> Let's all cheer and let the band begin to play,
> Hip-hip-hooray and a good ship ahoy!
> Happy, happy, happy, happy, make a lot of noise![47]

In addition to these disc records, the Ramblers produced five cylinders during 1907–1909 for the Indestructible Record Company, under the name "The Dixie Minstrels." Once again, they used material familiar from other labels. The same was true for three cylinders made for Edison between 1907 and early 1909, as "The Edison Minstrels" (subtitled "Dixie Minstrels," "Jubilee Minstrels" and "Model Minstrels").

For all of the many recordings they made during their relatively short existence, the Rambler Minstrels stuck closely to their formula, emphasizing close quartet harmony and very current songs. They ultimately broke up not due to a lack of popularity but because the members (especially Murray) were busy with other work. In addition to his considerable solo work, in 1909 Murray became the lead singer of the American Quartet, an extremely popular group that was one of the most recorded ensembles of the acoustic era. The other members of that quartet were Porter, tenor John Bieling, and bass William F. Hooley.

The Peerless Minstrels

The Ramblers' place as the leading minstrel recording troupe was taken by another very popular foursome, the Peerless Quartet. This group was founded in 1906 by Frank C. Stanley (1868–1910), a New York–area concert singer and veteran bass/baritone who had been recording since the 1890s. The other initial members were Steve Porter (there he is again!), Henry Burr, and Albert Campbell. Shortly after its founding, the quartet also began recording as minstrels, initially for Columbia, which announced in November 1907 that it would offer a "new combination, known as 'The Peerless Minstrels.'"[48] The interlocutor was usually the authoritative-sounding Stanley (addressed as "Mr. Stanley"), although on at least two early recordings Porter assumed this role.

There were two key personnel changes early in the quartet's history. In 1909, the busy Porter left to join the American Quartet and was replaced by Arthur Collins. A

Practically all of Victor's popular male artists were involved with minstrelsy in some way. Murray and Burr were leaders of the Rambler and Peerless Minstrels, respectively, while Collins, Harlan and Macdonough often recorded with them. Countertenor Will Oakland was a star on the minstrel circuit, while Geoffrey O'Hara appeared with Dockstader and others and was a member of the "Spook Minstrels" movie troupe (1905). *Source: Victor Records, June 1916.*

more dramatic change occurred at the end of 1910. On December 6, 1910, Stanley appeared at the Waldorf-Astoria Hotel in New York as the featured basso in a concert called "An Evening in Song with the Well-Known Composers Caro Roma and Ernest R. Ball." Leaving the concert for his home in New Jersey, he realized that he had forgotten his coat but decided to finish the trip in the frigid weather without it. He caught a cold, which turned into pneumonia, and in less than a week—on December 12—Frank Stanley was dead. In the days before penicillin and similar antibiotics, something as simple as a bad cold could quickly become deadly.[49]

Stanley had recorded with the Peerless Quartet shortly before his death (his last Victor session with them was on October 27), and the surviving members had to decide what to do. Henry Burr (1882–1941), an ambitious and business-oriented tenor, took charge and hired John H. Meyer as the new bass-baritone and formal-sounding interlocutor. In the new lineup, Burr assumed the role of stuttering endman—quite a contrast with the serious balladeer he was as a solo artist. Collins, who specialized in "negro delineations," was the drawling endman, and Campbell the querulous, high-pitched cast member. It was a nicely balanced cast, and under Burr's strict management the Peerless Quartet and Minstrels went on to become the most successful popular vocal group of the acoustic era. Aside from their minstrel records, the Peerless group, dominated by Burr's sweet Irish tenor, tended to specialize in ballads while their friendly rivals, the American Quartet (led by Billy Murray), emphasized upbeat and comic numbers.

None of the Peerless members—Burr, Collins, Campbell, Meyer, or their predecessors Porter or Stanley—had a background in professional minstrelsy. But, except for newcomer Meyer, they were all experienced recording artists, had almost certainly seen minstrel shows, and perhaps even participated in a local production or two. Given the experience the record companies had by this time in producing "minstrel first part" recordings, the pattern was set.

The Peerless Minstrels had a looser, more conversational tone than the tightly scripted Ramblers. While they typically opened with a quartet chorus and ended with a currently popular song, they varied this routine from time to time. They used older popular songs as well, and most of their songs seemed appropriate in a minstrel setting (which unfortunately meant more coon songs, like "The Humming Coon" and "My Dusky Rose"). Old classics found their way into the routines, too, like "Oh, Dem Golden Slippers" and "In the Morning by the Bright Light." To vary the sound, they would sometimes add a whistling chorus, sound effects, or even a sand dance, providing a much closer approximation of a stage minstrel show than did the Ramblers.

Ten out of the 11 sides that the Peerless Minstrels made for Columbia between 1907 and 1915 were 12 inches in size, giving them a full four to five minutes to develop the performance. They used the extra time to work in parts of three songs rather than two (i.e., first an opening chorus, some jokes, then another short chorus, more jokes, and finally the concluding number). Over time, the four men seemed to grow increasingly comfortable working together and bouncing off each other. Burr and Collins would sometimes spar back and forth, leaving the interlocutor to observe.

The Peerless Minstrels seldom recorded under their own name, usually employing a name assigned by the label (e.g., "Columbia Minstrels") or no name at all ("minstrels"). In fact, two of the sides made for Columbia (A5123 and A5138) were labeled as by the Rambler Minstrels, although they were in fact by the Peerless troupe. Real names were generally used during the routines, however. Burr was addressed as "Harry" (his real name was Harry McClasky), while Collins was "Arthur" and Campbell was "Albert." Meyer played a much less prominent role in the proceedings than Stanley had. On the occasions when Meyer was addressed directly, he was called "John" or "Mr. Wilbur" (after the pseudonym he often used on solo discs, "John Wilbur"). The Jewish-sounding "Meyer" would probably have seemed out of place in a minstrel show.

In 1910, the Peerless Minstrels began recording for Victor and became that company's principal minstrel troupe, usually billed as the Victor Minstrels or the Victor Minstrel Company. Victor named individual routines after southern states, so individual discs were called the Virginia Minstrels, Alabama Minstrels, Georgia Minstrels, Arkansas Minstrels, Louisiana Minstrels, Texas Minstrels, North Carolina Minstrels, South Carolina Minstrels, Mississippi Minstrels, Kentucky Minstrels, Tennessee Minstrels, Florida Minstrels, New Orleans Minstrels, and Missouri Minstrels, among other names. Basically they covered every state in Dixie, plus a few other southern locales. Victor also began numbering its minstrel discs, reaching as high as "number 27," but the numbering system was inconsistent.

In all, the Peerless troupe made 20 minstrel sides for Victor between 1910 and 1913, 19 of them 12-inch (four-minute) discs. They developed a lot of new material for the label, although it all followed familiar minstrel themes. Minstrelsy was very male-centric, and there were plenty of jokes about the trials and tribulations of marriage, always from the man's point of view. For example, this is the familiar "thousand kisses" joke:

> BURR: Say, Arthur, y-you don't look the least bit cheerful tonight. Wh-wh-what's the matter?
> COLLINS: Oh, I gotta letter from my wife.
> BURR: Yeah, well, wh-what's she say?
> COLLINS: She said, "Send me fifty dollars at once."
> BURR: Well, did you send it?
> COLLINS: No, I didn't send it, 'cause I didn't have no money. So I wrote her a nice lett-ah.
> BURR: Yeah, well, wh-wh-what'd you say?
> COLLINS: I said, "My darlin' wife, the truth is not doin' good work, and we have no fifty dollars my dear, but enclosed please find check for one thousand kisses." Now wasn't that real pretty, Harry?
> BURR: Yes, you'se was some bit of sentimentality.
> COLLINS: Um hum. Here's the answer to my letter. "Greenville, North Carolina, September fowteen. Friend husband, I received your letter this mo'ning. Also the check for a thousand kisses. Um hum. I had the ice man cash your check this mo'ning!"
> (laughter, clapping)[50]

Occasionally they would even casually toss off a joke about domestic violence:

> INTERLOCUTOR: Well, Arthur, you seem to be thinking very deeply. What is on your mind?
> COLLINS: I was just thinkin' 'bout the Rainbow Coon the boys were just singin' about. The women is all right, John, but they is so extraordinarily fickle. They goes back on ya for the slightest provocation.
> INTERLOCUTOR: Explain yourself, Arthur.
> COLLINS: Well, I, I called on Miss Miami Jefferson Tompkins last night, and she had the audaciousness to demand of me a new pair of gloves.
> INTERLOCUTOR: And what did you do?
> COLLINS: Well, so as not to 'pear too willin', I smacked her in the mouth, jabbed her in the nose, kicked her on the ankle, knocked her downstairs and near broke her neck, and just for a little thing like that she done said she'd break the engagement!
> (laughter, applause)[51]

One of the most interesting Victor discs is "Military Minstrels." Comic sketches about bumbling soldiers (often, but not always, black soldiers) had been a familiar part of stage minstrelsy since the 1870s, popularized by Harrigan and Hart and their "Mulligan Guard." These sketches were seldom found on the brief recorded minstrel vignettes, but the Peerless troupe worked one up into a full routine. It's particularly interesting in light of the personalities involved. In real life, Collins chafed under the domineering leadership of Burr, who was 18 years his junior. Collins would eventually quit the quartet as a result of this discord.[52] Here Collins got to play the colonel berating the cowering, stuttering corporal (Burr), and on the recording there is a real edge in his voice. It sounds like he was enjoying it!

COLLINS (ANGRILY): Corporal Burr!
BURR (STUTTERING): Yeh-yeh-yeh-yeh.
COLLINS (LOUD AND ANGRY): *Enough sir!* How dare you come on parade today with your uniform in such a disgraceful condition?
BURR: W-w-w-well, I, I …
COLLINS: Close that speech trap, and don't ya open your face at your peril, now answer my question.
BURR: W-w-why … I, I …
COLLINS: In other words, sir, I'll slap ya in the guardhouse. When I ask you a question and you answer …
BURR: Why, I …
COLLINS: *Shut up!* I'll have you tried and court martialed for sassin' yoh superior officer.
BURR: I, I didn't …
COLLINS: *Shut up!* And if you *don't* answer, I'll bust your black head for disobedience. Now you see, I got ya both ways!
(laughter, clapping)[53]

At the risk of overanalyzing comedy, the line "I'll bust your black head" merits some discussion. It may sound threatening on paper, but the line was delivered in a raucous, fast-paced, comedic setting and flew by like lightning. Clearly it was not meant to be taken seriously. The Peerless troupe was acting out a comic skit, and once the skit was over, they came together in harmony—literally. Then there are the characters they were portraying. Since this is a sound recording, you can't see them, but Corporal Burr is described as black. The colonel uses dialect too ("sassin' yoh superior officer"), and Collins was well known for portraying blacks, so he is also presumably portraying a black man. (Collins' performances were so convincing that some consumers apparently thought he actually was an African American.[54]) A white colonel berating a black soldier would be one thing; a black colonel doing the same thing was quite another. And what if listeners knew that these were white actors portraying black men? Still another. Today the phrase "I'll bust your black head" would probably be considered offensive in all but the most limited contexts. In 1913, however, it was just banter.

The Peerless Minstrels recorded for numerous minor labels, generally using the same material that had appeared on Victor or Columbia. They made six sides for the Victor subsidiary Zonophone, all released between 1909 and 1911, and all featuring Frank C. Stanley as interlocutor (thus recorded before his death in December 1910). Curiously, these were labeled as by the Rambler Minstrels, even though it was obviously the Peerless troupe. They were all 10-inch discs, and therefore somewhat shorter than the Victor recordings.

The small Keen-O-Phone label, founded in Philadelphia by Monroe Keen, issued one side by the Peerless troupe around 1912, this time using their own name and featuring the songs "My Rainbow Coon," "All Coons Look Alike to Me" and "Take Plenty of Shoes." In 1914, the failing Keen-O-Phone was reorganized as Rex, which reissued this disc and many other Keen-O-Phone masters, using the same catalog numbers. Shortly thereafter, Rex issued a second Peerless minstrel routine, featuring the 1890s hits "Push Dem Clouds Away" and "I Don't Care If You Never Come Back." The jokes were the same string of marriage-mocking one-liners found on the 1912 Victor routine "Louisiana Minstrels."

In 1914 and 1916, the Peerless troupe recorded at least six mini-minstrel sides for Little Wonder, a phenomenally popular small, single-faced disc that was essentially a song sampler. Available at department store music counters (not in record stores) for only 10 cents (versus 75 cents for normal releases), they sold in the millions. Each disc was only five and a half inches in diameter and had no artist identification (only the generic "tenor," "baritone," "minstrels," etc.). They lasted a minute and a half each, undoubtedly the shortest minstrel records ever made. They consisted of a fast opening chorus, a few jokes, and another fast chorus at the end. Not surprisingly, they sound very rushed. The full story of Little Wonder is contained in my book *Little Wonder Records and Bubble Books*.[55]

The Peerless troupe cut its final minstrel sides in 1917. One was for the Emerson label, an inexpensive seven-inch disc that, it was hoped, would cash in on the vogue for low-priced records pioneered by Little Wonder (Victor Emerson was a principal in both labels). Although the content was similar to popular Victor and Columbia sides released in 1911, the market for minstrel records had pretty much dried up by 1917, and copies are quite rare today. The songs featured were "Oh, Dem Golden Slippers" and "My Dusky Rose." Also rare are two minstrel sides made in 1917 for Par-O-Ket, a small (seven-inch) budget label founded by Henry Burr himself. One side was a remake of the previously cited "Military Minstrels," while the other featured "The Bully Song," "Black Jim" and "Just Kiss Yourself Goodbye." The scripts were the same as those used on Victor in 1912 and 1913.

Besides these discs, the Peerless Minstrels recorded a few routines for minor cylinder labels between 1909 and 1912. The market for cylinders was in steep decline by this time, and even Edison introduced a line of disc records in 1913 while continuing to manufacture cylinders for the dwindling and now largely rural market. The Indestructible Record Co. initially used the Rambler Minstrels, but when that troupe dissolved in 1909, it switched to the Peerless Minstrels, which cut for the company two two-minute cylinders (as "The Dixie Minstrels") and three four-minute cylinders (as "The Carolina Minstrels"). These date from 1909 and 1910, featured Frank C. Stanley as interlocutor, and used scripts found on other labels. In fact, one of the songs featured, "The Humming Coon," seems to be found on almost every label the Peerless troupe recorded for at this time.

Between 1910 and 1912, the Peerless Minstrels cut one two-minute and three four-minute cylinders for the other independent cylinder label of the time, U.S. Everlasting. Once again, the material duplicated their disc routines and songs (there's "The Humming Coon" again!). One has Stanley as interlocutor, while the others have Meyer in that role.

Other Artist Combinations

The Edison company, which continued to produce cylinders (only) until 1913, generally preferred to assemble its own minstrel units using various combinations of studio talent called, generically, "Edison Minstrels." In 1903, after a gap of two years since its previous minstrel cylinders, the company started bringing out new releases. This time, endman Len Spencer traded jokes with interlocutor S.H. Dudley. Other participants included tenors Harry Macdonough and Will F. Denny, as well as a newcomer, baritone Arthur Clifford (a pseudonym for George Alexander). Since the cylinders only allowed for two minutes of playing time, the routines were more abbreviated than those on Victor and Columbia discs, consisting of a short (15 seconds or so) opening overture by the orchestra, a couple of jokes, and an abbreviated closing song. In one routine Spencer joked about himself, thus both personalizing and localizing the performance.

> SPENCER: I say, Mr. Dudley, I had a terrible dream last night.
> DUDLEY: Tell us all about it.
> SPENCER: I dreamt I died and went to heaven. And as I approached the golden gates, St. Peter met me, he said, "Ah, who are you?" I said, "Len Spencer." "From where?" I said, "From Patterson, New Jersey." He grabbed me by the collar and said, "Come in here quick, why, you are the first one we ever had from Patterson!"
> (laughter, whistles)[56]

The troupe was called the "Edison Modern Minstrels," which was ironic since the repertoire was much more heavily weighted toward older songs than before. Examples include "Uncle Billy's Dream" (1871), "Darling Clo" (1879) and "My Love Remains the Same" (1887). The first release in this new series, in fact, was called "Reminiscences of Minstrelsy." Although a few releases featured current songs, mostly black themed (e.g., "Down in Mobile Long Ago," 1903), Edison seemed to be aiming more for a nostalgia market than its competitors. Individual routines were mostly named after states ("Alabama Minstrels," "Georgia Minstrels," etc.), as was the case with Victor later.

In 1905, Dudley was replaced by Billy Murray as Spencer's principal foil. Dudley proudly announced them on the cylinder itself as "the famous endmen, Len Spencer and Billy Murray."

In 1906, three years after Victor and Columbia made a splash with their half-hour "An Evening with the Minstrels" series, Edison finally brought out its own complete show, called "At the Minstrel Show." This was a set of six numbered cylinders, but since each one was a little more than two minutes in length, this amounted to only about 13 minutes of total playing time.

The exact cast list is known because Edison files survive from this period. The performers were all studio regulars, including Billy Murray, Len Spencer, Arthur Collins, Byron G. Harlan, Harry Macdonough, Will F. Denny, George W. Johnson, Vess Ossman and the Edison Quartet. Black performer Johnson is not audible, but he may have participated in the crowd laughter. There is no interlocutor; instead, staff announcer Ed Meeker introduced the acts.

It is a curious set, tightly produced and not particularly natural like a stage show, but nevertheless flowing smoothly from one cylinder to the next (except for the interruptions by Meeker to announce, "At the Minstrel Show number two, Edison Records," "Number three, Edison Records," etc.). Part 1 is "Around the World" by the entire company, a favorite routine of Edison's, used as early as the 1880s on experimental cylinders. In this routine, the narrator or singers take the listener on a trip to different countries, complete with boat whistles and so on, singing bits of familiar national airs from each destination. Here, since it's a two-minute cylinder, they visit only England, Scotland, Ireland, Germany and Russia before hurrying home to the "good old U.S.A."

Part 2 consists of jokes by Collins and Harlan, followed by an old song ("When the Days Grow Longer," 1892); part 3 has jokes by Spencer and Murray, followed by the even older "Lighthouse by the Sea" (1886). Part 4 is a monologue on marriage by Will F. Denny, and part 5 is more jokes by Spencer and Murray. The latter makes fun of minstrelsy itself. After a few ancient jokes, they break into song about "jokes that are as old as father."

> SPENCER: You've got an awful nerve to spring that joke here. That's one of the jokes our daddies laughed at.
> Murray: That's no joke. It was your daddy taught it to *me*.
> (They sing, to the tune of "Everybody Works but Father"):
>
>> They're everybody's jokes but father's,
>> These gags we love to tell.
>> He told them to the sexton and the sexton tolled the bell,
>> Some of them are older than father,
>> They're old enough to die,
>> But gamble every dollar you'll hear them in the sweet bye and bye![57]

Part 6 ends the proceedings with "Plantation Sketch—A Darktown Serenade" by the entire company.

Edison issued three more two-minute minstrel cylinders between 1907 and 1909, all by the Rambler Minstrels, with Porter as interlocutor and Murray as endman. (One of these had Meeker substituting for Arthur Collins.) Oddly, the label released few minstrel records on the new four-minute cylinders it introduced in 1908, even though minstrel records were still selling quite well at the time. Edison's marketing practices are a mystery to modern researchers (and probably were to its competitors as well).

One four-minute minstrel cylinder that was released in 1909 was a nod to the widespread production of minstrel shows by lodges and other local groups. It is credited to the Elks Minstrels, although the participants were studio stalwarts Steve Porter, Billy Murray, Edward Meeker, John Young (as Harry Anthony), and Ada Jones (a rare example of a female appearing on a minstrel record). Murray was the endman, parrying with interlocutor Porter, appreciative audience member Henry, and Henry's wife (Jones). Henry complimented Murray on a particularly hoary joke:

> Murray: Say, Mr. Middleman, you know what a hard drinker my father used to be?
> PORTER: Indeed I do.
> Murray: Well, sir, yesterday he went by twenty saloons and never stopped in one of them.
> PORTER: Was he in a trance?
> Murray: No, he was in a patrol wagon!
> (laughter, clapping)[58]

Henry then exclaimed, "I want to say, that's the funniest joke I ever heard in all my life." Murray replied, "Thank you, I'm glad you like it," to which he responded, "Like it? Why, when I was a boy I used to laugh every time Grandfather told it!" At this point, the audience erupted in laughter.

A second four-minute cylinder was cut by Frank Stanley's Peerless Minstrels in 1910 as a premium to be given away with the purchase of certain Edison products. This cylinder featured their familiar "Humming Coon" routine also found on Victor, Columbia, and other labels. Both this and the Elks' cylinder were later reissued on Edison's celluloid Blue Amberol cylinders.

Minstrel records that are found on other labels from the early 20th century are generally reissues from the labels already mentioned. Reissue labels included Aretino, Busy

Bee, Clarion, Concert, Cort, D&R, Diamond, Duplex, Harmony, Harvard, Kalamazoo, Manhattan, Marconi, Nassau, Oxford, Peerless, Royal, Silver Tongued, Silvertone, Standard, Star, and Sun.

Virtually every label of this period had a "minstrels" section in its catalog. Of them all, Victor was most heavily into minstrel first part recreations, with 34 in its catalog at the peak of this trend in 1913; Columbia had 15. After that, the minstrel records vogue gradually began to wane. Victor ceased recording new routines after 1913, and Columbia did so after 1915, although, as we have seen, some smaller labels persisted.

Content and Repertoire

It is worth taking a look at the content of the minstrel first part recordings made from the 1890s through the mid–1910s. The first wave of recordings, by the Imperial Minstrels in the mid–1890s, reflected the previous decade or two of minstrelsy. Featured songs basically fell into two categories. One group was made up of minstrel standards of the 1870s and 1880s, such as "Old Log Cabin in the Dell" and "Hear Dem Bells." Many had religious or pseudo-religious themes, like "Buckle on de Golden Sword" or "Play on the Golden Harp." This type of imagery was quite popular in minstrel shows during the late 19th century, reflecting the newfound white fascination with African American religious practices.

The other category was current popular songs, whether or not they had anything to do with black America, a music category long featured in minstrel shows. One can hardly think of songs with less to do with the African American experience than "Two Little Girls in Blue" or "Sweet Marie."

It is notable that what is often presented as classic minstrelsy, represented by Stephen Foster songs and antebellum America, was little represented in the minstrel recordings of the 1890s and early 1900s. Minstrelsy certainly had its traditions, but on record, as on stage, it strove to be contemporary and reflect what was then the modern culture.

As many more recordings were made during the years that followed, by the Imperial Minstrels and other troupes, this contemporary orientation became even more pronounced. Featured songs on Columbia and Victor minstrel recordings of the early 1900s were overwhelmingly current pop tunes. They touched on all sorts of passing fads in music, including western and cowboy themes ("San Antonio"), waltz songs ("Waltz Me Around Again, Willie"), and flag-waving patriotism ("In the Good Old United States"). The Rambler Minstrels (1906–1909) were almost entirely a current pop group. Only Edison seemed to tie its minstrel productions more consistently to 19th-century music.

Of course, "coon songs" mocking blacks were a prominent strain in popular music of this period, and they found their way into minstrel recordings (and stage shows) as well. There is no question that the minstrel show continued to present a demeaning picture of African Americans, but it is important to note that this was only one part of a very complex cultural quilt. There were also songs and routines that sympathized with blacks trapped in a Jim Crow system (such as "Coon, Coon, Coon").

Minstrel records' mixed attitudes toward blacks are perhaps even more evident in the dialogue. As this recording fad took place during the heart of the "coon song" craze, on some records the jokes were quite racial, including liberal use of words such as *coon* and *nigger*. But, similar to stage shows, others were not. It is perhaps surprising, in fact, how seldom the "n-word" is actually encountered in these recordings. (*Coon* is more frequent, but even that is not found in a majority of examples.) Jokes and stories are usually puns, conundrums, or putdowns. Flag wavers ("Why are the stars in the flag like the stars in the heavens?") are frequent, as are jokes about neckties, wives, girlfriends, mothers-in-law, drunkenness, and various human foibles. In some ways, these recordings might seem more offensive to women than to blacks, given all the jokes about domineering wives and oppressed husbands. Mocking marriage was a strain in popular music at this time (e.g., Irving Berlin's "My Wife's Gone to the Country, Hurrah! Hurrah!").

Importantly, the endmen—the principal jokesters—are *not* presented as stupid. They may mangle the language or stutter, but they usually outwit the interlocutor, who is supposed to be the stuffy representation of white authority. Remarkably, in some recordings the interlocutor is not even oppositional to the black endmen. Frank C. Stanley, in the early Peerless Minstrel recordings, is clearly in charge, but he acts almost as a friend. In fact, in many of these recordings the atmosphere is that of a "bunch of friends sitting around cracking jokes." This feeling is enhanced, no doubt, by the fact that there are only four participants in most of the records.

It is also worth noting that the Imperial Minstrel releases started out using fairly rough, "streetwise" black language, but by 1900 (on Columbia) the dialogue had been cleaned up considerably and made more mainstream. Subsequent minstrel recordings presented their participants as friendly and comfortable to be with, not as some "Other" to be observed at a distance. This was important, of course, to make minstrel shows accessible to families and to the large white audience.

Songs About Minstrelsy

Early recordings referenced minstrelsy in many ways beyond minstrel first part recreations. Passing references to minstrelsy, which was so much a part of the shared cultural landscape of the time, are found in so many songs as to be virtually beyond counting. For example, the big hit of 1900, "Just Because She Made Dem Goo-Goo Eyes," is about an endman in a minstrel show who thinks a pretty girl in the front row is flirting with him. There were also songs and sketches specifically about minstrelsy, often making fun of its conventions. Some of these were recorded, and they can be divided into three broad categories: songs, sketches, and instrumentals.

The songs include the following examples:

"That Minstrel Man of Mine" (1900), written by Lew Sully, a "coon song" about a woman who falls for a minstrel dandy. Recorded by Len Spencer and others.

"It's Got to Be a Minstrel Show Tonight" (1902) by Ren Shields and George "Honey Boy" Evans (a major minstrel star), a rousing parody of minstrel shows. Recorded by J.W. Myers and Dan W. Quinn.

"Me an' da Minstrel Ban'" (1904) by black composers Alex Rogers and James Vaughan, about a boy's infatuation with the minstrel band marching through town. Featured in many minstrel shows and by George Walker (who is pictured on the sheet music) of Williams and Walker. Recorded by Billy Murray.

"I Got to See de Minstrel Show" (1907) by Vincent Brien and Harry Von Tilzer, about a preacher's wife who can't stay away from the minstrel show ("'Cause de minstrel show ain't wrong, it makes you grin when you feel blue, and if dat's a sin, why I'm through with you"). Later she sings, "Dat ragtime sounds so coon-ey, dat it makes me spoon-ey," and jokes about old gags like "why did the chicken cross the street?" Recorded by Arthur Collins for at least 10 labels.

There were many songs about minstrelsy, including this one, which was featured on stage by George Walker (of Williams and Walker).

"The Stranded Minstrel Man" (1908) by Murry K. Hill, about the comic travails of a minstrel whose manager leaves the show stranded. Recorded as a song and monologue by vaudevillian Hill for Edison, which commented "This record is a whole show in itself."

"I'd Rather Be a Minstrel Man than a Multi-Millionaire" (1909) by Keller Mack and Frank Orth, about a black minstrel who, as the title suggests, would rather be a minstrel than rich. And if he were rich, he'd start his own show. Recorded by prominent vaudevillian Eddie Morton in real buck-and-wing style.

"Rap, Rap, Rap on Your Minstrel Bones" (1912) by Lew Brown and Albert Von Tilzer, which celebrates the bones player in a minstrel show. Recorded by Edward Meeker for Edison.

"The Minstrel Parade" (1914) by Irving Berlin, from the Broadway show *Watch Your Step*, which is another celebration of the colorful minstrel parade that often preceded an appearance in town ("Here they come, here they come, marching to the big bass drum"). Includes another joke about the "chicken crossing the street" gag. Recorded by Collins and Harlan.

Part of the appeal of minstrel shows seemed to be their very predictability, including jokes that even then were considered old and corny. The lyrics of "It's Got to Be a Minstrel Show Tonight" take on endmen, the traditional basso solo ("Rocked in the Cradle of the Deep"), cakewalks and, of course, "why did the chicken cross the street?"

> We want to see a minstrel show tonight,
> Do some ragtime steps and do them right,
> At the funny endmen we want a peek,
> Want to hear that fella rock his cradle in the deep,
> Or else this show will end up in a fight ...
>
> We came here with a minstrel appetite,
> We wanna see a cakewalk done tonight,
> We want to hear the tenor sing so sweet,

And the joke about the chicken that crosses the street,
It's got to be a minstrel show tonight![59]

Recorded sketches also poked fun at the clichés of minstrelsy, particularly as seen in the amateur productions familiar to every town. "The Squashtown Minstrels" was a sketch worked up in 1904 by Len Spencer and Columbia orchestra leader Charles A. Prince, who certainly knew a thing or two about amateur minstrel shows. The Columbia catalog described it thus: "The village turns out en masse to the town hall to be entertained by the local talent, whose attempts to emulate the 'regular professionals' are exceptionally funny. The village quartette sings 'Little Boy Blue Come Blow Your Horn' with real imitations."[60]

Another parody of local productions appeared on Edison in 1907, called "An Amateur Minstrel Rehearsal" by the Edison Vaudeville Company. This one is a necessarily fast-paced sketch (since it had to fit on a two-minute cylinder) in which stage manager Birch Wood (Steve Porter) puts giggling tenor Wambold Merriman (Byron Harlan) and eager endman Backus Black (Billy Murray) through their paces. Harlan starts the old chestnut "Take Back the Heart That Thou Gavest," only to be cut off for a corny joke by Murray, followed a quick chorus by the quartet, and then everybody is chased out by the janitor.

This song about minstrelsy included a fairly accurate depiction of the first part on its cover.

Ten years later, the reconstituted Empire Vaudeville Company recorded a tribute to both minstrelsy and the late black entertainer George W. Johnson, in a sketch named after Johnson's "Laughing Song." Participating were Edison regulars Ed Meeker and the Premier Quartet (Billy Murray, Steve Porter, John Young, and Donald Chalmers). In this sketch, Porter and the boys want to put on a minstrel show but can't find anyone to sing Johnson's "Laughing Song." Murray exclaims, "We've got to have it. Why, it won't be a regular minstrel show without that song!" Finally, they find Meeker in the billiard room and he agrees to do the song, accompanied by banjo master Vess L. Ossman. The routine was released on cylinder in 1918 and on disc in 1921.

Band records were very popular in the early days of recording, and a number of them paid tribute to minstrelsy. This practice began as early as 1889 with Duffy and Imgrund's Band on an Edison cylinder playing "The Jolly Minstrel." Somewhat ironic was the popular selection "Five Minutes with the Minstrels" in 1891—ironic since, due to the limitations of cylinders, it ran for only two and a half minutes! Later there was Hoffman's "The Minstrel Parade" (1905), Gumble's "The Minstrel Band" (1910), and the rather pretentious "Whistling Minstrel Caprice" (1906).

Lew Dockstader and the Phonograph

Although most minstrel records were made by studio regulars, most of whom had minstrel stage experience, a few genuine minstrel "stars" did record. The best known was Lew Dockstader (1856–1924), one of the biggest names in minstrelsy in the late 19th and early 20th centuries. Dockstader first headed his own troupe in 1886 and continued as a major star in stage minstrelsy (and sometimes in vaudeville) until the 1920s. Originally a song-and-dance man, he became known in later years as a portly monologist. Although he used blackface, he did not employ black dialect, and his subjects were usually not about race. He was also a very astute manager. His shows were contemporary and flashy, and he spotted and nurtured new talent, including Al Jolson. One writer described him as "turning the declining minstrel show into an instrument of social and political satire, portraying not comic negro characters but comic whites in blackface, one representing President Theodore Roosevelt [whom he resembled]."[61]

Dockstader was also a great promoter and embraced new technologies as they emerged. In December 1888, he and songwriter Monroe Rosenfeld visited the Edison laboratory to pitch the inventor an idea about recording a full minstrel show that they could then take on the road. Edison didn't bite, but while in the lab Dockstader recorded some songs and even some minstrel show repartee. Unfortunately, these experimental cylinders were not offered for sale and are long gone.[62]

In 1905, Dockstader made an arrangement with the American Graphophone Company (maker of Columbia records) to feature in his show one of its new "20th Century" cylinder graphophones, which had a special mechanical amplification system allowing it to be heard in a large theater.[63] A story in the *Music Trade Review* (a trade paper) described the bit. It is a fairly long quote but worth repeating as a vivid account of what it was like to attend a performance of Dockstader's minstrels more than a hundred years ago. It must have been a very carefully rehearsed (and funny) routine. As it began, Dockstader, as the blackface endman, got into a spat with the interlocutor:

> The altercation started from a natural comment upon the weather by Mr. Dockstader, who, as end man, casually remarked that it was "a very warm evening." His interlocutor, apparently crazed by the heat, and resenting any reference of the kind, snarled back, "Mind your own business and let the weather do the same."
>
> Mr. Dockstader was taken aback and sought to smooth matters over, in the eyes of his audience, by saying apologetically, "Kindly refrain from any personalities upon our opening night; also recollect, sir, the burden of the entertainment rests entirely upon me as end man, and the warmth of the weather naturally led me to remark as I did." Whereupon the interlocutor, gritting his teeth and glaring balefully at Mr. Dockstader, replied, "Mr. Dockstader, I maintain that any dummy with a spark of intelligence can sit in your position and tell a joke and even get applause, providing the interlocutor knows how to round off the jokes and bring out the humorous points in them." Dazed by this out-

Above: Minstrel star Lew Dockstader in costume at a benefit in 1908. *Right:* Dockstader regaling the audience with one of his stories.

burst of spleen from his interlocutor, Dockstader sprang to his feet and shouted, "Stung; ungrateful man that you are to thus belittle your friend and benefactor," to which the interlocutor unfeelingly responded, "Even so, I maintain emphatically that any idiot can sit on the end and elicit applause from the audience, providing he has the interlocutor's assistance."

Lashed to frenzy by the insults in the face of the audience, Dockstader leaped to the center of the platform and kicked his interlocutor bodily off the stage, yelling, "You're discharged; wash the cork from your face and get out!" Dockstader fell breathless into his chair, mopping pearls of sweat from his brow, and the show bid fair to terminate disastrously on the spot. The entire company became black in the face with chagrin at the unpromising prospect of dismissing the large audience, who were already preparing to mob the box office and demand their money back.

At this critical juncture the stage manager hastened to hand Mr. Dockstader a card at which he glanced and immediately arose, his mobile face wreathed in smiles, and announced, "Mr. Graphophone, the premiere interlocutor, show him in!"

The audience resumed their seats in a haze of expectancy, when on the scene appeared two stage hands escorting a magnificent "Twentieth Century" Columbia graphophone with a handsome silk-finished floral horn. Depositing same in the place of the interlocutor, Dockstader, with a sweeping salutation, commanded, "Gentlemen, arise and salute your new interlocutor."

The entire company arose, expectancy pictured on every countenance. When the Columbia interlocutor remarked in clearest stentorian tones, "Gentlemen, be seated," the audience burst into spontaneous applause. "There," said Dockstader, "that's the kind of interlocutor to have—one who knows how to speak and when to shut up," but he was completely floored when from the new interlocutor came the ringing words, "Well, you can't shut me up." "Hello!" said Dockstader, "what's this we've struck, more trouble? Well it's all right anyhow, let us make the best [of] it, and let me tell you all I know." "Go ahead," said the new interlocutor, "it won't take you long." "Well," said Dockstader, pacifically, "I want to tell you about my dog—fine dog, blue ribbon winner, can almost talk, and is very fleet of foot." "Yes, full of fleas from head to foot," exclaimed the premier interlocutor, and the laugh was all on Dockstader, who shouted, "Hold on there, my dog has no fleas." "No," thundered the machine, "the fleas have the dog." "Look here," rejoined Dockstader warmly, "that dog sleeps with me." "Ha! Ha! That's where he gets his fleas," added the machine, and the audience fairly shouted with glee as the discomfiture of Dockstader, who bellowed out, "Here, you shut up!"

"You can't shut me up," shouted the graphophone, "I'm a true-born American citizen, and no jackass can shut me up." "Well, see here," said Dockstader, "don't you call me a donkey or a jackass, or I will come over there and pull the springs out of you," to which the machine replied, "Yes, you will! Yes, you will! Yes, you will!" "Yes I will!" roared Dockstader in a rage, advancing threateningly towards the machine. "You've called me a jackass, you've insulted me, and you've got to apologize." "Well, Lew," consolingly from the machine, "Isn't a jackass all right in its place?" "Yes," admitted Dockstader, "a jackass is all right in its place." "Then, sir," concluded the machine emphatically, "go over in your place and sit down."

Dockstader, in a towering rage, seized the graphophone in his arms and bore it headlong off the stage, the machine continuing to vociferate in blood-curdling tones, "Help! Murder! Police! Hands off! Police! Murder! Help! Lemme go!" concluding with the same taunting laughter which so lashed Dockstader to uncontrolled fury, amid the tumultuous applause of the vast audience, who insisted on the reappearance of Mr. Dockstader and his premier interlocutor.[64]

In July 1905, Dockstader himself entered the Columbia studios to record the comic number "Everybody Works but Father," which he was singing in his current show and which was a major hit in the fall of 1905. The next year, he recorded a follow-up number from the show, "Uncle Quit Work Too," and he returned in 1912 to wax a third number for Columbia, "Fiddle, Dee, Dee."

Dockstader continued to feature the graphophone in his show for the full 1905–1906 season. He also made silent film shorts, including *Minstrel Mishaps* (1908), in which he raced into town barely in time for a performance, only to be chased off the stage by the manager, resulting in pratfalls for all. Later he starred as the slave Dan in the 1914 drama *Dan*, set during the Civil War. Both of these films are now presumed lost.

Other Minstrel Stars on Record

Modern writers sometimes lament the fact that major minstrel stars such as McIntyre and Heath, "Honey Boy" Evans and Billy Kersands did not record. Black stars such as Kersands did not record, but that is not surprising given that few blacks were recording in the early 1900s. What is often overlooked, however, is that, in addition to Dockstader, several white minstrel stars did make records. Because white minstrelsy of this period has been so poorly documented, their burnt cork careers are simply not well known. In addition, many performers moved back and forth between minstrelsy, vaudeville and theater.

Manuel Romain (1872–1926), a tenor sometimes described as countertenor, was a major star with Primrose and West and with Dockstader in the 1890s and early 1900s. He plunged into record making with a vengeance in 1907, and over the next 19 years he made more than 150 sides for numerous labels. His specialty was sentimental ballads like "The Curse of an Aching Heart." However, one of his releases, "Hippodrome Minstrel Medley" (1916), was an interesting and eclectic medley of minstrel tunes, consisting of short excerpts from "Hot Time in the Old Town," "Hear Dem Bells," "Lazy Moon," "Mammy's Little Pumpkin Colored Coons," "Hello Ma Baby," "Oh, I Don't Know, You're Not So Warm," "Oh, Dem Golden Slippers," "Under the Bamboo Tree," and "Oh, Didn't He Ramble." The record was a tie-in with *The Big Show*, a spectacular 1916 production at the New York Hippodrome that included a nostalgic, 400-man minstrel show.

Richard Jose (1862–1941) was a pure countertenor. Historian Allen Debus noted that he was "one of the great countertenors of minstrelsy and truly a star of the 19th century." Early minstrel chronicler Edward LeRoy Rice added, "Never in the annals of minstrelsy has any singer met with more phenomenal success." Born in England, Jose had a rags-to-riches life story, which was much embellished over the years. He was not Spanish; his name was variously pronounced "Joe's," "Joss" or "Ho-zay." A hefty man (250 pounds) with enormous lung power, he appeared with

Top: Minstrel star and recording artist Manuel Romain. *Bottom:* Richard Jose, one of the greatest minstrel stars, led his own troupe in the early 1900s.

several minstrel companies from 1886 to 1902, including Dockstader's, Thatcher's, and William H. West's Minstrels, before forming his own company in 1901 or 1902. He then went into vaudeville and the theater, to great success. His recording career was relatively brief, from 1903 to 1909, exclusively for Victor, but in that time Jose produced more than 50 issued sides, some of them best sellers. His trademark song (recorded five times) was "Silver Threads Among the Gold."[65]

Another countertenor, Will Oakland (1883–1956), was, according to Debus, "perhaps the only American minstrel counter-tenor to rival Richard Jose." A generation younger than Jose, he toured beginning in 1905 with the Primrose, Dockstader, Cohan and Harris, and "Honey Boy" Evans troupes. Oakland's recording career began with Edison in 1908, and over the next 18 years he recorded approximately 200 issued cylinders and discs for various labels, mostly sentimental songs (including many remakes of Richard Jose titles). His theme song was "Let's Grow Old Together."[66]

One old-timer who recorded late in his career was Tom Lewis (c. 1864–1927), who headlined with the Wilson, Cleveland, Carncross, and Primrose and West minstrel companies during the 1890s. A review of an appearance in 1890 (with Wilson) called Lewis "a new star in the minstrel firmament."[67] In 1924, while he was appearing in *The Ziegfeld Follies*, Lewis recorded two routines for Brunswick: "His First After-Dinner Speech" and "An Old-Time Minstrel Scene." The latter consisted of some very fast back-and-forth dialogue between Ernest Hare (as interlocutor) and Lewis, followed by Lewis launching into the mock ballad "Sweet Antoinette." Note that there is nothing remotely about race in this routine. Although the record opens with "Gentlemen, be seated" and a short overture by the orchestra, it might as well be a fast-talking vaudeville routine.

>HARE: Thomas, you look downhearted. What's the trouble?
>LEWIS: Trouble? I got robbed last night.
>HARE: Robbed?
>LEWIS: Yes, a burglar broke into my house, stole my watch and chain—in fact, everything I had. Went out through the back winda', and I went out after him. When I caught up with him, he struck me.
>HARE: On purpose?
>LEWIS: No, on the back a' the head.
>HARE: Well, was it premeditated?
>LEWIS: No, it was a club.
>HARE: Did you strike him in defense?
>LEWIS: No, he hit me under the fence.
>HARE: Did you or did you not retaliate?
>LEWIS: I couldn't get thru' the alley gate. When he got me under the alley gate, he set his dog on me.
>HARE: Why didn't you set your dog on him?
>LEWIS: My dog was dead. I got him home.
>HARE: What are you doing with a dead dog in the house?
>LEWIS: I got him stuffed.
>HARE: You've got him *what*?
>LEWIS: Tax-a-dermitized.
>HARE: Please repeat that.
>LEWIS: Not for thirty cents.
>HARE: What was the complaint?
>LEWIS: No complaint, neighbor seemed to be satisfied.
>HARE: No, no, no, what was the cause of his death?
>LEWIS: No cause at all. He had a good home, three meals a day.
>HARE: How did he come to meet death?

LEWIS: He didn't come to meet it, death overtook him.
HARE: No, no, no, what did he die *of*?
LEWIS: He died of a Thursday afternoon.
HARE: No, no, what was the cause of the dog's demise?
LEWIS: That's it. That's it.
HARE: That's what?
LEWIS: Closed dem eyes, couldn't get 'em open again.
HARE: Here, here, Mr. Lewis, do you take me for a fool?
LEWIS: Dog is dead, ain't he?
HARE: Yes.
LEWIS: And I have a right to get him stuffed?
HARE: Why, certainly.
LEWIS: Well, if I don't like it, I'll go home and kick the stuffin' out of him.[68]

Numerous lesser lights, some of whom had long careers in minstrelsy, also made records. See appendix 3 for details.

There were other crossovers between the phonograph and minstrelsy. One of the more unusual examples came in 1907, when the ever-resourceful Len Spencer helped mount a big "Columbia Minstrels—Automatique" exhibit in the Satin Theatre at Steeplechase Park, Coney Island, New York.

An item in the October 27, 1906, *New York Dramatic Mirror* reported that John M. Leavitt, a well-known set designer (previously responsible for an exhibit called "The Galveston Flood"), was working on the exhibit, which would consist of a row of nine animated dummies seated on stage in a semi-circle in a minstrel first part. They would move and gesture and tell jokes and sing songs via hidden phonographs located behind their shirt fronts.[69] The exhibit was ready in time for the summer 1907 season. Dummies with the likenesses of Columbia artists Billy Murray, Arthur Collins, Byron Harlan, Steve Porter, Frank C. Stanley, Henry Burr, Albert Campbell, and J.W. Myers made up the troupe, with Spencer seated in the middle as interlocutor. Five hidden Columbia Twentieth Century graphophones provided the sound. Spencer was identified as co-owner and "moving spirit" of the production. After a season at the park, the intention was to take this show on the road.

It must have been something to see, but unfortunately the exhibition didn't last long. On the morning of July 28, Steeplechase Park was completely destroyed by a huge fire, which leveled everything. The popular park was back up and running in less than a month, but the automated minstrels were not rebuilt.

Besides the hundreds of minstrel first part recreations, to say nothing of the songs about minstrelsy that were recorded during this period, there were hundreds more sketches and "blackface" songs recorded that could easily have been part of a minstrel show. In fact, some sketches were explicitly labeled "minstrel specialty" or "minstrel scene," although the same material might be called "vaudeville specialty" or "descriptive specialty" on another issue. It all melded together. Nevertheless, it is clear that minstrelsy, especially the classic "minstrel first part" with its "Gentlemen, be seated" opening and party atmosphere, was very prominent on record during stage minstrelsy's later years.

The Revival of Minstrel Recordings in the 1920s

After a 20-year run, recorded minstrelsy finally began to decline in the 1910s. Popular entertainment was becoming dominated by motion pictures, a craze for social dancing, the nascent jazz movement, and a general fascination with "modernism." This was, after all, an era in which the world was experiencing vast changes wrought by automobiles, airplanes, and all manner of electrical appliances unheard of just a generation before. A new world called for new forms of entertainment, and nothing could be more "horse and buggy" than your grandfather's minstrel show, no matter how it was dressed up.

Of course, the minstrel show, so familiar to all, did not disappear entirely from popular media. But rather than striving to be contemporary and featuring the latest songs and fads, it became unabashedly nostalgic. In 1919, Edison released what was billed as "an old-style minstrel performance" by the Premier Quartet Minstrels, opening with the traditional children's song "See-Saw, See-Saw (Now We're Off to London Town)," followed by some familiar jokes, George Wilton Ballard singing "Goodnight Dear" (published in 1909 but sounding much older), and a closing chorus about Dixieland, "the land of minstrelsy." Billy Murray and Steve Porter took the lead.[70]

In 1924, Edison released the even more explicitly titled "Minstrelsy of Other Days" by the Empire Vaudeville and Minstrel Company, a collection of old songs including "The Landstrum Galop," "Down Where the Cotton Blossoms Grow," "Trans-Mag-Ni-Fi-Can-Bam-U-Al-I-Try," "When the Harvest Days Are Over, Jessie Dear," and "My Castle on the Nile." The unidentified cast included Harry Docken and James Doherty as endmen, along with Jay Clay and others.

The racial content was reduced in these recordings, with no "darky dialect" or use of the "n-word" (although "coon" still sometimes appeared). Although some songs from antebellum minstrelsy were heard (e.g., Stephen Foster), most were from the late 19th and early 20th centuries. The goal seemed to be to tap into a gentle nostalgia for record buyers' younger days, 20 or so years earlier, by highlighting songs of their youth.

In 1923, Columbia released a couple of interesting discs by Lee "Lasses" White (1888–1949). White, who took his nickname from a childhood fondness for molasses, was from a new generation of minstrels. He had shot to fame when he replaced the beloved "Honey Boy" Evans in Evans' troupe in the 1914–1915 season, during the latter's final illness. White then went on to become a star with the Neil O'Brien Minstrels (1915–1917) and Al G. Field Minstrels (1917–1920) before founding his own troupe in 1920. He was riding high when Columbia engaged him to record the two-part "Old Time Minstrels." It was filled with antique songs cheerfully delivered, including "Oh, Dem Golden Slippers," "Darling Nellie Gray," "Silver Threads Among the Gold," "My Gal," "Asleep in the Deep," "Clap Your Hands" (a White original), and the finale, "Polly Wolly Doodle." (Note the inclusion of the basso solo "Asleep in the Deep," which had become a cliché of traditional minstrelsy.)

White and Al Bernard were the endmen and Wilfred Glenn the interlocutor, with the Shannon Four providing harmony. At least the jokes were new (if corny) examples of wordplay:

> WHITE: Hey, Mr. Glenn, I hear you're living out on a farm now.
> GLENN: Why, yes, Lasses, that's right, and by the way a peculiar incident happened on my farm last week.
> WHITE: Don't tell me!
> GLENN: Lasses, one of our cows ate some buttercups, and would you believe it, ever since then she has been giving buttermilk.
> WHITE: That's right, boy, when you tell 'em always do your best.
> GLENN: Some cow, eh?

WHITE: Boy, we had a cow that went out last winter and got her tail froze, and now she's giving ice cream sundaes!
(laughter)[71]

White also recorded the sketches "Levee Scene" and "Plantation Scene" for Columbia with the same cast, including some interesting blues material, as well as a "minstrel song" called "Sweet Mama, Tree Top Tall." The latter was written by White, who was a composer of some note. (In 1912, he wrote what is generally considered the first published 12-bar blues song: "Nigger Blues.")

Lasses White went on to a long and successful career in radio and motion pictures, which will be discussed in the chapters on those subjects.

Also in 1923, Columbia released, as part of its "Race" series, two sides by the Gulf Coast Minstrels, which was composed of black vaudevillians Cliff Ross and Perry Bradford. "Darktown Camp Meeting" and "I Ain't Skeered of Work" were black-themed sketches rather than minstrel first parts, but they were a reminder of the kind of material used on the black minstrel circuit. Ross and Bradford were accompanied by the quartet from *Dinah*, a black musical that ran in Harlem's Lafayette Theatre during the 1923–1924 season and introduced the dance "The Black Bottom." Bradford (1893–1970), a composer, producer, and performer in vaudeville and minstrelsy, went on to make a number of jazz and blues recordings during the later 1920s.

Okeh Records chimed in with its release of a 12-inch disc by "Al Bernard's Minstrel Co." in 1924. Bernard (1888–1949) was born in New Orleans and by the age of 18 was managing his own local minstrel troupe there, called "Al Bernard's Southern Minstrel Co."[72] He then entered vaudeville, where he specialized in blues and "coon songs," using the moniker "The Boy from Dixie" (when appearing with his wife Gertrude, they were "The Boy and Girl from Dixie"). There are many references to Bernard in local and theatrical papers between 1909 and 1918 as he toured throughout the South.

Bernard plunged into recording in 1919 and quickly become a prolific artist, appearing on numerous labels and becoming known nationally. He continued to specialize in black material, such as W.C. Handy's "St. Louis Blues," which he championed. In this Okeh recording, he was endman in a troupe assembled by Okeh recording director Justin Ring, the other cast members being interlocutor Lloyd Willing, baritone Harry Docken, bass Harry Donaghy, tenor Dan DeSylva, and the National Male Quartet. The featured songs were oldies or specialty material: "We Are Merry Minstrel Men," "Sweet Genevieve," "When You and I Were Young, Maggie," "Shine On, Mr. Moon," "When the Bell in the Lighthouse Goes Ding Dong" (the basso specialty), "Jerusalem Morning," "Flip Them Jacks," and the finale, a reprise of "We Are Merry Minstrel Men." It was all very fast paced, and (unusually for a minstrel record) the orchestra at times got a little jazzy. Bernard went on to a long and prominent career in media minstrelsy, on record and later on network radio, which will be discussed in due course.

The year 1926 brought the revue *Rufus LeMaire's Affairs*, produced by LeMaire and starring high-kicking stage (and later movie) star Charlotte Greenwood and bandleader Ted Lewis. The first act closed with an elaborate minstrel parade and minstrel first part featuring the entire cast. The show opened in Chicago in 1926 and then moved to Broadway, where it played for two months. It is probably best known for the song "Bring Back Those Minstrel Days," which was recorded on minor labels at the time but turned out to be a popular and long-lasting hit, used as a theme for many later professional and amateur minstrel productions.

> We all remember there were Primrose and West,
> Dockstader, Evans, the boys we loved best.
> Although they've gone to rest their memory stays,
> Bring back those minstrel days![73]

The last year of the decade brought several more minstrel first part recordings, all mining the nostalgia vein. The Carolina Minstrels on Banner and associated labels featured a lineup of familiar old songs: "Dixie," "Ida Sweet as Apple Cider," "Rufus Rastus Johnson Brown," "Silver Threads Among the Gold," "Oh, Didn't He Ramble," "My Gal Sal," "Goodnight Ladies," and "Auld Lang Syne." None of the cast is identified except by generic names such as Tambo and Bones, but veteran tenor Henry Burr is recognizable as the interlocutor. The opening, by Burr, makes no secret that this presentation is an exercise in nostalgia: "Ladies and gentlemen, I take great pleasure in introducing to you the Carolina Minstrels, presenting songs and jokes that your mothers and dads listened to and laughed at in the olden days. Gentlemen, be seated!"

Also in 1929, Cameo and its associated label (Romeo) released a similar production by the Dixie Minstrels. The old songs featured here were "Make a Lot of Noise," "Goodbye Eliza Jane," "Lindy," "My Gal Is a High Born Lady," "Dear Old Girl," and "Massa's in de Cold, Cold Ground." James Stanley was the interlocutor, with recording veterans Billy Murray, Albert Campbell (probable), Jack Kaufman and Walter Van Brunt forming the cast. The whole affair is rather subdued, in part because Stanley acted more like a radio announcer than an interlocutor interacting with the endmen.

A third minstrel release in 1929 was by "Dailey Paskman's Radio Minstrels" on Columbia. Paskman produced a very popular minstrel show on radio and was instrumental in launching minstrelsy into that medium. He will be discussed in detail in the next chapter.

The most elaborate minstrel recreation on record in 1929, and doubtless the best selling (judging from the frequency with which it turns up today), was "Minstrel Show of 1929" by the Victor Minstrels, a nearly nine-minute production on two sides of a 12-inch disc. Victor had not produced a new minstrel recording since 1913, but the combination of its high production values, electrical recording, and the very "live" acoustics of New York's Liederkranz Hall (where Victor recorded) made the listener feel like this performance was taking place in a real theater.

The show opened and closed with rousing numbers featuring the entire cast. The song lineup was "Make a Lot of Noise," "Down Where the Watermelon Grows," "Lazy Moon," "Oh, Dem Golden Slippers," "Allus the Same in Dixie," "By the

Victor returned to minstrelsy in 1929 with this best-selling disc.

Light of the Silvery Moon," "Abraham Lincoln Jones," "Under the Bamboo Tree," "Carry Me Back to Old Virginny," and "Climbing Up the Golden Stairs"—all familiar oldies (including Cohan's "Make a Lot of Noise" again) but all well done. The interlocutor was James Stanley, sounding much more energized and engaged than he had been on the Cameo release; the rest of the cast consisted of Billy Murray and Monroe Silver as the endmen, accompanied by Henry Burr, Carl Matthieu, Stanley Baughman, Frank Crumit, and the National Cavaliers quartet.

The entire production was full of energy, easy interaction between the cast members, and a considerable amount of musical variety, including a brief soft shoe and sand dance. It took five takes to get side 1 just right, and three for side 2. The jokes were corny but contemporary (for example, about cars), and they came so fast and naturally that they were hard to not like.

> STANLEY: Say, Monty, I'm in the market for an automobile and I hear you have one for sale.
> SILVER: Mr. Jim, I'm going to give you a big surprise. I'm gonna offer you this automobile for twelve hundred dollars.
> STANLEY: Yes, and I'm going to give you a bigger surprise. I'm going to offer you fifty dollars for the car.
> SILVER (CHUCKLES): Mr. Jim, I'm gonna give you the biggest surprise of yo' life. I'm gonna *take* it! (great laughter)[74]

Post-1920s

Minstrel recording pretty much died out in the United States during the 1930s and 1940s, although emerging radio minstrel and blackface artists recorded individual songs and routines. For example, Amos 'n' Andy (Charles Correll and Freeman Gosden) made a few records, both under that name and as their earlier personas, Sam 'n' Henry. Early radio blackface stars Cotton and Morpheus likewise recorded for Brunswick from 1928 to 1930.

The next minstrel first part recreation I have found on record, however, did not appear until after World War II. In 1948, Al Bernard, who had recorded widely in the 1920s and participated in a few minstrel records at that time, appeared on a two-disc 78-rpm album called "Al Bernard's Merry Minstrel Show" on the small Celebrity label run by New York songwriter, publisher, and all-around hustler Joe Davis. It sounds a lot like a radio show. "Interlocutor" Tom Shirley spoke in pearly, rounded tones like the friendly announcer/sidekicks so familiar on network radio (think Don Wilson on *The Jack Benny Show*). There seemed to be a large audience, the orchestra sounded contemporary, and each side faded out at the end as if it was excerpted from a longer show. Shirley even ended the show with the standard radio closing thanking the audience and reminding them to "be with us next time." Whether or not it was actually broadcast, it sounds like this was recorded in a radio or TV studio with a full audience in attendance.

Most of the songs on this album were originals written by Davis himself around the time the recording was made. The "show" opened and closed with the upbeat "There's Nothing Like a Minstrel Show" (written by Joe Davis in 1945), with the featured songs being "Trombone Jitters" (Davis, 1945), played by jazz trombonist Lou McGarity; "Truthfully" (Davis, 1944), sung by tenor Henry Shope; and "Bill Bailey, Won't You Please Come Home" (the only non–Davis song), sung by Al Bernard. Bernard cracked some pretty old jokes with likeable humor and enthusiasm. At one point he started bantering with Shirley about the travails of marriage, a familiar minstrel trope:

> SHIRLEY: Well, Al, personally I'm through with all that forever. I'm so anxious to live to be a hundred that I've signed a pledge never to smoke, drink, stay out late at night, or even put my arm around a girl.
> BERNARD: An' you doin' all that just so you can live to be a hundred?
> SHIRLEY: That's right.
> BERNARD: Well, answer me just one question, will yuh?
> SHIRLEY: Why, sure, what is it?
> BERNARD: Well, if that's the way you're goin' through life, what do ya want to live to be a *hundred* for?
> (great laughter)[75]

The resemblance to a radio show was not accidental. Bernard, the endman, was a major star on radio minstrel shows in the 1930s (in fact, his involvement with minstrelsy was even greater on radio than it was on record). Tom Shirley was a prominent radio announcer during the 1930s and 1940s, heard on such shows as *Jack Armstrong*, *Mr. Keen*, *Myrt and Marge*, *The Telephone Hour* and *Grand Central Station*. Even Henry Shope, the "golden voiced tenor," had been a radio singer since the 1920s, both solo and as part of ensembles.

"Al Bernard's Merry Minstrel Show" was reissued on a 10-inch LP around 1954, on Davis' Jay-Dee label, with an additional track that had not been used in 1948 ("Neptune," yet another song composed by Davis). Since the five 1948 tracks took up only one side of the LP, the other side, called "Merry Minstrel Songs," was filled with an organ medley of 19th-century songs.

Minstrelsy on record, which began before minstrelsy on radio or in motion pictures, outlasted both of its successors. At least 10 minstrel-themed LPs were issued between 1954 and 1963, which was well after the last radio and TV minstrel shows had left the air. About half of these records were primarily collections of old-time songs, built around a minstrel theme. The other half, like "Al Bernard's Merry Minstrel Show," were actual recreations of a minstrel first part, complete with interlocutor, endmen, jokes, and "Gentlemen, be seated!" All were considerably "cleaned up," with carefully sanitized lyrics, dialogue and graphics to avoid the appearance of racial insensitivity. In fact, in some cases the dialogue was so stiff that it was hard to recognize the performance as a minstrel show at all.

The first of these minstrel first part recreations was "Minstrel Show" (1957) on Somerset, a fairly widely distributed budget label. Recorded at the Capitol Studios in Hollywood, it was also issued in stereo on Somerset's sister label Stereo Fidelity. The talent was, for the most part, not identified (except for interlocutor Bill "Blackface" Ornsby), but the jacket accompanying the record mentioned that the singers and soloists were all members of the Lee Gordon Singers, a highly professional backing group found on many recordings of the day. This recording consists primarily of the chorus and individual soloists, all of whom are very good, singing a mix of minstrel songs ranging from antebellum (including Stephen Foster) to the early 1900s. There is also dubbed-in audience noise, applause and a few creaky jokes ("What has four legs and flies?" "Two pair of pants!" followed by laughter). The orchestra was conducted by Joseph Kuhn, a noted composer and conductor who is best known—ironically—for arranging many of Somerset's "101 Strings" albums. It is hard to believe anybody could be offended by this album (except possibly by the rather low-key drawing of a performer in "brownface" on the cover), and, in fact, it is still available on iTunes as of this writing.

For "The Minstrel Men" (1958), old-time vaudevillian Benny Fields (1894–1959) came out of retirement for the umpteenth time, shortly before he died, to emcee a collection of songs and sketches by fellow older stars. Although the jacket called it "a full length minstrel show," there were no jokes or endmen. This record consisted mostly of a whitebread male chorus singing old favorites from the 19th and early 20th centuries. Fields sang a few songs ("By the Light of the Silvery Moon," "Under the Bamboo Tree," "My Blushin' Rosie") and introduced routines by Jack Benny, Milton Berle, George Burns, and Phil Silvers, all obviously recorded at some other time. Applause was dubbed in. The orchestra was conducted by Owen B. Masingill, a talented arranger who worked with many pop stars of the 1950s, including Roy Hamilton, Della Reese, and Perry Como. The LP was released on Colpix, one of the more successful independent pop labels of the time, and rated a *Billboard* "pick" with the caveat, "if exposed, this might be a sleeper." Major promotion was promised, on *The Ed Sullivan Show* and by the four featured stars, each of whom then had his own series on TV.[76]

Another old-timer who lent his talents to the late stage of minstrelsy recording was Eddie Foy, Jr. (1905–1983), on "Minstrel Days" (Everest, 1959). Foy had been on stage since he was five, appearing with his family in "The Seven Little Foys" vaudeville act. He had an active career after his vaudeville days, appearing in more than 40 feature films and numerous TV shows, and he even starred in a sitcom of his own (*Fair Exchange*, which aired on CBS in 1962–1963). Foy looked like an antique on the LP cover, dressed in his colorful "Interloc-u-tator" outfit, but in fact he was only in his mid-fifties when this LP was made. "My father," he said, "was in minstrel shows before vaudeville existed. He even played in Dodge City when Wyatt Earp and Bat Masterson were there." According to the notes, "[Foy] welcomed this chance to recreate the minstrel days because he feels strongly that the charm and humor and wholly entertaining ease of the minstrel show can still appeal to newer generations of Americans as well as to those who remember the golden age of minstrelsy."

There certainly was talent in the grooves. The endmen for "Minstrel Days" were veteran stage and film actor David Burns and renowned songwriter Harold Adamson, evidently having the time of

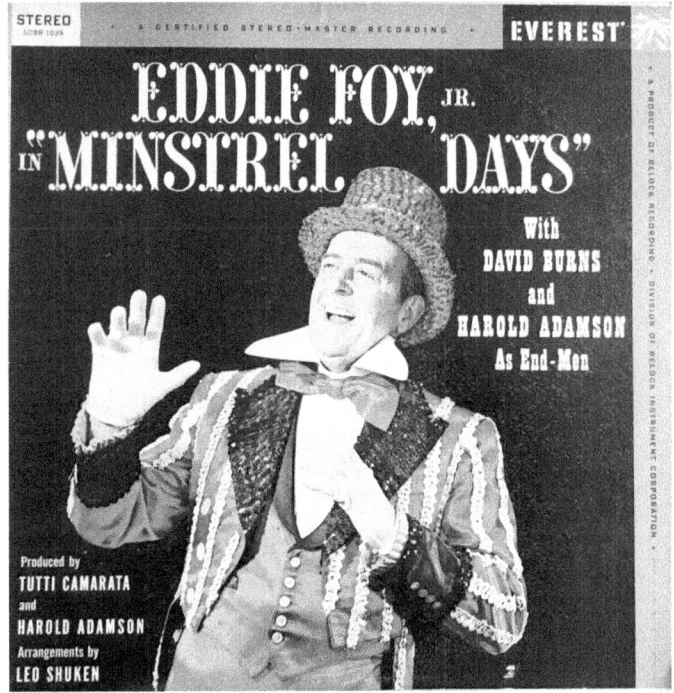

One of the minstrel LPs of the late 1950s.

their lives, and the orchestra leader and producer was top-flight arranger/conductor Tutti Camarata. The performance was snappy and fast paced, with soft shoe, a sand dance, and jokes that flew by so fast you hardly noticed how corny they were. Most of the featured songs were from the early 20th century (e.g., "Sleepy Time Gal," "By the Light of the Silvery Moon," and the inevitable "Mandy"). The opening and closing theme was Joe Davis' "There's Nothing Like a Minstrel Show." None of the material was about race. *Billboard* gave the disc four stars ("Very strong sales potential") and said it did "a bang-up job of reviving the flavor and excitement of the minstrels." It seems to have sold reasonably well.[77]

Even more explicitly instructional was "Minstrel Show!" (1961), by Frank Simms and His Minstrels, on RCA Camden, the budget subsidiary of industry giant RCA Victor. According to the liner notes, "This album was produced to serve as format for amateur groups if they desire to present their own Minstrel Show for community/charity purposes. The following serves as outline in planning the production of such a show."

It was a pretty stiff performance, sounding more like an overproduced radio or TV show than an authentic, party-like minstrel stage show. Simms was a veteran TV announcer, perhaps best known as announcer on the daytime and prime-time *Garry Moore Show* in the late 1950s, and as interlocutor for "Minstrel Show!" he used the exaggerated, mannered delivery common to network announcers of the period. The rest of the cast was unidentified, but they all spoke (or sang) in careful, precise English as well. It was a very "white" show, without a trace of the African American culture on which minstrelsy was based (even when it was being mocked). However, there was variety—banjo and whistling solos, bass solo ("Old Black Joe"), a soft shoe, and plenty of jokes—and the featured songs were authentic to 19th-century minstrelsy, ranging from "Oh! Susanna" (1840s) and "Dixie" to "Hello Ma Baby" (1890s).

"A Tribute to the Original Christy Minstrels" (c. 1963), on the obscure Dyna-Disc label, was a disguised reissue of the 1957 Somerset LP "Minstrel Show." It seems to have been a quickie issued to capitalize on the popularity of the folk group known as the New Christy Minstrels, whose career was booming in late 1962 and 1963.

In addition to LPs recreating the minstrel first part (more or less), there were "minstrel show" albums that were primarily collections of minstrel-era songs, minimizing or eliminating interlocutor and endman dialogue. Probably the best selling of these was "Gentlemen, Be Seated!" (1956) on Epic, the budget subsidiary of Columbia Records. Billed as "A Complete Minstrel Show," it was arranged by the same O.B. Masingill who was responsible for the Benny Fields "Minstrel Men" album. There were 18 songs altogether, mostly from the 1890s or early 1900s ("Hot Time in the Old Town," "Waiting for the Robert E. Lee," "Shine On, Harvest Moon," etc.), with only two or three short jokes. The unidentified interlocutor is probably baritone Stanley Kimes. The artists were not celebrities, but they were solid, experienced studio men, including tenor Gordon Goodman (from the Fred Waring organization), concert basso John Neher, the much-recorded Merrill Staton Choir, and Milton Berle's orchestra leader, Allen Roth. African American jazz drummer and vocalist Osie Johnson contributed a novelty vocal, making this an integrated affair.

Billboard gave this album a rating of 74 (its normal high seemed to be 80) but said, "On novelty value, should be a winner." Epic then provided a big-label push with a full-page ad in *Billboard*, claiming that it had the "largest advance orders for an album we have ever enjoyed" and that 73-year-old minstrel veteran Will Oakland had been engaged to promote it in cities around the country. The push apparently worked, as the album spent more than two months on *Billboard*'s Best Selling Pop Albums chart in the summer of 1956. This, remember, was at the height of the early rock 'n' roll era.[78]

That sort of success inevitably resulted in a follow-up, "Gentlemen, Be Seated! (Again)" (1959), also on Epic. This album was also arranged and conducted by O.B. Masingill, with a slightly different cast of singers and musicians. There were again 18 songs (mostly new) from the same era, along with a few jokes. Basso profundo J. Alden Edkins acted as interlocutor, introducing each number. The opening this time was a lively medley of "Down South" and the familiar "Bring Back Those Minstrel Days."

Bill Cullen (1920–1990) was one of the busiest men on television in the 1950s and 1960s, hosting or appearing as a panelist on more than a dozen prime-time programs. He nevertheless found time to appear on the ABC Paramount album "Bill Cullen's Minstrel Spectacular" (1959). This was a collection of 15 songs ranging from antebellum ("Old Dan Tucker") to the early 20th century ("Rufus Rastus Johnson Brown"). There was no interlocutor per se; Cullen acted as narrator, describing the progress of the minstrel parade and the various acts once the show began, with occasional sound effects to add to the atmosphere. The male chorus (called "The Endmen"—get it?) was directed by Frank Raye, with arrangements by James N. Peterson. The orchestra included old-time banjo virtuosos Harry Reser and John Cali.

One other music-oriented LP was "The Dixie Minstrels' Greatest Hits" (1962) on the Kapp label. According to the *Billboard* review, it included 38 old-time songs "played and sung with the enthusiasm that befits a minstrel show." This record included both 19th- and 20th-century music, such as "Aura Lee," "Dixie," "Roll Dem Bones" and "Waiting for the Robert E. Lee."

The wave of minstrel LPs issued during the late 1950s and early 1960s probably did help keep the memory of minstrelsy—or at least the good parts of minstrelsy—alive, if only for a while. Several of the liner notes informatively described minstrelsy's origins in the 1840s, and all treated the genre with respect. However, they were so cleaned up, slick, and (in most cases) devoid of the raucous, party-like nature of a true minstrel show that it was an imperfect picture at best. That would be left for scholars to preserve as best they could.

The Question of Authenticity

The answer to the question of whether the surprisingly large wave of minstrel first part recordings of the 1890s and early 1900s really represented what a contemporary minstrel show sounded like has to be, I believe, affirmative. The repertoire was the same (mostly current songs), the jokes were the same type found in minstrel joke books of the period, and the performers (mostly recording professionals) almost all had firsthand experience on the minstrel stage. Much can be learned from the tone of their routines, how the participants related to each other, and how much racial innuendo was present in the recordings. The interlocutor, for example, might be one of two types: a somewhat formal, perhaps even stiff, representation of the white "boss," whom the black endmen would typically outwit, or "one of the gang," a facilitator but also in on the jokes. The sense one gets from these recordings is that of hanging out with a group of guys (almost always guys) who are fun to be with.

Listeners of these records did not get the sense of a "big show," of course, since sound recordings could not replicate the spectacle of many of the stage shows or their large casts. The recordings were more intimate, usually performed by only four or five people. But many have background laughter and applause that suggest a larger audience, and a few recordings (like the "Evening with the Minstrels" cakewalk routine, with its crowd noises and stage asides) sound quite theatrical.

Importantly, there is a very strong suggestion that the minstrel recordings of the 1890s and early 1900s were, in the main, being sold as contemporary entertainment, not purely as nostalgia or historical recreations. In the 1920s and beyond, minstrelsy did become an exercise in nostalgia (and eventually history), and that development was reflected on the recorded versions as well. Stephen Foster made a comeback in the minstrel setting.

The content in these recordings directly related to race, in terms of overt mockery or demeaning of African Americans, is surprisingly limited. It is suggested by the use of dialect or the mangling of language, but on record you don't see blackface, which is a big part of the racial disparagement. The use of overtly insulting language like "nigger" or "coon" (especially the former) is rare. Even "coon songs," which were very popular in the early 1900s and might seem to be a "natural" for a minstrel record, are heard in a distinct minority of the minstrel recordings of that period.

Up until now, scholars of minstrelsy have worked almost exclusively from printed sources. A major purpose of this book is to shine a light on the body of audiovisual resources that can add significantly to our understanding of this seminal American form of entertainment and expression. Minstrel-related sound recordings are clearly an important part of those resources. Others are radio, movies, and television, which I will explore in the chapters that follow.

Minstrel Records in Britain

As described in the previous chapter, minstrelsy thrived in Britain for even longer than it did in the United States. However, recording of minstrel recreations got off to a slower start there, largely because control of the recording industry was held very tightly by the Edison interests through its patent monopoly. These were assigned in 1892 to a local affiliate known as Edison Bell (since it held the phonograph patents of both Edison and Bell-Tainter), which did little to develop the market for entertainment cylinders. While there were some exhibitions and a few cylinders made for them during the mid-1890s, regular commercial record making did not begin until the end of the decade, when Emile Berliner brought his disc record to Britain. Minstrel records soon followed.

Berliner's company was called the Gramophone Company, and its principal labels were Berliner (1898–1901), Gramophone (1902–1910) and finally His Master's Voice, or HMV (1910 onward).[79] Its first group of eight locally made minstrel recordings were issued in early 1899, on seven-inch, single-sided Berliner discs. The troupe was called simply the Christy Minstrels, a common name for minstrels in the United Kingdom, but on the single example available the cornerman is addressed as "Tom" and sounds like Tom Birchmore of the Moore and Burgess minstrel troupe. Some scholars believe that the recording ensemble was led by Gustave Chaudoir of Moore and Burgess.[80] The featured songs were a mix of current fare, both American ("Hot Time in the Old Town,"

"My Coal Black Lady," "Hello My Baby") and British ("Lads in Navy Blue," "Little Dolly Daydream"). The jokes were standard fare, often mocking marriage:

> TOM: But I say, can you tell me the difference between a married man and a single man?
> MIDDLEMAN: Well, I suppose the single man has no buttons on his shirt.
> TOM: Yes, the single man, as you say, has no buttons on his shirt, but a married man, he has no shirt! (laughs)[81]

A second group of six minstrel first part routines was issued in 1902, on the Gramophone label, as seven-inch discs, 10-inch discs, or both. The troupe was again called the Christy Minstrels, but this time it consisted of the Haydn Quartet, brought over from America for the purpose. The members were W. F. Hooley as middleman, S.H. Dudley as cornerman, Harry Macdonough as soloist, and one other man (unidentified). This was essentially the group that made the Georgia Minstrels records for Victor in the United States in 1900–1901. The repertoire was mostly American, either mid–19th-century ("Massa's in de Cold, Cold Ground," "Carry Me Back to Old Virginny") or traditional minstrel songs ("I'se Gwine Back to Dixie"). The jokes were familiar from American minstrel records, mostly insult humor or mocking marriage.

In addition, many U.S. minstrel records were imported from Gramophone's affiliate Victor, including the best-selling "An Evening with the Minstrels" set. There was little in either the imports or the locally made recordings that was distinctively British.

At least the set of eight brown wax minstrel cylinders issued by Edison Bell in February 1900 featured artists whose accents and delivery were distinctively British, even if the material was not. Called "The Excelsior Minstrels," the performers included Wilson Hallett, Harry Bluff, Eric Farr, Ernest Chester, Albert Pearce (tenor), Russell Hunting, William Doust, and one woman, Alma Jones. Hallett and Hunting (an American) were the cornermen. The featured songs were mostly American, including "Old Folks at Home," "Break the News to Mother," and "Hello Ma Baby," although they also included George Lashwood's music hall hit, "Three Women to Every Man."

The inclusion of a woman (Jones) in the cast was characteristic of British minstrelsy, and quite unlike the all-male American version. Jones' laughter could be heard amid the din, her voice was audible in the chorus, and on one recording she even got to sing the featured song ("The Honeysuckle and the Bee," a British show tune).

Four more cylinders were issued by Edison Bell in 1905–1906, two of them remakes and two new. Most notable is that on two of these cylinders the featured song was sung by Pete Hampton, an American-born black vaudevillian and banjo player whose career, including much recording activity, was centered in Europe during the early 1900s. On one cylinder, in fact, he sang "Old Black Joe."

The Edison company itself (separate from locally owned Edison Bell) began importing American-made minstrel and minstrel-related cylinders in 1903, as soon as it was contractually able to do so, but did not, as far as can be determined, record any locally.

The third major label, Columbia, was close behind Gramophone and Edison, issuing its first locally made minstrel cylinders in December 1901. These represented quite a coup, being billed as by the combined Mohawk, Moore and Burgess Minstrels, Britain's most famous troupe (although members of this troupe were apparently involved in making Berliner discs in 1899). The featured songs were more distinctively British than on other early minstrel records: "When the Children All Come Home," "They've Had 'Em Since Adam," "The Girl Who Won't Have Me," "A Sop in the Pan," and "Just Walk Along by the Side of Me." It is unfortunate that the cylinders appear to be lost, so we cannot hear these historic recordings.

We know that participants on the Columbia cylinders included Tom Birchmore, Ford Robinson, and Fred Melton. The director was listed as Celian Kottaun, a noted composer and cornetist who had been with the Mohawk and Moore and Burgess Minstrels for more than 25 years.

Birchmore was born in America but had been performing in Britain since the 1870s and was famed as a stump speaker and cornerman. Born Tom Moore, he changed his professional name to "Birchmore" when he joined Moore and Burgess (to avoid confusion with the leader, "Pony" Moore). Among Birchmore's specialties was "'Uncle Pete,' the ancient nigger ... a joyous, active old man, the very incarnation of humour and suppressed merriment, prepared on the slightest provocation to burst into song and dance of the most vigorous and eccentric description."[82] He also became known for his stump speech on "The Softer Sex" (women), which he recorded for Berliner and later for Jumbo. This was a rather appreciative view of women, quite different from the misogynistic mockery common in minstrelsy. Birchmore's style was in some ways similar to that of U.S. storyteller Cal "Uncle Josh" Stewart, with a kind of Yankee drawl and a tendency to laugh at his own jokes.

Birchmore took easily to recording and recorded both solo and as part of minstrel ensembles for numerous labels during the early 1900s. He was often billed on the label, in fact, as "Tom Birchmore, cornerman of Moore and Burgess Minstrels." He was probably the biggest "star" of British minstrelsy to record, but he was certainly not the only experienced British stage minstrel to do so. Frank Andrews, the noted British record researcher, has listed some of the others: George d'Albert, Sam Atherton, Baker E. Belphor, Herbert Campbell, Tom Campbell, Jack Charman, Gustave Chaudoir, Laddie Cliff, Johnny Danvers, G.H. Elliott ("The Chocolate Coloured Coon"), Bert Errol, Tom E. Finglass, George H. Fox, Louie Freear, Wilson Hallett, Jimmy James, Donald Keir, Celian Kottaun (cornetist), Dan Leno, Mays and Hunter, John V. Morton, George Mozart, H. Chance Newton, Harry Reynolds, Billy Richardson, Tom Simmons, Eugene Stratton, the Great Little Thomas, Dick Tubb, Jack Waller, and Billy Whitlock. (In his article, Andrews adds that he probably missed some.)[83] As in America, many (if not most) of the artists who made early minstrel records in Britain had firsthand experience on the minstrel stage.

After releasing these early and historic recordings (which were probably not sold in large numbers due to the limited duplication facilities of the day), starting in 1901 Columbia relied on imported U.S. minstrel cylinders and discs to fill out its catalog. These included its "Evening with the Minstrels" series and many Rambler Minstrels discs, among others.

Independent cylinder and disc labels, which had been shut out of the British market by the Edison and Berliner patent monopolies, began pouring into the market as soon as those patents started expiring in 1900–1902. As in the United States, all these companies wanted to have minstrel records on their lists. Pathé, an established French cylinder label, brought out at least three (and possibly more) minstrel cylinders in 1902, right after the Edison patents expired in March of that year. Unfortunately, all cylinders from this era are quite rare today, due to the relatively small size of the British record market and the fragility of the wax cylinders themselves.

Pathé was followed by several smaller cylinder operations between 1902 and 1907. One was the International Indestructible Co., formed in 1902 by a group of American entrepreneurs, which specialized in making "unbreakable" celluloid cylinders, many of which were bootlegs of Edison and Edison Bell recordings. This company also marketed under the Biophone label. It is not known whether its minstrel cylinders were original recordings or bootlegs, but the titles ("The Old Log Cabin in the Dell," "Echoes of Minstrelsy") certainly look familiar.

A particularly shadowy company was the Phonograph Record Manufacturing Co. (PRMC), active from 1904 to 1906, which appears to have been founded to sell off stock from the failed New Century Co. (1900–1904). The minstrel titles in a 1904 PRMC catalog may have originally been recorded by New Century, although they have not been traced to that source. The featured songs were American titles ("Break the News to Mother," "My Coal Black Lady," "The Old Folks at Home"). Star Cylinders, a small label based in Norwich, United Kingdom, claimed to have recorded "minstrel performers from the nearby seaside resort of Great Yarmouth." The only known title was either "Always Jolly" or "Hear Dem Bells" (sources differ). It certainly would be good to hear these local recordings, as minstrels were regular fixtures at seaside resorts in Britain, but no copies seem to have survived.

Only slightly more is known about the Clarion cylinder label, which issued several minstrel cylinders (and also "descriptives" that may have had minstrel content) between roughly 1907 and 1913. Titles included "Fun on the Plantation" and "A Cotton Fields Episode." These were said to have been conducted by George Ison.

No doubt the most successful independent cylinder label was Sterling, founded in 1904 by American Louis Sterling, who would later become a major figure in the British phonograph industry as the longtime head of Columbia Records. The Sterling company claimed to have shipped more than one million cylinders in its first year. Among its 1905–1906 releases were six titles by the Black Diamond Minstrels, whose members included middleman Russell Hunting, cornermen Johnnie Coles and Tom Hetherington, and the Tally Ho! Trio (Ernie Chester, Eric Farr, and William Doust—this trio recorded widely in the early days). The featured songs on the cylinders were mostly antebellum American titles ("Old Folks at Home," "Old Black Joe," "Hard Times," "Massa's in de Cold, Cold Ground," etc.)—just the kind of thing that was *not* featured on U.S. minstrel records of this period. If Stephen Foster was being left out of U.S. minstrel recordings at this time, he was being celebrated in Britain. Some of the Sterling cylinders were later dubbed onto Pathé discs.

Discs were rapidly taking over the British market, as they were in the United States, and many more labels sprang up in that sector of the market. Beka, a recently established German label, invaded Britain in 1905 with eight minstrel-related recordings evoking famous British names. The Tivoli Minstrels were named after the well-known Tivoli Theatre on London's West End, while the Royal Cowes Minstrels suggested the Royal Cowes yachting regatta and week of shoreside entertainment that took place every summer on the Isle of Wight. Whether the artists on these records had anything to do with either the theater or the regatta is unknown. The single disc heard by this author (the Royal Cowes' "Every Day Life") is not a minstrel routine but a song. Most of the songs listed as featured on these records were contemporary hits, either in the United States ("Navajo," "Hello Ma Baby") or in Britain ("Go 'Way, Good Massa Bee").

Russell Hunting's Black Diamond Minstrels also turned up on Odeon discs in December 1906, with the exact same repertoire and personnel used on Sterling cylinders. In February 1908, Gramophone subsidiary Zonophone brought out a set of four discs with somewhat more imaginative programming. Each disc had portions of two songs, the first an American hit and the second distinctively British. For example, one disc began with "Somebody Loves Me" (presumably the 1890s U.S. hit by that name) and ended with "Meet Me at the Golden Gate" (c. 1890), which was described on the sheet music as "The Popular Corner Man's Song of the Moore & Burgess Minstrels." Another one opened with "Cheyenne" (a 1906 U.S. hit) and ended with "Waiting at the Church" (1906), Vesta Victoria's great hit from the British music halls. The recording troupe was called "The Christy Minstrels," the same name that Gramophone had used earlier, but the records were advertised as conducted by Gustave Chaudoir of the Moore and Burgess Minstrels.

In 1910, Pathé released four more minstrel routines by the Black Diamond Minstrels, this time led by star cornerman Tom Birchmore, supported by Tom Hetherington and the Tally Ho! Trio. The featured songs were all by Stephen Foster, but the routines were apparently original ("The Definition of a Kiss," "M-O-N-E-Y," "The Total Abstanuisance Man," "The Absent-Minded Preacher"). They were described as "patter, with sung verse." These recordings were reissued in 1915 on Pathé's Diamond label and possibly again in 1920, credited to the Black Star Minstrels.

Birchmore was better identified on record with his "Coontown Minstrels," which appeared on several labels, including Jumbo (a Fonotipia product) in 1909 and 1911–1912. These were later reissued on Odeon, Silvertone and perhaps elsewhere. Supporting Birchmore was the familiar Tally Ho! Trio. The middleman in the 1909 set is addressed as "Mr. Johnson," a generic name, but in the 1911–1912 set it's "Mr. Farr" from the trio (a different voice). The featured songs are all American, mostly from the 19th century and identified with minstrelsy ("Old Folks at Home," "Down Where the Sugar Cane Grows," and "Good Old Jeff"—the latter used by the original Christy Minstrels in the 1850s).

These 12 sides from Jumbo were much reissued and do tend to turn up today, at least more so than some of the other early recordings. Listening to these discs reveals some interesting aspects of Birchmore's performance style, which presumably reflected his style during his many years on stage with Moore and Burgess. First, the cornerman (Birchmore) is very much the star of the show. Sometimes on U.S. recordings the middleman (or interlocutor) would take a more active role in the show, but here the middleman says little except to briefly set up Birchmore's stories and jokes. The rest of the cast supports Birchmore as well, including a woman (Alma Jones?) whose voice is plainly heard in the background and who occasionally gets in a reaction line or two herself. Birchmore's patter is extremely easy and conversational, with little interjections and side comments, making the proceedings seem very natural.

Although the songs are nearly all American, it's clear that this is a British troupe just by the British accents. The jokes are about marriage, relatives, relationships, and such, with hardly anything (even obliquely) about race. For example, there was the following story about Uncle George, which gradually built to a payoff:

> FARR: Well, Mr. Birchmore, how are you getting along now?
> BIRCHMORE (LAUGHS): I thought I had great expectations the other day. You remember my uncle George?
> FARR: Very well— (interrupted)
> BIRCHMORE: He's gone, you know.
> FARR: Gone? Gone where?
> BIRCHMORE: I dunno, he's got friends in both places! (laughs) But he left a will, so I went over to the house with the rest of the relations to hear the will read. Well, the old ex-e-cutor got up…
> FARR (INTERRUPTS): Don't you mean the *executor*?

BIRCHMORE: Yes, the old exceptioner, he got up, and the first bequeath in the will was to my brother, Jim.
FARR: Your brother Jim? You mean your brother James?
BIRCHMORE: Well, we used to call him Jim, we knew him better than you did (chuckles). Well, the will went on to say, "To my beloved nephew James I leave the sum of ten thousand pounds."
FARR: That was very kind.... What did James say now...?
BIRCHMORE: Oh, Jim cried something awful, he said he thought it was a great pity that poor Uncle George couldn't live to enjoy it himself.
FARR: I bet he prays as his duty....
BIRCHMORE: Yes, then the will went on to say, "And to my beloved niece Annie"—you know, that spunky veiled sister—"I leave a thousand pounds and a dwelling house."
FARR: That was very kind. And what did Annie say...?
BIRCHMORE: Oh, she cried worse than tears. (chuckles) She also thought it was a great pity that poor Uncle George couldn't live to enjoy it himself.
FARR: I'll bet she prayed for him also.
BIRCHMORE: Then the will went on to say, "And to my good-for-nothing nephew Tom..."
FARR (INTERJECTS): Why, that was *you*!
BIRCHMORE: (laughs) Yes, that was me. Said, "I leave the sum of tuppence..."
FARR: Two pence? What for?
BIRCHMORE: Why, "To buy arsenic to poison himself with."
FARR: What did you say?
BIRCHMORE: Oh, I said I thought it was a great pity that poor Uncle George couldn't live to enjoy it *himself*!
(great laughter from company)[84]

Birchmore also appeared in 1910 on Bell Discs, a subsidiary of Edison Bell, with his troupe there called the Manhattan Minstrels. The featured songs in the four routines were again 19th-century American ("Old Folks at Home," "I'se Gwine Back to Dixie," etc.). These routines were later reissued on Velvet Face, Exo, Curry's, and Famous. Birchmore was back in 1912 on Winner (another Edison Bell subsidiary) with the "Christy Minstrels," which sound very much like his Coontown Minstrels from Jumbo. Eric Farr was the middleman, and sweet tenor Ernie Chester (from the Tally Ho! Trio) sang the featured song, "Old Folks at Home." Birchmore's routine was about drinking, and that familiar female voice could be heard laughing in the background.

Birchmore was not the only veteran stage minstrel to participate in recorded first part recreations. The oddly named "Great Little Thomas" (Jay Thomas), who began performing as a boy (but kept the name thereafter), was a real pioneer of British minstrelsy. Born around 1836, he sang "God Save the Queen" at the opening of the Crystal Palace in 1851. He joined the Mohawk Minstrels in 1879 and later appeared with Moore and Burgess. In later years, he was sometimes known as the "Father of the Minstrels." In 1909, age 73 and portly, Thomas recorded several sides for Favorite, both solo and with the Favorite Minstrels. Also in the troupe were Billy Whitlock, Wallace Scott, and "other Palladium minstrels." The featured songs were a mix of American and British minstrel favorites, including "The Laughing Song," "Whistling Coon," "Rocked in the Cradle of the Deep" (every minstrel show had to have a basso solo!), "Camptown Races" and "I Carry My Sunshine with Me" (a Harry Hunter song from the Mohawks). Thomas' solo recordings for Favorite were also interesting, including his stump speech on "Contradictions" and his own "We Must Have Some of Each" and "Burlesque on 'When Other Lips.'" Several of these Favorite sides were reissued on Ariel Grand.

One of the more obscure labels of the period was Diplomat, produced for J. Blum and Co. between 1911 and 1915, drawing most of its releases from Bell, Kalliope and Disc

Record Co. However, it also apparently made some of its own recordings, among them at least one side by the "Kentucky Minstrels" and four others by the "Oxford Minstrels." Participants in these recordings are unknown. The featured songs were mostly old American minstrel songs. The sides were reissued on Besttone, Burlington, Famous and Pelican.

A ferocious price war that reshaped the entire British market broke out in 1912 when the German Beka Company began supplying matrices to low price labels such as Coliseum and Scala. These sold for as little as one shilling and six pence each, or about half the price of HMV and Columbia. The major labels tried to prevent the distribution and advertising of these cut-price discs, but eventually they responded with cheap(er) subsidiary labels of their own, including Cinch (1913) from the Gramophone Co., Phoenix (1913) from Columbia, Winner (1912) from Edison Bell, and Pelican, Arrow, Lyceum, and The Stars from others. Although the vogue for minstrel records was beginning to wane in Britain around this time, as it was in the United States, some minstrel records turn up on these lower-price labels.

Scala used master recordings from various sources, but in 1915 it issued six "minstrel sketches" that were apparently its own. These featured the Scala Minstrel Troupe, including comedians Harry Bluff and Billy Whitlock, and revolved around the imaginary village of Dark-Town. There was the Dark-Town Minstrel Show, Dark-Town Police Court, Dark-Town Fire Brigade, Dark-Town Races, Dark-Town Picnic, and Dark-Town Shaving Saloon.

Ariel Grand, sold widely by the John G. Graves mail-order company from 1911 to 1938, drew its masters from many suppliers in the early 1910s, including minstrel recordings from Zonophone, Favorite and Jumbo. Many were labeled "Ariel Minstrels" or something similar. Those drawn from Zonophone were not actually minstrel first part recreations, however. The "Zono Minstrels" group was a mixed quartet consisting of Ernest Pike, Annie Rees, Violet Oppenshaw, and Stewart Gardner, who rendered in rather formal fashion 10 "plantation songs" written by British composer Alfred Scott Gatty ("De Ole Banjo," "Dat's Berry Queer," etc.).

From the evidence of these records, it is obvious that British record buyers of the early 1900s embraced minstrel recreations just as enthusiastically as their American cousins. They had their choice of either American minstrel recordings (which were widely imported) or locally made fare. But unlike American minstrel recordings of the period, which tended to emphasize current song hits and strove to present themselves as "contemporary" entertainment, the British versions were more traditional (a lot of Stephen Foster) and even nostalgic, evoking minstrelsy's long tradition. The Brits, it seems, really liked the general idea of tradition. There was local star power as well, and British record makers were fortunate in having access to quite a few well-known stage minstrels. Star cornerman Tom Birchmore of Moore and Burgess played a particularly large role in these records. The featured songs on the British recordings were a mix of American and British songs, many from the music halls, but there were surprisingly few "coon songs." In fact, in both repertoire and dialogue, there was much less reference to race than in American minstrel recordings.

For Britain, of course, World War I began in 1914, and the following years brought major social change and modernization. Minstrelsy receded quickly into the past. Whereas in America major stage troupes (such as those led by Al G. Field, Lew Dockstader and "Honey Boy" Evans) continued to tour into the 1910s and beyond, in Britain the last major troupe—the merged Mohawk, Moore and Burgess Minstrels—closed up shop in 1904. Minstrel recordings sold well for another 10 years beyond that, but by the early 1910s they, too, were fading away. For the next 15 years or so, there was little activity.

British Minstrel Records: 1920s and Beyond

One oddity did pop up during this dry spell. In December 1926, HMV issued a rather strange 12-inch disc by one of its most popular dance bands, Jack Hylton and His Orchestra, called "The Hylton Minstrels." It was subtitled "Being a Musical Burlesque on the Old Time Nigger Minstrels, Introducing Plantation Songs, Jokes, and Effects by Jack Hylton and His Orchestra." One wonders what Hylton's young fans thought of this disc, which opened with "Gentlemen, be seated," followed by instrumental performances of various minstrel songs (many in dance band tempo), plus vocal interjections, laughter, and jokes between "Jones and Bones." It was as if Paul Whiteman, or Glenn Miller in a later decade, had interrupted an evening of familiar big band dance numbers to put on a minstrel show! Trumpets, saxophones and massed violins crooned "The Old Banjo," "Oh, Dem Golden Slippers," "Come Along, Sister Mary," "My Old Kentucky Home," "Old Folks at Home," "Camptown Races," instrumental imitations, and "By the Watermelon Vine," ending with "Razors in the Air." One band member, in heavy dialect, actually posed the question, "Why did the chicken cross the road?" However, the release apparently sank without a trace, as copies are rare today.

The drought in new minstrel records ended rather abruptly in late 1929. The Gramophone Co. released Victor's "Minstrel Show of 1929" on HMV in December of that year, about six months after its U.S. release, labeling it as by "The Darktown Melody Makers." It apparently had healthy sales.

The very same month, arch-rival Columbia released the four-part "An Old Time Minstrel Show" by the Mississippi Minstrels on its Regal subsidiary. This was an elaborate local production supervised by Stan Greening, one of the principal dance band contractors in the United Kingdom during the 1920s. Among the participants were Greening on banjo, W.T. Best on piano, and the Greening band conducted by Charles Prentice. According to the files, unnamed others were "Columbia studio singers and musicians contracted by Greening."

The featured songs and skits were antique, and a real throwback to the 19th century and blackface minstrelsy: "Camptown Races," "Come Where My Love Lies Dreaming," Stump Speech—Passing Events, "There Was a Little Nigger," "Massa's in de Cold, Cold Ground," "Poor Old Joe" (aka "Old Black Joe"), "Oh, Dem Golden Slippers," Stump Speech—W.O.M.A.N., "My Old Kentucky Home," and "Marching through Georgia." The rather thick British accents made it clear that this was a local production, providing a curious contrast with the all-American material. In some cases, the effect was rather bizarre (at least to American ears), as with the pure, high-pitched boy tenor Master Autry singing "Poor Old Joe" ("I he-arh the gentle voices calling …"). There was an unusual amount of racial material (for example, "There Was a Little Nigger" done to the rhythmic clicking of the bones).

Laughter and interjections from the seemingly large cast gave the production a very live feel. There was even a running gag through the show in which the pompous middleman kept admonishing the cornermen to stop asking him questions they couldn't answer themselves, until one of them turned the tables on him:

MIDDLEMAN (STERNLY): Didn't I tell you, just now, not to ask questions you couldn't answer yourself?
RASTUS (CHUCKLES): So you did.
MIDDLEMAN: Yes, and by the way, that reminds me, I saw you going home the other night in a beautiful inebriated state. Where had you been to?
RASTUS: I don't know. Do *you*?
MIDDLEMAN: No.
RASTUS: Well, take my advice, and don't you ever ask questions you cain't answer yourself!
(great laughter)[85]

Regal's "Old Time Minstrel Show" was well done and engaging, and with four 12-inch sides (on two discs), it was essentially a 16-minute minstrel show. It was released in the United States on Columbia in the early 1930s but had little impact there, in part because it was so British, in part because it was buried in a very obscure Columbia numerical series (the 55000-D series), and perhaps most of all because of the parlous state of U.S. record sales at the time (sales were, in a word, collapsing). This album stayed in the British Columbia catalog for more than a decade, however, and was even reissued in edited form on a 10-inch disc (MR 2547) in 1937.

At virtually the same time that HMV and Regal brought out these two major minstrel first part productions, Edison Bell, via its Edison Bell Radio label, issued "The Darktown Minstrels, Parts 1&2" on an eight-inch disc.

The 1929 minstrel discs from three major British labels seems to have started a revival of minstrelsy on record, mostly oriented toward nostalgia. HMV was so pleased with the reaction to its Victor import that, two years later, it produced the "Minstrel Show of 1931," headlined by the English Minstrels, which starred the blackface radio and music hall duo, Alexander (James Carew) and Mose (Billy Bennett). They were accompanied by a chorus and the Ray Noble Orchestra, giving the performance a distinctly contemporary sound. The featured songs were "Camptown Races," "My Moon," "Speedwell" (a banjo solo), "Swanee River" (aka "Old Folks at Home"), "De Old Banjo," "Lily of Laguna," a tap dance, and "Goodnight" (aka "Shine, Shine Moon"). Modeled after successful American blackface duos such as Moran and Mack and Pick and Pat, Alexander and Mose mostly used short, fast-talking, insult and marital jokes, which contrasted with the very straight and proper vocal solos by other cast members.

ALEXANDER: Say, Mose, did you hear that Mr. Johnstone had lost his wife?
MOSE: Yes, *sir*.
ALEXANDER: Why, it must be hard to lose a wife.
MOSE: Yeah, it's almost *impossible*!
(laughter)[86]

Six years later, in 1937, HMV issued "Minstrel Show of 1937," by the then very popular radio troupe known as the Kentucky Minstrels (12 voices), with Harry S. Pepper, C. Denier Warren, Doris Arnold, Ike Hatch, and orchestra. This troupe will be discussed in detail in chapter 3, but here they presented songs familiar to minstrel fans: "Oh, Dem Golden Slippers," "Hear Dem Bells," "Oh, Lordy," "Dixie," "Massa's in de Cold, Cold Ground," "Kemo, Kimo," and "Hear Dem Bells."

The popular Kentucky Minstrels also made many more recordings in the 1930s. For HMV they recorded, between 1938 and 1942, more than 20 10- and 12-inch discs of parlor ballads, such as "The Holy City," "O Dry Those Tears" and "Plantation Medley." These were by vocalists and instrumentalists from the show, especially John Duncan and Gwen Catley, and were not minstrel first part recreations.

For Decca, in 1934, the Kentucky Minstrels recorded "The Big Radio Minstrel Show," four sides on two 12-inch discs. This was a 16-minute performance that mimicked an actual show (it will be described in more detail in chapter 3).

Others jumped on the newly resurgent minstrel train in the 1930s, notwithstanding the depressed condition of the record industry during the Great Depression. In 1931, Zonophone issued eight sides by the Zonophone Minstrels, subtitled "The White Blackbirds." The White Blackbirds were a stage and radio troupe that originated in the seaside resort of Blackpool, England, in the late 1920s and were popular throughout the 1930s. The name came from *Blackbirds of 1928*, a hit American revue, but the British show bore little resemblance to its American predecessor. The star cornerman of the White Blackbirds was Norman Savage, who is addressed on the recordings. Featured songs were a mix of American and British standards, including "Come Where My Love Lies Dreaming," "I Want to Be Down Home in Dixie," "The Old Black Crow," "My Old Kentucky Home," "Belle of the Barber's Ball" (a George M. Cohan song), "Way Down in Dixie," and "Goodbye Eliza Jane"; most of these songs were performed by a male chorus. There were also novelties such as banjos, tambourines, dancing and yodeling. Savage had a friendly, easygoing style somewhat similar to Tom Birchmore a generation earlier, and his cornerman patter was filled with puns, conundrums and banter with other cast members. As in most British minstrel recordings, there was little material that was explicitly about race.

Also in 1931, Beltona, a private label that drew masters from various sources, released two sides by the "Kentucky Minstrels" as well as a sketch by Rastus and Sambo from that troupe. It is unlikely that this group was related to radio's Kentucky Minstrels, as the radio show did not premiere until 1933. The sides were recorded for Beltona by Edison Bell. Two years later, in 1933, Edison Bell released two sides by the White Minstrels on its own Edison Bell Winner subsidiary, the last version of the venerable Winner label. The major British labels and their subsidiaries, aside from Decca, had by this time been merged into the Electric and Musical Industries (EMI) conglomerate. "The White Minstrels" was a generic name used by many amateur groups in the 19th and early 20th centuries, and it is not certain who this particular group was—only that minstrelsy still commanded enough interest, even during the Depression, to warrant billing on records as well as radio shows.

By the time of World War II, minstrel records had once again faded from view in Britain. They stayed out of sight for 20 years, with the curious exception of a two-disc nostalgia release by Columbia in 1951.

This release was titled "Way Down South (A Minstrel Show)," and it featured veteran blackface entertainer G.H. Elliott ("The Chocolate Coloured Coon") and three young pop singers—Marie Benson, Bryan Johnson, and Teddy Johnson—who handled most of the songs. (Marie was a member of the pop group the Stargazers.) They were backed by Norrie Paramor's orchestra and chorus. Elliott (1882–1962) was born in Britain but got his start in America at the age of nine with the Primrose and West Minstrels. Returning to Britain in 1901, he appeared for a time with Harry Reynolds' Minstrels before becoming a major star in the music halls. He made more than a hundred records in a recording career extending from 1904 to 1960.

"Way Down South" was quite a mishmash of 19th- and 20th-century songs, stretching from the 1840s to the 1920s: "On the Mississippi," "I Want to Be in Dixie," "Beautiful Dreamer," "I Want a Girl Just Like the Girl That Married Dear Old Dad," "Waiting for the Robert E. Lee," "Camptown Races," "I'm Just Wild about Harry," "Carry Me Back to

Old Virginny," "Sue, Sue, Sue" (one of Elliott's trademark songs), "Dixie's Land," "Oh, Dem Golden Slippers," "Swanee," "Ma Curly-Headed Baby," "Josie," "Polly Wolly Doodle," "My Old Kentucky Home," "On the Banks of the Wabash," "By the Light of the Silvery Moon," "Are You from Dixie?" and "Oh! Susanna."

Britain did not have a surge of minstrel LPs in the late 1950s, as occurred in the United States, but it made up for that lack with three mega-sellers in the 1960s. These were spin-offs from the phenomenally popular BBC TV series *The Black and White Minstrel Show*, which ran from 1958 to 1978. The first LP, released in 1960 and consisting of a chorus singing medleys of old-time songs, spent 142 weeks on the best-seller charts and sold more than 100,000 copies—the first British LP to ever do so. Two follow-up LPs also stayed on the charts for six months or more. All three records reached number one on the charts. (More information on *The Black and White Minstrel Show* and its recorded spin-offs will be found in chapter 5.)

3

The Minstrel Show on Radio

The idea that radio might become an entertainment medium began to percolate before 1910, but it took a long time to come to a boil. When it finally burst upon the consumer scene in the early 1920s, one of the first program genres to make its way into the new medium was minstrelsy.

Guglielmo Marconi had demonstrated the feasibility of long-distance wireless communications in 1901 (from Newfoundland to England), but the next 20 years were occupied with experimentation and refinement of radio equipment. During the 1910s, the government handed out licenses to experimenters, some of whom broadcast phonograph records during their tests. The first commercial stations were licensed in 1920; however, throughout 1921 stations launched very slowly, and they broadcast only intermittently. Few people had receivers, and there were no program listings in the newspapers. Not until major urban stations began to launch in late 1921 and early 1922 did radio start to take off. In New York City, early stations included WJZ (October 1921), WOR (February 1922) and WEAF (March 1922), each of which would eventually become the key station for a national network. The *New York Times* began providing radio program listings on March 30, 1922, and other local newspapers followed suit.

Even though most of these stations were not yet broadcasting full time, it quickly became apparent that radio was a voracious medium. The search for inexpensive, yet appealing, programming was on, in order to entice consumers to buy sets. Music was cheap and plentiful, and there was plenty of that via vocalists and orchestras, usually live in the studios. Although minstrelsy was now passé as big-time stage entertainment, it still had appeal as occasional, special programming. It was also relatively straightforward to produce. Scores of stations in the early 1920s therefore broadcast minstrel shows, usually from their studios, and almost always using local talent.

The earliest example I have been able to find—though not necessarily the first to be broadcast—was on KDKA in Pittsburgh, often cited as the first commercial station. On November 22, 1921, during its first year of operation, the station carried a "Shriner's Minstrel Show" from a local temple, apparently as a remote.[1]

Another early example came on May 3, 1922, on WVP in New York, a station operated by the U.S. Signal Corps from around 1920 to 1922 and run by volunteers. This minstrel show had a direct tie-in with a record label, demonstrating the crossover between radio and the older medium of records. Presented under the auspices of the *New York Evening Globe*, it was one of a series of musical programs aired that spring supervised by the musical director of Okeh Records, Fred Hager. Participating were Okeh artists Ernest Hare and the Shannon Four quartet, and most of the songs featured were either recorded by Okeh or written by Hager and studio orchestra leader Justin Ring. Among the songs (which were mostly contemporary) were "Swanee Smiles," "Oh Brother, What a Feeling" and "Kiss Me by Wireless." It sounds a lot like a label promotion, which is perhaps how the performers were compensated for their appearances.

Serving as interlocutor for this show was Nat Sanders, while the endmen were Billy Tilden and Al Ward, all minor league vaudevillians and entertainers from the New York area. Tilden delivered dialect stories and a sketch called "Snider's Grocery Store," while Sanders offered a couple of songs. A duo called "Ike and Jake" held their "Third Wireless Confab," and the show ended with the whole company joining in on "Kiss Me by Wireless," which was being promoted heavily by the label.[2]

A sampling of other local stations broadcasting minstrel shows during 1922 and 1923 includes KYW, Chicago (June 1922); WHAZ, Troy, New York (possibly late 1922); WGY, Schenectady, New York (February–July 1923); WSB, Atlanta (March 1923); WDAR, Philadelphia (October 1923); WMAQ, Chicago (*Ted Brown Minstrel Show*, October 1923); and WEAF, New York (Eveready Minstrels, December 1923). There were many more.

Detailed information was published about the WGY broadcasts, giving us insight into just how these early, live programs were structured. (There are no off-air recordings from this early period.) WGY, the General Electric station in Schenectady, reached much of the East Coast and was a major producer of plays, sports, and other special programming in the early days of radio. During 1923, its second year of operation, the station scheduled a minstrel show roughly once a month, using a different (presumably local) troupe for each broadcast. Most of the featured songs were either 19th-century or specialty material, suggesting that the shows were making no effort to be contemporary but were tapping into the nostalgia vein, as was true of minstrelsy on record and on stage at this time.

In February 1923, the performers were the Cambrian Minstrels, who offered "old Southland Melodies" and George M. Cohan's "Oh, You Coon" (1908), among others. There were endman jokes, a bass solo, a monologist, and a xylophone specialty, plus English variety artists "Will and Fred." In March, it was the Raggety-Taggety Minstrels, performing "My Old Kentucky Home," "School Days," "Kentucky Babe," the traditional "Asleep in the Deep" and the novelty "When My Shoes Wear Out from Walkin', I'll Be on My Feet Again" (the latter by endman Lew Washington). A nod to contemporary music was a medley of recent popular southern songs, including "Lovin' Sam" and "Carolina Rolling Stone." Performers had names

The 1920s saw the explosion of radio (1923).

like Rastus and Nichodemus, and there was a traditional "humorous dialogue" and "jokefest." One interesting title was "Radiominstrelsy," performed by the entire company.[3]

The reaction to these broadcasts was enthusiastic. In July, the *Schenectady Gazette* reported, "After a recent minstrel show broadcast by WGY 1,400 letters were received by the station within 24 hours. Over 2,000 letters were received within a week referring to this particular entertainment.... In addition to the letters addressed to the station many thousands are sent direct to the performer."[4]

Virtually all of the minstrel performers who appeared on radio were whites, who may or may not have been in blackface. Obviously listeners couldn't see them, but some shows were put on in front of live audiences, and there was a belief that blackface in the studio would enhance the performance. There were plenty of black musicians on radio at this time—Fats Waller, Fletcher Henderson, Duke Ellington, Louis Armstrong, and so on—but black minstrels were pretty much relegated to circus sideshows and traveling tent shows, off the air.[5]

Dailey Paskman and the Explosion in Radio Minstrelsy

He is forgotten today, but more than anyone else, one young man was responsible for the explosion of interest in minstrelsy in the late 1920s and 1930s—and for many other innovations in radio in the years when that industry was taking shape. Dailey Paskman (1894–1979) certainly led an interesting life. Born in Philadelphia, he started as a child actor in the Forepaugh Stock Company before talking his way into a job as an office boy in the Shubert theatrical organization. Working his way up, he soon became advance representative and then company manager of a Shubert troupe traveling across the country. Around the age of 20, he was hired by prominent producer Morris Gest, assisting in producing and adapting many of Gest's Broadway shows, including *Chu Chin Chow* (1917), *Mecca* (1920), and *The Miracle* (1924). Paskman, who dabbled in music, also wrote lyrics for the hit imported revue *Chauve Souris* (1922) and collaborated with such notable composers as Rudolf Friml, Vincent Youmans and Victor Young.

In 1924, Paskman received an interesting offer. The Gimbels department store was about to

Dailey Paskman outside a theater.

launch a radio station (WGBS) in New York. Would he be interested in becoming the first station director? Here was a brand new medium, still experimenting with programming, and the Gimbel family was interesting in building a classy, attention-getting operation that would reflect well on their stores. With his deep contacts in the theatrical world, Paskman couldn't resist.

The inaugural broadcast took place on Sunday, October 26, 1924, from the theater in Gimbels, and it was nothing short of spectacular. Emceed by Eddie Cantor, the show featured the Vincent Lopez and George Olsen orchestras, as well as Cliff Edwards, Raymond Hitchcock, George Jessel, Rudolf Friml, Ben Bernie, Rube Goldberg, George Gershwin, the Dolly Sisters, Judith Anderson, Sigmund Spaeth, and many others. An audience of 400 attended. Cantor wisecracked about there being so many Gimbels around: "Wherever you go there's a Gimbel. You almost fall all over them. But there are Gimbels—and Gimbels. The New York Gimbel is all right, but the Philadelphia Gimbel is the worst kind."[6]

Paskman followed this triumph with a string of radio plays and operas, including an audio version of the acclaimed Broadway play *The Miracle*, which was particularly challenging since much of the play was silent (music and some narration guided listeners). There were numerous interview shows, programming from Europe (prerecorded on a "Homophone"), and a live broadcast from an airplane circling over New York. In 1925, a laudatory article in *Theatre Magazine* cited Paskman's production of two O. Henry stories, "a really gorgeous presentation of *Peer Gynt*, with Arvid Paulson and Maida Craigen in the cast, and Grieg's music accompanying it," and Paskman's musical drama *Jazzmania*. "Best of all, thanks to Mr. Paskman, it was radio's own, created and produced for the new art, not carried wholesale from the stage and dumped without apologies into a loud speaker."[7]

Amid all this high culture and periodic stunts, Paskman needed a continuous flow of programming—lots of it—to "feed the beast." He had always been fascinated by minstrel shows, and when the need arose to fill some time in a noncritical time period, he decided to try one. WGBS was on the air about 40 hours per week, and during days off it would sometimes feed programming from its studios to other stations. One such link was to WMAF, a powerful station run as a hobby by Colonel Edward Green (heir to the Hetty Green fortune) on his estate in South Dartmouth, Massachusetts. On July 22, 1925, while WGBS itself was off the air, it fed from its studios to WMAF the first in a series of "Old-Time Minstrels" broadcasts. It went so well that Paskman moved the show to WGBS. Publicized as "compiled and directed by Dailey Paskman," it premiered on WGBS on October 1, 1925, at 9:00 p.m., and ran weekly or biweekly for either 60 or 90 minutes. It was an immediate hit.

Instead of congratulating himself on a good idea for an occasional program and leaving it at that, wheels began to turn in Paskman's head. He loved minstrelsy, with its upbeat mix of comedy (which he thought there was too little of on radio) and music. If this show was working so well, maybe it could be built into something even bigger.

Prior minstrel broadcasts on local stations had been performed either by ad hoc groups pulled together for a one-time broadcast or by local amateurs. (WGY, for example, had recruited a different outside group for each broadcast.) Neither type of group was used to working together on a show for radio. Experience working together, and knowledge of the peculiar demands of performing for a microphone, would be key to creating a smooth, professional-sounding broadcast.

Paskman may have been the first to assemble a regular troupe of performers specifically for broadcasting. Their names were generally not publicized (the better to focus on the format), but from later stories and the Paskman papers now at the New York Public Library, we have some of them. The original interlocutor was WGBS staff announcer Floyd Neale, replaced after a few weeks by character comedian Albert Farrington. Later (in 1927), singer Leroy Montesanto served for a time as interlocutor. The original endmen, referred to as Tambo and Bones, were Ward Kirby and Georgie Zorn, succeeded by William Browning and Zorn, and then Browning and Harry Jenkins. Other principals in the cast included tenor Milton Yokeman, bass/baritone William Sweeney, and comics William Heins (Mr. Hambone) and Charles Marks (Sambo).

None of these men were major stars. Most were second-tier vaudevillians or radio performers from the New York area, and nearly all had other roles on WGBS, either with their own "musical interludes" or as actors in some of the station's many plays. They were reliable, journeyman performers whom Paskman knew well. They knew how to work a microphone and over time could develop the chemistry necessary for a smooth-running series. The "star" would be the minstrel format itself.

A couple of Paskman's troupe members did have larger careers outside of WGBS. Leroy Montesanto was a dance band vocalist who made many recordings in the late 1920s, and William Heins was none other than "Billy Heins," an old-time minstrel who had made recordings in the 1890s and later recorded blackface material with Billy Golden (as Golden and Heins) in the 1910s. In addition, there were occasional celebrity guests. In 1928, Paskman's pal and author Dr. Sigmund Spaeth made a guest appearance as interlocutor, and on another episode Tin Pan Alley legends Albert Von Tilzer and Seymour Brown, as well as old-time minstrel star Neil O'Brien (veteran of the Haverly, Al G. Field and Dockstader troupes), were guests.

Dailey Paskman's Radio Minstrels became a regular feature heard in New York and throughout the Northeast on Thursday (later Sunday) nights. It ran for more than three years, from July 1925 to August 1928.

In the late spring of 1927, while the radio show was at its height, Paskman launched the second phase of his master plan to bring back minstrelsy. He formed a 20-man touring troupe, using some talent from the radio cast but mostly new cast members. The dignified interlocutor was thin, mustachioed Jack Rice, and the original endmen were Nate Busby and Dave Irwin (later Bob Conn replaced Busby). From radio came George Zorn (portraying "Honey Boy" Evans) and Milton Yokeman. They were joined by the "Hi and Low" banjo-piano team, the Diamond Studded Quartet, and the Savannah Shufflers dance team Kramer and Stone.

The stage troupe embarked on what was billed as a transcontinental tour, although most of the traced appearances appear to have been in the Northeast. Judging from the positive reviews and extensive bookings, it was well received. The gimmick was that the Radio Minstrels replicated an actual radio show on stage, with a microphone, speakers and a radio-style announcer, which was novel at the time. In fact, one of the "characters" was called "Mike-rophone." One reviewer commented that the troupe brought "their full quota of jokes, wheezes and comedy monologues, some new and some mellowed by age; and songs old and new.... [It was] clean, wholesome entertainment."[8] All performers were in blackface except for the interlocutor. As was customary, the endmen (including the animated Busby and the operatic-voiced Irwin) carried much of the show, with a few jokes specific to the New York area:

Paskman's radio troupe on stage, with emcee/interlocutor Jack Rice.

SAMBO: Where does you live now, Tambo?
TAMBO: Hoboken.
SAMBO: Isn't that the town where they ring curfew every night at 7?
TAMBO: They used to, but they don't anymore.
SAMBO: Why not?
TAMBO: 'Cause it woke everybody up![9]

Although most of the cast members (like those on the radio show) were journeyman performers, it is worth noting that interlocutor Jack Rice (1893–1968) went on to a significant career as a character actor in movies during the 1930s. He is best known as the freeloading brother-in-law in Edgar Kennedy shorts and as "Ollie" in the *Blondie* films. He also made many later film and TV appearances.

The Radio Minstrels company toured for about two and a half years, from around April 1927 to late 1929; meanwhile Paskman was concocting parts three and four of his ambitious plan. Stage three, surprisingly, involved a book. Over the years, Paskman had assembled an impressive personal archive of minstrel materials, including sheet music, jokebooks, scripts, and photos, which he used to put together his shows. In 1928, he partnered with musicologist Dr. Sigmund Spaeth, an old friend, to coauthor a book on minstrelsy called *Gentlemen, Be Seated! A Parade of the Old-Time Minstrels.*

This volume was a cross between a scrapbook and an academic history of the genre, the first ever published in book form. Books were not as common then as they are now, and minstrelsy had not been considered worthy of such serious treatment. Probably the most notable predecessor was Edward Rice's *Monarchs of Minstrelsy* (1911), but that was an encyclopedia of individual performers. *Gentlemen, Be Seated!* was an accessible, 247-page overview of the history and structure of the minstrel show, generously illustrated with pictures and line drawings and including musical excerpts. In his preface, Spaeth, the academic, gave profuse credit to Paskman: "While this book is announced as a work of collaboration, it is only fair to state that its workmanship belongs almost entirely to Dailey Paskman, who has been in and out of the theatre since his cradle days."

Published by Doubleday and released in May 1928, *Gentlemen, Be Seated!* received major attention (Paskman knew how to generate publicity!). The book was promoted on air and through interviews, and Gimbels made it the centerpiece of a big window display of minstrel memorabilia. The reviews were uniformly favorable. The *New York Times* called it "a volume as amusing as it is illuminating ... immensely jolly reading," and then added, presciently, "as soon as this book gets out through the country there will be, we predict, an amateur revival of minstrelsy of impressive dimensions."[10] Other reviews were just as complimentary. Judging from the number of copies that turn up today, it was a best seller. A revised edition, with additional material, was published in 1976.

Spaeth, who was previously known for *Read 'Em and Weep* (1922) as well as more erudite books on music, became famous as "the tune detective" on radio in the 1930s. Curiously, when *Gentlemen, Be Seated!* was reissued in 1976, shortly before Paskman died, Spaeth's name was dropped as coauthor and there was no mention of him in the acknowledgments. (Spaeth had died in 1965.)

The final stage of Paskman's plan involved recording. In mid–1927, he approached the Victor Talking Machine Co. and recorded a two-part, 12-inch trial recording of his minstrels. However, Victor decided not to issue it, and the recording is now lost. Paskman had better luck with Columbia. In December 1928, his minstrels recorded another two-part mini-minstrel show for that label, which was issued in February 1929. It is the best representation we have of what Paskman's pioneering radio minstrels really sounded like.[11]

Participants are not identified on the record other than as Tambo, Bones, and so forth. However, radio broadcasts had ended the previous summer and the touring group was in the New York area between engagements in December when the recording was made, so the participants were *probably* from that troupe—namely, Jack Rice as interlocutor, booming tenor Dave Irwin (Bones), either Bob Conn or Nate Busby (Tambo), George Zorn, and the Diamond Studded Quartet. The featured songs were all 19th-century minstrel classics: "Oh! Susannah," "My Old Kentucky Home," "Arkansas Traveler," "The Bully Song," and "Climbing Up the Golden Stairs." The introduction left no doubt that this was an exercise in nostalgia.

> Interlocutor (speaking in a highly formal manner): How do you *do*, ladies and gentlemen. We have the pleasure of bringing to you the happy and highly popular Dailey Paskman Radio Minstrels. The old-time minstrels have assembled here to bring back to your memory those golden tunes and mirth-provoking jokes of minstrel days gone by, recalling songs and jokes you forgot to remember. So listen, ladies and gentlemen, for the opening of our minstrel show by the *en-tire* company!

The jokes were pretty creaky—they even used the one about a "check for a thousand kisses" mentioned in the previous chapter. However, at least one story touched on current popular culture. The interlocutor spoke in a highly formal (and seemingly clueless) manner, while Sambo was much more conversational, with only a rather mild use of black dialect:

SAMBO: Say, Mr. Interlocutor, a-ain't you a married man?
INTERLOCUTOR: Why, certainly, Mr. Sambo, you know I'm a married man.
SAMBO: Uh huh. How long you been married?
INTERLOCUTOR: Three years.
SAMBO: You got anything to show for connubial felicity?
INTERLOCUTOR: For *what*?
SAMBO: Anything runnin' around the house, you know what I mean…
INTERLOCUTOR: Oh, you mean children?
SAMBO: T-T-That's it.
INTERLOCUTOR: Yes, *indeed*, I'm the happy father of six beautiful children.
SAMBO: Doggone, that's all right, but how long you say you been married?
INTERLOCUTOR: Three years.
SAMBO: And six children?
INTERLOCUTOR: Six children.
SAMBO: Uh uh. Th-Th-That can't be done.
INTERLOCUTOR: Well, I'll explain that. You see, the first year of our married life I took my wife to see Charlie Chaplin in *The Kid*, and the stork presented us with a bouncing baby boy.
SAMBO: Did he have funny lookin' feet?
INTERLOCUTOR: Yes, yes … [catches himself] NO, of course not. The second year of our married life I took my wife to see *The Two Orphans*, and the stork presented us with twins!
SAMBO: Well, that's all right.
INTERLOCUTOR: Yes! The *third* year of our married life I took my wife to see *The Three Musketeers*, and the stork presented us with triplets! Six children. Three years. Why, it's very simple.
SAMBO: And what a system!
INTERLOCUTOR: Yes.
SAMBO: Mr. Interlocutor, do yo'self a favor.
INTERLOCUTOR: Why, certainly.
SAMBO: Don't let your wife see *The Big Parade*!
(great laughter, clapping)

Paskman had many other accomplishments while at WGBS. In 1926, he helped establish a network with Gimbels-owned stations WIP (Philadelphia) and WPG (Atlantic City), over which the minstrels were doubtless heard. WCAE (Pittsburgh) and other Gimbels stations may have also been linked in. (Quite a few companies were trying to establish networks at the time, but only NBC and CBS were successful.) By 1930, Paskman was planning a venture into television. He had by this time acquired an ownership interest in WGBS, and when, in 1931, the partners decided to sell the station to William Randolph Hearst (who changed the call letters to WINS), Paskman no doubt exited with a good deal of money. He then established an agency representing independent stations in New York, along with a literary agency that pitched musical comedy and operetta material to film studios for possible motion picture use.

Paskman pitched his book *Gentlemen, Be Seated!* to Hollywood several times and apparently came close to a movie deal in 1942, when there were reports that MGM had bought the rights and planned a major motion picture starring Gene Kelly. Another Paskman project, the following year, was the story of "Honey Boy" Evans, who would be portrayed by Mickey Rooney. Neither came to pass.[12] He remained active from the 1930s through the early 1950s, composing, writing, and pitching scripts. He was long associated with Lionel Barrymore in the latter's annual radio productions of *A Christmas Carol* and produced recordings by Barrymore on the ARA label in 1946.

Paskman never lost his interest in minstrelsy, and in 1936 he published a booklet of songs and minstrel material titled *Blackface and Music: The Spirit of Minstrelsy. A New*

Minstrel Book Complete with Songs, Words and Music and a Full Show Ready for Performance. In 1940, he was interviewed on station KPMC in Beverly Hills, California, about his career and was so delighted by the attention that he agreed to produce a minstrel show for the station, which aired in June 1942. There is no record of the participants, but a recording of the show survives. It was a professional production with a big orchestra, audience, sound effects, and a couple of rather old-sounding endmen. The featured songs were eclectic, ranging from "Shine On, Harvest Moon" and "Ida" to the current movie hit "Franklin D. Roosevelt Jones." Sambo also did a rather clever imitation of how Bert Williams might sing the current romantic big band hit, "I Don't Want to Walk Without You."

Lee Roy "Lasses" White and Lee Davis "Honey" Wilds headlined a popular minstrel show on WSM (Nashville) in the mid–1930s.

The massive popularity of Paskman's minstrels in the 1920s via radio, touring, books, and recordings was, I believe, primarily responsible for igniting a revival of interest in minstrelsy. His activities were centered in New York, the capital of show business at the time. Executives at other radio stations, and at the newly established networks, could not have missed his enormous success. Many soon jumped on the minstrel train.

Local radio minstrel shows continued to multiply. Examples include *WDAF Minstrels* (Kansas City, 1925), *Joe Bren's Minstrels* (WLS, 1925), *Minstrel Show* (KOA, Denver, 1925), *The Burnt Cork Review* (WLW, Cincinnati, 1926), *Honeyside Minstrels of Riverside* (WGR, Buffalo, 1926), *Haymaker's Minstrels* (WLS, Chicago, 1927), *The Steel Pier Minstrels* (WIP, Atlantic City, 1928), *Arpeako Minstrel Show* (WHAM, Rochester, New York, 1929–1932), *Weener Mastodon Minstrel Show* (WENR,

Top: Lasses White (left) and Honey Wilds (right) in a posed shot promoting their radio minstrel show. Source: *Lasses White's Book of Humor and Song* (1935). *Bottom:* Lasses and Honey also appeared as endmen with their minstrel troupe on *The Grand Ole Opry* in the mid-1930s; Lasses is on the far right, Honey on the far left. Source: *Lasses White's Book of Humor and Song* (1935).

Chicago, 1929–1930), *WOR Minstrels* (New York, early 1930s), *The Murphy Minstrels* (WLS, Chicago, 1930–1931), *WMCA Minstrels* (including Billy Heins; New York, 1931), *Johnston Cracker Minstrels* (WTMJ, Milwaukee, 1931), *Lasses White–Honey Wilds Minstrel Show* (WSM, Nashville 1932–1934), *Old Virginia Minstrels* (including a young Mel Blanc; KEX, Portland, Oregon, 1933), *O'Leary's Irish Minstrels* (KWK, St. Louis, 1933–1937), *WJZ Minstrels* (New York, 1934), *Cotton Queen Minstrels* (WLW, Cincinnati, 1934), *Morning Minstrels* (WLS, Chicago, 1935–1939), *Sunset Corners Minstrels* (WHO, Des Moines, 1938) and *WMBD Minstrels* (Peoria, Illinois, 1939). Local minstrel show broadcasts continued through the 1940s as well.

The 1932 Lasses White program on WSM is particularly interesting. White had toured with top minstrel troupes in the 1910s and headlined his own "Lasses White All-Star Minstrels" from coast to coast during 1920–1928. He also recorded minstrel material for Columbia in 1923 (see chapter 2). White's troupe was one of the most successful of the 1920s, but by the end of the decade the collapse of big-time stage minstrelsy finally caught up with him. He played vaudeville for a few years, with partners including Chaz Chase, but, finding that interest in old-time humor survived mostly in rural areas, in 1932 he accepted an offer from WSM (Nashville) to host a minstrel broadcast on that station. There he met a portly (270 pounds), genial comedian named Lee Davis Wilds, whom he partnered with and promptly dubbed "Honey" Wilds. As "Lasses and Honey," they were a hit both on their own two-man blackface "buddy comedy" show and as end-men on Lasses' WSM minstrel show. Photos show Lasses and Honey on the ends in blackface, with the rest of the minstrels in whiteface and tuxedos. In 1934, WSM signed the team to its signature program, *The Grand Ole Opry*, and they performed there as "Lasses and Honey" for the next five years. In addition to serving as Lasses' straight man, Honey Wilds (a fine comedian in his own right) played ukulele and sang.[13]

In 1935, White published a souvenir booklet, *Lasses White's Book of Humor and Song*, which included some of their catchphrases ("Well, ain't it the truth" and "Shut my mouth!"), several of White's own songs, and jokes and parodies. Some of these were political, like this one about Franklin Roosevelt and his vice president, John Nance Garner, sung to the tune of "Frankie and Johnny."

> Frankie and Johnie are Partners,
> They're up in Washington now.
> They had a big job when they went there,
> And they're doing it well somehow.
> They are two men—that won't do us wrong.

In 1939, Lasses White left for Hollywood to seek a new career in movies (see chapter 4 for his later career). Initially Wilds went with him, but he soon returned to Nashville and teamed with Bunny Biggs to play "Jamup and Honey" on the *Opry*. When Biggs died in 1942, Harry Levin took over the role of "Jamup" and the duo continued until 1963. Wilds died in 1982 at the age of 79.[14]

Early Network Stars: Al Bernard, Pick and Pat, and the Wiener Minstrels

Variety shows (e.g., Rudy Vallee, Fred Allen, Jack Benny) were extremely popular on network radio in the 1930s. They were modeled on vaudeville but featured familiar,

Top: The first major minstrel show to appear on network radio was NBC's *Dutch Masters Minstrels*, which aired from 1928 to 1932. *Bottom:* Among the stars of *Dutch Masters Minstrels* were Carson Robison and endmen Al Bernard and Percy Hemus.

continuing characters, including the host, sidekick, announcer and singers, along with mostly contemporary jokes, skits and songs. The minstrel show was in many ways the grandfather of this format, as it also featured familiar characters (interlocutor, endmen, etc.), jokes and songs. Minstrelsy was upbeat and cheerful and, with a little updating of material, fit right in to the radio tenor of the times.

The national radio networks, particularly NBC, gave minstrelsy extensive exposure. The first major series was *Dutch Masters Minstrels*, which premiered on the NBC Blue Network in September 1928, sponsored by Dutch Masters cigars. This was a big production, as only a network could mount, with new material every week for a traditional,

The minstrels of *Dutch Masters* in costume and blackface (top) and their ten-piece band (bottom, whiteface).

three-act minstrel show and stars drawn largely from the recording industry. In fact, the original endmen were intended to be Arthur Collins and Byron G. Harlan, the black-dialect comedians behind many best-selling coon song and minstrel recordings during the 1900s and 1910s.[15] But Collins' health was failing, and the positions went instead to the somewhat younger Al Bernard and Percy Hemus. Both of them had recording experience, and Bernard in particular had done much blackface work on stage in the 1910s; he also recorded minstrel routines with Lasses White and with his own "Merry Minstrel Men" in 1923–1924 and appeared frequently on radio in the 1920s.

The original interlocutor for *Dutch Masters Minstrels* was none other than Steve Porter, who had filled the same role in dozens of minstrel first part recordings in the early 1900s. Also in the cast were recording artists Carson Robison and Harry Donaghy, among others.

The *New York Herald Tribune* imparted some of the flavor of this pioneering radio minstrel show in its 1928 announcement:

> The program will open with the band tuning up just before the rise of the curtain and as it proceeds the minstrels swing into an opening chorus of an old familiar tune. Much of the first part of the program will be devoted to the amusing experiences of the two end-men, Hemus and Bernard, as told by them at the insistence of Interlocutor Porter.

As in all old-time minstrel shows, there will be a real olio, made up of vocal and instrumental specialties. Banjos and tambourines will be in evidence. Guest artists and the featured members of the cast will be heard in songs which will range from such perennial favorites as "When You and I Were Young, Maggie" and "Asleep in the Deep" to hits from the latest Broadway productions. The orchestral music will be varied.

Comedy skits will take place in the afterpiece. Carson Robison is scheduled to present "The Arkansas Traveler" in the inaugural program, and he and other entertainers well known to radio and theatre audiences will be featured in following programs.[16]

After the first season, Hemus was replaced by Paul Dumont as the second endman, and William Shelley took over from Porter as interlocutor. The original Hugo Mariani orchestra was eventually replaced by Harold Sanford and his orchestra. Dumont was an NBC announcer who teamed with Bernard on later minstrel shows and also starred in his own show, *Mr. Bones and Company*, in 1931–1932, with much of the same cast heard here; he later announced and directed several important shows. Bernard remained throughout as the "star" of this show.

The featured songs were largely from the 1890s and early 1900s, only 20 or 30 years earlier at this time, marking this as clearly a "nostalgia" program. The rundown for a typical 1930 broadcast was as follows: "My Creole Sue" (Maurice Tyler, tenor), "Peg Leg Jack" (Robison), "Whistling Rufus" (banjo solo), "Somebody Lied" (Hemus), "To Have, to Hold, to Love" (Frank Cuthbert, baritone), "Hiawatha" (orchestra), "Congo Love Song" (quartet), and "Ain't Dat a Shame" (Bernard). All of these pieces dated from 1898–1907 (except for "Peg Leg Jack," a recent novelty written and recorded by Robison).[17]

As was often the case in minstrel shows of this period, the jokes and stories were typically about human foibles, and they were delivered in standard English. For example:

SHELLEY: Well, Al, did you go to visit your Uncle Rufus last Sunday, as you said you were going to do?
BERNARD: Yes, sir, Mr. Shelley, and I went to church with him in the morning too.
SHELLEY: I hope you derived some benefit from the experience.
BERNARD: Oh, yes, and Uncle Rufus derived a good sleep.
SHELLEY: Do you mean to say your uncle went to sleep in church?
BERNARD: Yes, sir, right in the front row, and when the preacher saw him he said to me, "Wake that man up."
SHELLEY: And you did, of course.
BERNARD: No, sir; I said, "You put him to sleep. Wake him up yourself."
(laughter)[18]

Dutch Masters Minstrels aired for four years (1928–1932). There was no regular audience measurement at this time, but in 1929 the Association of National Advertisers commissioned researcher Archibald Crossley to conduct personal interviews across the country to determine the popularity of individual shows. It was one of the earliest audience surveys ever undertaken, and, based on 15,000 interviews conducted east of the Mississippi, *Dutch Masters Minstrels* ranked among the top 10 shows on the air, just ahead of *Amos 'n' Andy* (which had recently begun and was not yet at the peak of its popularity). The top 10 was dominated by music shows, with *The A&P Gypsies* ranking number one in the East. *Dutch Masters* did not rank in the top 10 in interviews conducted in large cities, suggesting that it had a somewhat rural appeal.[19]

Dutch Masters made Al Bernard a major radio star of the 1930s, something that is often missed in his record-oriented biographies. As early as 1930, he was given a featured position in *Who Is Who in Radio,* a book celebrating the first generation of national radio stars. His biography there began with the statement "Radio owes Al Bernard a debt that it can never hope to pay." It went on to say that he first broadcast on WJZ (New York) in 1921 and then, in 1923, toured the country visiting (and appearing on) every radio station he could. Bernard later organized the Record Boys with Frank Kamplain and Sammy Stept, which broadcast on WJZ in 1926, and the Raybestos Twins, with Billy Beard, which had a variety show on the NBC Red Network in 1928–1929.[20]

In 1931, the Glen Alden Coal Company, makers of blue coal (a home heating product popular in the 1930s), commissioned its advertising agency to produce a series of 20 15-minute minstrel shows for syndication across the country. It was called *The Blue Coal Minstrels* and was prerecorded by the Columbia Records Transcription Service in New York on oversize (probably 16-inch) shellac discs, which were then shipped from station to station for airing at different times in each market, sponsored by the local blue coal dealer. Some copies survive and can be heard today.

The sponsor wanted to keep the focus squarely on the product and did not identify the speaking cast members for *Blue Coal Minstrels*. However, one of the endmen (Tambo) is believed to have been Al Bernard. The interlocutor was addressed as "Mr. Glen Alden," which of course was the name of the sponsor! The musicians, who were identified, were Billie Dauscha ("Blue Coal Mammy"), tenor Fred Vettel, the Blue Coal Quartet, and the Larry Pryor Orchestra. Dauscha was a New York cabaret singer who had a long career in the metropolitan area, and Vettel was one of those booming, bombastic tenors heard all over radio in the 1930s. The opening theme was "Just Hear That Slide Trombone," and the closing was a special version of the recent pop hit "Blue Again" (advertising the sponsor's product).

Unlike many nostalgia-focused minstrel shows of the period, *Blue Coal Minstrels* featured many current hit songs, usually sung by Dauscha (who could be quite bluesy) or Vettel (who could hammer them into submission). Among them were "Georgia on My Mind," "Roll On Mississippi," "Now That You're Gone," and "I Apologize." Vettel worked his magic with, among other examples, "Marching Home to You" and "King for a Day," sometimes with a dramatic recitation. Some older songs, like "Just Because She Made Dem Goo-Goo Eyes" and "At a Georgia Camp Meeting," were mixed in, but the tone of the program was rather contemporary. The orchestra was also pretty hot at times. Benny Goodman and jazz violinist Joe Venuti were known to be present in some of these sessions.

The emphasis on the latest hit songs was a bit odd, as it must have dated these programs rather quickly. Occasionally, however, there would be a surprise. One unusual song, which was sung by the quartet in program number 14, was "You Can't Get Your Lodging Here." This is a 1928 song about an antebellum African American woman turning away a slave who is trying to escape. It was a serious, unexpected choice for an entertainment-oriented program such as *Blue Coal Minstrels*.

As for the jokes and stories, they were pretty standard minstrel fare, but, again, there was an occasional surprise, as when Bones launched into a discourse about Tambo's automobile, set to an increasingly rhythmic beat. He was essentially rapping—in 1931!

> For sale one flivver with piston rings,
> Two rear wheels and one front spring.
> Carburetor busted halfway through,
> En-jine missing, hittin' on two.

> Radiator rusty, sho' do leak,
> Differential drive, you can heah the squeak.
> Tires all off, an' a-runnin' on the rims,
> It's a mighty fine bus for the shape she's in!
> (laughter)[21]

Blue Coal Minstrels began airing on local stations in November 1931, accompanied by ads showing a caricature of a grinning black minstrel and the slogan "Listen folks, you'll sho' laff till you cry." The program was aired fairly widely in 1932 and 1933, with occasional broadcasts thereafter.[22]

Al Bernard and his *Dutch Masters* partner Paul Dumont were back on NBC for the 1934–1935 season as endmen in a new series of minstrel shows. In fact, they were on both the NBC Blue (WJZ) and the NBC Red (WEAF) networks, airing three times a week, which must have been a grueling schedule given the continuous need for new material. The NBC Red programs aired in the early evening (7:30 p.m. Eastern) on Mondays and Thursdays, running originally 15 and later 30 minutes; the NBC Blue show was half an hour on Friday nights at 10:00 p.m. The title of the show was quite confusing—sometimes *Burnt Cork Dandies* and sometimes *Molle Minstrels*, after the sponsor (Molle shaving cream). It was also occasionally called *The Molle Show* or *The Molle Dixie Dandies*. To further confuse matters, Molle had other, non-minstrel shows airing.

Bernard was supported by experienced talent. In the cast were announcer Wally Butterworth, Emil Casper, Mario Cozzi, the Melodeers (directed by Leith Stevens) and the Milton Rettenberg orchestra. Butterworth was an up-and-coming NBC announcer and sportscaster who would later become a successful game show host and producer; Cozzi was a noted opera and concert baritone; Stevens was one of the busiest conductor/arrangers in the radio industry in the 1930s and 1940s, responsible for (among other things) CBS's *Saturday Night Swing Club* and the music for many dramas; and Rettenberg was a veteran pianist and orchestra leader active on radio and records since the mid–1920s. The show was described as "an old time minstrel entertainment of songs and jokes."[23]

Bernard returned yet again in 1938, this time on CBS, with *Al Bernard's Merry Minstrel Men*, which ran on weekday afternoons from 1938 to 1940. It was described as a streamlined version of the old-time minstrel show. The theme song was Bernard's own "We Love to See a Minstrel Show." Bernard made no bones (pardon the pun) about what he was trying to achieve with these shows. In a 1939 interview, under the headline "Nothing New Is Wanted for Show," he was quoted as saying, "Where other comedians look for new jokes, we look for old ones. We use only the old gags that minstrels used in the old days."[24] Bernard continued to write songs and make personal appearances during the war years, and in the late 1940s he brought minstrelsy to early television (more information on that subject can be found in chapter 5).

Another major blackface act on radio in the 1930s, now largely forgotten, was the comedy duo known as Pick and Pat. Pick Malone and Pat Padgett were two Irishmen who teamed up in 1929 with a two-man blackface act reminiscent of Moran and Mack. After working for a time on New York radio (see *WOR Minstrels*, c. 1931), they got their first big break in early 1932 as "Molasses and January" on the hit NBC program *Show Boat*. In late 1933, they recorded a show called *Pick and Pat and Their Minstrels*, which was widely syndicated during 1933 and 1934.

Like the *Blue Coal Minstrels*, *Pick and Pat and Their Minstrels* was recorded in batches

A cardboard Pick and Pat promotional display, featuring their sponsor Model Pipe Tobacco.

by Columbia Records Transcription Service in New York on 16-inch shellac discs. The 13 15-minute episodes were then shipped from station to station for airing at different times in each market, with local advertisements to be inserted. During the research for this book, I was fortunate enough to acquire a complete set of these discs, and the provenance of that set sheds light on the manner in which programming was distributed to local stations in those days.

The seven heavy, fragile discs in this set were neatly packed in their original shipping carton, which was found under a bed in an old house that was being cleaned out in Michigan. (There were seven discs because 12 episodes were on six two-faced discs, while the 13th was on a single-faced disc.) The label on the box indicated that it was shipped via Railway Express from WDRC in Hartford, Connecticut, to the Fintex Stores in Detroit.

(Fintex was a chain of clothing stores that advertised on the Detroit station WWJ in the early 1930s.) Stickers on the disc labels specified that the show was to be aired during the six months beginning September 26, 1933, and a 15-minute Pick and Pat show was in fact listed as airing on WWJ during the fall of 1933. These appear to be the very discs from which those airings took place.

Rather than discarding these discs after use, which was the accepted practice, someone apparently packed them back in their box and stuffed them under a bed, where they remained for the next 80-plus years. Having only been played twice, perhaps (once on WDRC and once on WWJ), they are in mint condition. When played back today (carefully), the sound is pristine, even though they are old shellac records and play at only 33.3 rpm. Listeners in 1933 could easily have thought they were listening to a live broadcast.

Although Pick and Pat's theme song was "Bring Back Those Minstrel Days," and they employed a standard minstrel first part opening with an interlocutor called "Mr. Stafford," the show was basically a vehicle for their comedy dialogues. Other members of the cast were the Grenadiers Quartet, banjo virtuoso Johnny Cali, and booming tenor Fred Vettel. The typical format consisted of the entire company opening with a fast chorus of the theme, then Stafford announcing, "Gentlemen, be seated!" followed by some jokes by the two stars (or else Stafford asking one of them a question), a song by the Grenadiers, a few more jokes, an instrumental piece by Cali, more jokes, a song by Vettel, maybe a closing joke, and finally the "Grand Finale," a reprise of the theme. On a couple of shows, accordionist Gene Von Hallberg was given a solo.

The featured songs were a mix of early 1900s oldies and current pop tunes. Unlike *Blue Coal Minstrels*, Pick and Pat's show generally chose current tunes that were appropriate to a minstrel setting, like "Dusky Stevedore" (1928) or "That's Why Darkies Were Born" (1931). Cali played some interesting early 20th-century rags that were not often heard, and Vettel thundered through showpieces like "Rich Man, Beggar, Pauper, King" and "In the Garden of My Heart," rolling his Rs. Occasionally Pat added a nice change of pace by playing a bit of bluesy harmonica during the sketches. The quartet tended to get a little jazzy with their material, mimicking the vocal tricks of contemporary groups like the Revelers, but overall the atmosphere was that of a small, tight-knit group of minstrels who liked each other and were having fun. There were even a few minor slip-ups, making this performance sound like a "live" broadcast.

The jokes were mostly about relationships, misunderstandings, and human foibles rather than race, although, of course, the endmen affected "darky" dialect and garbled meanings. The interlocutor came across more as an indulgent friend than as boss. In the first episode, he asked Pat why he wore two overcoats while he was painting his house. Because, replied Pat, on the can it said, "For best results, put on two coats." In another, Pick asked Mr. Stafford a question, followed by much wordplay.

> PICK: Mr. Stafford?
> STAFFORD: Yes.
> PICK: I wants to akst you a little question.
> STAFFORD: Well, you go right ahead and ask me the question, and I'll try to elucidate.
> PICK: Is *that* old gal back in town?
> STAFFORD: What old gal?
> PICK: Lucy Pate. Did she come back?
> STAFFORD (CHUCKLING): No, she didn't.

PICK: Well, Mr. Stafford, what I want to akst you is ... d-do you know where I could get ten thousand cock-a-roaches?
STAFFORD: Ten thousand cockroaches?
PICK: Yassir.
STAFFORD: Why, you must be a student of entomology.
PICK: No, suh, I, I just want ten thousand cockroaches. That's what I am.
STAFFORD: Well, what do you want with ten thousand cockroaches?
PICK: Because, Mr. Stafford, I gotta move next week.
STAFFORD: I know you have to move, but *why* do you want ten thousand cockroaches?
PICK: Well, the lease I got on my apartment say ... "Leave the place just like you found it."
(laughter)

In January 1934, Pick and Pat were picked up by NBC for a network half-hour on Friday with the same format,[25] sponsored by U.S. Tobacco, and in June 1935 the show moved to CBS on Monday, where it remained until 1939. Over the years, baritone Edward Roecker and the Landt Trio joined as musical talent, while orchestra leaders Josef Bonime, Bennie Krueger and Ray Bloch served for various periods. A live studio audience added to the theatrical atmosphere. The music gradually shifted to mostly contemporary songs such as "Whistle While You Work" and "There's a Goldmine in the Sky."

Although the theme song remained "Bring Back Those Minstrel Days," the minstrel setting was phased out over time, until the show became basically banter between the two stars (although the announcer might still be called the "interlocutor"). At various times the show was known as *Pipe Smoking Time*, *One Night Stands with Pick and Pat*, and *Model Minstrels* (after the sponsor, Model Tobacco). Pick and Pat were riding high, and in 1937 they appeared in the Frances Langford film *The Hit Parade*. In March 1939, however, Tom Howard and George Shelton took over the show (then called *Model Minstrels*) and continued it into 1940.

Audience levels for the program remained strong throughout its run. Regular audience measurement for network shows had begun in the early 1930s, at the behest of sponsors. By the time the show moved to Mondays, *Pick and Pat* regularly placed among the top 10 programs for the night, and often in the top five. Its audience was generally between six and eight million people, good enough to rank it in the top 40 among all programs on the air. At its peak in 1936–1937, *Pick and Pat* was one of the top 10 comedies on radio.[26]

Pick and Pat's run as blackface radio stars did not end there. You can't keep a good minstrel down, and during 1940 and 1941 they appeared on a number of network shows, including NBC's *National Barn Dance* and *The Vincent Lopez Show*. They were guests of Rudy Vallee and Kate Smith when those two stars staged "mini-minstrel shows" on their programs. Beginning in August 1942, Pick and Pat starred in a curious five-minute NBC daytime series called *America's Advisors on the Home Front*, on which they offered "advice for husbands of defense workers." Newspaper ads showed them made up looking very much like Amos 'n' Andy. In October 1942, the comedy team launched a full half-hour NBC program called *Yankee Doodle Minstrels*, which ran until January 1943. Edmund "Tiny" Ruffner was the interlocutor, and the cast included singer Clark Dennis, "Hi, Lo, Jack, Dame, and the Joe Rines orchestra." Guest endmen included comedians Harry Hershfield and Senator Ed Ford. The stars were referred to as both Pick and Pat and Molasses and January during their later career.

In January 1944, Pick and Pat began a new series on the Mutual Broadcasting System, with Tiny Ruffner (emcee), vocalist Mary Small and the Vincent Lopez Orchestra. This program moved to the new ABC Radio Network in the summer of 1945, and a morning show ran into early 1946. Still later they ventured into television (which will be discussed in chapter 5).

Al Bernard and Pick and Pat and their minstrel shows were a constant presence on American radio in the 1930s and early 1940s, but neither had the number one minstrel program on the air. That honor belonged to *Sinclair Wiener Minstrels*, which aired on the NBC Blue Network from 1932 to 1937. It was one of the top hit radio series of the 1930s.

The origin of the show was *The Weener Mastodon Minstrel Show*, which aired locally on WENR (Chicago) in 1929–1930. (The name "Weener" or "Wiener" had nothing to do with hot dogs; rather, it was the local slang name for WENR.) The show, helmed by writer/interlocutor Gene Arnold and co-starring endmen Big Bill Childs, Ray Ferris, Joe Warner, and Chuck Haynes, attracted the attention of NBC, which was looking for a new minstrel entry as its *Dutch Masters* show wound down.

Arnold was given a 30-minute slot on the NBC Blue schedule starting in March 1932, sponsored by the Sinclair Oil Co. The title was changed to *Sinclair Wiener Minstrels*, and later *Sinclair Greater Minstrels*. Big Bill Childs came over from the WENR show, but otherwise Arnold recruited a new cast. Mac McCloud and Cliff Soubier were the original endmen. Malcolm Claire was "Spare Ribs," and others in the 26-man cast (plus a 15-piece orchestra) included Fritz Clark, Ray Marlin, bass Joe Parsons, tenors Chauncey Parsons and Billy White, and the Harry Kogen Orchestra. They played in full costume before a live audience of 500 in Chicago. This was network-level production! At its height, there were up to 20,000 people on a waiting list for tickets.[27]

The format was that of a traditional minstrel first part, complete with an interlocutor, endmen, songs, and novelties. In 1936, Red Grange joined to analyze football results.

This is an actual photograph of an audience witnessing a broadcast of the Sinclair Minstrels from the world's largest broadcasting studio, Chicago.

The *Sinclair Greater Minstrels* was one of the top shows on radio in the mid–1930s, drawing large (white) studio audiences to its live broadcasts from Chicago. The minstrels are in the background; the endmen are in full costume and blackface.

The featured songs were a mix of minstrel oldies and more recent tunes. For example, a 1936 episode included oldies "Buffalo Gals" (1844), "Teasing" (1904), and "On the Old Fall River Line" (1913); contemporary songs included "The Hills of Old Wyoming," a Hollywood western tune from the 1936 Frances Langford film *Palm Springs*.

Virtually all network programming was live at this time (by policy), and off-air recordings—mostly made for sponsors—were primitive and infrequent. Tape recording was still 10 to 15 years in the future. Thus there are very few recorded examples extant even of top-rated network shows from the mid–1930s. One example of *Sinclair Greater Minstrels* that has been located indicates that it sounded like a big, contemporary production in the traditional minstrel format—more like a comedy-variety show than classic 19th-century minstrelsy. The live audience, big orchestra, and absence of dialect all contributed to that impression.[28]

The *Sinclair Greater Minstrels* troupe, clockwise from top left: McCloud, Ferris, Haynes, Childs, "middle man" Gene Arnold, James, Soubier.

Gene Arnold needed a lot of material for a weekly series like this, and he addressed that need (and involved his audience) by suggesting that listeners send in jokes they'd like to hear. Of course, he got thousands of them, but an article in *Radio Mirror* about the practice was telling. Although Arnold used some of the submissions, it said, "Some have to be rejected because he has already used them or because they might tend to offend a race, sect, or nationality."[29] Racial concerns were clearly being taken into account.

The material was modern, fast-paced stand-up comedy:

> ENDMAN #1: A crook gave me a lead half dollar.
> ENDMAN #2: Let me see it.
> ENDMAN #1: I spent it this morning.[30]

Others were gags that would work in any era:

> CLIFF: How can I cure myself of snoring?
> GENE: Does it bother your wife?
> CLIFF: Bother my wife? It bothers the whole congregation!

According to trade journals, *Sinclair Greater Minstrels* at times rated in the top five among all network shows.[31] During its first two seasons, it was the second-highest-rated program on Monday night (after *Amos 'n' Andy*) and in the top 15 among all shows for the entire season. Radio was still spreading across the country at this time (only about

60 percent of households had sets in 1932), and yet *Sinclair Greater Minstrels* averaged about seven million listeners per week. At its peak in 1933–1934, the show outdrew such hits as the Bing Crosby and Jack Benny shows, and it was not far behind *Amos 'n' Andy*. However, as strong as these figures are, they probably understate the program's popularity. By this time, minstrel appeal skewed toward rural and downscale areas, while audience surveys were taken in cities and among households that had a telephone (only about 30 percent of U.S. households at this time).[32]

Previously mentioned audience figures for *Dutch Masters Minstrels* confirm a rural skew for minstrelsy in the 1930s, as do the prevalence and longevity of minstrel shows on more rural-oriented stations such as WSM (Nashville). Nevertheless, minstrel shows were popular everywhere.

In 1936, Gene Arnold was replaced as interlocutor by vaudevillian Gus Van of the famous song-and-comedy team Van and Schenck (Schenck had died in 1930). No doubt this was seen as bringing star power to the show, as Van and Schenck were well known from big-time vaudeville, *The Ziegfeld Follies*, radio, and films. In addition, Van was an expert dialectician. However, ratings declined, Sinclair ended its sponsorship, and the show was canceled in January 1937. This decision produced such an uproar among listeners that NBC decided to bring the program back in April with Arnold again at the helm. The show was retitled *NBC Minstrels* and ran for another two years, until April 1939. It continued to be broadcast from Chicago in front of a live audience.

Besides Arnold, the cast included Jimmie Dean, Vance "Catfish" McCune, Shorty Carson, Bill Thompson and Ken Christy as endmen at various times. Eventually Cliff Soubier returned as well. Music was handled by baritone Edward Davies, tenor Clark Dennis, and a 12-man choir. The orchestra leader was originally Al Short, who died suddenly in August 1937. After some months, his place was taken by Harry Kogen from *Sinclair*.

While *NBC Minstrels* retained the basic minstrel first part structure, the format was tweaked to make the show sound somewhat more contemporary. The program opened with "Follow us inside the theater for Gene Arnold and the NBC Minstrels," followed by a lively opening chorus and then "Gentlemen, be seated!" Featured songs were a mix of old-time tunes and current swing hits ("All You Want to Do Is Dance," "It's the Natural Thing to Do"). A different city or town was honored each week based on votes received from the audience, in proportion to the population. The honored towns on episodes heard by this writer were Woodward and Moreland, Oklahoma, and Bay Minette, Alabama, suggesting the areas where a program of this type was still popular. As for the jokes, they were often quick one-liners ("She's so dumb she was fired from a dime store 'cause she couldn't remember the prices!"; Q: "Do you know how long cows should be milked?" A: "Same as a short one").[33]

From December 1939 to May 1940, the Mutual Broadcasting System presented a half-hour minstrel show on Tuesday nights that is believed to have starred Gene Arnold. However, this program received virtually no publicity—appearing as merely "minstrel show" in the listings—and so we cannot be certain.

Other Network Minstrel Shows

Besides these high-profile hits, there were numerous other minstrel shows on the networks from the late 1920s to the 1940s.

Cotton Blossom Minstrels (1929–1930) originated on the NBC Pacific Coast Network but was also heard on stations in the East. It was described as an "old fashioned 60 minute minstrel show." Barry Hopkins was the interlocutor (later replaced by Harry Stanton). Also in the cast were Harold Peary, Clarence Hayes ("The Voice of the South"), and an African American group called the Southern Harmony Four. (African American vocal groups such as gospel quartets were fairly common on radio at this time.)[34]

Morning Minstrels (1930–1932) aired on CBS multiple times a week at 8:30 a.m., which seems rather early in the day for a minstrel show. A radio columnist in 1931 humorously suggested one purpose this timing might serve:

> Radios have provoked more feuds in … apartment buildings than tap dancing, setting-up exercises and poker parties combined. One family sits up until midnight listening in on the *Perfectly Impossible Story Hour* and its police sirens, gun shots, and dull thuds, while the other family is trying to grab off a quantity of sleep. Next morning the victims get their revenge by turning on the *Merrie Morning Minstrels* at their noisiest while the *Perfectly Impossible Story* fiends are trying to make up the slumber they snubbed the night before.[35]

Whatever the reason for airing a minstrel show in the morning, *Morning Minstrels* may have been primarily an instrumental musical interlude. It was a mere 15 minutes in length, and the only participants ever identified were three rotating orchestras, led by Vincent Sorey, Nat Brusiloff, and Emery Deutsch. This program should not be confused with the WTAM *Morning Minstrels* that ran locally in Cleveland in 1932–1933, or the WLS *Morning Minstrels*, which aired in Chicago in the late 1930s.

Mr. Bones and Company (1931–1932), by contrast, was a traditional half-hour minstrel first part, airing on the NBC Red Network on Saturday evening. The cast was essentially carried over from *Dutch Masters Minstrels* on NBC Blue, except that star endman Al Bernard was replaced by someone named Jim Dandy. The other principals were endman Paul Dumont, interlocutor William Shelley, vocalist Harry Donaghy and the Harold Sanford Orchestra, all from *Dutch Masters*. This casting gave NBC two bites at the juicy *Dutch Masters* apple, one on each of its networks. The featured songs were mostly from 1890–1920, as on *Dutch Masters* (for example, "Darktown Poker Club," "Nothin' from Nothin' Leaves You," "Too Much Mustard," and "Rufus Rastus Johnson Brown").

Magnolia Minstrels (1933–1934) originated from San Francisco's KPO and was heard on Saturday nights on NBC's West Coast "Gold Network." The cast included interlocutor Barry Hopkins, endmen Charles Marshal and Smilin' Sam, tenor Bob Stevens, bass Armand Girard, the Knickerbocker Quartet and the Joseph Hornik Orchestra. Featured songs were mostly from the 1890s or early 1900s. On a sample broadcast, Girard showed off his low notes with "The Big Bass Viol," while sweet-voiced tenor Stevens crooned "The Old Irish Mother of Mine." The band also played John Philip Sousa's "El Capitan March."

Modern Minstrels (1934–1935) on CBS took a slightly different tack. According to the network, "The program will be patterned after the old-time stage productions except that modern tunes will be used." Apparently this strategy worked, as the show began at 9:00 a.m. and then was moved to Saturday evening and expanded to a full hour because of its success. In addition to "modern" music, it apparently favored novelties, including a musical saw and impersonations of old-time stars like Bert Williams. On one early broadcast, "*Modern Minstrels* at 9 a.m. are to see how dangerous it is to present 'Duet for Piano and Pistol.'"[36]

It was a big production, with a 35-man cast including Bert Swor and Lou Lubin as endmen, Harry Von Zell as interlocutor, and the Leith Stevens Orchestra. Swor (1871–1943) had been in minstrelsy since the early 1900s and was once the partner of George Moran in the Two Black Crows. Lubin (1895–1973) was a comic actor who would go on to a long career in movies and television. Von Zell (1906–1981) was a young CBS staff announcer who became famous as the comic foil of Eddie Cantor on radio in the 1940s and of Burns and Allen on TV in the 1950s.

The Gold Medal Minstrels (1935) was an attempt by Mutual to appeal to women with a daytime show. Originating at WGN in Chicago, this program aired daily around noon for 15 minutes, sponsored by Gold Medal Flour.

> In the experience of "Tiny" Stowe, writer and producer of this popular air feature, was seen an indication that dramatic serials and cooking talks might not be the only way to appeal to the feminine audience. For years, as interlocutor of the "Lasses White All-Star Minstrels," Stowe trouped the country from one end to the other. Invariably in the crowds that greeted the old-time minstrel troupe, women were in the majority. So to the daytime audience was presented the *Gold Medal Minstrels*.[37]

One might wonder about the appeal to women, given minstrelsy's propensity for jokes mocking marriage and belittling wives and girlfriends. Perhaps those themes were downplayed in this show. In any event, *The Gold Medal Minstrels* lasted only four months. The cast included Arthur W. "Tiny" Stowe as "Tony, the interlocutor," Danny "Sunshine" Duncan and Billy Chandler as endmen, the singing Dean Brothers (Eddie and Jimmie), and the Five Rangers. The Dean Brothers were not related to the later country/pop star Jimmy Dean; however, Eddie Dean went on to a notable career as a singer and actor in low-budget western movies in the 1940s.

Colonel Merriwether's Minstrels (1938–1939) originated from superstation WLW (Cincinnati) on Saturday nights. Virtually nothing is known about this show's content, other than that old-timer Eddie Leonard was a guest on one episode, singing his hits "Ida" and "Roll Them Roly Boly Eyes." WLW broadcast at this time with 500,000 watts—one of the most powerful signals in the world, blanketing the East and Midwest. Its power was so great that it sometimes dimmed street lights and could be picked up on mattress springs. Therefore, a lot of people were exposed to *Colonel Merriwether's Minstrels*, which also aired on other Mutual Network affiliates, but apparently few listened. The show was canceled after three months.[38]

Minstrel Episodes and Segments

Besides standalone minstrel shows, many network and syndicated radio series included minstrel episodes or segments. One of the earliest examples is an episode of *Maytag Radioettes*, a prerecorded anthology series syndicated to more than 50 stations around the country in 1929. It was apparently the second prerecorded series in radio history, launching a few weeks after *Amos 'n' Andy*. Most episodes in the series were either dramas or musicals, but one that first aired in March 1929 was titled "The Minstrel Show." This episode began with a man and his son entering a theater and describing the opening of the show ("The curtain is about to go up, son"). This is followed by a classic minstrel first part, complete with interlocutor "Mr. Scott," jokes with endmen Bones, Kratch and Moeller, and mostly 19th-century songs including "Kentucky Babe," "The Old Folks at Home," "Dixie," and, of course, "Asleep in the Deep," along with the more recent "She's in the Jailhouse Now." Singers were introduced as George "Dusty" Rhoads and George

Ireland, but no one in the cast was well known—they were probably local talent from Chicago, where the show was recorded.[39]

The National Barn Dance, which began on WLS in Chicago in 1924, aired in part on the NBC network on Saturday nights from 1933 to 1946. Periodically included in the network portion of the evening-long broadcast, during the 1930s, was a traditional, three-act blackface minstrel show. *Barn Dance* regular Uncle Ezra introduced this segment, promising "a corkin' good old-time minstrel show." Then Tiny Stowe took over as interlocutor, bantering with endmen Cliff Soubier and Malcolm "Spare Ribs" Claire, veterans of the *Sinclair Greater Minstrels* show. Others from the *Barn Dance* cast (including the Maple City Four, the Hoosier Hot Shots, the Rangers and the Dean Brothers) joined in. *The National Barn Dance* also fielded a minstrel touring troupe.[40]

In November 1936, the top-rated Jack Benny Jell-O program devoted an entire episode to a comic sketch set in 1906 in Spongecake, Missouri, where "Doc Benny's World Renowned Minstrels" paraded down a street, launched into a minstrel first part, traded jokes and songs, and ended by presenting a blackface *Romeo and Juliet* as the afterpiece. Benny played the interlocutor and sang a comic version of "Asleep in the Deep." Kenny Baker and Phil Harris were the endmen, and Mary Livingston and Don Wilson joined in as well. The performance was tightly scripted and funny, and the live studio audience howled with delight. "Doc Benny's World Renowned Minstrels" made a return appearance in March 1942, with Benny reprising "Asleep in the Deep" and gravelly voiced black actor Eddie "Rochester" Anderson—who had since joined the cast—singing "Somebody Else, Not Me," a song made famous by Bert Williams.

Beginning on December 4, 1936, another top show, *Amos 'n' Andy* (a 15-minute comic serial that ran Monday through Friday at 7:00 p.m.), experimented with staging minstrel shows on Friday nights. In the storyline, the entire cast trooped down to the Mystic Knights of the Sea clubhouse, where Amos and Andy (Freeman Gosden and Charles Correll) became the endmen and announcer Bill Hay served as interlocutor. On the premiere episode, Amos sang "Dinah," while deep-voiced Andy massacred "Asleep in the Deep." There were in-character jokes, sound effects (Andy shot several people who annoyed him), and a special guest—tenor Frank Parker—doing a big production number around that minstrel favorite, "Mandy."[41] Also participating was an unbilled African American quartet, the Four Vagabonds, performing "Sing, Baby, Sing" from the movie of the same name and backing Amos on "Dinah." This was all staged in front of a live studio audience, which applauded enthusiastically. In the following week's episode, Andy did a juggling act—breaking all the plates—and slow-moving janitor Lightnin' sang a specialty number, "Sleepiest Man in Town." The theme song for both episodes was "Roll On Mississippi."

There was talk of making the minstrel show a regular Friday feature, but after two trial episodes in December, *Amos 'n' Andy* moved from Chicago to a California origination in January 1937 for the winter, and those plans were dropped.

The Maxwell House Show Boat was one of the biggest musical variety hits on radio in the mid–1930s, known for its elaborate production values and top-flight guest stars. However, it declined precipitously in popularity after its loveable host, Charles Winninger ("Captain Henry"), left in 1935. Nevertheless, NBC and sponsor Maxwell House were determined to recover. The show was set on a Mississippi River showboat and minstrel elements had always been a strong part of the entertainment, so in January 1937 the cast presented a full-fledged minstrel show, as the boat supposedly docked at Little Rock,

The Show Boat Cast (left to right)—Molasses, Captain Henry, Annette Hanshaw, Lanny Ross, Tiny, Mary Lou, and January (Picture taken June 9)

The popular *Maxwell House Show Boat*, with Charles Winninger as Captain Henry and Pick and Pat (as "Molasses and January") on the far left and right.

Arkansas. Resident blackface comics Pick and Pat (as "Molasses and January") were the endmen, and popular singer Lanny Ross served as the emcee. Others taking part made it look like a kids' talent show. They included 15-year-old Mary Small singing "Alabama Barbecue," 10-year-old violinist Stuart Canin, the seven-year-old Lauriat Brothers, the youthful De Marco Sisters, James and Andy Donnelly (doing a "Juvenile Court" routine), guest star Jackie Coogan, and Al Goodman and his orchestra.

Another of radio's top comedy-variety shows was NBC's *Texaco Star Theatre*, starring Fred Allen, along with Portland Hoffa, Kenny Baker, Minerva Pious, Alan Reed, announcer Jimmy Wallington, and the Al Goodman Orchestra. In June 1942, guest star Maurice Evans joined Allen for a minstrel show, including the sketches "The March of Trivia" and "The Life of Luther Boomer ... The Flop of the Year." It worked well enough that Allen staged another minstrel show in February 1949.

Minstrelsy could turn up in the most unlikely places on radio. On May 23, 1945, NBC's *Chesterfield Supper Club*, a suave, contemporary music program starring rapidly rising crooner Perry Como, turned into, of all things, a minstrel show. The episode opened as usual, with the atmospheric sounds of an audience waiting in anticipation and a smooth announcer purring, "Welcome to the supper club. Your table is ready. You'll be entertained by Perry Como, your supper club date Mary Ashworth, and Ted Steele's orchestra. And there's the master of ceremonies, Martin Block." The next thing the audience knew, Block turned the show over to Perry as interlocutor, with special guests Pick and Pat, and the jokes started flying, including one about the war:

COMO: And now on my right, our endman, Pat.
PAT: Hello dere, Mr. Como.
COMO: Say, Pat, how are you getting along with your Victory Garden this year?
PAT: Well, suh, I planted myself a pure Victory Garden right down in the basement of my house, and it grows right up into the bedroom.
COMO: It *did*?
PAT: Yas, suh, and this morning I opened my aunt's dresser drawer and found a pair of early bloomers!
(laughter)

Perry then crooned a rather bizarre rendition of Al Jolson's "Mammy" ("I'se a comin'"), followed by a lovely interpretation of the classic 1896 lullaby "Kentucky Babe," which was much better suited to his style. The original lyrics were changed to accommodate changing racial sensitivity ("little coon of mine" became "little child," "kinky head" became "curly head," and so on). The Satisfiers, a bouncy 1940s quartet that included Mary Ashworth, did an upbeat version of "Waiting for the Robert E. Lee," and everyone was accompanied by Ted Steele's big swing orchestra, which gave this minstrel show a very 1940s feel. Pick and Pat were recurring guests on *Chesterfield Supper Club* in 1945, and at least one other episode (June 29) was staged as a minstrel show as well, that one opening with "Are You from Dixie?"

Bing Crosby's *Philco Radio Time* (1946) is remembered largely for being the first major network show to be tape recorded in advance, breaking the networks' rule that all major shows had to be broadcast live. In fact, Crosby had to switch networks, moving from NBC to ABC, to enable him to introduce this change. He had a parade of top stars on his show, and when Al Jolson was booked for an April 1947 appearance, it was natural that they would present a minstrel show. Jolson, of course, had spent half his career in blackface (and got his start with Lew Dockstader), but Crosby was no stranger to blackface, either, having used it in his 1943 movie *Dixie*, as well as *Holiday Inn* (1942) and *Here Come the Waves* (1944). No one complained, perhaps because both Jolson and Crosby were known as strong supporters of African Americans. The entire *Philco* program (including the commercials) was done as a minstrel show. The first tune was "A Hot Time in the Old Town Tonight," and Jolson sang his trademark "Mammy."

Jolson himself was riding high in the late 1940s, having been the subject of two movie biographies, once again having hit records, and starring in NBC's *Kraft Music Hall* from 1947 to 1949. His *Music Hall* cast included Oscar Levant, announcer Ken Carpenter, and the Lou Bring Orchestra. On the March 24, 1949, episode, Jolson reminisced about the "old days" with guest star George Jessel and then staged a minstrel show. Among the featured tunes were "Chinatown, My Chinatown" and Jolson's theme, "April Showers." This program essentially brought down the curtain on network radio minstrel shows—although not on TV, as we shall see in chapter 5.

Proposed Minstrel Shows

While women were occasionally heard on later minstrel show recreations, the genre was still overwhelmingly male. In 1935, NBC tried a novel departure by recording a half-hour pilot for a show to be called *The NBC Lady Minstrels*. An audition disc survives in the NBC Collection at the Library of Congress, and while the program apparently never aired, it does show that the network was actively looking for ways to refresh the venerable minstrel format.

The star and interlocutor was Sadie Banks, a rather strident, harsh-voiced woman who might have been one reason why the pilot didn't make it to air. (Sadie was a burlesque artist who later became a cabaret favorite at New York's Old Romanian club with her saucy style and "blue" material and also made blue LPs.) Others in the cast were Mammy Jinny, Miss Jean Bennett, Josie Flynn, and Carrie Lilly. The show opened with "Ladies, be seated!" followed by the usual jokes and songs, all by females.

> SADIE: Hey, Carrie, have you read in the newspapers about the new law?
> CARRIE: New law? You can't keep up with it.
> SADIE: Well, the law now requires all policemen to be vaccinated.
> CARRIE: Oh, why don't they leave the police alone? They never catch anything.

Featured songs included "Shine," "High Brown Blues," and "Way Down Yonder in New Orleans," some accompanied by a rather jazzy orchestra. There was also some use of dialect. Viewed from the perspective of gender equality, it's a shame that the network did not take another look at this idea, perhaps with a different cast.

Two other audition discs, dated 1945 and 1946, exist for proposed Mutual Network shows, both of which included female minstrels. Both were called *The Minstrel Train* and dramatized the progress of a train as it crossed the country, pulling into a different city each week, where the cast would set up and put on a traditional minstrel show. Scenes were set on the train, at the station, and backstage, as well as during the actual performance, and there were even continuing storylines (for example, a young girl who wanted to join the troupe). The theme for both versions of the show was "Alabamy Bound."

The first pilot program, recorded June 28, 1945, starred Pick and Pat as fast-talking endmen "Molasses and January," with popular network host "Tiny" Ruffner as interlocutor (called "Colonel Tiny"). Also in the cast were baritone John Baker, John Brewster, Jane Randolph, Judy Lange, Gene Lowell's minstrel band, and the Minstrel Train Monarchs of Harmony. The jokes and songs were pretty standard minstrel fare (for example, "Oh, Dem Golden Slippers," "A Hot Time in the Old Town," and "Old Man River"). However, the program was not picked up by a sponsor.

The second *Minstrel Train* pilot, recorded on June 11, 1946, once again had Ruffner as interlocutor, but this time the show placed women in the forefront, with Cecil Roy, Elizabeth Morgan and Florence MacMichael as the endmen (endwomen?), Miss Jones, and two women called Miss Bones. Also in the cast were the Clark Sisters and the Emerson Buckley Orchestra. While the "train" premise remained, the content was much more contemporary. Featured songs, all by the Clark Sisters, included current hits "The Coffee Song," "Rockin' Chair" and "Stardust," accompanied by Buckley's big swing orchestra. The banter between the interlocutor and endwomen consisted mostly of corny conundrums, but it also included typical minstrel putdowns of women—and comebacks.

> INTERLOCUTOR: Maybe you can tell me the difference between a modern car and a modern girl?
> JONES: What *is* the difference between a modern car and a modern girl?
> INTERLOCUTOR: You really want to know?
> JONES: Oh, I sure do, honey.
> INTERLOCUTOR: Well, a modern car has something under the *hood*! (chuckles)
> BONES: Mr. Interlocutor, do you know the difference between a girl and a horse?
> INTERLOCUTOR: No, I don't know the difference between a girl and a horse.

BONES (LAUGHS): I'll bet you have some *be-autiful* dates!
(laughter)

The cast was made up of radio pros, although none apparently had any minstrel (or blackface) experience. Ruffner was a longtime network announcer, and at the time that this pilot was made he was serving as host of the popular Mutual Broadcasting System quiz show *The Better Half*. He was six feet, five inches tall (hence his nickname, "Tiny") and had previously worked with Pick and Pat. Cecil Roy, "The Girl of a Thousand Voices," was all over radio in the 1930s and 1940s, playing old women, giggling girls, a young boy on *Ma Perkins*, and even a monster on *Quiet, Please*. She later did voice work in Hollywood cartoons. Morgan was a radio actress on a number of shows, including the soap opera *Stella Dallas*. MacMichael, who was somewhat younger, was just beginning her career but would go on to do a lot of television work, including playing the next-door neighbor on *Mr. Ed* and *My Three Sons*. The Clark Sisters (who recorded with Tommy Dorsey as the Sentimentalists) were a typical 1940s pop vocal group.

The actors' lack of minstrel experience showed, as their delivery sounded like they were just reading lines. The weak script, current pop music, and swing orchestra didn't help. This version of *Minstrel Train* wasn't picked up by a sponsor either.

Network Minstrel Shows in the 1940s

As the 1940s dawned, the networks—especially NBC—continued to treat the minstrel show as an important part of their programming mix, but they increasingly looked for new approaches and gimmicks to refresh the format. One of the more obvious examples was NBC's *Celebrity Minstrels* (1940). This idea was an outgrowth of the 1938–1939 show *If I Had the Chance*, in which Mort Lewis interviewed celebrities about goals they had once wanted to attain. The most frequently expressed wish was to be a minstrel, so in August 1939 the program staged a minstrel show in which cartoonists Peter Arno and Ham Fisher, actress Bebe Daniels, comedian George Jessel, band leader Tommy Dorsey, *Time* editor Frank Morris, and announcer Graham McNamee got to act out their suppressed desires. That experience led to a four-week tryout for *Celebrity Minstrels* (aka *Mammoth Minstrels*) in March–April 1940.

Jay C. Flippen served as interlocutor for *Celebrity Minstrels*, along with the Norman Cloutier Orchestra. The guest lineup was impressive. Week one included illustrator James Montgomery Flagg and cartoonist Ham Fisher as endmen; actor Ezra Stone of *The Aldrich Family*; bandleaders Will Bradley, Sammy Kaye, and Nat Shilkret; lyricist Clement Wood; and a quartet composed of announcers Milton Cross, Graham McNamee, Harry Von Zell, and Howard Petrie. During week two, it was Flagg, Fisher, bandleaders Johnny Green and Tommy Dorsey, singer/pianist Ray Perkins, and sportscaster Bill Stern. Week three featured former governor Alfred E. Smith, New York Stock Exchange president George P. Rea, "Tune Detective" Dr. Sigmund Spaeth, socialist leader Norman Thomas, criminal lawyer Samuel Leibowitz, author Elliot Paul, actor Ray Bolger, band leader Frank Novak, and assemblyman Fred Moritt. In week four, the participants included Flagg, swimmer Eleanor Holm, bandleader Raymond Paige, songwriter Jack Norworth, and others. Presumably they all had a grand time, but the show was not picked up for a regular run. Syndicated columnist Walter Winchell commented that the show had some famous guests, adding, "And most of the jokes are equally well known."[42]

Minstrel Melodies (1942–1946) had more modest goals, as well as a longer run. Originating from NBC's San Francisco studios, the half-hour show aired on Saturday afternoons for five years (albeit with a few gaps). The cast consisted of NBC West Coast staffers, who were seldom named. The only regulars were apparently bandleader Anton "Tony" Freeman and vocalist and endman Clarence Hayes ("The Voice of the South").

The emphasis in *Minstrel Melodies* was on music, although there was occasionally an interlocutor and endmen. Based on copies of a few episodes surviving at the Library of Congress, the interlocutor in 1944 was G. Archibald Presby, and in 1945 it was John Boyer Grover (both were NBC West Coast staff announcers). The featured songs were classic minstrel tunes from the 19th and early 20th centuries, such as "Camptown Races," "In the Evening by the Moonlight," "That Mysterious Rag," and "Shine On, Harvest Moon," rendered by various West Coast vocalists and "The Old Oaken Quartet."

The Mutual Network did not give up on either minstrelsy or female minstrels. In September 1946, it premiered *The Gold and Silver Minstrels* (1946–1947, aka *Gold Star Minstrels*) as a Saturday night half-hour program. The original announced star was actress and comedian Gee Gee James, along with emcee Jack Arthur, comedian "Happy Jim Parsons," singers Jimmy Carroll and Betty Mulliner, and the Ray Bloch Orchestra. There seems to have been cast turnover during the program's four-month run, as James and Arthur disappeared and Roland Winters took over as host and interlocutor.

There were several surprises in the cast for *Gold and Silver Minstrels*. To start, this was the only known example of an African American female headlining a radio minstrel show. Regina "Gee Gee" James (1911–1971) first attracted attention in the early 1930s when she appeared on a number of radio shows, including Louis Armstrong's groundbreaking musical revue in 1937. Nicknamed "The Female Rochester" (after the character on the *Jack Benny Show*, on which she also appeared), James drew raves for her "fine, throaty voice" and was often compared to Ethel Waters. She also appeared on soap operas and in Broadway plays (including *A Streetcar Named Desire*).[43]

"Happy Jim Parsons" was none other than Irving Kaufman (1890–1976), a prolific recording artist in the 1920s who got into radio around 1922 and was known on CBS in the mid-1930s as "Lazy Dan, The Minstrel Man." Kaufman used multitudinous pseudonyms during his long career and supposedly had more than one hundred pseudonyms on record. In 1940, he created "Happy Jim Parsons" for a show on NBC. This continued to air (later locally on WOR) until 1943.

Roland Winters (1904–1989), the later interlocutor, was a busy radio actor and announcer of the 1930s and 1940s, on programs including the *Milton Berle Show*. In 1947, he broke into films and won enduring fame playing (with suitable makeup) the title role in the last six Charlie Chan films. He later did much film and television work.

Jimmy Carroll and Betty Mulliner were young radio singers, both of whom (separately) had just begun to attract attention in the mid-1940s. Carroll had his own CBS show in 1945; Mulliner was best known for *The Squibb Show* (1943–1944) and *Here's to Romance* (1944–1945). She married choir director Norman Luboff and later became principal soloist of his choir.

Each episode was dedicated to a different city, usually in the Midwest or South. The emphasis was on music, both old ("A Bird in a Gilded Cage," "Silver Threads Among the Gold") and new ("That's What I Like about the South"), although Bloch's big swing orchestra gave all the songs a modern feel. There were also sketches and special themes. In one episode, James and Parsons did "Breakfast in Harlem," a parody of the "Mr. & Mrs. Shows" that were so prevalent on radio at the time. In another, Cliff Hall and Ken Roberts offered a musical salute to Al Jolson, followed by Ray Bloch offering a medley of Jolson songs. In still another episode, honoring Dallas, emcee Roland Winters introduced a musical tribute to "that great Texan" Victor Herbert, leading to the following exchange with bandleader Bloch based on convoluted logic:

> BLOCH: Wait a minute, Roly, since when is Victor Herbert a Texan? He was born in Dublin, Ireland.
> WINTERS: Yes, and since Dublin, Ireland, is in Texas ...
> BLOCH: Stop, Roly, you're talkin' to a real Irishman. (Irish accent) Ray Bloch-o.
> WINTERS: All right, (Irish accent) Ray Bloch-o. I'll prove to you—you've got me doing it—that Dublin, Ireland, is in Texas.
> BLOCH: This I gotta hear.
> WINTERS: All right. Dublin is in Ireland. Ireland is the Emerald Isle. Emeralds are green. Green is the favorite color of Pat O'Brien ...
> BLOCH: Wait, wait, wait a minute. What has Pat O'Brien got to do with the man in the moon?
> WINTERS: Well, the man in the moon is happy, Happy Jim Parsons is with the Gold and Silver Minstrels, the Gold and Silver Minstrels are in Texas, therefore Dublin, Ireland is in Texas, which makes Victor Herbert a native son, right?
> BLOCH: Aw yes, sure. Sounds just logical. Sounds fine. OK, fellas, we better play...

There was little use of dialect, and although there were an interlocutor and endmen, *Gold and Silver Minstrels* sounded more like a variety show than a traditional minstrel show (only a portion of a single episode survives, so it is hard to be certain about the sound of the show).

Another interesting show, *Mirth and Melody* (1948), is a bit of a mystery. A recording exists and is credited to the ABC Network on December 2, 1948. However, no record of the show airing on that date or any other can be found in newspaper listings. It may have been an audition program that was not picked up by the network, or perhaps a one-time special that aired under some other name. In any event, *Mirth and Melody* is an example of a late attempt to revive the minstrel show on radio, and at least two of the three endmen appear to have been African Americans. Ernie "Iodine" Whitman definitely was, and Nicodemus Brown is believed to be Eddie Green, who was also black. The third endman, William "Algernon" Jefferson, is unknown (although, intriguingly, "William Jefferson" was the full name of the character Lightnin' on *Amos 'n' Andy*). The interlocutor was veteran actor/announcer Ken Christy, with tenor Harry Babbitt, the Dark Town Quartet, and the Buzz Adlam Orchestra rounding out the principal cast.

The premise of *Mirth and Melody* bore some similarity to *Minstrel Train*, in that the show supposedly visited a different Midwestern or southern city each week, with the sample episode set in New Orleans. Featured songs were generally from the late 19th or early 20th century, such as "By the Light of the Silvery Moon," "Alabamy Bound," and "Way Down Yonder in New Orleans." The opening and closing theme was "A Hot Time in the Old Town." As in many of these late shows, however, the period flavor was undercut by the big swing orchestra and occasional current pop tunes ("On the Sunny Side of the Street"). In addition, the presence of current pop singer Harry Babbitt and guest star Martha Tilton made it seem more like a contemporary variety show than a minstrel show.

The trio of endmen did crack jokes in black dialect. The jokes were pretty familiar (a bandit shot at sleepy Nicodemus, and Nicodemus outran the bullet), although Nicodemus did a rather funny parody of a torch song: "My Heart Is Bustin'." Whitman, an accomplished actor, played bass-voiced "Miss Iodine," while Jefferson was "Sugarfoot." Clearly the goal was to give the minstrel format a more contemporary sound, as well as to involve African Americans, but the result was a bit of a mishmash.

Perhaps the best way to honor minstrelsy was to remember it, and that's what happened on a remarkable episode of *This Is Your Life* on March 1, 1949. The format of the radio version of the show was the same as the later television version: surprise a celebrity on stage with the story of their life, and bring out a parade of people they had worked with along the way.

The honoree for this episode was old-time minstrel Lee Roy "Lasses" White (born 1888), who, as we've seen, was active on stage, records, and radio. He also had a very successful movie career (which will be described in chapter 4), but *This Is Your Life* focused on his minstrel days. He was lured into a Hollywood theater with the connivance of his wife, who helped the producers locate more than a dozen people from his past, many of whom White hadn't seen in years. Out they came, one by one, as the program was broadcast live on NBC. A real trooper, White rose to the challenge and exchanged hoary gags with unctuous host Ralph Edwards:

> EDWARDS: How are you feeling, Mr. Bones?
> WHITE: Like a sewing machine.
> EDWARDS: How's that?
> WHITE: Sew-sew!

Edwards recounted White's career from 1906, when he joined the Albert Taylor Stock Company, to the present day, introducing various old showbiz friends along the way. Then came the pièce de résistance—a live, six-minute, on-the-spot minstrel show with a group of White's friends, most in costume and blackface, sitting in the traditional minstrel semi-circle in front of a live studio audience. Edwards acted as the interlocutor. Participating in this improvised "Lasses White All-Star Minstrels" troupe were John Swor; White's former endman Skeets Mayo; monologist Billy Beard; dancer/singers Chester Wilson, Jimmy MacDonald, and Ernest Reeves; minstrel man Peenie Elmo; actor Chill Wills; and White's former colleagues William Spaeth, Verne Phelps and Neal Abel. Having been in on the surprise, and having had time to prepare, they carried much of the show, but White chimed in as well. They, and the audience, had a riotous time.

At the end of the show, White and his wife got a cartload of gifts, including a Westinghouse combination radio-TV-phonograph, a free carpet White had been needing for his house, and a week's vacation in Las Vegas. It was fitting capstone to a long and productive career. Lasses White passed away just nine months later, on December 16, 1949, of leukemia.

"Blackface" on Radio

Besides full-blown minstrel shows, black-themed routines and black dialect were used on many radio shows, most notably *Amos 'n' Andy*. Particularly popular were blackface comedy "buddy" teams along the lines of Pick and Pat, which appeared on both network and local shows. These programs were in a sense a spin-off from the minstrel show, taking the two endmen and building a show around them.[44]

Arguably, the prototypes for this type of act were two African American comedians: Flournoy Miller (1885–1971) and Aubrey Lyles (1884–1932). Childhood friends, they formed their two-man cross-talking act around 1905, appeared in vaudeville, and began writing material for plays and revues. The team used many comedy devices, such as skits contrasting Miller's height with Lyles' short stature, the "indefinite talk" routine in which each continually interrupted the other and answered before a question was even finished, and generally "mutilatin'" the language. The peak of their career was probably the hit Broadway musical *Shuffle Along*, which they wrote (with music by Noble Sissle and Eubie Blake) and which ran from 1921 to 1924. The play made history as the most successful all-black musical of its day, setting the stage for others. Miller and Lyles produced other shows and made recordings of their routines for Okeh. Already stars, they made their radio debut on CBS on July 29, 1931. One major black newspaper proudly declared, "Critics along Broadway were of the opinion that Miller and Lyles' entrance on the air spelled doom to Amos 'n' Andy's dominance of the 'blackface' comic field on the radio."[45]

Despite the confident prediction, the popularity of *Amos 'n' Andy* was not even dented by Miller and Lyles' appearance. Feeling that the white creators of *Amos 'n' Andy* had "stolen" their act, Miller and Lyles sued them. However, the lawsuit went nowhere and was dropped following Lyles' death in 1932. Miller (billed as F.E. Miller) continued to appear, partnering at times with Mantan Moreland and Johnnie Lee. His appearance in a motion picture minstrel show will be covered in the next chapter.

Amos 'n' Andy was not really a two-man buddy show, but rather a five-night-a-week comedy serial in a black setting. Its creators were white actors Freeman Gosden and Charles Correll, who voiced all the characters. Their inspiration was not Miller and Lyles but *The Gumps*, a popular serialized comic strip about a white middle-class family. Beginning as a local show called *Sam 'n' Henry* on WGN (Chicago) in January 1926, the show was renamed *Amos 'n' Andy* and moved (along with announcer Bill Hay) to WMAQ and national syndication in 1928. In 1929, it was picked up by the NBC Blue Network and went live nationwide. The setting was initially Chicago and later New York, where the two principals operated a low-rent taxi company. Over time, many supporting characters were added to the program. *Amos 'n' Andy* was phenomenally popular with its serialized stories, but it really had little in common with minstrelsy other than its use of dialect and portrayal of at least some blacks as lazy, shiftless, or conniving. It also portrayed them with some emotional depth, as real human beings, which of course was not the strong suit of a fast and happy minstrel show.

There were few successful imitators of *Amos 'n' Andy* because it was so dependent on the sophisticated writing of Gosden and Correll and the investment that listeners built up in the continuing characters they had created. However, there were plenty of two-man black buddy comedy teams on network radio, nearly all enacted by white men.

One of the earliest teams was Cotton and Morpheus, portrayed by Phil Cook and John Mitchell, who appeared on NBC in 1927–1928 on a show called *The Sealy Air Weavers*. The alert Cotton and the somnolent Morpheus were two wandering Negroes who joked and then listened in on their portable radio to the Sealy Air Weavers Orchestra as it played popular music. Examples of their routines can be found on Brunswick records.[46]

Perhaps the most popular blackface buddy team of the 1920s was George Moran and Charles Mack, known as "The Two Black Crows." Mack had originally teamed with John Swor in the 1910s, as Swor and Mack, but fame came around 1920 when Swor was replaced by Moran. Moran and Mack appeared in the *Ziegfeld Follies of 1920* and later revues, including the *Greenwich Village Follies* (1924–1925) and *Earl Carroll's Vanities* (1926). They recorded one of their routines, "The Early Bird Catches the Worm," for

Columbia in 1927, after having been turned down by Victor. It was an absolute sensation, selling more than one million copies—a phenomenal total for that period and one of the biggest-selling records of the entire pre–World War II era. More records naturally followed. Their act involved one partner being naive but practical, while the other was slow and lazy (but quick with a quip). Catch phrases included "Why bring *that* up?" and "What *caw-ses* that?"

Moran and Mack made their radio debut in 1927, on NBC's *Eveready Hour*, via a special remote broadcast from their dressing room at the theater where they were appearing in *Earl Carroll's Vanities*. They were regulars on CBS's *Majestic Theatre Hour* (1928) and later had their own *Moran and Mack Show* (1933) on CBS. In 1930, Moran was replaced by John Swor's brother Bert Swor (who adopted the name "Moran"). Mack died in 1934, but Bert Swor (as Moran) continued to perform with various partners in the years that followed. Moran and Mack never reached the heights on radio that they had on stage or in records, in part because of personnel changes, but they were household names during the late 1920s and early 1930s.[47]

Honeyboy and Sassafras (George Fields and Johnnie Welsh) began on local radio in the Dallas, Texas, area around 1929, appearing on KGKO, KSAT and WFAA (among other stations).[48] Both had minstrel stage experience, Fields with Al G. Field and Welsh with Lasses White's Minstrels. Their program was a comedy set at their Black Panther Detective Agency. Fields, who wrote and directed the show, explained his formula rather vividly to *Radio Digest* in 1930:

> You see, Sassafras is the levee type of Negro—lean, lanky, active. I am the Alabama "blue gum" Negro—slow, sloppy, lazy. Humor in Negro skits depends on three situations. A Negro to be funny must be either broke, hungry or scared and the problem for the creator of blackface comedy is to stick to these situations and still furnish sufficient variety.[49]

In 1934, Fields and Welsh were picked up by the NBC Blue Network and heard nationwide as a 15-minute daily midday feature, similar to *Amos 'n' Andy*. This program ran until 1937, when Fields, the team's guiding force, died suddenly of a heart attack. Welsh formed a new duo, Sugarfoot and Sassafras, with Bob Padgett (brother of Pat Padgett of Pick and Pat), and there was also a revived Honeyboy and Sassafras with new actors (Tom Woods and Tex Burch). Both of these teams received some exposure in the late 1930s but were not nearly as successful as the original pair.

Another popular blackface buddy team on radio in the mid-1930s was Moonshine and Sawdust, who were first heard on NBC's *Corn Cob Pipe Club* (1934) and also possibly on *The Gulf Show*. In 1937, they made some well-publicized appearances on NBC's *Jane Froman Show*, at which time they were identified as Lawrence Drinard and Stuart Brauer from WRVA (Richmond, Virginia) and as close friends with Freeman Gosden of *Amos 'n' Andy* fame. They had appeared with Gosden in minstrelsy in the mid-1910s—before he became famous. Possibly it was Gosden who got Drinard and Brauer their exposure on NBC, but in an overcrowded field they quickly faded from sight.

Buck and Wheat were heard on *Cabin at the Crossroads* (1937–1938), one of a long series of network shows starring "Aunt Jemima" (actress Tess Gardella). Both Jemima and her co-stars made heavy use of dialect as they joked and pitched the sponsor's pancakes and other Quaker Oats products. "Buck" was Vance McCune, while "Wheat" was Forrest Lewis. McCune was a busy radio actor who had starred on a number of minstrel series, including *The NBC Minstrels*. Lewis was referred to as the Midwest's version of a "man of a thousand voices," appearing in comedies and dramas alike, sometimes on the same day. He told a reporter an amusing story of one consequence of this situation: *Cabin at the Crossroads* was broadcast live in front of a studio audience, and the sponsor insisted that the actors be in full costume, which in Lewis' case meant blackface and gaudy endman regalia. On one occasion, the moment the episode ended he had to run across the hall to another studio to fill in for the romantic lead on a dramatic serial, with no time to change clothes. As he rushed into the studio, the audience burst out laughing at his appearance.[50]

Conjur and Caroline were a male-female team initially heard in the daytime on the Mutual Network in 1935–1936. Conjur was a handyman and Caroline a cook at a southern hotel; the pair would spar together before generally ending in a song. Later, the show was given a nighttime slot. The actors are unknown.

Local Radio Buddy Teams

Colorfully named black dialect duos flitted across the local airwaves like fireflies on a summer night. They were everywhere. Some were clones of *Amos 'n' Andy*—serialized shows with more or less continuing storylines and subsidiary characters. Others were simply two guys (almost always guys) trading stories and jokes, like endmen in a minstrel show, usually in a 15-minute format. The following is just a sampling to give a flavor of the phenomenon that was so prevalent, especially in the 1930s. The performers are in some cases unknown.

One of the earliest examples was *The Gold Dust Twins* (1923–1926), which began on WEAF in New York shortly after the station went on the air, first heard locally and later on an eight-city hookup. "Goldy" and "Dusty" were the advertising icons of Gold Dust scouring powder, usually depicted as two young African American boys cleaning the dishes. Here they were portrayed by white actors Harvey Hindermyer and Earle Tuckerman, singing songs like "Hear Dem Bells" in black dialect and playing the banjo. Their theme was the gospel song "Brighten the Corner Where You Are."

One of the earliest blackface buddy teams on radio was Goldy and Dusty, the "Gold Dust Twins" (1923–1926).

George and Rufus (WOV, Brooklyn, 1929–1930) was a pretty straightforward copy of *Amos 'n' Andy* during the early days of the latter program's success. *Lulu and Leander* (WXYZ, Detroit, 1931, 1933) revolved around Lulu and her "no 'count" husband. Here's a summary of a typical episode:

> The series opens with Lulu attempting to persuade her no 'count husband, Leander, to find himself a job, an endeavor in which she has never had much success. In the meantime Lulu's trusty washboard keeps the wolf from the door.[51]

Smokey Joe and Tee-Tain (WWL, New Orleans, 1930) was a southern version of this phenomenon, portrayed by Ralph Nogués and Rene Durél, who specialized in what *Radio Digest* called "Creole nigger-talk." Smokey Joe was the pompous and slightly smarter partner, while Tee-Tain was the simpler one who always had a comeback. They were supported by a cast of local characters that made this show somewhat akin to *Amos 'n' Andy*'s imaginary world.[52]

A favorite in the South was *Snowball and Sunshine*, in which white married couple James and Mary Dodgen portrayed "the comedy and pathos in the lives of an indolent southern negro preacher and his thrifty, hard working wife." James, as "Rev. Snowball," also delivered mock sermons (a direct lift from minstrel shows) in separate broadcasts. The Dodgens broadcast from stations in Memphis, Kansas City, New Orleans and St. Louis, eventually settling in Atlanta in 1931, from which point their show was picked up by the CBS network and carried on its southern affiliates in 1931–1932.[53] The *New York Age*, a leading black newspaper, sarcastically observed,

> The portrayers of "Snowball and Sunshine" are not Negroes, however. They are Caucasians—Mr. and Mrs. James H. Dodgen—who are said to have formerly lived in Georgia, which of course "qualifies" them as authorities as giving true delineations of Negro characters. For some reason, best known to officials of broadcasting companies, preference is given white people to interpret Negroes.[54]

Snowball and Sunshine made several recordings, including hymns and one of Snowball's mock sermons. Their performance was apparently good enough to fool some modern scholars, who have listed it in discographies and reissue CDs as being by African Americans.[55]

Snowball and Willie (WIBO, Chicago, 1931), starring Bob Greer and Malcolm Claire, was another *Amos 'n' Andy* clone. Also in Chicago was *Speed and Lightnin'* (WCFL, 1931). *Lizzie Titus and Mrs. Emma Potts* (WLW, Cincinnati, 1934) featured a female minstrel duet. Out on the West Coast, the stars of *Anaesthetic and Cerebellum* (KGW, KEX, Portland, 1934) were known as the "Blackbirds of Harmony" (many of these shows included music). Slick and Slim and Watermelon and Cantaloupe were other teams of the 1930s about which little is known.

When it premiered, *Magnolia and Sunflower* (WGY, Schenectady, 1936) was billed as a minstrel show, with Gene Cobb and Goff Link as the namesake endmen ("with song and patter") and John Sheehan as the interlocutor, accompanied by the Four Jacks vocal group and a studio orchestra. However, this program also apparently had a continuing storyline.

> The daily WGY broadcast deals with the tribulations of these two Negro characters, Magnolia as a simple-minded, hard-working darkey, Sunflower, her husband, is a boastful, no-good, lazy black Adonis. The locale of the story is a back street in the Negro quarters of Tuscaloosa, Ala.[56]

Emphasizing the show's alleged authenticity, the station said that Cobb and Link were both from the South, which had given them "ample opportunity to acquire the real Southern accent and dialect."

On the West Coast, *Sambo and Mandy* (KPO and KGO, San Francisco, 1932) were Sam P. Moore and his wife Carolyn Moore, two vaudevillians who "left vaudeville to go on the airlanes," where they were accompanied by pianist Dixie Marsh and guitarist Chuck Russell. Their daily show was also known as *Dixie Memories*. KGO and KPO were the originating stations for NBC's West Coast Orange and Gold Networks (equivalent of the Red and Blue networks in the rest of the country), and *Dixie Memories* continued for the rest of the 1930s, so the duo may have been heard throughout the Pacific region for a number of years.[57]

Emmaline and Easy (WGY, 1938) consisted of sketches and songs by old-time recording artist Vernon Dalhart and Betsy White (a pseudonym for Adelyne Hood): "Emmaline of the story is the cook in a commercial hotel at Cottondale. Easy is the lazy, carefree handyman. The vocal numbers, solos and duets, are cleverly written into the sketch and the simple story of each program is complete." Once again, the station emphasized that both actors were from the South, "so their dialect is authentic," adding, "The scripts, all of them written by Miss White, evince a sympathetic understanding of the Southern Negro's gaiety, piety and devotion."[58]

In some ways, nothing had changed in a hundred years of American blackface stage performance. White audiences were still being sold the idea that white men in blackface (whether literal or aural) were presenting a true picture of life in a corner of society that most white people never personally encountered. Moreover, according to this fictional perspective, everyone was happy "down on the old plantation."

The End of Radio Minstrelsy

Two examples—one small, one larger—show how sensitive the radio networks became to racial matters after World War II. One involved black characters on *The Tom Mix Ralston Straight Shooters* show, an early evening western adventure serial for kids that ran for almost two decades (1933–1951). From 1944 to 1951, this show aired on the Mutual Network. The "colored cook" and camp handyman Wash, portrayed by white actors Vance McCune and later Forrest Lewis, was easily frightened and rather stereotypical. His friend Chloe was played by white actress Betty Lou Gerson.

In May 1946, a white mother whose two small sons listened to the program wrote to the sponsors, saying, "Must Wash and Chloe be quite so ignorant, so illiterate, so cowardly, so typically old time Negro?" She praised the inclusion of Wash as a step in the right direction for the betterment of race relations but added,

> Why, then, must Wash, just to furnish comedy relief, be so overdone, and so typed in the worst way? Can't he be funny and still not so silly, so scared, so servile, so almost degraded at times? If you could give Wash a little more dignity and respect, make him a little more human and a little less "Uncle Tom" or "Black Sambo," you'd be doing a real civic job, as well as pleasing me no end. And I'm sure you'd sell just as many packages of Ralston.[59]

The American Council on Race Relations commended this letter as an excellent example of constructive criticism regarding racial portrayals, and the sponsor promised to improve the characterization of Wash and Chloe. The show's longtime director, Charles Claggett, assured the concerned mother that she could expect a change because none of the persons connected with the program wanted such an important character as Wash to be "lacking in dignity and respect."

The last attempt by a radio network to schedule a series called a "minstrel show" occurred in 1948, at NBC, resulting in a tremendous battle. Jewish businessman Moe Gale, owner of the Savoy Ballroom in Harlem and a major promoter of black talent, had been trying to convince NBC to schedule a series celebrating the Savoy's long and glorious history. It would be hosted by black bandleader Lucky Millinder and feature current black talent in a "recreation" of an evening at the famous night spot. Gale finally succeeded, and NBC announced the program as a summer replacement for *The Dennis Day Show*, to premiere on July 7, 1948. The name of the show would be *The National Minstrel Show*.[60]

The black press, including the *New York Age*, *Pittsburgh Courier*, and *Chicago Defender*, all got behind the show and urged their readers to support it. Despite the title, it was promised to have an all-black cast and "not be of an anti-progressive vintage, which most people associate with anything which is so titled." Millinder made it clear that "nothing would go on the program that would bring discredit to the race or the entertainment profession." Billy Rowe, theatrical editor of the *Courier*, called it "the most important step that radio has taken in the direction of the race in more than a decade."

Then the National Association for the Advancement of Colored People (NAACP) stepped in and protested that a minstrel program would perpetuate racial stereotypes. Activist Ralph Cooper also mounted a campaign against the planned show. A series of frantic meetings ensued at NBC, including everyone from Walter White (executive secretary of the NAACP) to eminent black writer Langston Hughes, who was brought in to doctor the script. The premiere was delayed until July 14, and then July 21. Sponsors refused to touch the program for fear of being associated with controversy.

Meanwhile, black supporters of the show complained bitterly. "This is an opportunity that the colored performer cannot afford to lose," wrote Rowe. "At this moment it has been placed in dire jeopardy by the thin-skinned, the fearful, the misunderstanding and the down-right ignorant." The writers were being hampered, he said, "because of the great fear of bringing down the wrath of the Negro intelligentsia upon their heads."

Finally, frustrated at the haggling, NBC canceled *The National Minstrel Show*. Then, at the last minute, it was reinstated with the new title *Swingtime at the Savoy*, premiering on July 28. The co-hosts were Millinder and fellow bandleader Noble Sissle, assisted by comedian Moms Mabley, the King Odom Quartet, the Hall Sisters, and the comedy team of F.E. Miller and Johnnie Lee. The show consisted largely of music, with Millinder belting out hard-driving swing and jazz, a calypso by the Hall Sisters, a ballad by Paul Breckenridge of the Millinder band, Bert Williams' half-talking/half-singing lament "A Cousin of Mine" by Mabley, "Uncle Ned" softly sung by the King Odom Quartet, and "Lady Be Good" by guest star Ella Fitzgerald with the Ray Brown Trio. There was also an old-fashioned minstrel-style routine by Miller and Lee, in which the bombastic Miller tried to help the befuddled Lee fill out a questionnaire, using the familiar "forefathers" joke:

MILLER: What I got to get at, is yo' an-cesters!
LEE: W-w-what?
MILLER: Yo' fo-fathers.
LEE: Steve, I ain't had no fo-fathers!

MILLER: You did have fo-fathers, everybody had fo-fathers!
LEE: Well, if I did have fo', didn't but one of 'em come home.

Cut short by the delays, *Swingtime at the Savoy* ran for five weeks, until August 25. Guest stars, besides Fitzgerald, were the Ink Spots, Count Basie, Billie Holiday, W.C. Handy and Carol Brice, all of whom reportedly worked for expenses to help the show. But the show did not attract a sponsor, and critics in the mainstream white theatrical press were not particularly kind. "The main shortcoming," *Variety* opined, "was in *Swingtime*'s failure to establish itself as something distinctive for radio." The music was "loud, brash and practically all in one tempo," the reviewer complained. The Miller and Lee routine was also criticized as "strictly out of the minstrel end men book."[61]

Billboard was a little kinder, approving the musical talent but saying of Sissle, "He does a competent job, but seems to lack the spark with which some radio quarterbacks can ignite their team." Miller and Lee were also criticized as "like a faster paced Moran and Mack dialogue." *Radio and Television Best* magazine said, "[The show] fell short chiefly because it insisted on emphasizing the first word in its title—as if Negro talents were incapable of anything but jazz, swing and minstrel-style comedy ... there is greater Negro artistry to be tapped."[62]

Listening to *Swingtime at the Savoy* today, even applying today's standards, the criticism seems excessive. Millinder's band could certainly be hard driving, but it is generally acknowledged as one of the best of its era. It could also play appropriately for Breckenridge's softer Billy Eckstine–style ballad. Mabley's "A Cousin of Mine" was a riot, and Ella Fitzgerald was, well, Ella, scat singing through the classic "Lady Be Good" in a way that is timeless. The one thing today's listeners might take offense at is the Miller and Lee routine, but times have changed, and judging from the howls of laughter, the studio audience loved it.

The experience of *National Minstrel Show/Swingtime at the Savoy* illustrates not only the increased sensitivity of the networks to possibly offensive material in the late 1940s but also how divided the black community still was. While "the Negro intelligentsia," represented by the NAACP, was quick to complain about anything they deemed offensive, working actors and musicians just wanted to get on the air and showcase their talent. Once the more egregiously offensive material had been eliminated, black entertainers could accept the use of dialect and the juxtaposition of smarter versus dumber comic characters (like Miller and Lee) if it made the audience laugh.

In any event, the outcomes for these two shows would have been unthinkable just a few years earlier, when the whole point of black portrayals seemed to be to make them "ignorant, illiterate, and cowardly." While there had always been complaints in the black press, some were just glad that blacks were being included at all. But in the 1940s groups such as the American Council on Race Relations (founded in 1944, mainly to fight segregation in Washington, D.C.) became more militant. They were supported by the liberal Truman administration, and both national networks and local stations were keenly aware that stations were federally licensed. Perhaps most important, pressure groups learned how to hit broadcasters where they were most vulnerable—with sponsors.

Although the most blatantly racist elements of minstrelsy, such as the coon songs and happy slave skits of an earlier time, had already been expunged, dialect and blackface remained. While blackface could not be seen on radio, it was assumed and used in publicity. Since those two elements were at the core of what a minstrel show was, the entire format had to go.

As a postscript, Millinder and his band went on a 40-city tour the following year (1949) with a show called "Lucky Millinder's Mighty Modern Minstrels," which opened with "Gentlemen, be seated!" and included endmen, dancers, costumes and all the paraphernalia of a classic minstrel show. However, it was emphasized that while Millinder retained "the pattern and style of basic minstrelsy," he "completely eliminated the offensive features of the minstrel show, such as dialogue, situations and controversial characters" (presumably meaning blackface and dialect). No one seems to have complained.[63]

Minstrelsy on British Radio

As we have seen, minstrelsy was as popular in Britain as it was in America, both on stage and on record. However, the British radio industry was much more concentrated than that in the United States. Instead of a multiplicity of privately owned stations, the British Broadcasting Company (founded in 1922) originally oversaw just nine regional stations, so there was less experimentation with specialized programming.

Blackface minstrelsy did not make much of a splash on British radio until 1930, when the two-man "buddy" team of Alexander and Mose began to broadcast. The act was originated by Billy Bennett (1887–1942), a music hall comedian who was known for his monologues mocking some of the more pretentious examples of Victorian literature. For example, in his hands "The Green Eye of the Yellow God" (a Kipling-esque tale of Oriental mystery) became "The Green Tie on the Little Yellow Dog." Beginning around 1930, Bennett teamed first with James Carew, and later with Albert Whelan, in the blackface act Alexander and Mose. The two were clearly modeled after American two-man black buddy acts that were then emerging, particularly Moran and Mack (aka the "Two Black Crows"). They mangled the language and traded stories, conundrums, and insults, with the more or less logical Alexander eternally frustrated by the slow-talking, drawling Mose (Bennett): "Clarify yo'self, boy—clarify yo'self!"

Besides their radio appearances, during 1931–1932 Alexander and Mose recorded "Minstrel Show of 1931" and four individual records for His Master's Voice (HMV). The latter consisted mostly of "duologues" with piano, including "In Dark Subjects," "Chicken Chasers," "Fish Sauce" and "Negro Nothings," all written by Bennett. Sources differ on who played Alexander on these recordings; those made in 1931 have a distinctly different voice (probably Carew) from the last one, dated 1932 (probably Whelan).

The height of radio minstrelsy in Britain, however, was clearly a BBC show that premiered in 1933. *The Kentucky Minstrels* was conceived by Harry S. Pepper (1891–1970), who produced other variety series for the BBC in the 1930s, including *The White Coons Concert Party* (1932–1936). *Kentucky Minstrels* was enormously popular, running for 17 years, spawning a stage show and even a feature film. Remarkably, the small cast was unchanged for most of that long run. The principal comedians were three African Americans: Harry Scott (Pussyfoot), Eddie Whaley (Cuthbert), and Ike Hatch (Tambo). Bones was played by C. Denier Warren. They were all referred to only by their character names. Accompaniment was provided by the Kentucky Banjo Team (Dick Pepper, Edward Fairs, Bernard Sheaff), a piano duo (Harry Pepper and his partner, co-producer and arranger Doris Arnold) and Leslie Woodgate and the BBC Revue orchestra. "Mr. Interlocutor" was otherwise unnamed but probably changed over time.

Scott (1879–1947) and Whaley (1886–1961) were the stars of the show. They met in

By far the biggest radio minstrel show in Britain was *The Kentucky Minstrels* (1933–1950), starring African American émigrés Eddie Whaley and Harry Scott as Cuthbert and Pussyfoot.

1905, played in U.S. circus bands, and then formed a comic duo that appeared in vaudeville and in *The Dark Town Swells* minstrel show. They emigrated to Britain in 1909, where they played music halls and minstrel shows to increasing acclaim for their "snappy and syncopated songs." Their act contrasted the smart and debonair Cuthbert (Whaley, who did not wear blackface) with the drawling, slow-moving Pussyfoot (Scott, who did). This setup was an outgrowth of the old model of the urban dandy and the rural coon, although Scott and Whaley smoothed off the racial edges. As scholar Michael Pickering, who has studied this program about as much as anyone, put it, they projected a "happy-go-lucky gregariousness, a good-humored argumentativeness which could spill over into threats of physical aggression, a propensity to be light-fingered, an incorrigible fondness for drinking, smoking and shooting dice ('African golf'), and an entrenched aversion to work."[64] Their banter was full of creative malapropisms, puns and putdowns: "You is the terrible result of what might have been a good idea"; "You is a fugitive from the Brains Trust."

Hatch (1892–1961), a musician, got his start in American vaudeville, played in W.C. Handy's band, and then moved to Britain in 1925. There he formed a piano duo with Elliot Carpenter that played in cabarets, recorded and broadcast, before striking out on his own in 1930.

Warren (1889–1971) was brought to Britain by his showbiz parents in 1897 and was on stage from the time he was a child. In the years that followed, he appeared in variety, revue, musical comedy, and radio. He wrote most of his own material, using the byline "Book written and remembered by C. Denier Warren."

Thus all four principal comedians were Americans, although all but Hatch had been performing in Britain for many years.

The Kentucky Minstrels had all the elements of classic minstrelsy: banter between the cornermen, cross-talk routines, monologues, stump speeches, sketches, and comic altercations with Mr. Interlocutor. However, this was no attempt to "modernize" minstrelsy or strip it down to look like a contemporary variety show, as was sometimes the case in America. This was unabashed nostalgia for a simpler time, when there was (it was thought) good clean entertainment, both comic and sentimental. The opening made that feeling abundantly clear. An announcer would introduce the show, followed a rousing chorus of the opening theme, "Rastus on Parade" (an 1895 ragtime two-step by Kerry Mills), by the entire company:

> Keep on a-shoutin', fall in line
> Hi there! Just clear the way.
> Slap down them flat feet, keep on the move,
> My Rastus is out today!

Next came "Gentlemen, be seated," followed by a tambourine flourish and Mr. Interlocutor tapping his cane for silence. The interlocutor would then evoke memories of old-time minstrelsy, such as an idyllic Southland scene where "the old songs and melodies were crooned by the plantation darkies," or "Let us turn back the clock and transport you for a few happy moments to the days when minstrelsy was in flower." Then came jokes and banter among the cast with the interlocutor acting as straight man, asking well-intentioned questions that were met with comic rejoinders or led into routines by cornermen Tambo and Bones, as well as Pussyfoot and Cuthbert.

Music, and there was a lot of it, was supplied by the Kentucky Banjo Team, soloists, or a male chorus. Many of the featured songs were 19th-century minstrel classics such as "Camptown Races," "Oh, Dem Golden Slippers," "Li'l Liza Jane," "Hear Dem Bells," "Kemo, Kimo," and, of course, "Dixie." Others were sentimental or religious songs: "The Lost Chord," "The Holy City," "Abide with Me." If more recent material was used, it was either minstrel appropriate or topical ("All God's Children Got Rhythm," "Thanks, Mr. Roosevelt"—the latter a wartime tribute). Many of these songs were recorded by the minstrels between 1938 and 1942 for HMV, with John Duncan serving as the soloist on most of them.

The program would often finish with one of the sentimental favorites, rather than an upbeat number, to leave listeners in a mellow mood. This conclusion contrasted with the more hard-driving American approach. *The Kentucky Minstrels* was escapism from the very difficult times Britain was experiencing during the Depression and World War II, which no doubt accounts in large part for its extraordinary longevity.

Pickering argues that *Kentucky Minstrels* was more misogynistic than racial. Jokes were full of references to insufferable wives, unreliable girlfriends, harridans, shrews, and nagging mothers-in-law. To some extent, these jokes were typical of minstrelsy, but here they were the province mainly of Bones (Warren), whose monologues were so extreme that the other characters began to joke about it. "Trust Bones to get one in against the ladies," cracked Mr. Interlocutor at one point. Bones' response to being called a misogynist was to ask what that meant. Responded Mr. Interlocutor, "A misogynist, Bones, is a man who dislikes women even more than they dislike each other."

Although there was no regular audience measurement in the early 1930s, it is clear that *The Kentucky Minstrels* was enormously popular. As noted, there were record, film, printed material, and touring company spin-offs. The show was so well known that sample episodes were rebroadcast by CBS and NBC in the United States in 1933–1934, and it was often included in short-wave listings in the United States and Australia. When regular audience figures did become available during the war years (well past the program's prime), it was still drawing 20–30 percent of the British population for each broadcast.

The Kentucky Minstrels began to decline after the war, especially after Scott and Whaley left in 1946. They were replaced by characters called Rastus and Mr. Lillywhite, who could not match their predecessors' popularity. The series finally ended in 1950. Two years earlier, in 1948, it had celebrated its one hundredth radio broadcast. In that same year, looking toward the future, the BBC telecast a Kentucky Minstrels performance from Alexandra Palace, its main studio. In less than a decade, minstrelsy would be back on the BBC in a way that nobody expected.

4

The Minstrel Show in Motion Pictures

In the same way that minstrelsy moved into the new media of sound recordings and radio, it also found a home in motion pictures. However, the migration took a little longer for movies, because movies were initially "silent"—and music and sound were of course the soul of a minstrel show. The list of films discussed in this chapter is not exhaustive, but it will shed light on the wide range of minstrel depictions, the many different types of films in which they appeared, and how those depictions changed over time.

Minstrelsy in Silent Films

Motion pictures as we know them rolled out to the public gradually, in contrast to the rather sudden (from the public's point of view) introduction of records and radio. After photography was invented in the mid-1800s, various kinds of viewing devices exhibiting limited motion were introduced, including the zoetrope, kineograph/mutoscope, and kinetoscope. Projected motion pictures—at first silent and less than a minute in length—began to be exhibited in the mid-1890s. For the next decade or so, they were shown mostly as a novelty in vaudeville theaters, as an "act" within a standard, live vaudeville show. Not until around 1905, as films became longer and filmmakers developed the ability to tell stories, did separate, dedicated movie theaters begin to spread. These theaters were initially called nickelodeons.

African Americans appeared frequently in early silent films—sometimes in stereotypical roles, sometimes not. Most of the earliest films were short scenes from real life, and of course African Americans were present. One of the earliest films released by Edison was *The Pickaninny Dance, from "The Passing Show"* (1894). Filmed in Edison's "Black Maria" studio in New Jersey,[1] this movie showed two young black men bending, clapping and enthusiastically dancing a lively jig and breakdown, while a third played the harmonica. Less than 30 seconds in length, it is an extraordinary piece of film, showing dance moves somewhat resembling modern breakdancing, and thus quite modern in appearance. Although billed as "pickaninnies," the three men were actually professional dancers from the farce-comedy *The Passing Show* featuring white actress Lucy Daly, which was then running on Broadway. Their names were Joe Rastus, Denny Tolliver, and Walter Wilkins, and they were very good. It was a vivid display of black talent.[2]

Edison's main competitor in the early film business was the American Mutoscope

Company (later known as Biograph), and it, too, brought out a film showing black dance, titled *Dancing Darkies* (1896). This piece showed five black dancers against a white background, dancing to the unheard music of a visible banjo.

More stereotypical, and one of the "hits" of the early period, was Edison's *Watermelon Contest* (1896), showing two black men chomping on large slices of watermelon and spitting out the seeds. It was so popular that a longer (two-minute) version was filmed in 1900, with four men and more comedic action. Biograph had its own version of that film, too, called *Watermelon Feast* (1896), depicting an entire family "reveling in a feast of the favorite food of their race."[3]

Another popular early title was Biograph's *A Hard Wash* (1896), in which a black mother energetically washed her squalling child in a tub. Edison's version was *A Morning Bath* (1896), described as "Mammy is washing her little pickaninny. She thrusts him, kicking and struggling, into a tub full of foaming suds." Both films were about 30 seconds in length. Some modern writers have read all sorts of meanings into these scenes (trying to scrub off the blackness?), but they could equally be seen as humanizing African Americans for a white audience that seldom met them in person.[4]

Several early films depicted the high-stepping cakewalk, a staple of the minstrel show. Among them were *Cakewalk* and *Cakewalk Parody* (both from 1903). The five-minute *Infernal Cakewalk* (1903), by French auteur Georges Méliès, was positively surrealistic, set in Hades, with a dancing devil as well as blackface dancers. There was also a cakewalk sequence in the first screen adaptation of the famous play *Uncle Tom's Cabin* (20 minutes, 1903), which used white actors in blackface for the principal roles. The play, which was so familiar that it was referred to as simply "U.T.C." in the theatrical press, had long been a staple of parodies and afterpieces in minstrel shows.

An interesting piece of early film tied directly to minstrelsy is an 18-second clip held by the Library of Congress that is believed to have been made between 1897 and 1903. There are no titles, but it is called by modern curators "Minstrels Battling in a Room." Approximately half a dozen blacks (or whites in blackface—it's hard to tell) are seen in a small room, all dressed in minstrel-style tuxedoes. Two couples are dancing, while a musician, off to the side, accompanies on guitar. One of those dancing is a man in drag— another frequent trope in minstrel shows. Suddenly, a short, bald, white man (the manager?) bursts into the room and tries to break up the dancers, while the others look on in surprise and the guitar player flees. A general melee erupts, the white man has powder thrown in his face and is thrashed, and the action ends.

It's pure slapstick comedy, with much tussling and waving of hands, and could have been part of a longer comedy film (although most films of this era were only about half a minute long). Without titles or a period description, it's hard to know exactly what was intended, or if the film was even released, but it was clearly a nod to some of the principal elements of minstrelsy.

Getting a handle on the total number of early films featuring blacks, or of whites impersonating blacks, is difficult for a number of reasons. Film historian Jan-Christopher Horak points out that many early films do not survive, and the descriptions given at the time were often not entirely clear. There are also "ghost films" that were announced but not made, and even when a film is actually found, it's not always clear whether the performers are blacks or whites in blackface. Some (like *Uncle Tom's Cabin*) had blackface whites as the leads but blacks in supporting roles. Do they count?[5]

Nevertheless, some scholars have tried to create a final tally. Ron Magliozzi, curator at New York's Museum of Modern Art, conducted a survey of all films produced in the United States between 1894 and 1915 featuring black performers or characters (whether in blackface or not) and came up with a total of 263, of which 122 (46 percent) survive today. Horak also compiled a list, focusing on (presumed) black performers only, which yielded 121 films for the same period, with a 40 percent survival rate.[6]

Thus early silent films do contain elements of minstrelsy, such as dance, the cakewalk, and even physical comedy routines. Representations of an actual minstrel first part are rare, due to the lack of sound. There are, however, exceptions.

One of the most fascinating is *Spook Minstrels* (January 1905). This was a 15- to 20-minute presentation consisting of several short films. In the first film, an onscreen announcer stood in front of a large curtain and introduced the act. The curtain (in the film) then rose, revealing a cast of approximately 32 minstrels, in three ascending rows, with the front row dressed in 18th-century court attire and powdered wigs, plus blackface endmen; the second row consisted of a band dressed in black, while the third row featured minstrels in blackface and tuxedos. Dancers stood to the side, at the ready. In the short films that followed, different members of the company performed various acts in the minstrel first part, including songs, dances and monologues. Sound was provided by the theater's house orchestra and by five singers hidden behind the screen, who carefully synchronized their speaking and singing so it appeared that it was the singers and comedians on screen who were speaking. After the last film, the five live singers stepped out in front of the screen, in costume, and sang some current songs.

Spook Minstrels drew widely favorable reviews as a genuine novelty, bringing "big cast, big time" minstrelsy into even small theaters, combining the new technology of motion pictures with live entertainment and still appearing quite current due to the songs at the end. Songs in 1906 included the current hits "Waltz Me Around Again, Willie" and "Will You Love Me in December as You Do in May?" The onscreen movie troupe appeared on the cover of the sheet music for the latter song. The five behind-the-screen singers were identified in early 1905 as Geoffrey O'Hara, interlocutor; Parvin Witte, first tenor; Charles Bates, second tenor; Charles Smith, baritone; and Leon Parmet, bass. A few months later, this group (with Smith replaced by Wallace White) made a commercial cylinder recording of "The Rosary" for Edison, as "The Knickerbocker Quintette," so we can actually hear them today.[7]

There were occasional complaints by theater managers about the difficulty of synchronizing the sound perfectly, the ability of the singers to be heard in the back of the hall, and just the fact that it wasn't what they were used to, but, overall, the reaction was quite positive. The live singers were first rate, and one of them (Geoffrey O'Hara) went on to a notable career as a recording artist and songwriter. One key to the synchronization was apparently that the on-screen conductor kept very steady time, so that the live conductor in the theater could follow along. *Spook Minstrels* ran widely during 1905 and 1906. It was apparently seen in England in 1906, and it continued to play in U.S. vaudeville theaters intermittently until at least 1911, with some turnover among the singers over time.

If films could be integrated into a vaudeville show, why not into a stage minstrel show? As we've seen, minstrelsy was making great efforts during this period to appear modern and up to date, and no one was more devoted to that effort than America's most famous minstrel impresario, Lew Dockstader. In the spring of 1904, as Dockstader was planning his new season (to premiere in July), he came up with a topical theme. He would project a specially made film of his black "tramp" character riding in a balloon over Washington, D.C., making humorous comments about the sights below. The tramp would then fall out the basket and land on the Capitol steps, just as President Theodore Roosevelt was riding by in his carriage. Roosevelt would get out, pick him up, and put him in the carriage. As Dockstader described it, "the colored brother—who is impersonated by myself—revives, says he is all right, thanks the President for his kindness, and gets out." This was obviously a play on the highly publicized meeting of Roosevelt and black leader Booker T. Washington, whom Roosevelt had invited to dinner at the White House in 1901.[8]

Dockstader, a cast member named Harry Ellis, an assistant, and a cameraman traveled from New York to Washington on May 18 and registered at a hotel. The following morning, Dockstader blacked up and donned his tramp outfit, while Ellis was made up to impersonate President Roosevelt. They made their way to the Capitol steps at seven o'clock in the morning, when no one was around, and marked a spot on the steps where the tramp was to "land." With the camera set up and rolling, Dockstader fell down on the designated spot, Ellis (as Roosevelt) drove up in the carriage, and the action was completed. Two takes were done for safety. The entire shoot took about 20 minutes, by which time some onlookers had begun to gather. The actors' appearance was so realistic that a Capitol guard saluted Ellis as they were leaving, thinking he was actually the president.

Then, we might say, the film hit the fan.

When word about Dockstader's film reached the White House, the president and his aides were furious. It was an election year, and the last thing they wanted was a reminder of the highly controversial dinner with Washington. Southern voters and newspapers were still fuming over the fact that Roosevelt had hosted a black man in the White House, an event that had been met with vicious headlines such as "Niggers in the White House" and "Damnable Outrage." Firebrand Democratic senator Benjamin Tillman of South Carolina had declared, "The action of President Roosevelt in entertaining that nigger will necessitate our killing a thousand niggers in the South before they will learn their place again." Northern newspapers and blacks were more supportive, although some black radicals were not satisfied, calling Roosevelt a hypocrite for dining with a black man but not repealing all Jim Crow laws (which, of course, he couldn't do).[9]

The White House immediately ordered the Secret Service to seize and destroy the film. Since Dockstader had already returned to New York, a call was placed to the New York City Police Department, which obligingly confronted the showman and requested the film. Dockstader willingly handed over what he said were the negatives. They were subsequently cut up and burned, with much being made to the press of this "swift action." The story appeared in newspapers all over the country. Some of them pointed out that there was no legal basis for such an extraordinary action, as it was perfectly lawful to film on public grounds. As for Dockstader, he said that it was all an innocent misunderstanding. "What have I got to do with politics any[way]? Do you think I am running a Democratic minstrel show? I am out for the dust, and as all money looks alike to me, whether paid into the box office by Republicans, Democrats, or Populists, I have no desire to run a one-party minstrel show." He then added, "I want it to be distinctly understood that I am not an enemy, but a friend, of the President," and pointed out that he had in the past impersonated Harrison, Cleveland, Bryan, and Roosevelt himself without any objections.[10]

The authorities said that if copies of the film had by some chance been made before they got the negatives and were shown, they would be seized and destroyed too. What they did not know was that Dockstader had apparently handed them blank, undeveloped film, not the footage shot in Washington. The originals were retained by Edison's chief cameraman, Edwin Porter, in his personal archive. Unfortunately, they were destroyed in a fire at the Famous Players Studio 10 years later.[11]

A Minstrel Sound Film in 1913

One of the most interesting attempts to capture a realistic minstrel show on film during the early days of film occurred in 1913, using Edison's newly refined Kinetophone system. Ever since motion pictures were introduced, the inventor, who had also invented the phonograph, had been trying to develop a workable marriage of sound and film. The new Kinetophone linked a film projector to a specially designed phonograph through a series of belts and pulleys. The phonograph played an oversized, highly durable, six-minute cylinder recording containing the "soundtrack" for the film. The sound was recorded as the film was being shot, by means of a large, moveable horn suspended over the stage, out of camera range.

Production began on the six-minute featurettes in 1912, and the first batch debuted on February 17, 1913, simultaneously in four Keith-Albee vaudeville theaters in New York City. The first film shown was a lecture explaining the new sound system, complete with a dish being dropped (crash!) and a demonstration of various musical instruments. Then came the minstrel film, revealing 18 performers squeezed into a small set in a static shot (the camera could not move). In the front row sat the interlocutor and two endmen, behind them were six minstrels, and in back there was an eight-piece band plus the conductor, who stood with his back to the camera for most of the performance. Most were in whiteface and 18th-century court attire, except for the conductor, who was in a suit. The two endmen were in blackface and minstrel costumes, with wide lapels, huge bowties, and striped pants. One held bones, the other a tambourine.

The poker-faced interlocutor opened with "Gentlemen, be seated!" followed by an overture, "Toreador Song" by the company, jokes, "Believe Me If All Those Endearing Young Charms" by baritone Owen J. McCormack, more jokes, an energetic "When the Midnight Choo Choo Leaves for Alabam'" by Bones, "Silver Threads Among the Gold" by tenor George Wilton Ballard, and a grand finale by the entire company—"Three Cheers for the Red, White and Blue," "Dixie," and the national anthem. At the end, wind machines set the British and American flags flapping in the background. The jokes were the usual cornball minstrel fare, such as the following double-meaning exchange:

> INTERLOCUTOR: What's the trouble, Mr. Tambo?
> TAMBO: Oh, boss, that song sure do remind me of one that I used to sing.
> INTERLOCUTOR: Well, won't you sing it for us?
> TAMBO: Mah voice is not too great, but I'll excite you a little somethin'.
> INTERLOCUTOR: You mean recite?
> TAMBO: Yes, suh, that's it. I had a little bird … and its name was Enzie. I opened the cage … and in-flew-enzie!
> (laughter)

The first minstrel sound film, *The Edison Minstrels* (1913), with interlocutor Arthur Housman. Immediately behind him are Edison recording artists Owen J. McCormack (right) and George Wilton Ballard (left).

The emotionless interlocutor was Arthur Housman (1889–1942), who would go on to a long career as a character actor in films. Tambo was played by comedian Edward Boulden, who made numerous short films between 1903 and 1924. The identity of Bones is uncertain, but it may have been John Young, who made many commercial recordings under his own name and under the pseudonym Harry Anthony. McCormack and Ballard, both Edison recording artists, were introduced by name, and the stern-faced conductor was Edison house conductor Eugene Jaudas. Also believed to be in the company were Edison singers Leon Parmet and H.L. Wilson. It appears that there was a good deal of crossover between Edison's record label and his film operation, with the same performers sometimes employed by both entities. Parmet was one of the original Spook Minstrels.

The production was certainly fast paced, but it was also rather stiff and mechanical (especially that interlocutor). The company stood up and sat down in perfect unison several times, the space constraints being obvious. This issue was noted at the time by reviewers who generally applauded the technical advance but in some cases criticized the unnaturalness of the production. It was in a sense a video version of one of the minstrel records so popular at this time, quickly hitting the highlights of a minstrel first part, with which viewers would have been familiar. The "Gentlemen, be seated!" opener, endman jokes, featured songs, and a big ending by the entire company were all there. The court attire might look unusual compared to later film recreations, but it was often used at the time.

Technically, at least, the Kinetophone premieres seem to have gone well. Thomas Edison himself oversaw one of them, at the Colonial Theatre, scurrying around backstage clad in overalls. When the audience learned Edison was there, they loudly cheered, calling for him to take the stage and give a speech, which he declined to do. Instead, he slipped out the back, in a 1913 version of "Edison has left the building!"[12]

More than 200 Kinetophone films were reportedly made in 1913 and 1914, but the reception was mixed, and after a disastrous 1914 fire at the Edison factory, in which many materials were lost, work on the system was discontinued. Only a handful of these films and their accompanying sound cylinders survive today. Fairly recently, the sound and film for *The Edison Minstrels* were located and restored. However, the film is the version made for U.S. distribution in which the chorus ends with "My Country 'Tis of Thee," while the cylinder is a version made for Britain in which they all sing "God Save the King." The rest of the performance is identical. So, in the restored version, at the end, the actors mouth one song, but the cylinder plays the other. Everything else matches up quite well, a testament to how carefully drilled the performers were.

Buster Keaton

By the early 1920s, motion pictures had matured into a fairly sophisticated storytelling medium, with its stars and fads. Within this new media environment, minstrelsy remained a cultural touchstone that everyone understood. This fact was illustrated by the clever 1921 comedy short *The Playhouse*, featuring one of the biggest stars in film—Buster Keaton.

The 22-minute film opened with Keaton in front of a theater, deciding to see a minstrel show. Once inside, Keaton was everywhere—he was the conductor and all four members of the orchestra, the stagehand, all nine minstrels, several members of the audience, and both partners in a dancing duo. The program read, "Keaton's Opera House. Buster Keaton Presents Buster Keaton's Minstrels," and it listed Keaton in every conceivable onstage and backstage role. A patron (also played by Keaton) remarked, "This fellow Keaton seems to be the whole show."

The minstrel show began with a line of nine minstrels on stage clad in tuxedos, and only the endmen in blackface. The traditional "Gentlemen, be seated!" was followed by a couple of jokes, including the following fast exchange:

> INTERLOCUTOR (KEATON): Mr Bones! I understand you had a cyclone in your town.
> BONES (KEATON): Yes, sir! The wind blew so hard it blew a silver dollar into four quarters!

This dialogue led into a brief, two-and-a-half-minute minstrel sequence, followed by a steady stream of Keaton's trademark physical comedy. When the stagehand encountered a punch clock, he punched it. Flats fell down. Keaton lost a stage monkey, so he took the monkey's place and did the whole routine hopping around the stage. Told to mount a Zouaves routine (a frequent feature of late minstrel shows), Keaton recruited a group of workmen outside the theater and turned them into Zouave soldiers who performed all sorts of clumsy stunts. At the end of the show, he smashed an onstage water tank, washing the entire audience out of the theater, and then grabbed a surprised showgirl and married her.

It's a Buster Keaton tour de force, with plenty of visual gimmicks, including Keaton playing all the main roles and even appearing next to himself. The minstrel show is not mocked or portrayed as particularly old fashioned. It's simply a setting with which contemporary viewers would have been familiar.

Early Talkies

With the widespread introduction of talking pictures in the late 1920s, movie minstrelsy really came into its own. Through the efforts of Dailey Paskman and others, radio had brought minstrel shows back to the forefront of American popular culture. Its familiar mixture of music, comedy, and nostalgia fit perfectly with both the optimism of the Roaring Twenties and the distress of the Great Depression—especially for older Americans.

During the first wave of talking pictures, the studios wanted to show off the capabilities of the new medium, and the investment they had made, with plenty of music. "All Singing! All Dancing!" shouted the ads. A minstrel show provided an excellent opportunity make sound a key feature in a film, even as the backdrop for a drama. At least four major motion pictures in 1929–1930, from four different studios, were built around minstrel shows.

Paramount was first, in May 1929, with *The Rainbow Man*, starring Eddie Dowling. Dowling (1889–1976) was a well-known Broadway writer and actor known primarily for revues and musical comedies, including *The Ziegfeld Follies* and *Honeymoon Lane*. In addition to starring in *Rainbow Man*, he wrote and produced the sentimental story of down-on-his-luck minstrel performer Rainbow Ryan (Dowling), who adopted orphaned Billy (Frankie Darro), his "little pal," after Billy's dad, who was Rainbow's best friend, died. They were eventually found by Billy's aunt, who fell in love with Rainbow. About 25 minutes into the film there was a nearly 15-minute minstrel show, with 40-plus whiteface performers on stage in tuxedos and white gloves, as well as four endmen in blackface. Songs included "Rainbow Man" and "Sleepy Valley." A second, seven-minute minstrel sequence was seen at 89 minutes in, reprising the same songs, and with the same cast (even though the poster outside the theater said, "50 singers, 30 musicians"). The other featured song in the film was "Little Pal," by Dowling, which is not to be confused with the more famous Al Jolson song of the same name and year.[13]

The Rainbow Man was one of several sentimental man-with-cute-kid movies of the day, and it was a success in its initial release. It was doubtless inspired by Jolson's massive 1928 hit *The Singing Fool*, a man-with-kid film that spawned the million-selling song hit "Sonny Boy." *Rainbow Man*'s use of a minstrel show as its setting was entirely natural, a place where an itinerant and not-always-reliable entertainer like Rainbow might be found, and where an adorable kid might worship him and want to be like him. (In *The Singing Fool*, the flawed man-with-a-heart-of-gold was a nightclub singer.) The minstrel depiction might not be completely accurate, but it seems reasonably close, including many backstage scenes, and it served the plot admirably.

The Grand Parade, from the Pathé studio, released in January 1930, made an even bigger deal of its minstrel content. This film starred Helen Twelvetrees (1908–1958), a young actress who was quite popular in the 1930s but is now forgotten. This was a comeback tale set in 1910 in which Twelvetrees appeared as the loyal girl who picked up a has-been minstrel singer (Fred Scott), and got him off the bottle and away from the evil influence of a blonde bombshell (Marie Astaire). The film is now lost, but advertising at the

Top: Theater program for the 1930 film *The Grand Parade*, which brought minstrelsy to the big screen in spectacular fashion. *Bottom:* An ad for *The Grand Parade*. The film is now lost.

time shouted, "100 singers and dancers—first time a complete minstrel show has ever been seen or heard on the living screen!" Stills from the picture show a large cast in blackface and minstrel costumes, and advertising posters displayed a minstrel motif, with Twelvetrees kissing her tall, dashing minstrel man in front of a line of caricatures of banjo-strumming black minstrels. It also boasted, "All Music ... All Sound ... All Dialog."

One promotion involved a minstrel band playing on the sidewalk in front of "The Grand Parade Exhibit," a display of photos of "the first minstrel stars of bygone years." Clearly, the appeal here was minstrel nostalgia.

An even more spectacular salute to minstrelsy was delivered by Fox Film Corporation's *Happy Days*, released in March 1930. This effort involved practically every star on the Fox lot in a giant minstrel show, which occupied nearly a third of the film's total running time. The thin plot involved a contemporary Mississippi River showboat, described as "a relic of an almost forgotten era" and run by loveable Colonel Billy (Charles E. Evans), which was on the verge of going broke. Spunky, diminutive showgirl Margie (Marjorie White) learned what was happening, made her way to New York, hustled her way into an actor's club, and, after much comic business, told the stars about the dire straits facing Colonel Billy, who gave many of them their starts. Deciding to help him, they all flew to Memphis, staged a big minstrel parade through town, and then put on a "Grand Gala of Broadway Stars" to benefit the showboat.

The 25-minute minstrel first part, which began about 28 minutes into the film, was truly spectacular. George MacFarlane served as interlocutor, leading 76 blackface minstrels seen on a giant stage, seated in five ascending rows, all waving tambourines. There was dancing, singing, and comic skits. Among the featured music was "The William Tell Overture," "La Golondrina," "A Hot Time in the Old Town," "Minstrel Memories," "A Toast to the Girl I Love" and the big finale, "Mona" and a reprise of "Minstrel Memories." Stars appearing in this sequence included Janet Gaynor, Charles Farrell, George Jessel, Warner Baxter, Whispering Jack Smith, Ann Pennington, Will Rogers, and the George Olsen Orchestra. Among those taking parts in skits were band leader Olsen (in a "Dixie" skit), Tom Patricola, Walter Catlett and Willie Collier, and Edmund Lowe and Victor McLaglen. Former heavyweight champ James J. Corbett took over for a time as interlocutor. After the minstrel first part ended, the movie continued with individual acts, essentially constituting an "olio."

In one of the most remarkable special effects ever seen in a movie of this type, the featured stars magically changed from blackface to whiteface as they began their numbers. It was the modern equivalent of the old minstrel posters that showed side-by-side pictures of the stars in whiteface and blackface, to assure the audience that these were really the (white) movie stars the mainstream audience knew and loved. There does not seem to have been an African American in the entire cast.

Another unique feature of *Happy Days* was that it was filmed in a 70-millimeter widescreen format, which Fox called "Grandeur." It had special widescreen premieres in New York and Los Angeles, which must have been quite spectacular. However, most theaters were not equipped with the special projectors and 42-foot-wide screen (versus the normal 24-foot screen) needed, so they ran *Happy Days* in the normal format. No widescreen print of the film is known to survive today.[14]

Happy Days was a celebration of "old-time" minstrelsy, filled with contemporary stars and songs. With its giant cast and special effects, it served as a template for many over-the-top Hollywood depictions of minstrelsy that would follow.

Finally, if singing and blackface were back in vogue, could Al Jolson be far behind? Jolson, "The World's Greatest Entertainer," had starred in two additional films since his smash hit *The Jazz Singer* launched the talking picture era in 1927: *The Singing Fool* in 1928 and *Say It with Songs* in 1929. All three were highly sentimental melodramas, the latter two pairing him with an adorable child, and they were beginning to look alike. The

Al Jolson, "The World's Greatest Entertainer," with his minstrels in *Mammy* (1930).

most recent, *Say It with Songs*, earned less than half the box-office receipts of the first two. Jolson needed to try something different, and that something harkened back to his early years in show business—a film exploiting the newly revived interest in minstrelsy. One of Warner Brothers' top directors, Michael Curtiz, was assigned to direct.

The plot of *Mammy* featured Jolson as endman Al Fuller in a traveling minstrel show, who became involved in a love triangle with his best friend Westy (the interlocutor) and the beautiful daughter of the owner. Another minstrel, who cheated at cards, wanted to draw attention away from himself, so he framed Al for shooting Westy during a skit with a gun that was supposed to contain blanks. Al went on the run, staying with his beloved mom, to whom he sang "To My Mammy" in a scene straight out of *The Jazz Singer*. Eventually the culprit confessed and Al was cleared, returning to the show in triumph.

Given its premise, the movie was suffused with the world of minstrelsy, both in front of the camera and behind the scenes. There was a 10-minute minstrel first part (interrupted by plot developments) depicted about 14 minutes in, and a second 11-minute segment at about 55 minutes. Twenty minstrels in blackface appeared in the first segment, and there were one hundred in the second. A major feature of the movie was that it included selected sequences, including the second minstrel sequence, in two-strip color. Although crude by modern standards, this development was revolutionary for the time, and the sudden appearance of color made the second minstrel sequence appear vivid indeed! There were also grand parades through town preceding the performances.

Songs in the minstrel sequences were a mix of new and old, including two Jolson hits from the 1910s ("Who Paid the Rent for Mrs. Rip Van Winkle?" and "Why Do They All Take the Night Boat to Albany?") in addition to "When You and I Were Young, Maggie," "Old Folks at Home," and a riotous mock-opera version of "Yes! We Have No Bananas." A running theme throughout the film, and a new hit for Jolson, was "Let Me Sing and I'm Happy" (by Irving Berlin). Another hit from the show (also by Berlin) was "Across the Breakfast Table Looking at You." All this, plus interlocutor-endman gags, dancers, and a tambourine chorus.

Jolson's high energy and charisma dominated the movie, but the big, flashy minstrel sequences also contributed—especially when they burst into color. Color is, of course, taken for granted today, but here it stood in sharp contrast with the rest of the film, which was in black and white, like nearly all films of the period. The minstrel show in 1930 could hardly have had a better salesman than Jolson in this nostalgic, yet very contemporary, production.

As with many other early films—even big ones—parts of *Mammy* were at one time lost. Modern restorations include 84 of the original 95 minutes and two color sequences (the second minstrel show sequence, and the big, happy ending in which Jolson arrived back in town in black and white and then marched down the street in the minstrel parade and sang his final song in color).

Besides these feature films, there were a number of short subjects in the late 1920s and early 1930s related to minstrelsy. In October 1926, a year before *The Jazz Singer* debuted, Jolson starred in a 10-minute Vitaphone sound short called *A Plantation Act*, in which he appeared in blackface and workingman's clothes on a static set in front of a southern cabin. A cotton field could be seen in the background, and live chickens pecked in the yard as Jolson launched into three of his famous hits: "When the Red, Red Robin (Comes Bob, Bob, Bobbin' Along)," "April Showers," and "Rock-a-Bye Your Baby with a Dixie Melody." The film presented him as if he was in a live stage performance, complete with impromptu asides ("Wait a minute, you ain't heard nothin' yet!"), callouts to the conductor, and three curtain calls at the finish. Jolson even threw in a good-natured defense of "mammy songs," which were much mocked at the time, saying John McCormack sang them too ("Mother Machree"), before offering his own "Rock-a-Bye Your Baby."

No doubt there were many blackface stage performances like this in minstrelsy, as well as in vaudeville, though few could command the screen like Jolson. Looking at the footage today, the songs are corny and the technology is old, but you can't take your eyes off him.[15]

The Voice of Vaudeville, from Herman Fowler Studios, was a series of 15-minute shorts that circulated in 1930–1931. They were also known as *Fowler Varieties*. Each one contained three or four standalone acts, and one of them (possibly the first) included a full blackface minstrel sequence. The film began with the Four Harmony Boys—three dressed as Chinese and one in blackface and a suit—doing a sketch in a Chinese laundry. In the second act, the Dusky Four (African Americans) were seen rolling dice in an alley, warming up with a "calliope song" and then singing "Roll Dem Bones." This sequence was followed by Charley Wellman, a popular West Coast radio comedian and singer ("The Prince of Pep"), in a radio studio doing an energetic, Jolson-style rendition of "Alabamy Snow." At about nine minutes into the film, the scene abruptly cut to a full-scale, four-minute minstrel show, with approximately 36 minstrels on stage in all sorts of costumes. There were three banjo players dressed as circus clowns, four blackface dancers, 10 female dancers (whiteface), blackface endmen in traditional minstrel outfits, and a 17-piece band. The interlocutor (whiteface) appeared to be Wellman. They all sang and danced to an encore of "Alabamy Snow," followed by a short chorus of "Ida."

The final act of the film is a mystery, as there is only a title card for "Modern Minstrels" with Cliff Nazarro—the footage for that sequence is missing. A colorful lobby card also survives for Nazarro's "Modern Minstrels," but with little information about the content.[16]

Hollywood's Golden Age

The 1930s brought a steady stream of big-screen celebrations of minstrelsy, featuring some of Hollywood's biggest stars. In fact, it is hard to maintain that the minstrel show was "dead" in the 1930s when one could hear it on top-rated network radio shows and see it at the movie theater in big-budget productions. Following are some of the motion pictures that recreated classic minstrel shows, often in extravagant productions that exceeded anything seen on the 19th-century stage. All starred whites in blackface, although some included blacks in the cast.

Eddie Cantor was one of the biggest stars of the decade, both on radio and in movies. He had been in and out of blackface since the early days of his career in the 1910s, and many of his films included blackface sequences—audiences expected it. In 1934's comedy romp *Kid Millions*, he played a naive Brooklyn boy who inherited $77 million from his archeologist father but had to sail to Egypt to claim it. He was pursued by bumblers who were also after the loot, including his father's scheming common-law wife (Ethel Merman). Arriving in Egypt, he had various misadventures involving the powerful Sheik Mulhulla and his beautiful daughter Princess Fanya. Cantor was about to be boiled in oil when he escaped back to the United States in an airplane conveniently parked outside the palace. Home, and now rich, he opened an ice cream factory for kids in a concluding two-strip color sequence.

While on the ocean liner en route to Egypt, everyone put on, for no particular reason, a full-fledged minstrel show. (Why should anything in this movie make sense?)

Drawn from life by Samuel Rogers Without Benefit of Burnt Cork

Another modern proponent of blackface, Eddie "Banjo Eyes" Cantor, headlined a minstrel show in *Kid Millions* (1934).

Beginning at about 37 minutes into the film, it lasted for 12 minutes and was built around the Irving Berlin hit "Mandy," a minstrel favorite that Eddie Cantor had originally sung in *The Ziegfeld Follies of 1919*. Cantor was in blackface, and some of the women, including Merman, were in "brownface" (subdued coloring presumably meant to suggest mixed-race, or mulatto, heritage). There were big production numbers featuring dozens of white showgirls. Little Harold Nicholas, an African American child, opened the show dressed in a white suit and top hat, singing "I Want to Be a Minstrel Man." This introduction was followed by Cantor offering some creaky endman jokes ("Do you know the difference between a horse and a girl?" "No." "You certainly must have some funny dates!"). Cantor and Merman then sang "Mandy." Ann Sothern and George Murphy duetted on the romantic "Your Head on My Shoulder," surrounded by both black and white couples, and the sequence ended with Cantor being comically upstaged by the dancing Nicholas Brothers, Fayard and Harold, in a reprise of "Mandy." It's pure Hollywood, with scores of beautiful girls and elaborate production values not seen in any minstrel stage show.

There is virtually nothing in the songs or dialogue of this sequence that is overtly about race, although while Cantor was in his dressing room blacking up before the show, he remarked to his black attendant, "This is tough to put on ... and take off. You know you're lucky!" The attendant, an older man, simply smiled. The *New York Age* and *Pittsburgh Courier* celebrated the featured inclusion of the Nicholas Brothers in the film, paying no attention to the blackface.[17]

The biggest movie sensation of the mid–1930s was Shirley Temple (born in 1928), a precocious youngster who sang and danced her way into America's hearts. In the midst of the Depression, her sunny disposition, eternal optimism, and eagerness to help everyone around her struck a welcome chord. Several of her films featured actors in blackface, or even actual African Americans, notably dancer Bill "Bojangles" Robinson, with whom she performed. These films included *The Littlest Rebel*, *The Little Colonel*, *Just Around the Corner* and *Rebecca of Sunnybrook Farm*. In *The Littlest Rebel* (1935), Shirley played the daughter of a slave-owning family, where the slaves were, of course, happy and dancing, and she even donned blackface herself.

Dimples (1936) included a full-fledged, if brief and fanciful, recreation of a minstrel show. Set in 1850 New York City, the film had ever-cheerful little Shirley living with her loveable but larcenous grandfather (Frank Morgan) and leading a ragamuffin street band. Though a series of unusual circumstances, she became involved with a rich woman and wound up cast (in whiteface) in productions of *Uncle Tom's Cabin* and a minstrel show. At about 37 minutes into the film, Shirley sang a brief chorus of "Get on Board" with a chorus of blackface field hands; at 62 minutes, she played Eva in *Uncle Tom's Cabin*, with Topsy and other cast members in exaggerated blackface (and much backstage business). At 74 minutes, this sequence morphed into a full-fledged, four-minute blackface minstrel show, with 35 men in tuxedos waving tambourines and Shirley (in whiteface) addressed as the interlocutor. From a modern perspective, the racial imagery is striking: a happy young white child with three dozen black men at her command, almost as if they were her playthings. Shirley did a song and dance to the tune "Dixie-Anna," and even cracked a corny joke with a befuddled black endman:

> SHIRLEY: Mr. Bones, why does the fireman wear red suspenders?
> BONES: Well, I tell yuh, Miss Interlocutor, I dunno, say, how cum a fireman wear red suspenders?
> SHIRLEY: The reason a fireman wears red suspenders, keep his pants up, I dunno!

Originally shot in black and white, *Dimples* was colorized in the 1990s, adding to the impact of the *Uncle Tom's Cabin* and minstrel show segments. Somehow, in black and white, they seemed to be of another time, but with expert colorization they are of ours as well. Shirley Temple was at the height of her popularity at the time, and *Dimples* was one of the top-grossing films of 1936.[18]

The movie minstrel show was not only for older moviegoers, or those who might remember the halcyon days of Primrose and West. It also featured in the rise of America's most popular teenagers—Judy Garland and Mickey Rooney—in 1939. Seventeen-year-

Even little Shirley Temple got in on the act in *Dimples* (1936).

old Garland was on the cusp of her fabulous career, and Rooney, 18, was best known for his recent *Andy Hardy* B-films. *Babes in Arms* (1939) was the third film that they headlined together, and it made them both stars. Set in current times, the film featured the hyperenergetic Rooney and other neighborhood kids putting on a big, outdoor minstrel show as a benefit for their out-of-work vaudeville parents. Garland played Mickey's talented but insecure girlfriend who stepped in when the star's father pulled his daughter out of the show at the last minute.

Throughout the movie, there was a great deal of wrangling, many setbacks, comedy bits, and dramatic moments as sparkplug Rooney overcame all obstacles to pull the show together. Big band swing dancing routines—some built around the featured song "Good Morning (We Danced the Whole Night Through)"—gave *Babes in Arms* a very contemporary feeling. Finally, about 70 minutes into the film, the big show began—and what a show it was! The build-up within the film did not make clear that it was going to be a minstrel show, and the sight of all those kids in blackface marching enthusiastically into the outdoor theater with a blaring minstrel band was the first shock to movie audiences. This was followed by seven minutes of a high-energy minstrel first part, with 26 boys and girls in costume and blackface (some of the girls were in brownface) singing and dancing their hearts out. Songs included "My Daddy Was a Minstrel Man," "Camptown Races," "Oh! Susanna," "Ida," "Moonlight Bay," "I'm Just Wild about Harry," and bits of others. The imposing interlocutor and the two endmen (Rooney and Garland) sang their

Mickey Rooney and Judy Garland in blackface (and "brownface") in *Babes in Arms* (1939).

corny jokes, and all were accompanied by the big MGM studio orchestra offscreen. The entire production was directed by ace choreographer Busby Berkeley.

Just as the film's minstrel show hit a singing and dancing high point, however, a crash of thunder was heard, and the skies opened up. A hurricane had moved in. As this was an outdoor production, everyone ran for cover and Rooney's dreams were again shattered—at least for the moment. Of course, he bounced back, with a big, patriotic show on Broadway built around the song "God's Country," including Rooney and Garland doing a riotous parody of Franklin and Eleanor Roosevelt, and ending with another Busby Berkeley dance routine on the steps of the Capitol.

Rooney received an Oscar nomination for this film. It was a major hit and did even better at the box office—at least initially—than Garland's concurrently released *Wizard of Oz*. According to *Box Office Digest*, *Babes in Arms* was the fifth highest-grossing movie of the year. It certainly made the minstrel show (or at least Hollywood's version of it) look cool.[19]

Three years later, Garland and Rooney were paired in a follow-up movie, *Babes on Broadway* (1942), also directed by Busby Berkeley, which contained many of the same elements as the original and was an equally big box-office success, ranking number six for that year.[20] Mickey played a young song-and-dance man in present-day New York, with two partners, trying to break into the big time. Despite meeting with constant rejection, he was not discouraged, and when he encountered Garland at his "office" (a diner), he convinced her to join the team. They all then got involved with producing a fundraiser

4. The Minstrel Show in Motion Pictures   155

for the cute kids at a settlement house. This show led to an opportunity to audition for cranky Broadway producer Thornton Reed, and after many missteps and near disasters, at about one hour and 46 minutes in, they finally staged the audition. It began with a song in which six characters tried to decide what kind of show they should put on. After running through several comic possibilities, Judy sang,

> JUDY: What's wrong with doing something old, something tried and true?
> MICKEY: Well, how about a minstrel show, does that appeal to you?
> JUDY: A good old-fashioned minstrel show …
> ALL (TOGETHER): That suits us!
> MICKEY (EXCITED): Well, then, let's go!

The scene then turned into a spectacular 11-minute minstrel show, with more than 80 people on stage in white tuxedos and blackface, including endmen Tambo (Garland) and Bones (Rooney). The fast-moving segment began with "Black Up for a Blackout over Broadway," followed by a couple of old jokes sung by the interlocutor and endmen, a tap dance set to "By the Light of the Silvery Moon," Judy belting out "Franklin D. Roosevelt Jones," "Ring de Banjo," a frantic banjo routine built around "Old Folks at Home" and "Alabamy Bound," and the big finale, "Waiting for the Robert E. Lee." The makeup changed for some numbers, with dancing girls in whiteface and Garland sometimes in brownface. There were huge dance routines, complete with director Berkeley's trademark aerial shots. Several jitterbug sequences earlier in the film gave the production a very modern feel.

Set solidly within the new tradition of Hollywood-style minstrelsy, with flashy special effects, spectacular cinematography, and two extremely popular young stars, this sequence cemented the status of the minstrel show as being for the younger as well as older generations.

The year 1944 brought another feature film that presented the minstrel show as contemporary entertainment. *Minstrel Man* was a comeback vehicle for Benny Fields (1894–1959), a big man with a booming voice who had been a vaudeville star in the 1920s with his wife, Blossom Seeley. It was an unusually elaborate production for the independent Producers Releasing Corp., one of Hollywood's "poverty row" studios. Set in modern times, it was the story of minstrel man Dixie Johnson (Fields), who, after many years of struggle, reached the top of his profession with his own show on Broadway. However, on opening night, while he was on stage, his beloved wife gave birth to a baby girl (named Caroline) and then died. Guilt ridden because he wasn't by her side, Dixie turned the baby over to his friends, Mae and Lasses White, and went into a long downward spiral. Sixteen years later, while singing for tips in a shabby dive, he learned that his daughter (who thought he was dead) was about to open in her own show as "Dixie Girl Johnson." Traveling to New York to watch her from a distance, he was discovered and they were reunited.

At about six minutes into the film, there was a fairly traditional, old-style 11-minute minstrel first part, with 30–40 performers on stage in gleaming white minstrel outfits and blackface. It included songs ("Minstrel Man," "Remember Me to Carolina"), dancing, and familiar jokes.

> INTERLOCUTOR: Lasses White.
> WHITE: Yees, Mr. Interlocu-tor.
> INTERLOCUTOR: Why were you running down the street so fast last night?
> WHITE: I was runnin' to stop a fight.

INTERLOCUTOR: Who was fighting?
WHITE (SHEEPISHLY): Me and anotha' fella.
(laughter)

At 52 minutes in, there was another 11-minute minstrel show, this time an updated "modern" production starring Dixie's grown-up daughter Caroline and done in 1940s style, with a swing band and a 50-person mixed male and female cast. Some (including Caroline) were in minstrel costumes and blackface; others were not. The movie concluded with Dixie and Caroline reuniting on-stage in a duet ("Remember Me to Carolina"), where he was in blackface and she was in whiteface. Fields also did individual numbers in blackface at other points in the movie, including "Cindy," "Melancholy Baby" and "Remember Me to Carolina." Music from the film was nominated for an Academy Award. Some of the authenticity of the film no doubt stemmed from the fact that a genuine minstrel star of earlier days—Lee "Lasses" White—was an advisor to the film. White also played one of the minstrels, and "Lasses White" was a principal character in the film, with that role being played by actor Roscoe Karns.

In an interesting postscript, Pictorial Films excerpted four of Fields' musical routines from the film and repackaged them into a 12-minute short called *Minstrel Melodies*, which was distributed in 1948.[21]

A late but notable entry in Hollywood's minstrel tradition was *Yes Sir, Mr. Bones* (1951), from the low-budget Lippert Studios (the production company was appropriately called Spartan Productions). This film was an exercise in pure nostalgia. The movie's opening set the tone:

> By far the most colorful era in show business was that of the Minstrels. These black-face troupes traveled in picturesque river showboats and heralded their arrival by the vibrant notes of the steam calliope. There was nothing like the excitement of a Minstrel Show: the singers, the dancers—the comedy of the end men, the dignified interlocutor—the rhythms of the banjo, the tambourines and the "bones." Today the Minstrels are nearly forgotten. They have "drifted on down the river," but have left, in their wake, a great American tradition.

Yes Sir, Mr. Bones (1951) **featured several authentic minstrel stars from a prior era.**

The cast included an interesting mix of older performers, both white and African American, some with significant minstrel experience. They included the teams of Flournoy Miller and Scatman Crothers, endmen Cotton Watts and Slim Williams, and Emmett Miller and Ches Davis, as well as Freeman Davis ("Brother Bones"), interlocutor Archie Twitchell, and Ned Haverly (grandson of J.H. Haverly, the 19th-century minstrel mogul).

The movie began with an inquisitive young boy wandering into a retirement home for aging minstrels and asking, "What are minstrel men?" After a few songs in the home's lounge, at about 16 minutes into the film, the scene shifted to a full-blown, 36-minute minstrel show set on a 19th-century Mississippi showboat. There was an interlocutor and a five-piece band (augmented by an offscreen orchestra), plus approximately 22 men on stage, all in minstrel outfits. Some were in blackface, while others were whites or African Americans without makeup. There were also six white chorus girls. The show opened with the entire company singing "I Want to Be a Minstrel Man," followed by comedy bits, a dance routine by the team Boyce and Evans, a medley of 19th-century songs by the Four Hobnobbers (white), another comedy routine, "Is Your Rent Paid Up in Heaven?" by Ellen Sutton, "Ragged but Right" and a sand dance by Ned Haverly, "Maggie Murphy's Home" by Billy Green, comedy and dance by Cotton Watts and his rather tough wife Chick (he in blackface, she in white), "I Dream of Jeannie" by Irish tenor Jimmy O'Brien, a stump speech, "Listen to the Mocking Bird" by Brother Bones, more comedy by Miller and Davis, a piano solo "Flying Saucer" by Elliott Carpenter, a comic court scene, "Memphis Bill" by the cast, and a finale including "Camptown Races," "Ring de Banjo," and "I Want to Be a Minstrel Man."

One of the most interesting segments was an "indefinite talk" routine by Scatman Crothers and Flournoy Miller. It was a classic routine that Miller and his late partner Aubrey Lyles had used in the 1920s, based on fast talk between two friends who finish each other's sentences so quickly, and implausibly, that the audience can hardly keep up.

> CROTHERS: No, no, not him. He gonna get married.
> MILLER: Yeah?
> CROTHERS: Yeah, he goin' to marry the daughter of what used to be—
> MILLER: That's a nice girl. But listen. I heard that one time she—
> CROTHERS: That was her sister. You see, I'm keepin' company wi' her.
> MILLER: I didn't know you know'd her.
> CROTHERS: Sure, I been goin' with her evah since—
> MILLER: That long?
> CROTHERS: Sure I is!
> MILLER: You know, the funny thing, I was talkin' to her father the other day and the first thing I know—
> CROTHERS: That was *yo'* fault. Now, what you should have done was—
> MILLER: I DID!

Yes Sir, Mr. Bones was not exactly an authentic recreation, what with its staging (no showboat ever had a theater like that!) and the female dancers, but it was arguably closer in spirit than many of the spectacular productions of the major studios. While it contained many of the old minstrel tropes such as a fat mammy terrorizing her cowering man, and whites in blackface, it also provided a showcase for some veteran black talent that was seldom seen by the general audience, including comedians Crothers and Miller, hot pianist Carpenter, and the Jester Hairston Choir in a respectful, "straight" performance of black spirituals (set outside a southern cabin).

Biopics

Another popular venue for minstrel shows on film was the biographical picture, or "biopic." In the hands of Hollywood producers, these movies often became elaborate, big-budget affairs, sometimes with a tenuous—to say the least—connection with reality. They were particularly popular in the 1930s and 1940s. There were three different films made about the life of Stephen Foster, all including minstrel show recreations. Composers Dan Emmett and Chauncey Olcott and showman Al Jolson each got the biopic treatment as well.

The first of the Foster biopics was *Harmony Lane* (1935), a modestly budgeted production from Republic Pictures starring Douglas Montgomery. Opening in 1848, the rather teary script followed the much-put-upon Foster (Montgomery) as he struggled to make a living as a songwriter, even as his family and shrewish wife Jane showed no faith in him. Only his lost love Susan believed in him, but she was married to another man, so their love could never be. Pudgy, sometimes comical E.P. Christy (William Frawley) played a major role in the plot, introducing Foster's songs. At about 33 minutes into the film, there was a fairly realistic, five-minute Christy minstrel show recreation, with just 12 men on stage in black tuxedos, white gloves, and blackface, working in a modest theater. (Minstrel troupes, even famous ones, were in fact still fairly small at that time.) Christy opened the show with the traditional "Gentlemen, be seated," followed by corny endman jokes ("Who was that lady I saw you with last night?" "That was no lady, that was my wife!"—although that one's so old that maybe it was new in 1848).[22]

According to the film, Christy persuaded the reluctant Foster to personally introduce his new song, "Old Folks at Home," which was followed by two minstrels tap dancing to the tune. Foster then descended into despair and drink, ultimately dying just as his friend Christy was about to open a tribute performance to help him out. At about one hour and 20 minutes in, Christy was seen for about two minutes, now with 20 to 25 men onstage, in minstrel costumes and blackface. They paid tribute to Foster with a reprise of "Old Folks at Home," and everyone wept.

Harmony Lane is an odd mix of reasonable historical accuracy and Hollywood fantasy. As noted, Christy's early minstrel productions were modest by later standards, with only a few men on stage and no elaborate sets. The theaters were generally small too, without the cavernous stages depicted in many Hollywood films. Some details were lifted straight from published biographies—for example, Foster did in fact die, as indicated in this film, by falling and cutting himself in his room, not drunk and destitute in a frozen alleyway. However, the script played fast and loose with other aspects of his life, most notably the final "tribute performance." Since Christy predeceased Foster by two years (and Christy had given up his troupe long before that), the impresario could hardly have held a tribute at the time of Foster's death. Foster was heard murmuring "dear friends, gentle hearts" on his deathbed. Those were the same words scribbled on a scrap of paper found in Foster's pocket at the time of his death, which were later the inspiration for the popular song "Dear Hearts and Gentle People."[23]

Hollywood movies are not documentaries, of course, but, while basically a soap opera, *Harmony Lane* did come closer to reality in its depiction of the pre-war minstrel show than many motion pictures.

The second Stephen Foster biopic, *Swanee River* (1939), starring Don Ameche as the composer, was more extravagant. Highly romanticized and in Technicolor, it co-starred

Fanciful movie biographies were popular in the 1930s and 1940s. *Swanee River*, based on the life of Stephen Foster, featured Don Ameche, Al Jolson and technicolor minstrel sequences.

Andrea Leeds as a much more supportive wife Jane and Al Jolson as a high-energy E.P. Christy. Again, his family had no faith in his ambition to be a songwriter, but Foster was much more upbeat and persistent in this film. Famous songs poured out of him practically full blown whenever he heard a random phrase like "Camptown Races" or "Ring de Banjo." *Swanee River* is full of incredible coincidences. For example, just as his father sternly dismissed "Oh! Susanna," Christy's Minstrels happened to march by their house and Christy bought the song!

At about 26 minutes in, there was a seven-minute Christy Minstrels show featuring 30 men in blackface and gaudy red, white and blue costumes. Christy sang and danced to "Camptown Races," after which Foster sneaked on stage to introduce the ballad "My Old Kentucky Home" (which Christy didn't like).

But Foster got a swelled head after this point, and his life began to disintegrate. He wrote a classical suite that flopped, the Civil War broke out and his songs were dismissed as too southern, and he left Jane and started drinking. Christy valiantly tried to get him back on his feet, and at 79 minutes in there is another five-minute minstrel show (including plot interruptions), with 45 men on stage in gold outfits. They sang "Merry Minstrel Men" and "Ring de Banjo." Foster was supposed to join them but had a heart attack and died, so Christy sang what is said to be Foster's last song, "Old Folks at Home," as a tribute. Everybody wept.

The plot was full of contrivances. For example, in *Swanee River* Foster went on tour with Christy, which he never did in real life; the movie claims that he wrote "Old Folks at Home" as his last, comeback song when in fact it was written a dozen years before his death; he dies during a Christy performance when in fact Christy was already dead by then; and so on. The minstrel show sequences are pure Hollywood—not quite as over the top as in the Garland-Rooney *Babes* movies, but certainly more elaborate than anything seen during Christy's time. However, Jolson's irrepressible energy gives them a spirit and optimism that is perhaps reflective of the appeal of minstrelsy in its early days.

The third Foster film was *I Dream of Jeanie (With the Light Brown Hair)* (1952), a fanciful biography, in Technicolor, of Stephen Foster's early days. Starring Bill Shirley, it co-starred tall, booming Ray Middleton as Foster's biggest booster, E.P. Christy. As with the previous films, much emphasis was placed on Foster's love life, this time revolving around sour Inez, who despised his music, and her sister, the perky girl-he-can't-have named Jeanie (do you detect a song title about to pop into Foster's head?), who adored him despite his faults. Brother Dunning and "minstrel man" Christy took charge of Foster's business affairs, with sometimes comic brio, and his songs swept the country. At about 46 minutes in, there was a stylized, 13-minute recreation of a Christy minstrel show, with 20 men on stage in blackface and colorful gold-and-white costumes. The minstrel show sequence included "Ring de Banjo," "Old Folks at Home," a sand dance, "Come Where My Love Lies Dreaming" (performed by endman Rex Allen), a tap dance to "Camptown Races," and "Some Folks." The recreation was marked by elaborate choreography, and it was essentially a Hollywood reimagining of 19th-century minstrelsy. As in most of films of this type, the original lyrics were changed (for example, in "Old Folks," the line "Oh, darkies, how my heart grows weary" became "Oh, chillin'...").

The song-filled score included both Foster favorites and more obscure titles: "Oh! Susanna," "Head Over Heels," "I See Her Still in My Dreams," "A Ribbon in Your Hair," "Jeanie with the Light Brown Hair," "Oh Boys, Carry Me 'Long," "Old Dog Tray," "Camptown Races," "The Glendy Burke," "Nelly Bly," "Melinda May," "My Old Kentucky Home," "Massa's in de Cold, Cold Ground," "Beautiful Dreamer," and "Old Black Joe."

Dan Emmett, the founder of the original minstrel troupe (the Virginia Minstrels) and composer of "Dixie," got his due with an even bigger production in Paramount's Technicolor extravaganza *Dixie* (1943), starring Bing Crosby, Dorothy Lamour, and Billy De Wolfe. In this far-fetched "biography," Emmett (Crosby) was seen in the early 1800s struggling to get a foothold in show business while juggling two girlfriends. He hooked up with a hustler named Bones (De Wolfe), who got them and two friends, Whitlock and Pelham, a booking in a New Orleans theater. At about 23 minutes into the film, the four performed for six minutes as singers in blackface and minstrel-style outfits. During the performance, Emmett began joking to cover for another cast member who had fallen into the orchestra pit and disrupted the show, thereby creating the first "minstrel show"— a combination of music and comedy. Songs included "Old Dan Tucker," "The Last Rose of Summer," and "She's from Missouri." At 35 minutes in, they were walking toward the theater when a kid asked, "How do I know you're any good?" whereupon they started singing as they walked, creating the first minstrel parade.

At 37 minutes in, there's a big six-minute show with 30 men on stage in elaborate costumes with big collars and bowties, top hats and blackface. Everyone entered through a giant "darky mouth" at the back, a device rarely (if ever) seen in the 19th century. Their landlord wanted to join the show, so he was added as an "interlocutor" and imperiously announced, "Gentlemen, be seated." That segment included "Buffalo Gals," "A Horse That Knows the Way," and even a female impersonator. Bones then promoted an even bigger show, which, after much travail, opened at 72 minutes in and ran for almost 14 minutes. Billed as presented by the "Virginia Minstrels," it included more than 40 men on a huge stage, plus the orchestra. Tambo (Crosby) sang the new love song "Sunday, Monday or Always" (a major hit in 1943) in blackface(!), followed by jokes that fell flat with the cultured audience. Then came a ballet burlesque in drag and a slow ballad rendition of Emmett's new song "Dixie," which also flopped until a fire broke out backstage and he sped the song up to get through it quickly. At the new, fast tempo, the New Orleans audience joined in enthusiastically, and the song became an immediate hit. The fire was put out, and all ended happily.

Among the film's many implausibilities, Emmett initially put on blackface to cover up a black eye, he won a critical booking in a card game, and he stumbled onto the minstrel show format with spontaneous joking! This was pure Hollywood musical fantasy, but fun nevertheless. *Dixie* was heavily promoted in print and on Crosby's radio shows, noting the tie-in with the one hundredth anniversary of the minstrel show as originated by Emmett and the Virginia Minstrels in 1843. In December 1943, *Lux Radio Theatre* broadcast a full radio dramatization of the movie, with Crosby and Lamour reprising their roles. *Variety* said, "*Dixie* is a Technicolor money-getter, ideal for the summer b.o." In the black press, the *New York Age* commented that minstrelsy was "the gayest, most glamorous entertainment the Old South ever knew," while Billy Rowe of the *Pittsburgh Courier* demurred, saying the film "slurs a race of people who are fighting as hard as any others to create a free world." Despite these negative comments, the film did reasonably well, ranking as one of the top-grossing films of 1943. Unlike most other Crosby films, *Dixie* was not officially reissued on VHS or DVD, presumably because of the heavy use of blackface.[24]

The success of *Dixie*, and the Garland-Rooney movies, brought about renewed interest in minstrelsy in Hollywood. MGM was reported to have a biopic based on "Honey Boy" Evans in the works, and it also bought the rights to Dailey Paskman's book, *Gentlemen, Be Seated!* (a survey of minstrelsy). In the end, neither of these films would be produced.[25]

However, the late 1940s brought more Hollywood blackface, with the comeback of one of the most famous modern blackface proponents, Al Jolson, in *The Jolson Story* (1946). Jolson was portrayed by young actor Larry Parks in what was widely hailed as a great performance. It was a simplified but basically accurate biography of Jolson, from his showbiz youth in the early 1900s to his first "comeback" in the 1930s. After starting out in vaudeville, in blackface, Jolson got a job with the famous Lew Dockstader minstrel troupe (1908–1909). At 37 minutes in, there was an approximately two-minute depiction of a Dockstader show with about 24 men on stage, in blackface, wearing white gloves and matching tan or white outfits. There was also a pit orchestra, and even a glimpse of female impersonators in the background. Jolson was assigned to sing "I Want a Girl Just Like the Girl That Married Dear Old Dad," at first as part of an eight-man chorus, but he soon persuaded Dockstader to let him do the song in a quartet, and then in a duo, so that he could stand out more. However, Dockstader was a traditionalist, and when he refused to let Jolson jazz up his numbers, the ambitious young performer quit. Later, Jolson scored huge success on Broadway and in films while dealing with his marriage to Julie (modeled on real-life wife Ruby Keeler). Near the end of the film, his aging parents visited, and he sang for them a sentimental rendition of "The Anniversary Waltz," which became his first major record hit in years.

Although the minstrel sequence was brief, Larry Parks (as Jolson) performed in blackface for much of the first hour of the film. Dockstader and minstrelsy were presented in a respectful way, though they were clearly portrayed as part of an earlier era.

The Jolson Story was a box-office and critical hit. It won Academy Awards for Best Music and Best Sound Recording, and it was nominated for awards in the categories of Best Actor (Parks), Best Supporting Actor (William Demarest), Best Cinematography and Best Film Editing. The African American press didn't seem to mind the blackface, perhaps because of its admiration for Jolson, Parks, and particularly Parks' wife, actress Betty Garrett, a well-known progressive and advocate of black rights.[26]

Parks reprised his Jolson role for the sequel *Jolson Sings Again* (1949) and also portrayed the singer in a *Lux Radio Theatre* dramatization of *The Jolson Story*, which aired in February 1948. *The Jolson Story* was also re-released in 1954 in widescreen format with stereophonic sound. Unfortunately, Parks' promising career (and, to some extent, that of his wife) was derailed in the 1950s due to blacklisting resulting from his admitted affiliation with the Communist Party.

The minstrel parade marched through theaters in another hit film the following year, this time *My Wild Irish Rose* (1947), a rollicking Technicolor biography of Chauncey Olcott (1858–1932), the premiere Irish singer/composer of the late 19th and early 20th centuries. Dennis Morgan starred as Olcott, with Arlene Dahl as his lady love, Rose; Andrea King as stage star Lillian Russell, who helped him professionally; and Ben Blue as comic relief. During Olcott's rise to stardom, he appeared in Haverly's Mastodon Minstrels for several seasons, a plotline that occupied about a quarter of the film. Olcott was in fact with several minstrel troupes from around 1876 to 1886, but in this movie Haverly represented them all.

Only a few brief minstrel performance segments were shown in the film. At about 22 minutes in, there was a colorful street parade by Haverly's Minstrels, and at 36 minutes there was a two-minute minstrel first part with about 30 men on stage, plus a 10-piece band. The performers were in blackface and gleaming crimson-and-white minstrel costumes and white gloves. Songs were "Minstrel Days" and "Polly Wolly Doodle." At 42 minutes, there was an elaborate six-minute afterpiece depicting a race between the riverboats *Natchez* and *Robert E. Lee*, with scores of dancers, big band accompaniment (occasionally breaking into jitterbug), the song "Miss Lucy Lou" with a comic female impersonator (Ben Blue), and eye-popping stage effects. All of these segments were highly stylized in typical Hollywood fashion.

The film featured many early 20th-century songs, both by Olcott ("Mother Machree," "When Irish Eyes Are Smiling") and others ("Wait 'Til the Sun Shines, Nellie," "By the Light of the Silvery Moon"). *My Wild Irish Rose* was one of the top-grossing films of the year, placing number 15 according to *Variety*, and was nominated for an Academy Award for its score.[27]

Minstrel Shows in Westerns

Often overlooked is the appearance of minstrelsy in Hollywood westerns. Depicting a minstrel show in a western is not as illogical as it might seem, as small minstrel troupes did in fact tour mining camps and frontier towns in the 19th century. In fact, the movie depiction of these smaller, simpler troupes is probably more representative of pre–Civil War minstrelsy than the sprawling, big-budget productions of mainstream films. In addition, a minstrel show fit right in with the "singing cowboy" and comedy sidekick vogue in westerns of the 1930s and 1940s.

One of the earliest Hollywood westerns of this era to include a minstrel show was Republic's *The Singing Vagabond* (1935), starring Gene Autry. The four-minute minstrel show was seen at the beginning of the film, in the setup for the story. In 1860 St. Louis (then on the frontier), the Pritchard & Ringle Minstrels were putting on a 12-man show in a smallish theater. The cast was seen in blackface and minstrel tuxedos, waving tambourines. Songs included "Louisiana Belle," "Camptown Races" (song and dance, with a pint-sized child minstrel, also in blackface), and a dance to "Old Folks at Home." The endman's patter mocked black aspirations to culture:

> INTERLOCUTOR: You mind telling me what you're writing there, Mr. Tambo?
> TAMBO:: I'se writing a new poem.
> INTERLOCUTOR: Well, I didn't know you were a poet.
> TAMBO:: Yes indeedy, I'se practically Bill Shakespeare.
> INTERLOCUTOR: Well …
> TAMBO:: You all like to hear my latest effusion?
> COMPANY (ALL TOGETHER): NO!
> TAMBO: Then I'll recite it for yuh. 'He sipped the nectar from her lips, as 'neath the moon they sat. And wondered if evah a man before, had drunk from a mug like that!' (laughter).

Someone familiar with minstrelsy was having fun here. "Pritchard & Ringle" is an obvious takeoff on Richards and Pringle's Georgia Minstrels, a famous African American troupe of the 1880s. Tambo refers to the interlocutor as "Mr. Christy," which had become a generic name for interlocutors. Talented children were indeed sometimes used in shows, and the term *Ethiopian* (used here) was often used to describe early shows.

In any event, in the film, sweet Lettie (Ann Rutherford) was dumped by her boyfriend Barton, the star of the minstrel show, when he discovered that she was not rich. She then ran off with a theatrical troupe headed for California. They eventually met up with Autry's rangers and survived many close calls.

Harlem on the Prairie (1937) is known primarily as the first all-black western. Made on a shoestring budget, it starred suave singer/actor Herb Jeffries, supported by such well-known black talent as comedy duo "Miller and Mantan" (Flournoy Miller and Mantan Moreland), Connie Harris, and Spencer Williams, Jr. The plot involved wandering cowboy Jeff (Jeffries), who helped the daughter of a former outlaw, now running a traveling medicine and minstrel show. She wanted to find the gold that her father stole 20 years earlier and return it to its owners. Sidekicks Crawfish and Mistletoe (Miller and Mantan) provided stereotypical comic relief. Songs included "Harlem on the Prairie," "Romance in the Rain," "There Is a New Range in Heaven" and Stephen Foster's "Old Folks at Home."

The black press celebrated this breakthrough, citing the "uniformly splendid performance of the cast" and calling the film "a considerable improvement on past race-produced pictures." Special praise was reserved for comic relief Miller and Mantan (they "steal the show"), even though some modern critics have criticized their "scared darky" stereotypes. Handsome Herb Jeffries also drew plaudits ("cuts a gallant figure astride a pure white 'hoss.'"). Black reviewers also appreciated the fact that the film played in some white theaters as well as in the usual black theaters.[28]

Unfortunately, I cannot analyze the minstrel content because no copy of this historic film could be located for my research. There are contradictory claims as to whether it still exists or is a "lost" film.[29]

Definitely not lost is *Boss of Rawhide* (1943), starring Dave "Tex" O'Brien, a low-budget western that contained a surprisingly realistic depiction of pre–Civil War frontier minstrelsy. In the film, a group of Texas Rangers, led by O'Brien, fought a gang of crooked ranchers. Three of the rangers joined a couple of itinerant minstrels as cover, and they presented five-man blackface performances in the town theater. At about 18 minutes into the film, there is a two-and-a-half-minute performance in which tall Panhandle "Romeo" Perkins and short Jed Bones played Jones and Bones, the endmen, while handsome Jim Steele was the interlocutor and featured singer. Jones, Bones, and two others were in blackface and outlandish minstrel costumes, while Steele was in whiteface and a tailored cowboy outfit. The instrumentation used by the minstrels was minimal, consisting of banjos, tambourines, two guitars and a small accordion. The stage decoration was likewise minimal, and the location was a small, plain, rough-hewn town hall auditorium. The sign outside said, with obvious irony, "Oakley's Gigantic Minstrel Show."

While this show was not meant to be a precise recreation, the small size of the troupe, the rough and ready setting, the limited instrumentation, and the loose and easy informality of the cast are much closer to what we know of early touring minstrel shows than the elaborate productions seen in most Hollywood films. At least one of the minstrels was played by an actor (Dan White) who had real minstrel experience during his youth.

The short minstrel segment opened with a corny joke between Jones and Bones, after which loose-limbed Jones did a dance and interlocutor Steele sang "I Ain't Got a Gal to Come Home To," which was written for the film. At the half-hour mark, there was another show, this one five minutes long, in which Steele sang "Stardust Trail" (another commissioned song) followed by jokes and horseplay (much of it physical) by the minstrels. The troupe maintained a fairly high energy level, laughing, whacking each other on the head with their tambourines, and kicking up their heels. The jokes were familiar minstrel wheezes, which also evoked the spirit of the real thing. For example, there is the old "forefathers" gag:

> JONES: Mr. Interlocutor, Mr. Bones over there is tellin' me about his forefathers. What does he mean?
> INTERLOCUTOR: Why, that's easy to understand. Everyone has forefathers.
> JONES: Say which? Does you mean to say that *I* got fo' fathers?
> INTERLOCUTOR: Certainly. Your father's father's father's father.
> JONES: Well, doggone. Man, well, if I did, three of 'em never come home!
> (laughter, slapping of tambourines)

Ranger Steele ended the proceedings abruptly after about five minutes to segue back into the plot, which involved O'Brien's father coming on stage to exhort the assembled ranchers (who had been lured into town to see the show) to vote out the crooks who were exploiting them. Gunfire, of course, ensued.

Another western that used a minstrel show as a device to lure ranchers into town so that they could be urged to vote out the bad guys was *The Lonesome Trail* (1945), starring Jimmy Wakely (then a rising star on the country and western record charts). This film had an authentic 1920s minstrel in the cast, Lee "Lasses" White, along with Wakely and his sidekick, John "Dusty" James. At about 29 minutes in, there was a nearly 11-minute minstrel show performed in the town saloon, which happened to have a full (if rustic) stage. Although the troupe was small (10 people plus a five-piece band), it was a little less authentic and more Hollywood than the one in *Boss of Rawhide*. The minstrels consisted of six men and four women, all of whom were in whiteface except for the two endmen (Lasses and his pal Billie). The men were in minstrel-style tuxedos, the women in gowns. Perhaps intentionally, the western band sounded a lot like the one on Wakely's records—trumpet, fiddle, accordion, guitar, and banjo. The songs, all by Wakely and his associates, were in the style of western pop songs of the 1940s.

The show was billed as by "Lasses White's Minstrels" and opened with the cast singing "When You See a Minstrel Show." All were then seated, followed by "Too Bad, Little Girl, Too Bad" by Wakely and girlfriend Elsie, jokes by interlocutor Dusty James and Lasses White, "Goodbye, Good Luck My Darlin'" by Wakely and the Sunshine Girls (a trio), a joke by endman Billie, and the lively "Mine All Mine" by an animated White. The gags were familiar minstrel fare, including this one about marriage:

> JAMES (INTERLOCUTOR): That's pretty good, Lasses, but other girls are a pretty delicate subject for a man who has as many arguments with his wife as you do.
> WHITE: I mean, Mr. James, me and my wife been marr'd for ten years and we ain't nebber had but one argument.
> JAMES (SURPRISED): You've been married ten years with only *one* argument?
> WHITE: And it's still goin' on ...
> (great laughter)

The show was eventually broken up by gunfire, as was often the case in westerns, but not before the cast delivered a rather lengthy performance.

Four years later, a virtually identical plot was used in another western from the same studio, Monogram. This was *Mississippi Rhythm* (1949), starring Jimmie Davis and, once again, Lasses White. Not only were large chunks of the plot the same as in *The Lonesome Trail*, but specific scenes and dialogue were also taken from the earlier film. At least the film's opening was different, introducing this Jimmie as a passenger on a Mississippi riverboat. He then arrived in a Montana frontier town, where he battled crooked developers for control of the town. In order to rally the locals and convince them to vote to incorporate so that their leaders would be elected, Jimmie and his crew staged a minstrel show to bring everybody into town.

At about 45 minutes into the film, the 11-minute minstrel show began. As in *The Lonesome Trail*, the setting was a rough frontier theater, attached to the town bar. The cast consisted of nine persons, five men and four women, plus the nine-piece Sunshine Band. Only the two endmen (Dixie Dalrymple, played by Lasses White, and Deanne "Peenie" Elmo) were in blackface. The costuming was very similar to the earlier film, with the men in minstrel tuxedos (some of which appear to be identical to the ones in *Lonesome Trail*) and the women in gowns.

The show began with the entire cast singing "Howdy Folks," followed by a joke by endman Dixie and the interlocutor, "Mr. Lawrence." Next came the song "One Has My Name the Other Has My Heart" (a big hit on the country charts in 1949), performed by Jimmie Davis. Then Peenie recited a familiar comic temperance poem from the 1930s:

> Well, early last December
> How well do I remember,
> I was walkin' down the street with manly pride.
> My heart went all a-flutter,
> Then I fell into the gutter.
> And a pig came up and lay down by my side. (laughter)
> As I lay there in the gutter,
> With my heart still all a-flutter,
> A lady, by chance, was heard to say,
> "You can tell a man that boozes, by the company he chooses."
> And the pig got up and slowly walked away ...
> (more laughter)

This piece was followed by a man and woman dancing to "Old Folks at Home," Miss Jeanette singing the comic "Why Don't Someone Marry Mary Anne?" and another joke by Peenie, and then a song and dance by Dixie called "The Old Levee Shuffle." Most of the songs were newly written but sounded old (stylistically speaking), and the accompaniment was in a country-western style familiar to country music fans of the 1940s.

Jimmie then stopped the show to urge the assembled townspeople to vote, only to be interrupted by gunfire from the bad guys. Just as in *Lonesome Trail*, there was a subplot about a crooked judge and his winsome daughter who convinced him to go straight, as well as a climactic scene in which the bad guys barricaded the town to prevent the ranchers from voting but were foiled by Jimmie and his men.

Monogram was also responsible for another late minstrel-infused western, *Sierra Passage* (1950), starring Wayne Morris. At least this one had a new script, and one with far more character development than its predecessors. In 1865, after his father was killed by outlaw Yance Carter, young Johnny Yorke joined a traveling minstrel show run by Thad Kring. Pudgy, fatherly Kring "adopted" the boy, and star sharpshooter Sam Cooper took him on as an apprentice. In the years that followed, Sam taught Johnny to be an expert sharpshooter. But Johnny's real goal was to track the elusive Carter across the west and avenge his father's death.

Scenes from performances of "Kring's Minstrels" are woven throughout the film, often interrupted by plot developments backstage. There were generally 10 to 15 minstrels

Often overlooked are the minstrel show sequences in westerns, which were often rather authentic. This one is from *Sierra Passage* (1950), starring Wayne Morris.

on stage, all in blackface, with minstrel tuxedos, white gloves, and tambourines (except for interlocutor Kring, trick shooter Sam and apprentice Johnny, who were in whiteface). At about 12 minutes into the film, there was an approximately four-minute segment that opened with minstrels doing a soft-shoe dance to "Old Folks at Home," followed by exhibitions of Sam's sharpshooting, with young Johnny (initially appearing as a boy) fearlessly holding the targets. At 35 minutes in, there were two minutes with the now-adult Johnny's sweetheart Ann singing "Love Is Magic," and at 44 minutes there was a one-minute segment with the now-expert Johnny exhibiting trick shooting with Ann holding the targets (now *that's* love!). At about 62 minutes, a nearly nine-minute segment began with Ann singing "Let's Break the Ice," followed by cornball jokes from endmen Lighter and Darker, sharpshooting by Johnny (with Ann and Sam holding the targets) to the music of Rosas' "Over the Waves," and a blackface quartet singing "Old Black Joe." Immediately after the show, Johnny finally found Carter in a gambling den and shot him in both hands—ending his gambling career—but did not kill him, leading to a happy ending for the four principals.

Most of the songs were new, and Ann's vocals were presented in a very 1940s style. Although the minstrel segments were "Hollywood-ized" and hardly a true representation of 19th-century minstrelsy (how many traveling shows back then had a pretty girl singer?), they were integral to the plot, not just a device. A traveling minstrel show was an appropriate setting for the evolving friendship between the three men, as the older Kring and Sam seemed to genuinely care about young Johnny and tried to help him deal with his demons (as did Ann). At several points Kring remarked that one of the greatest rewards of the minstrel life was the lifelong friendships that are forged—an aspect of minstrelsy seldom mentioned in other media vehicles.

Overall, the minstrel shows portrayed in B-westerns were generally more modest in scope than those in mainline features, presumably for budgetary reasons. Oddly, this smaller size made them more realistic than the over-the-top spectaculars presented in films like *Babes on Broadway*. Occasionally, as in *Boss of Rawhide*, they appeared quite authentic. Incorporation of elements like the trick shot artists in *Sierra Passage* had some basis in reality as well, as minstrel shows did in fact incorporate novelty acts of this type. Certainly, the appearance of minstrelsy in westerns as well as in mainstream films further validated blackface performance as normal in the 1930s and 1940s.

It should also be mentioned that westerns sometimes incorporated blackface without full minstrel show performances. Two actors who played this type of role were Frank Rice (1908–1993) and Ernest L. Stokes (1907–1964), known professionally as "Mustard and Gravy." They teamed up in 1933, at first on North Carolina radio, then appearing in B-western movies in the late 1940s and 1950s alongside such stars as Charles Starrett and Smiley Burnett. In some of these films (e.g., *Bandits of El Dorado* and *Feudin' Rhythm*, both 1949), they were in blackface. They also starred on a syndicated radio show in 1945.

Minstrel Shows in Short Films

Minstrel shows were also depicted in "shorts," films usually under 20 minutes in length, used to flesh out the programs in theaters during the 1930s and 1940s. The production values were often high in these short films.

One of the principal series of shorts was distributed by Warner Brothers under the Vitaphone brand. These were sometimes billed as "Broadway Brevities" (although that title did not necessarily appear in the films). They were produced between 1931 and 1943, and at least three of these shorts were built around elaborate recreations of a minstrel first part.

The first was called *Speaking of Operations* (18 minutes, 1933), which opened in a casting office where Mr. Maxwell (Dick Lane) didn't want to produce a minstrel show pitched to him by radio performers Pick and Pat. Suddenly Maxwell fell ill and was rushed to the hospital for an appendectomy, where he dreamed that the doctors, nurses and patients had turned into performers in a minstrel show. The operating theater then turned into a stage with nearly 50 minstrels, a mix of men and women, seated in ascending rows. All were in whiteface except for four blackface endmen (Pick and Pat, Al Bernard, and Lou Lubin). Maxwell himself was the interlocutor. There were jokes by the endmen and numbers by Gracie Barrie ("We Just Couldn't Say Goodbye"), the Rollickers ("Under the Cotton Moon"), booming baritone Joseph Pope Jones, and the Three X Sisters, who channeled both the Boswell Sisters and the Mills Brothers. The songs were all contemporary, and in fact the production resembled a variety show with contemporary music, comedy, and pretty chorus girls in big dance routines. Several of the principals (including Pick and Pat, Bernard, and the X Sisters) were well-known radio performers.

King for a Day (21 minutes, 1934) was even more unusual, with an all–African American cast including Bill Robinson, Ernest Whitman, and Dusty Fletcher. In this film, Robinson was turned away from an audition for a Harlem show; then he won the show in a crap game and made himself the star. The show was in an odd, minstrel-like setting, with interlocutor "Mr. Delacadeux" flanked by two female singers in gowns, three endmen in blackface, and Robinson in a suit. Behind them sat rows of 12 dancers and an eight-piece band. Robinson did a four-minute tap dance, and there were some typically corny jokes, one of which was racial in nature:

> FLETCHER: Boy, where was you born at?
> ROBINSON: I was born in Russia.
> FLETCHER: What part?
> ROBINSON: The darkest part, Asia.
> FLETCHER: Did you evah live near the Black Sea?
> ROBINSON: Brother, I *bathed* in the Black Sea.
> FLETCHER: And you forgot to dry off!
> (laughter)

Perhaps the most imaginative of these Warner shorts was *One for the Book* (18 minutes, 1940), which included one of the earliest film appearances of 19-year-old future star Betty Hutton. This film opened on a desktop in a study, cluttered with books. As the clock struck midnight, tiny figures, including Captain Kidd, Huckleberry Finn, Robinson Crusoe, and Rip Van Winkle, stepped out of their books and began conversing. (Rip Van Winkle: "I've been asleep for 20 years. When I woke up, everything was changed—except the jokes!")

They then noticed a new book, titled *Minstrel Days*, whereupon a tiny minstrel band marched in playing "Bandana Days" (from *Shuffle Along*), and the troupe was seated. The troupe consisted of an imposing interlocutor flanked by a 12-piece band (in striped minstrel outfits and top hats) and four endmen in blackface. Behind "Mr. Interlocutor" were two ascending rows of dancing girls, totaling about 34 performers in all. The cast launched into two more numbers from the musical *Shuffle Along*, "I'm Just Wild about Harry" and "Love Will Find a Way," with the latter turning into an elaborate dance routine. Cinderella (Hutton) then arrived and went into a swing arrangement of "Old Man Mose," followed by some business with the endmen and a wild jitterbug dance number. Along the way, eccentric dancer Hal Sherman portrayed Joe Miller, an 18th-century show business legend whose book, *Joe Miller's Jests*, was a notorious collection of ancient jokes. In fact, in show business any time-worn jest came to be known as a "Joe Miller." Here he told a couple from a little book:

> MILLER: What general in the army wears the biggest hat?
> INTERLOCUTOR: The one with the biggest head.
> MILLER: Well, that's out (crosses out entry in book). Let's see, here's another one. Why do they bury a Scotsman on the side of a hill?
> HUTTON: Because he's dead.
> MILLER: Uh ... (goes into a rubber-legged dance as the band launches into a sprightly tune)

It's a very contemporary (1940) production, with comedians, a big swing orchestra (unseen), and platoons of leggy chorus girls.

One of the more instructive shorts, also produced by Warner Brothers, was *Minstrel Days* (20 minutes, 1941). This was a docudrama about minstrelsy, opening with a reenactment of Daddy Rice meeting Jim Crow in Louisville in 1832 and adopting his "Jump Jim Crow" dance. That segment was followed by a big minstrel parade and recreations of performances by George Primrose, "Honey Boy" Evans, McIntyre and Heath, Eddie Leonard ("Ida") and Bert Williams ("Constantly"). Also included were clips of Al Jolson and Eddie Cantor in blackface, taken from their films. The short concluded with an elaborate, 10-minute minstrel first part, with chubby Bud Jamison as interlocutor, Al Herman and Billy Elliott as endmen, and Willie Best (black) also in the cast. Platoons of energetic dancers tapped and jitterbugged to a 1940s swing orchestra. The atmosphere was contemporary, but the songs were generally from the 19th century, including "Way Down Yonder in the Cornfield," "When You and I Were Young, Maggie," and "In the Evening by the Moonlight." The show concluded with the entire company singing "Minstrel Days." This short was reissued in 1946 and again in 1953.

Minstrel imagery also turned up in comedy shorts. In one *Our Gang* comedy, *Ye Olde Minstrels* (1941), the kids decided to raise money for the local chapter of the Red Cross by staging a minstrel show. They enlisted the help of Froggy's uncle, played by real-life minstrel Walter Wills. Spanky served as the interlocutor, with Mickey and Froggy as endmen and 35 kid minstrels in a pyramid bleacher. The cast included Buckwheat (the only black kid in the gang) and Darla (the only girl). None were in blackface. The show began with "Carry Me Back to Old Virginny," followed by a tambourine act, a tap-dancing specialty, Froggy singing "When De Profundis Sang Low C," a round of "Auld Lang Syne," and Uncle Walt singing "Lazy Moon."

Non-Minstrel Use of Blackface in Movies

In addition to full-fledged minstrel show recreations, there were, of course, numerous examples of blackface in Hollywood films of the 1930s and 1940s. Al Jolson and Eddie Cantor were known for "blacking up," but on occasion other major stars would do so as well. A sampling would include Buster Keaton in *College* (1927), Al Jolson in *The Jazz Singer* (1927), the three Moran and Mack films (1929–1933), Amos 'n' Andy in *Check & Double Check* (1930), Eddie Cantor in *Roman Scandals* (1933, in which he appears as an Ethiopian attendant in a Roman bath), Shirley Temple in *The Little Colonel* and *The Littlest Rebel* (1935), Irene Dunne in *Show Boat* (1936), Fred Astaire in *Swing Time* (1936, a tribute to Bill Robinson), Judy Garland in *Everybody Sing* (1938), George Murphy in *This Is the Army* (1943, singing "Mandy" in blackface as the soldiers look on), Donald O'Connor in *Curtain Call at Cactus Creek* (1950) and *Walking My Baby Back Home* (1953), and Keefe Brasselle in *The Eddie Cantor Story* (1953).

Sometimes blackface was used as a plot device, as in *Father Is a Bachelor* (1950), in which William Holden donned burnt cork to perform in a medicine show and then was not recognized later without the makeup. A little more bizarre was the sight of Joan Crawford as a temperamental Broadway star in *Torch Song* (1953), singing the big production number "Two Faced Woman" in "brownface" (apparently she was supposed to be a mulatto).

Perhaps the most notorious (today) use of blackface in a Golden Age film, however, was by Bing Crosby in the classic *Holiday Inn* (1942). However, the use of blackface must have seemed logical at the time. The premise of the film was that Crosby was running a Connecticut country inn that opened only on holidays, staging a big musical production for each occasion. Irving Berlin contributed a marvelous score celebrating a series of holidays, notably the mega-hit "White Christmas."

For Lincoln's birthday, Berlin wrote "Abraham," which was sung by Crosby in blackface, a top hat, and whiskers. Not only that, but the entire orchestra was also in blackface, and Crosby was joined midway through the song by girlfriend Marjorie Reynolds, who was also in blackface and dressed like Topsy from *Uncle Tom's Cabin*. The black waiters and staff who were serving the white patrons provided a backing chorus. There was also a cutaway to a black maid in the kitchen (Louise Beavers, a *real* African American), singing a verse to two little kids:

> When black folks lived in slavery,
> Who was it set the darkey free?
> Abraham! Abraham!

There was very little use of dialect in this scene (Crosby croons in his usual style), but the visual effect of all those white folks in blackface, in an upbeat movie otherwise unconnected to race, is startling, to say the least. However, *Holiday Inn* is a holiday classic, featuring major stars, and it is the film that gave us "White Christmas," so it can hardly be ignored. As a compromise, the movie is still broadcast, but often with the "Abraham" scene deleted. The scene is present, however, on home video releases. It frequently appears on YouTube, is taken down, is put up again, is taken down, is put up, is taken down, and so forth. This is a striking example of the difficulty of dealing with the reality of blackface (and minstrelsy) in earlier eras.

The success of the song "White Christmas" was so great that 12 years later Paramount produced a follow-up film loosely based on *Holiday Inn*, called *White Christmas* (1954). This one was in glorious color and starred Bing Crosby, Danny Kaye, Rosemary Clooney, and Vera Ellen. In this film, two Broadway entertainers staged a musical at a Vermont inn to boost the fortunes of their former army commander. Among other things, the four stars staged a big, flashy tribute to minstrelsy, with specialty material about corny jokes ("Mr. Bones, Mr. Bones") and the obligatory performance of "Mandy." This time, however, no one was in blackface. The film was a major box-office hit.

A snapshot of minstrelsy was offered in the low-budget production *Hollywood Varieties* (1950), a one-hour vaudeville show staged at the Belasco Theatre in Los Angeles, in which 14 acts performed, among them singing waiters, roller skaters, acrobats, trained dogs, trained seals, a country band, and a tap dancing harmonica player. Robert Alda was the emcee. In the midst of the proceedings, clean-cut young vaudevillians Glenn Vernon and Eddie Ryan bounced out on stage in gleaming white suits.

> EDDIE: You know, Glenn, when you talk about old-time show business there's one phase of it that you just cannot overlook.
> GLENN: Ha! And that is ...
> EDDIE: That is, the minstrel days!
> GLENN: Boy, weren't those good old minstrel shows wonderful?
> EDDIE: Oh, I should say they were. You know, Glenn, minstrels were the "daddy" entertainment.
> GLENN: That's right.
> EDDIE: They used to start their minstrel shows off with that famous old line, "Gentlemen, be seated!"

Glenn and Eddie then launched into a four-and-a-half-minute comedy act in which they donned bibs and methodically began putting on blackface makeup, wigs, white gloves, and oversized minstrel bowties, while simultaneously telling fast-paced endman jokes, as "a tribute to minstrel shows." At the end, they exited to a fast chorus of "Goodbye, My Lady Love."

Cartoons

Demeaning caricatures of African Americans appeared frequently in cartoons of the 1930s and 1940s. For the most part, they were presented as blacks in the American South or as natives of Africa, not explicitly as whites donning blackface makeup. One estimate is that about a third of the cartoons released by MGM in the late 1940s included a blackface, coon or mammy character.[30]

"The Censored Eleven" is a notorious group of Looney Tunes and Merrie Melodies cartoons that contain particularly egregious ethnic stereotypes and have been withheld from syndication by United Artists and its successors since 1968. They are *Hittin' the Trail for Hallelujah Land* (1931), *Sunday Go to Meetin' Time* (1936), *Clean Pastures* (1937, a parody of *Green Pastures*), *Uncle Tom's Bungalow* (1937, a parody of *Uncle Tom's Cabin*), *The Isle of Pingo Pongo* (1938), *Jungle Jitters* (1938), *All This and Rabbit Stew* (1941, a Bugs Bunny cartoon), *Coal Black and de Sebben Dwarfs* (1943, a parody of *Snow White and the Seven Dwarfs*), *Tin Pan Alley Cats* (1943), *Angel Puss* (1944) and *Goldilocks and the Jivin' Bears* (1944). Many of these cartoons are nevertheless available online.[31]

The cartoons mentioned above are only the tip of a vast black iceberg. Bugs Bunny pitched war bonds with a blackface Al Jolson imitation in *Any Bonds Today?* (1941). The following year, in *Fresh Hare"*(1942), he faced a firing squad that turned into a line of minstrels singing "Camptown Races." As late as 1953, in *Southern Fried Rabbit*, he put on blackface and pretended to be a slave to beg for mercy from "overseer" Yosemite Sam. In addition, from 1939 to 1950, Inki (an African boy hunter with big lips, a loincloth, and rings in his ears) appeared in five Looney Tunes cartoons by Chuck Jones.

There were nearly 20 "Jasper" installments in the stop-motion "Puppetoon" series (1942–1947) by George Pal. Jasper was a sweet little black boy with a large, round head, bulging eyes and a mouth outlined in white (like a minstrel). He was continually led astray by Scarecrow, as well as Scarecrow's friend (the crow sitting on his shoulder). "Puppetoons" was an ingenious production, with a separate hand-carved wooden puppet for each frame in which the character moved or changed expression. Sometimes there would be as many as 9,000 wooden figures or parts per cartoon. One of these, *Jasper's Minstrels* (1945), recreated a minstrel show. Little Jasper was intercepted in the field by Scarecrow, who, in order to impress the boy, regaled him with stories about his former life as an interlocutor with the Dixie Minstrels. The scene then dissolved into an all-scarecrow cast of minstrels, with corny jokes by endmen Tambo and Mr. Bones and a lavish series of musical numbers, including "Polly Wolly Doodle," "Carry Me Back to Old Virginny" and "Dixie."

Another cartoon minstrel show appeared in *Krazy Kat: The Minstrel Show* (1932). Krazy and Ignatz (the mouse) decided to put on a minstrel show in the town theater. They paraded into town to the tune of "A Hot Time in the Old Town," leading into the show with five minstrels in costume and blackface. The animals sang and danced to vintage songs (e.g., "Old Folks at Home," "My Old Kentucky Home," "At a Georgia Camp Meeting") and told corny jokes in exaggerated fashion until the audience began to pelt the stage, first with watermelon, and then with other objects. At this point, Chicken dropped an egg on Krazy's head, which cracked open to reveal a skunk who drove everyone out of the theater.

There were plenty of other examples of black caricature in cartoons (enough, in fact, for a book on the subject). In *Making Stars* (1935), Betty Boop was shown hosting a children's talent show including three caricatured black babies wiggling to "Old Folks at Home." They were lured offstage with a slice of watermelon. In case viewers missed the point, a squalling black baby in the audience was then pacified with—you guessed it—a slice of watermelon. *Scrub Me Mama with a Boogie Beat* (1941), a riff on the then-popular boogie woogie music, depicted big-lipped "coons" all sleeping in Lazytown until a sexy black torch singer arrived to show them how to jive. Animator Tex Avery, undeterred by complaints about his *Uncle Tom's Bungalow* (1937), followed up a decade later with *Uncle Tom's Cabaña* (1947).

No doubt the best-remembered example of animated blackface from this era, and something of a cause célèbre among film fans, is Disney's *Song of the South* (1946). This was a full-length feature film combining live action with about 25 minutes of animated segments; the plot was based on the Uncle Remus stories of author Joel Chandler Harris. Set on a Georgia plantation owned by the family of Johnny (Bobby Driscoll), a young white boy, the movie began with Johnny deciding to run away after his parents separated and his father left for Atlanta. Before he got far, Johnny was intercepted by Uncle Remus (James Baskette), a kindly, older black man who lived on the plantation. Uncle Remus spun a tale about Br'er Rabbit that convinced the lad to return home. Johnny and his pals Toby (a young black boy) and Ginny (a poor white girl) then became fast friends with Uncle Remus, who spun more tales for them, but Johnny's uptight mother tried to break them up. Eventually, the happiness and love that good-hearted Uncle Remus brought to all around him prevailed, and all ended well—Johnny's mom and dad even got back together.

Song of the South contained numerous musical numbers, mostly performed by the largely African American cast and the all-black Hall Johnson Choir. The featured number, "Zip-a-Dee-Doo-Dah," won an Academy Award for Best Song. Baskette, previously a little-known actor, won a special Academy Award for his performance.

Objections surfaced immediately from critics who complained about the movie's treatment of race. Part of this dislike stemmed from the widespread misconception that the story was set during slavery days. It was in fact set during the late 19th century, and the blacks on the plantation were sharecroppers, not slaves, although this fact was not made entirely clear. Nevertheless, critics said, it portrayed a world in which whites appeared superior to blacks.

Defenders maintained that the whole point of the film was how blacks and whites could come together, especially through their children. Blacks in the film, though of an inferior social status, were treated with respect by the whites. Moreover, the film itself was a technical and artistic tour de force, with a remarkable integration of animation and live action and a great deal of "heart" (even if sentimental). The Academy Award Baskette received was the first ever given to a black male actor.[32]

The controversy has continued to this day. The Walt Disney Company has steadfastly refused to reissue *Song of the South* on home video in the United States or allow it to be screened in recent years. The controversy even spawned two books, one pro (*Who's Afraid of the Song of the South? And Other Forbidden Disney Stories*) and one against (*Disney's Most Notorious Film: Race, Convergence, and the Hidden Histories of Song of the South*), both published in 2012. The controversy is emblematic of the conflict between acknowledging history and the fear that acknowledging it might perpetuate its evils.[33]

Later Film Reflections on Blackface and Minstrelsy

The use of blackface, and references to minstrel shows in particular, were pretty much expunged from motion pictures (and mass media generally) in the United States after the 1950s. When there was any reference to either, it was usually in the form of strident condemnation. However, that did not stop controversy or criticism from those who did not want the subjects addressed at all.

Black Like Me (1964) was very much a product of the 1960s—didactic, obvious, and delivering its message with a sledgehammer. Based on a nonfiction book of the same title, this film followed a white journalist (played by James Whitmore) in 1959 as he darkened his skin and traveled through the South as a black man, as research for a series of articles, to "see what it is like to be black." Though his ruse was undetected, the journey was at times harrowing. The *New York Times* called the film "melodramatic and unsubtle."[34]

Even darker, and angrier, was *Minstrel Man* (1977), a CBS-TV movie set in the minstrel world of the 1890s. In it, two black brothers took different paths, one (Glynn Turman) determined to succeed in the world of minstrelsy, while the other (Stanley Bennett Clay) was just as determined to discard blackface and minstrel routines and succeed as a respected ragtime musician. Clay was eventually lynched as an "uppity black," causing Turman to see the light, symbolically wipe off the burnt cork and put on a "respectable" show—after which he was fired.

Minstrel Man opened with a seven-minute traditional minstrel first part, which must have taken viewers in 1977 aback. The scene showed 12 black minstrels on stage in heightened blackface, plus a white interlocutor. There were corny endman jokes and songs that were certainly era appropriate—it sounded as if some of them might have been taken from phonograph records of the period. The show opened with "A High Old Time in Dixie" (1899), followed by the traditional "Gentlemen, be seated!" and then "Turkey in de Straw" and "Coon, Coon, Coon" (1900). As pointed out in chapter 2, the latter song, associated with Lew Dockstader, was actually a sly criticism of the racism of the Jim Crow era ("I wish I was a white man/'stead of a Coon! Coon! Coon!").

Although it won an NAACP Image Award and a Christopher Award, and the original score was nominated for an Emmy, *Minstrel Man* has evidently been suppressed. It is not available on DVD and is no longer aired. No explanation has ever been offered for its disappearance, although it may be related to that shocking opening or to the repeated use of "coon songs" (another example in the film is "Two New Coons in Town"). Copies may circulate online.

Not suppressed, but not watched much anymore, is the 1980 remake of *The Jazz Singer* starring pop singer Neil Diamond. Unlike the 1952 version of *The Jazz Singer*, which starred Danny Thomas and made no use of blackface at all, the 1980 film snuck blackface in though a rather unusual plot device. Diamond played Yussel, a young Jewish cantor, who wrote songs for a black R&B group on the side. When one member of the quartet took ill, Yussel filled in for him during a gig at a black nightclub by putting on an afro wig and blackface. All went well until a man in the audience noticed that Yussel's hands were white and yelled, "That ain't no brother, that's a white boy!" A brawl ensued and everyone was arrested.

The 1980 *Jazz Singer* film was a box-office and critical flop, and it is on several "worst movies" lists. Diamond was nominated for both a Golden Globe Award and a Golden Raspberry Award for Worst Actor for his role, but he won only the latter. However, the soundtrack album was an enormous hit, selling more than five million copies and remaining on the charts for more than two years. The movie also yielded three major singles hits: "Love on the Rocks," "Hello Again" and "America." Reputedly the album made more money than did the movie.

Soul Man (1986), starring C. Thomas Howell, was a comedy about a white kid who darkened his skin (via tanning pills) in order to qualify for a scholarship to Harvard that was available only to African Americans. He got the scholarship but was wracked with guilt when he met the struggling young black woman whom he had beaten out. He eventually decided to drop the charade and work his way through college.

There were protests against *Soul Man* lodged by the NAACP and director/activist Spike Lee, who complained about its mockery of affirmative action. They also complained about the use of blackface. Movie critics just thought it was a bad film, with Roger Ebert calling it a "dim-witted sitcom." Nevertheless, it was reasonably successful at the box office.[35]

Probably the most remarkable movie about blackface and minstrelsy in more recent years was Spike Lee's *Bamboozled* (2000). The story was reminiscent of Mel Brooks' *The Producers*, which was the story of a producer who created an outrageous show purposely designed to fail, only to see it become a big hit, with dire consequences. Essentially a long diatribe against racism and various other subjects (shallowness of the TV industry, self-aggrandizing protesters, etc.), *Bamboozled* leavened its heavy moralizing with moments of humor and jaw-dropping, over-the-top performance sequences.

Here pompous black TV executive Pierre Delacroix (Damon Wayans) wanted to get out of his contract, so he pitched *Mantan: The New Millennium Minstrel Show*, featuring black dancers and actors in exaggerated blackface; racist jokes; liberal use of "nigger," "coon," and watermelon; and offensive cartoons of black stereotypes. Instead of firing Delacroix for coming up with such a horror, the white network executives loved it; the show then went into production and became a major hit. However, everything began to fall apart as Delacroix's personal assistant, modern black woman Sloane (Jada Pinkett Smith), turned against him, and the two stars, tap-dancing Mantan and his angst-ridden sidekick Womack, both quit the show. Events then spiraled into violence: the militant rap group known as the Mau Maus abducted Mantan and executed him in a live Internet feed, the police found the rappers and killed them all (except for one white member), and Sloane shot Delacroix in his office while lecturing him on the evils of his creation. The movie was not exactly subtle.

Segments of *Mantan* were woven throughout *Bamboozled*, resembling a variety show more than a traditional minstrel show. At about 50 minutes in, following a careful illustration of the procedure for applying blackface makeup, there was a five-minute trial routine before a studio audience to test the concept, consisting of jokes and energetic dancing. The audience was initially stunned by the language and the blackface, but blacks and whites alike gradually warmed to it. At about one hour, three minutes, a four-minute chicken-stealing routine was depicted, and at one hour and eight minutes the animated show opening was seen, along with two bizarre commercials—one for a black-themed, sex-enhancing malt liquor called "Da Bomb," and another for "Timmi Hillnigger" ghetto-wear clothing. At an hour and 24 minutes, there was a five-minute segment of the final show. Now the studio audience (which included both blacks and whites) was in blackface as well, laughing and cheering. The stars entered the stage through a huge "darky mouth" (a device rarely used in authentic minstrel shows), told some jokes about their relatives, and segued into a big tap dance routine set to the music of a black "convict band."

Given the vivid imagery, no one who has seen this movie is likely to forget it. Its relationship to actual minstrel shows is tenuous at best, but its arguments about black representation (not offending others versus freedom of expression) attracted wide attention from critics. Although *Bamboozled* comes to its own clear conclusion, the film does present both sides of the debate.

The critical consensus was "good try, but it didn't work," though few were willing to dismiss the film entirely, perhaps because of Spike Lee's stature as a well-known black activist. The Rotten Tomatoes review aggregation site summarized critical reaction as follows: "*Bamboozled* is too over the top in its satire and comes across as more messy and overwrought than biting."[36] Audiences were less forgiving, giving the movie a limited run and poor results at the box office. However, it has since become something of a cult favorite.

Britain

Although Britain had a love affair with minstrelsy equal to that of the United States, its movie industry is much smaller and there are fewer examples of minstrelsy—or of blacks—on film there.

Film historian Stephen Bourne lists several early British silent films depicting blackface minstrelsy. The earliest is *The Wandering Negro Minstrels* (45 seconds, 1896), in which half a dozen blackface minstrels entertained on a London street—singing, dancing, and playing banjos, tambourines and bones—to the delight of passersby. Three years later, *The Lightfooted Darkey* (1899) showed a minstrel dancing at a racecourse. *Stump Speech* (1900) depicted the familiar minstrel show routine indicated in the title, while *Sambo* (1902) featured blackface comedian Sam Dalton smoking a cigar. *Nigger Courtship* (1903) showed a black couple spooning and kissing.[37]

In the 1930s, G.H. Elliott ("The Chocolate Coloured Coon"), one of the most famous British minstrel and music hall performers, appeared as one of the acts in the film *Music Hall* (1934), about a fundraiser to save a struggling theater. Harry Scott and Eddie Whaley, two African Americans who emigrated to Britain in 1909 and became major stars there, appeared in a Pathé short around 1933, performing a four-minute routine. It was set in a music room, in which Scott, the drawling, blackface partner, and Whaley, the debonair dandy (not in blackface), traded some jokes before launching into the 1906 song, "Crocodile Isle." This segment was later included in the Pathé compilation film *Pathétone Parade of 1936*.

By far the most notable British feature film of this era related to minstrelsy was *Kentucky Minstrels* (1934), a spin-off of the very popular radio series of the same name. This was a low-budget "quota quickie" produced by Universal, meant to satisfy a recent British law intended to encourage the development of the British film industry, which was being overwhelmed by Hollywood productions. The law did result in quite a few British-themed films that would probably otherwise not have been made, including this one. It is important as the first British film to feature black actors in starring roles.

The film opened with a couple at home listening to a radio broadcast of *The Kentucky Minstrels*. The scene quickly shifted to the studio with the minstrels on stage for a nearly nine-minute performance. About 35 men were seen in minstrel outfits, with perhaps 20 of them in blackface, doing a fast rendition of "Camptown Races." The interlocutor ("Mr. Johnson") delivered the traditional "Gentlemen, be seated!" opening line, followed by jokes from endmen Mott and Bayley (played by Scott and Whaley). Then came a song and dance to the tune "When I Marry Louisiana Lou" and a sketch by Mott and Bayley.

Following the show, Mott and Bayley were approached by white manager Mr. Goldman (C. Denier Warren), who told them that the minstrel show was closing and suggested that they should form a music hall act. But the partners were determined to start their own minstrel show, which failed. They then took a trolley to the seaside to perform for vacationers on the boardwalk (a longstanding English tradition), but the vacationers walked away and it began to pour. More setbacks followed, and they were eventually reduced to taking odd jobs, including pitching hay. Finally, they were tracked down by the now-rich manager Goldman, who wanted them for his new-style radio minstrel show.

The scene then shifted to approximately six minutes of the new show, which had about 35 or 40 men on stage in tuxedos and blackface. However, it was not the exaggerated style seen earlier; instead, the men were darkened without seeming cartoonish. The cast was scattered around the stage on risers, rather than in the traditional minstrel semicircle, and the show consisted of a succession of comedy bits and music, almost in the style of a black variety show. Sexy black singer Nina Mae McKinney did a big number, "I'm in Love with the Band," accompanied by the Debroy Somers Orchestra (white, but seen here in subdued blackface). Mott and Bayley then came out and danced in a major musical number. The film ended with a home scene of a contented couple listening to the "new minstrel show."

Universal certainly got a lot of mileage out of its modest investment in *Kentucky Minstrels*. Clips from this film, including the Nina Mae McKinney sequence, were used later in the short films *Swanee Showboat* (Ajax Pictures, c. 1940) and *Minstrel Days* (Comedy House, c. 1940).[38]

The two contrasting minstrel show sequences are certainly interesting in the context of the changes in show business during the 1930s, as is the enduring friendship between Mott and Bayley. The way in which they interacted with whites as equals speaks volumes about British social attitudes as compared with those in the United States at the time. *Kentucky Minstrels* was released in the United States under the title *Life Is Real*, but it has not been seen in many years and has never been available on home video. Today it exists as a 35-millimeter print at the Library of Congress and in fragments at the British Film Institute. Ideally one day it will be more widely available.

5

The Minstrel Show on Television

Minstrelsy had a shorter history on television than it did on records, on radio or in motion pictures, but many readers may be surprised that it had any such history at all. As television began its rapid rise as a mass medium in the late 1940s, the minstrel show appeared to be moving into the new arena as effortlessly as it had into earlier media.

Experimental Television

Minstrelsy on TV actually predated commercialization of the medium. A crude form of television was first demonstrated in the late 1920s, and experimental telecasts took place throughout the 1930s, although very few people had sets at that time (after all, radio was king). Finally, in 1939, NBC and CBS both began regular telecasts over their experimental stations in New York City, and in July 1941 both were awarded the first commercial television licenses.

On January 24, 1940, during the experimental period, NBC telecast a fascinating program called *The NBC Pages and Guides Minstrel Show* over its New York station, W2XBS-TV. The pages and guides were young men who were employed by NBC at its studios in a special training program. They were assigned to various departments, giving them exposure to network executives and making the program an excellent entree into the business. It was also highly competitive (today, only about 1 percent of those who apply are accepted). Young men were allowed to remain in the program for only a year or so before they had to either move up in the company or leave.

Pages and guides were an intelligent, motivated and extroverted bunch, most of them recent college graduates, and in 1940 the current group was given the chance to stage a minstrel show on NBC's experimental TV station. There were only about 2,000 TV sets in the area, so even if they failed, it would do little damage to NBC's reputation.

NBC needn't have worried. The 30-minute telecast was brimming with youthful enthusiasm, yet tight and professional. This was a very talented group of young men. No video survives (a practical means of video recording did not exist until the introduction of kinescopes in 1947), but the program was audio recorded, and scripts, notes and other descriptive documentation exist in the NBC collection at the Library of Congress.

It is worth describing the show, as it reflects what a well-done amateur minstrel show may have looked like at this time. (The show was written, directed and acted entirely by the pages, with no professional involvement.) It opened with staff announcer Ray Forrest introducing page/interlocutor Casper Kuhn standing in front of a curtain. The curtain then parted, and the ensemble went into the familiar song "Bring Back Those Minstrel Days," followed by the entrance of the endmen to "Oh, Dem Golden Slippers" and then the traditional "Gentlemen, be seated!" This sequence was followed mostly by music, including "Can't You Heah Me Callin' Caroline," "Ida," "The Sheik of Araby" (by a "jazz trio"), "Without a Song," a tap dance, an 1890s medley (quartet), "I'm Gonna Quit on Saturday," "Mighty Lak' a Rose," "Chinatown, My Chinatown" (trio), "Mandy" and "Going to the Dogs," plus the comedy monologue, "Ham on Rye."

Despite the presence of endmen, there were few traditional minstrel jokes. The humor was mostly in comic introductions, monologues, and (in later shows) burlesques of plays and operas.

The show closed with Kuhn inviting viewers (all of whom were in the New York area) to visit the NBC studios for a tour: "We'll take good care of you. Until then, we say goodbye and thank you for looking…. And now the grand finale, with the entire company singing 'Waiting for the Robert E. Lee'" (in a medley with "Darktown Strutters' Ball"). Announcer Forrest then invited viewers to send in cards sharing their opinions of the show.

The staging was in a small studio, with sketches indicating that the company was grouped together in a modified minstrel-style semi-circle. About 20 pages took part, most of them performing either solo or in the trio or quartet. The majority wore minstrel jackets and held tambourines, and some were outfitted with top hats, canes, and "negro wigs" (all rented). Apparently none wore blackface, and there was little or no use of dialect.[1]

Some of these young men were extremely talented, and they sounded well rehearsed. The most famous name among the pages was 24-year-old baritone Earl Wrightson, who would go on to a stellar career as a singer and actor on stage, television and recordings. Casper Kuhn (age 24), the glib interlocutor, would become a prominent announcer under the name Dick Dudley. Writer/arranger Bob Button (age 24) would later become director of the Voice of America and then a satellite and cable executive. Years later, at the age of 75, he founded the Bob Button Orchestra. Other pages included William Garden (later a TV director), Steve DeBaun (advertising writer and producer), and Walter Covell (actor and executive). NBC announcer Ray Forrest was himself only 24 when the show aired. He went on to a long career as a TV announcer, host and newsman.

Early TV broadcasters kept in close touch with their small bands of viewers, mailing out weekly schedules and soliciting feedback via postcards. Apparently viewers liked what they saw of this minstrel show, because the pages and guides telecast three more shows, on March 24, May 14, and July 16, 1940, gradually expanding to more than an hour in length. At the start of the second telecast, Forrest remarked on how well received the first show had been. In addition, the troupe appeared on stage at the Ritz Theater in a benefit for the New York Fund Campaign on May 16.

Essentially the same cast of pages appeared in each of these shows, with Kuhn as interlocutor and "Bring Back Those Minstrel Days" as the opening theme song. The subject of the second telecast was Broadway, with Kuhn imitating staccato-voice Walter Winchell and recalling Broadway songs and stars of the past. There was also an extended parody of a Metropolitan Opera broadcast, hosted by Milton J. Doublecross (Kuhn) and introducing a new, ridiculous opera, "True Blue." The May telecast was in the form of a medicine show, with Kuhn as Dr. Eustace McGargle of the World Wide Remedy Company.

This show was punctuated by medicine pitches from Kuhn, as well as a new opera by Bob Button, spoofing *Gone with the Wind* (General Sherman: "Will someone please tell me, which way is the sea?"). The July telecast was billed as a "Summertime Revue." Besides old classics, some newer songs such as "Two Cigarettes in the Dark" and "Smoke Gets in Your Eyes" were included in the later telecasts.

Like the members of a college fraternity or a local lodge, these young performers knew each other well and worked easily together. They put on a professional-sounding show, but they were also clearly having fun. There was laughter and encouragement from the sidelines, and when announcer Forrest began to close out the second telecast a little too quickly, there were impromptu calls to "give some credits!" (to which he willingly acceded). The good-natured spirit and youthful energy fairly jump off these audio recordings. There is not the slightest suggestion of mockery of African Americans (or of much relating to African Americans); it's more like a variety show using some minstrel tropes such as costumes, tambourines, and "Gentlemen, be seated!"

Obviously many minstrel shows of this period did retain conventions such as blackface and dialect, but *The NBC Pages and Guides Minstrel Show* is a reminder that this was not always the case.

"An Epidemic of Minstrel Shows"

As World War II came to an end and servicemen began to stream home, there was a vast wave of patriotism and concomitant fascination with American history and traditions. This trend was reflected in all media. Many popular Hollywood films from this time period were nostalgic. One of the top films of 1946 was Disney's *Song of the South* (set in the 19th century), and among the top-grossing films of the next few years were *Unconquered* (set in colonial America), *Mother Wore Tights* (early 1900s vaudeville), *Red River* (the Old West), *Easter Parade* (early 1900s America), and *Look for the Silver Lining* (a bio of 1920s star Marilyn Miller). Moviegoers also flocked to *The Jolson Story* and *Jolson Sings Again*.

Music was likewise filled with nostalgia. Among the best-selling records of the late 1940s were new versions of "Whispering Hope" (1868), "When You Were Sweet Sixteen" (1898), "Because" (1902), "I Wonder Who's Kissing Her Now" (1909), "Peg o' My Heart" (1913), "Twelfth Street Rag" (1916), "Baby Face" (1926), "I'm Looking over a Four Leaf Clover" (1927), "Prisoner of Love" (1931), and "Heartaches" (1931), as well as new songs that *sounded* old, like "The Old Lamplighter" and "Cruising Down the River." Old-timers like Al Jolson and Joe Howard made comebacks, and Dorothy Shay ("The Park Avenue Hillbilly") built a whole career on celebrating—or mocking—rural America.[2]

One aspect of this pervasive nostalgia for simpler times was the minstrel show, which flourished not only in the media but also in amateur productions in town halls across America. A 1948 story in a Pittsburgh newspaper called it an "epidemic" and explained it as follows:

> Theatrical costumers report that an epidemic of minstrel shows seems to be sweeping the country. There were 25 or 30 last week in the Pittsburgh district alone. The local costumers were hard-pressed to outfit all the actors and had to call for help from other cities. Only explanation is that minstrel shows seem to have a special appeal to ex–GI's, offering, as they do, some of the camaraderie they knew at times while in the service.[3]

Even sports heroes got in on the act. In 1949, 10 members of the league-leading New York Yankees put on a "Yankees Minstrels" show at a benefit for St. Gabriel's Church in Marlboro, New Jersey. Serving as interlocutor was infielder George "Snuffy" Stirnweiss, with first baseman Tommy Henrich as endman and Phil Rizzuto, Hank Bauer, and Bobby Brown among the others participating with songs and jokes.[4]

Early television tapped into this wave of nostalgia. There were even commercials using a minstrel theme, one example being spots for Tavern Pale Beer.[5]

Local television stations were just beginning to come on the air year by year in the late 1940s, and it was not surprising that some would mount their own minstrel telecasts. These programs can be difficult to trace due to the paucity of television listings (and the fluidity of schedules) in those very early days. However, in New York, Al Bernard—that indefatigable promoter of minstrelsy—began producing shows for DuMont station WABD at least as early as 1945. Telecasts of *Al Bernard's Minstrel Men* aired in February and March of that year, and in June 1948 Bernard wrote that he had "just recently" staged another minstrel show on WABD and was expecting another in September. As discussed in chapter 2, he produced a 78-rpm album of minstrel music in 1948 ("Al Bernard's Merry Minstrel Show"), which was structured very much like a radio or TV broadcast. Bernard also made personal appearances at fairs and at the popular Village Barn country music nightclub in Manhattan. Sadly, his renewed career, which had begun in the 1910s, was cut short by his death on March 6, 1949.[6]

In the Midwest, the newly opened Crosley TV stations in Ohio aired a rather popular Sunday night series called *The Olympus Minstrels* for a full year beginning in October 1948. Originating at WLWT in Cincinnati, it was carried on other Crosley-owned stations in the region as well. The star was 63-year-old endman Joe Dunlevy, who had begun his minstrel career in 1904 and later toured with the Barlow and Primrose Minstrels. In the early 1910s, he formed his own troupe, which toured Europe and Africa, and then (in 1914) went into vaudeville and later radio until his retirement in 1940. Dunlevy had settled in the Cincinnati area and was no doubt delighted to be invited back on stage again. With Bob Bently (and later Harry Hall), he formed the show's blackface comedy team of Dot and Dash, dancing and cracking old jokes.

In an interview, Dunlevy remarked on the changes from the days of stage minstrelsy: "Radio's penchant for gobbling up material still amazes Dunlevy, who once used the same song in an act for seven years. He recalls one (stage) minstrel team that in its whole career used only three acts."[7]

The Olympus Minstrels was WLWT's biggest production, with a cast of 25 and a 15-piece orchestra. Also in the cast were interlocutor Bill Thall (a veteran of the *WLS Barn Dance* and *WLW Midwestern Hayride*), singers Bob Shreve and Ann Ryan, and the Swanee River Boys, a noted white gospel quartet founded in 1938. Guest stars, such as banjo virtuoso Eddie Peabody, made appearances.

The show was billed as "entertainment for the whole family, taking you back to the old popular burnt-cork opries with their rhythmic songs, end men gags, and gay costumes." It was well received, and the Dodge dealers of Greater Cincinnati liked it enough to act as the sponsor. The show opened with "Dodge" spelled out on five tambourines, along with the names of 10 local dealers, also on tambourines. Later Dot and Dash held up giant tambourines emblazoned with the legends "Dodge Job Rated Trucks" and "Air-O-Ride Seats."[8]

There were no public complaints about *The Olympus Minstrels* (or at least none that

I have been able to locate). The reason it ended, in October 1949, was not announced, but it may well have been due to the health problems of star endman Dunlevy. He passed away in April 1950 after what was described as a "long illness."[9]

On the West Coast, ABC's KGO-TV in San Francisco launched *The Show Boat Minstrels* a few months after the station went on the air in May 1949. A half-hour evening program, it aired for at least two months in late 1949 and early 1950, but little else is known about this show.

No TV market was more interested in minstrelsy than Los Angeles, America's entertainment capital. There had been intermittent experimental TV broadcasts in Los Angeles since the early 1930s, operating for the few hundred sets in the area; however, the first commercial station—KTLA—did not go on the air until January 1947. This was followed by KTSL (operated by West Coast radio mogul Don Lee) in May 1948. In August, KTSL broadcast *The Mississippi Minstrels*, a half-hour minstrel show with a cast of eight, including endmen Jimmy Scribner and Dick Haynes and interlocutor Harry Stanton.

Scribner (1907–1975) was a veteran white radio performer, best known for the radio serial *The Johnson Family*, which ran on Mutual from 1937 to 1950 and was set among African Americans in a southern town—a sort of rural *Amos 'n' Andy*. Scribner was a wizard with voices, including black dialect, sometimes playing as many as 22 characters in a single show. He also hosted children's programs, including *Gypsy Joe* on radio and *Sleepy Joe* on ABC television (1949). Haynes was a popular local disc jockey, and Stanton a long-time radio singer and actor who had been interlocutor on NBC's *Cotton Blossom Minstrels* in 1930.

On *Mississippi Minstrels*' first (and possibly only) telecast, Stanton appeared in a ghost routine, Scribner told one of his familiar "Uncle Remus" tales, and Haynes and the Chordsmen Quartet offered some songs. A reviewer for *Variety* happened to catch the telecast, and he was not kind, writing that "worn down routines, weak interlocutor and unharmonious harmony group make *Mississippi Minstrels* a poor video entry." He went on to say that the sound was poor and movement limited and that the program was held together by the two endmen, who "could not be expected to carry the entire program." We should not underestimate the challenges inherent in mounting this complicated format on live television in 1948, especially at a local station.[10]

In March 1950, CBS affiliate KTTV-TV debuted *McMahan's Minstrels*, sponsored by McMahan's Furniture Stores. This program ran for about three months, live from El Patio Theatre, and was better received than *Mississippi Minstrels*. The writer and director of *McMahan's Minstrels* was Arthur "Tiny" Stowe, who also served as the jovial interlocutor. "Tiny" ("all 500 lbs of him") had a long career, beginning with the Lasses White Minstrels in the 1920s, and he appeared on several radio minstrel series of the 1930s (see chapter 3). In the 1940s, Stowe ran his own ad agency in Los Angeles, and he clearly knew how to interest sponsors in his projects. His endmen were Peenie Elmo and Marvin "Bud" Harrison, who had a blackface act in vaudeville and minstrelsy as "Seben 'n' Eleven" for nearly 20 years. (They had each also appeared in a few films.) Stowe explained that when he was putting the show together, he remembered them and tracked them down, finding them working as a bartender and a bricklayer.[11] Norwood Smith and big band vocalist Tudy Williams provided vocals.

The show was fast paced, with Elmo and Harrison (in costume and blackface) delivering traditional minstrel gags and stories. A Dixieland band also appeared. "With the return of the Charleston and other reminders of the good old days," enthused a McMahan's representative, "what could be more apropos than the return of the wonderful minstrel shows?"[12]

Although McMahan ended its sponsorship in June 1950, KTTV apparently liked what it saw and brought back Stowe for *Tiny Stowe's All Star Minstrels* in January 1951. Elmo and Harrison returned as endmen, heading a cast of 35 including singers and gorgeous dancers (this was Hollywood, after all!). Some episodes were built around themes— for example, for St. Patrick's Day the show had an all-Irish episode, with 21-year-old guest Anita Gordon singing "Too Ra Loo Ra Loo Ral." The show ran until July 1951, its end possibly hastened by the fact that endman Harrison was badly burned in a fire in May.

The most successful of the local Los Angeles minstrel shows, and the only one to attract controversy, was KTLA's *Dixie Showboat*, which premiered in March 1950 at virtually the same time as KTTV's *McMahan's Minstrels*. A newspaper called it part of the "latest craze of TV for old-fashioned minstrel shows."[13]

Dixie Showboat was a major production, set on a docked Mississippi River showboat and featuring music, dancing and comedy acts. The original interlocutor, Frank Bull, was quickly replaced by Dick Lane as the captain and host of the showboat. Comedy was provided by blackface comics Peanuts and Popcorn (John Swor and Harry Cody), as well as comic Ralph Peters. Others in the large cast included singer Jacqueline Fontaine, accordionist Tony Lovello, "stand-up pianist" Maurice Rocco, the Dixiettes dancing trio, and

KTLA's *Dixie Showboat* was helmed by Captain Dick Lane and starred endmen Peanuts and Popcorn.

Nappy Lamare and his Straw Hat Strutters Dixieland band (later replaced by Rosy McHargue's jazz band). There were African American performers in the regular cast as well, including Scatman Crothers and jazz violinist Ginger Smock.

Although there were minstrel-style routines by Swor and Cody, it is unclear whether the show ever presented a traditional "minstrel first part." Mostly it seems to have been a southern-themed variety show with plenty of beautiful dancing girls and hot Dixieland music, which was then in vogue. A typical interchange had the friendly Captain Lane walking up to the winsome young Smock, who was seated off to the side in the audience of "passengers," and asking her if she would "mind playing ... a little something" on her violin. She replied, "Well, I wouldn't mind, but in front of all these people and with a great big band with me?" Lane insisted, and she walked to the center of the stage with a big smile and launched into a hot version of "What Is This Thing Called Love?" The audience loved it.[14]

Unlike early local radio minstrel shows, which often used amateurs, this and other local television productions used professionals. Dick Lane was an actor and announcer who had appeared in dozens of films from 1936 onward. When Paramount Studios launched KTLA in 1947, he immediately became one of its principal announcers and was widely known for his colorful coverage of wrestling and the roller derby. Lane was nominated for a local Emmy for his work on *Dixie Showboat*. Old-time minstrel John Swor (1877–1965) had been George Moran's original partner in the 1910s, before Moran formed the Two Black Crows. Cody (1896–1956) was a film and TV actor with many minor credits.

Paramount's goal was to set up its own television "network," essentially a syndication service for the stations coming on the air across America. Several KTLA-produced shows were filmed and run on other stations. *Dixie Showboat* was seen on WNAC (Boston), WCPO (Cincinnati), WOC (Davenport), WFBM (Indianapolis), WDSU (New Orleans), WPIX (New York), and KING (Seattle), among others. In its trade advertising, Paramount pitched the show as "a glorious American era recaptured." Despite the fact that it was filmed (presumably by kinescope), only one episode is known to survive today, at the UCLA Film and Television Archives.

An anecdote about *Dixie Showboat*, which may or may not be apocryphal, sheds light on the way blackface, and television itself, were viewed in the medium's early days. On the same night (Monday) that KTLA televised *Dixie Showboat*, it also aired a bone-dry public affairs discussion program called *Teleforum*, hosted by 75-year-old Dr. Rufus B. von KleinSmid, chancellor of the University of Southern California. On one particular evening two senators were scheduled to appear to discuss a weighty topic. When they arrived at the station, they were ushered into makeup, where the makeup artist thought they were there for *Dixie Showboat* and made them up in blackface. The politicians, never having been on television, assumed that this was what was required for the new medium. When they walked into the *Teleforum* studio, however, Dr. KleinSmid was horrified and rushed them back to makeup to have it taken off—barely in time go on the air live. Their ears, it was said, still had traces of black makeup.[15]

Could this hilarious incident have actually happened? In the early days of live television, makeup was indeed used to counter the glaring lights of black-and-white TV and produce a natural look on the screen. Moreover, the blackface used on *Dixie Showboat* was subdued and might have been mistaken for something else. Everyone was learning their way, and sensitivity to mistakes (racial or otherwise) was not as high as it is today.

A more serious racial contretemps erupted during *Dixie Showboat*'s first few weeks on the air. Originally not only endmen Swor and Cody but also the entire studio band, led by Nappy Lamare, were in blackface. This arrangement raised the ire of some viewers, as reported in the following story, which appeared in *Down Beat* magazine shortly after the show premiered:

> Protest TV Show Minstrel Makeup
>
> Hollywood—TV station KTLA, in response to a deluge of complaints and threats of picketing by the National Association for the Advancement of Colored People, has announced that there will be no more "blackface" makeup worn by performers on the new weekly show, *Dixie Show Boat*, which features Nappy Lamare's band.
>
> On the first two shows, all of Nappy's bandsmen appeared in the old style minstrel man's makeup despite the fact that, in the traditional minstrel show, makeup never was worn by musicians and usually only by "end men." Situation was especially embarrassing to Nappy's drummer, Zutty Singleton (now with Art Hodes in Chicago), and brought sharp protests from many sources.[16]

To clarify, blackface *was* sometimes worn by musicians in minstrel shows, although the practice had become less common in the mid–20th century. Drummer Zutty Singleton was an African American and did not appear on the show (perhaps in protest?). The elimination of blackface apparently applied to band members only, as comedians Swor and Cody appear blacked up in later photos, although not in exaggerated fashion. Interestingly, there were no complaints (or at least none that reached the media) over their appearance. It may be that the use of blackface was still considered acceptable in 1950, at least on a local level, if it was limited and the comedy material did not directly mock African Americans. Furthermore, the show was giving exposure to African American performers by including them in its cast. After the initial demands were met, there were no further protests. The NAACP may simply have chosen to fight other battles. *Dixie Showboat* continued for more than three years, ending its run in May 1953.

Television ownership was not yet universal, and the programs telecast in the late 1940s were seen by a limited number of homes that had sets. But TV penetration was expanding rapidly, and stations were coming on the air across the country. In 1946, there were only an estimated six thousand sets nationwide, but a year later this had grown to 250,000; by 1949, it had increased to more than one million, and by 1953 to nearly 25 million, or about 50 percent of all U.S. homes.[17] It was time for the networks to get into the minstrel business.

Network Television

There were warning signs that blackface minstrelsy might face mounting opposition, as observed in the uproar over NBC radio's planned *National Minstrel Show* in 1948. Nevertheless, minstrelsy was often referenced within network shows without generating complaints. For example, in an episode of *The Bigelow Show*, which aired on CBS-TV in the fall of 1949, co-stars Paul Winchell and his dummy Jerry Mahoney "appear[ed] on the show as endmen in an old-time minstrel show." Local stations were also broadcasting minstrel shows without any real opposition.

It was widely reported in the spring of 1949 that the legendary Al Jolson had a network television minstrel show in the works, tentatively called *Al Jolson's Minstrels*. Jolson was riding high at this time, on the heels of *The Jolson Story* and *Jolson Sings Again*, and if anyone could pull it off, he could. He said he wanted to kick the show off with an old-time minstrel parade through New York's Times Square. Said Jolson, "There's a million jokes—all of 'em bad. But people will laugh at 'em when you put 'em in blackface. If I were only 35 years old ..." However, the show never came to pass.[18]

NBC-TV did try out a program called *Broadway Minstrels* in May 1948, a couple of months before the *National Minstrels* radio debacle. The show was a bit of a mess, with a constantly changing cast and format, and no regular host. It started out as an "all colored revue" featuring tap dancer Derby Wilson, singer Maxine Sullivan, basso Theodore Hines, comedian Tom Fletcher, and the Deep River Boys ("colored quartet, dressed in regular business suits singing the songs popular with a minstrel show"). After two weeks, the name was changed to *Broadway Jamboree* and the show began to feature both black and white singers, dancers and comedians, including old-timer Gus Van. Then Jack Albertson was added to tie things together as a "Broadway columnist" hunting down acts. These included a square dance team from Isaac Young High School in New Rochelle, New York. Then Albertson was dumped, and an unseen voice took viewers through the pages of *Variety* pointing out talent that would then appear. The show mercifully ended after seven telecasts.[19]

In January 1949, ABC-TV tried something closer to a real minstrel show with *American Minstrels of 1949*. It was actually a cross between a classic minstrel show and a modern, fast-paced variety show—the direction in which many thought minstrelsy was headed (i.e., a variety show with blackface). Veteran radio stars Pick and Pat headlined, performing in blackface and delivering jokes and routines throughout the program. The rest of the hour was occupied by singers, dancers, and comedians, some of whom were also in blackface. Some guests were real old-timers, like vaudevillians Smith and Dale doing their "Doctor Kronkheit" routine, but most were newer talent. The rest of the regular cast was made up of attractive 20-somethings, including emcee Jack Carter, a nightclub comic who was just getting his start in TV. Carter has been described as one of the "slapstick, mugging, gag-a-minute comics who made early TV look like a vaudeville stage." Vocalist Mary Small was a former child star of the 1930s, known as "the little girl with the big voice," while tenor Jimmy Burrell was best known for his appearance in the World War II film *This Is the Army* while he was still in the service. Vivacious tap dancer Estelle Sloan had also appeared in several films.[20]

Variety reviewed *American Minstrels of 1949* twice, first complaining that "the combination of minstrelsy and modern vaudeville doesn't jell." It said that the brash, fast-talking Carter was OK but that there was too much Pick and Pat and that their leisurely, old-time entertainment contrasted with the fast modern acts around them. In one routine, the retinue of minstrels arrayed behind the two comics even looked bored! Production values were also subpar. However, the second review, two weeks later, was much more favorable. It singled out show-stopping acts by dance team the Three Winter Sisters, tap dancer Hal Leroy, dancer-comedians the Three Wiles (who "opened with a novelty tap including some magic tricks and closed with a slick wooden soldiers routine"), and comic Kenneth Whitmer (who "played a musical cigar, an umbrella whistle, a miniature fiddle and an exploding flute"). Pick and Pat were "particularly funny in a blackout sketch with Carter, making liberal use of pratfalls."[21] Another paper complained about the inconsistent and even sloppy use of blackface, pointing out that sometimes the faces were black while the hands were white.[22]

But if white reviewers in 1949 had no problem with blackface, aside from its sloppy use, the black press felt differently. In February, the *New York Age* carried the following headline: "Raps Television Minstrel Act: Many Protest Pick and Pat Show on WJZ."

> Mounting protests at the insulting Dixieland caricature of the Negro as portrayed by the two white comedians, Pick and Pat, in their weekly televised show, titled "American Minstrel," heard and seen every Thursday night over WJZ-TV, channel 7, culminated this week in a number of theatre and nightclub performers telling their views of the matter to The New York Age.[23]

The protesters were led by popular black disc jockey and bandleader Willie Bryant,[24] who contrasted the situation with that from the previous year when black entertainer Lucky Millinder was criticized by the NAACP for his involvement with NBC radio's proposed *National Minstrels*. "Why are two white comedians, whom I understand are from the South, given the green light to ridicule the race in this manner?" Bryant pointed out that the distasteful aspects of minstrelsy—black faces, white lips, etc.—were a feature of the show and were being seen by thousands, including those in bars and restaurants in Harlem. A spokesman for WJZ responded to the protest by telling the *Age* that the act was simply "blackface, the same as *Amos 'n' Andy*."

Walter Winchell picked up on the "bitter protests" against the program in his nationally syndicated column: "Bitter protests have come in over the 'American Minstrel' program because of the Uncle Tom approach. To top things, the comedians are Pick & Pat—Southern whites!"[25]

American Minstrels of 1949 did have black defenders. Old-timer Noble Sissle, who had co-hosted NBC radio's *National Minstrels/Swingtime at the Savoy* a year earlier (and who had wanted that program to be a real minstrel show), came to the defense of the TV series and of Pick and Pat in an impassioned editorial, saying,

> I have never yet got the thrill in a theatre the minstrel gives me. How could I when since childhood every church, club, YMCA, school, college, north, south, east and west, England, Australia and around the world loved and imitated the American Negro minstrel? When Marian Anderson and the world stops singing Negro spirituals and loving them, then I'll stop loving the minstrel. They are both sacred to me and so American.[26]

American Minstrels was canceled two weeks later, on March 17, after a two-month run with no sponsor. The protests may or may not have played a role in the show's demise. *Billboard* commented that the program, which was sustaining and had a weekly talent budget of $2,200, was dropped in a wave of cost cutting. That explanation was plausible given the perilous state of ABC's finances at the time, but the protests surely could not have helped.[27]

That was the last "minstrel" series on American network television. However, minstrelsy did not disappear entirely from the networks. There were still skits and musical numbers invoking minstrelsy—for example, the routine in a 1953 episode of the top-rated *Colgate Comedy Hour* in which Teresa Brewer sang Eddie Leonard's "Roll Them Roly Boly Eyes" (1912) backed by six girls in minstrel outfits with tambourines, seated in a semi-circle minstrel-style, and two male dancers (no one was in blackface).[28]

Even more remarkable were the full-scale recreations of a minstrel first part staged on two of the top-rated Sunday night series: *The Fred Waring Show* and *Ed Sullivan's Toast of the Town*. Viewers may have been surprised when they tuned in to the Waring show on October 8, 1950, and saw Waring's familiar male chorus (the Pennsylvanians) in blackface and minstrel costumes (certainly viewers who see the video today are). The entire second half of the live hour was devoted to a full, 24-minute minstrel first part, with 20 men on stage in blackface, minstrel tuxedos and white gloves, waving tambourines. The onstage band, directed by Fred Culley, was also in blackface. Waring, in whiteface, served as interlocutor, seated in the throne-like middle chair. The endmen were the show's resident comedians Poley McClintock (Bones) and Lumpy Brannum (Tambo).

This performance was intended to be a historical recreation, so the songs were from the 19th century, opening with "Angels Meet Me at the Crossroads" by all, followed by jokes by Tambo and Bones, and then "Gentle Annie" by Leo Bernache, "Little Brown Jug" by Eric Carlson, "Old Dog Tray" by Hugh Fleming, "Camptown Races" by Clyde Sechler and Ray Sax, "I'll Be Dar" by Leonard Kranendonk, "Oh! Sam" by Gordon Goodman, and "Oh! Susanna" by all. The show ended with an exceptionally tender reading of "Kentucky Babe" by Joe Marine and the glee club. The jokes were classic minstrel fare, often involving wordplay.[29]

> BONES: Tell me, Mr. Tambo, what is your first name?
> TAMBO: Uh, "Sufficient."
> BONES: Suh-who?
> TAMBO: Sufficient.
> BONES: Why, how come that yo' first name, Tambo?
> TAMBO: Well, suh, I was the 17th child in my family. And when I was born, my maw, she says, "that's sufficient!"
> (laughter)

One of the funnier bits was by banjo player Stuart Churchill,

Top: Fred Waring as interlocutor on a 1950 minstrel show recreation on CBS. *Bottom:* Waring's minstrel show featured his chorus, the Pennsylvanians, in blackface. Here Joe Marine solos on "Kentucky Babe."

seated at the back of the group, who from time to time would stand up unexpectedly and ask, "Now, Mr. Interlocutor?" Each time Waring would patiently respond, "Not now, Mr. Churchill," and move on. Finally, as the show was about to end, Churchill stood up again. This time Waring acquiesced, and Churchill moved down to the front and ripped into a banjo solo with clever lyrics that led seamlessly into a final commercial for sponsor General Electric's TV sets.

The live show was expertly choreographed, and Waring's soloists and chorus were, as usual, top notch. It was perhaps one of the most accurate representations of classic 19th-century minstrelsy in modern media.

The episode was so successful, in fact, that it led to two more, in 1951 and 1953. The October 1951 telecast opened with a minstrel parade, during which Waring encountered the eminent actor Raymond Massey. Massey, a commanding presence best known for portraying Abraham Lincoln on stage and screen, reflected on how he had gotten his start in minstrel shows, and Waring and Massey (in normal whiteface) then sat in front of the chorus and described the show as it unfolded. Behind them were 16 men in blackface, tuxedos and white gloves, as well as an interlocutor (in whiteface), endmen McClintock and Brannum, and the band. The jokes and songs were mostly the same as in 1950, including "I'll Be Dar" by Mr. Vaughn Comfort (Kranendonk), "Camptown Races" by Primrose and Dockstader (Sechler and Sax), "Mah Lindy Lou" by Manuel Romain (Goodman), "Nobody" and a soft shoe dance by Massey and Waring, and "Oh! Susanna" by all. The entire segment ran about 15 minutes.

By March 1953, *The Fred Waring Show* had been cut back to 30 minutes, and that season's minstrel show was an 11-minute segment. It began with a parade in the park and the band playing "Dixie." Then 25 men were seen onstage in blackface, minstrel tuxedos and white gloves, with Waring (in whiteface) as the interlocutor. The endmen were again McClintock and Brannum. The repertoire was unchanged: "Angels Meet Me at the Crossroads" by all, "I'll Be Dar" by Kranendonk, "Camptown Races" by Sechler and Sax, "Mah Lindy Lou" by Goodman, "Old Folks at Home" by Marine, and "Oh! Susanna" by all. The telecast emanated live from Kansas City, Missouri, where Waring was then on tour.

Waring toured widely, and he incorporated the minstrel show recreation into his road show at least as late as 1956. Other segments of the road show included a folk song sequence, "Hymns of All Churches," college songs, an "electronics ballet," a Dixieland band, and even a bit of rock 'n' roll. Waring's 1955–1956 tour covered more than 25,000 miles and visited 125 cities from coast to coast. African American baritone Frank Davis had joined the company by this time, but it is not known whether he participated in the minstrel sequence.[30]

Waring even staged a minstrel show at President Dwight Eisenhower's inauguration in Washington, D.C., in 1953—to the dismay of some. The *Pittsburgh Courier*, a black newspaper, commented, "Many Negroes were not too pleased with the GOP show at the two festivals because of the Fred Waring 'black-faced minstrel' act which opened the show.... Others felt that Waring's show was intending to portray the history of entertainment in America which got its beginning from the old traditional Negro minstrel. At any rate they felt however distasteful the minstrel act was to the majority of Negroes, Waring vindicated himself at the close of the hour show when he presented [Frank] Davis with his Pennsylvanians in 'Old Man River.'"[31]

This raises the question: How did Waring get away with such performances at this late date? Blackface in general, and the minstrel show in particular, had been pretty much banned from mass media in the United States by the early 1950s, but there were apparently no serious complaints about Waring's presentations—at least none that I could find. Why?

I think that there are several reasons. One was Fred Waring's reputation. He was known as a serious musician who regularly featured American themes, such as songs of the Civil War, songs of patriotic holidays, folk music, and so forth. Observing Waring and his chorus was almost a tutorial on *The American Songbook* (in its broadest definition). The fact that, like Ed Sullivan, Waring was somewhat stiff in front of the cameras only added to his credibility. He was authentic, and when he took on the minstrel show, which was undeniably an important part of the American musical journey, he did so with care. Here is his opening to the 1950 telecast:

> The minstrel show. The wholesome and fascinating form of entertainment which has been used in churches and schools and clubs all over the country for many, many years. So because minstrelsy means good, clean fun and wonderful music, we continue in the spirit of all good minstrel shows with the greatest of dignity and respect. Gentlemen, the opening chorus!

Note the words "dignity and respect," which he repeated later in the telecast. This was not simply an attempt at deflection. Waring engaged as a consultant Lillian Gale, the daughter of George Gale, a noted minstrel of the late 19th century, to help shape the production. There were no exaggerated dialects, no jokes about race, and no out-of-date, potentially offensive lyrics ("little babe" was substituted for "little coon," etc.). However, the interlocutor/endman structure, the looseness, and the general sense of fun inherent in minstrelsy were faithfully reproduced. Only the now startling presence of blackface is unacceptable by modern standards.

Waring himself (like Al Jolson and Eddie Cantor) was known to be liberal on racial matters, which also helped mute criticism. There are many stories of Waring defying southern venues and accommodations when they would not accept African American members of his company. Finally, the extraordinary musicianship of his chorus and soloists distanced his presentations from anything remotely resembling exploitation. Eventually, the backlash against the use of blackface would force Waring, like others, to forgo its use, but for a time even in the black community many felt he was doing it for the right reasons.

The Fred Waring Show aired on CBS-TV Sunday nights at 9:00 p.m., immediately following Ed Sullivan's *Toast of the Town* (later known as *The Ed Sullivan Show*). Sullivan also staged a full-blown, half-hour minstrel show at least once, on June 14, 1953. The occasion was the fiftieth anniversary of sponsor Ford Motor Company. As a tribute, the second half of that night's *Toast of the Town* was a traditional American blackface minstrel show, with Sullivan as the interlocutor (in whiteface) and veteran fast-talking vaudevillians Smith and Dale as the endmen. In fact, the cast consisted largely of old-timers, including Joe Smith (age 69) and Charlie Dale (67), songwriter Joe Howard (75), tenor Will Oakland (73), Gracie Fields (55), and the 30-voice Ford Choir. Sullivan danced with old-timer Pat Rooney (72) to the tune of "Sweet Rosie O'Grady." Also performing were dancer Hal LeRoy; musicians Frank Evans, Joe Sodja, and the Longfellow Tambourine Troubadours; and the Ford chorus, in blackface, singing "Floating Down to Cotton Town."[32]

While certainly nostalgic, the idea of a blackface minstrel show on network television in 1953 did not sit well with some. Columnist Izzy Rowe of the *Pittsburgh Courier* complained that "the sight of a stage full of performers wearing the burnt cork which comes naturally to the Mr. Bones of a bygone era was anything but entertaining!" She continued, "Instead [of a colored star] there was the minstrel show which served no purpose except to get the switch flipped to another channel in Negro living rooms across the country." However, the *Courier* subsequently published a rebuttal, reminding readers that there were differing opinions on this issue within the black community. A reader pointed out that Ed Sullivan had always been a friend to African Americans and opined that Rowe was being "entirely too sensitive." "You must face facts about this business called show business," the correspondent wrote. "You might as well accept black face minstrels as a part of the chronology of American show business. As a historical event, it represents the greatest era in the birth of show business ... I see no sense in Negroes, or any other race, hair-triggerly becoming too self conscious."[33]

Although there were different opinions about the appropriateness of blackface minstrels on television (in any context), the networks got the message. This was a touchy, controversial area, and sponsors hated controversy. In 1955, *Broadcasting* magazine reported that the Ford Motor Company was planning a series of high-profile specials called *Ford Star Jubilee*, one of which would be called *The Big Banjo*, "a musical salute to America's minstrels, with an all-star cast," courtesy of Broadway producer Paul Gregory. This program never made it to the network air, nor did any other post–1953 minstrel-based programming that I could locate—at least in the United States.[34]

Britain

Britain, however, was another story. In Britain, when you think of minstrelsy on television, one program comes to mind. It ran for 20 years and was hugely successful, but it is now regarded as a national embarrassment. It was never rerun or released on home video of any kind, and little has been written about it even in academic journals or books. There is little video from the show online, either, since its run preceded the era of home taping, and the BBC has kept the original tapes locked up tight (although it did not destroy them, as has been rumored).

Interviewed today, people who saw the show tend to make excuses ("I happened to be walking by a TV set when it was on"; "What were they *thinking*?"). What was this pariah, this show that transfixed Britons for 20 years but is now the Program-Whose-Name-Must-Not-Be-Spoken?

First, a little background: *The Kentucky Minstrels* was an enormous hit on BBC radio in the 1930s and 1940s. In 1948, the Kentucky Minstrels themselves telecast from Alexandra Palace. Around the same time, BBC producer Charles Chilton produced radio histories of the American minstrel show called *Cabin in the Cotton* (1947) and *Gentlemen, Be Seated* (1950), using the George Mitchell Choir.

The Mitchell Choir, which was composed of white singers and dancers, appeared on TV several times during the 1950s, including on *Festival of British Popular Songs* (1956) and *The George Mitchell Glee Club* (1958). In 1957, producer George Inns wanted to breathe new life into old-fashioned television variety, and he invited Mitchell to assemble a minstrel troupe for BBC television. This led to a special, *The 1957 Television Minstrels*, telecast from the National Radio Show in London on September 2, 1957. This program starred the George Mitchell Minstrels and veteran entertainers Ike Hatch and G.H. Elliott, and it was the basis for a series that would follow.

The Black and White Minstrel Show premiered on June 14, 1958. The featured performers were the Mitchell Minstrels (male), the Television Toppers, a female chorus and dance troupe, and (as soloists) baritone Dai Francis, tenor John Boulter, and bass Tony Mercer. All of them remained with the show for virtually its entire run. A frequent host in the early days was Stan Stennett, although the program was more ensemble driven than focused on any individual. There was no interlocutor.[35]

The show typically featured a chorus of 12 men and 12 women. The men were in blackface, with white-outlined eyes and mouths and white gloves. The women were natural (whiteface) and fetchingly dressed, often in short-shorts or bikinis. There was much energetic singing and dancing, interspersed with an occasional ballad. Each medley was built around a theme (in Mexico, by the beach, etc.) with elaborate dance routines, usually at a manic pace. Sometimes a whole show was devoted to a theme (e.g., Irving Berlin or Gilbert and Sullivan). The show was not only carefully choreographed but also visually striking. There were bright, colorful sets and costumes, especially in the color episodes (the show was telecast in color beginning in 1967), and many costume changes during each episode.

Essentially this was a sing-along show, somewhat similar to American TV's *Singalong with Mitch* (1961), with an emphasis on medleys of middle-brow songs, both old and new. From long ago there might be songs like "Little Annie Rooney," "In the Good Old Summertime," "Sweet Rosie O'Grady," and "The Band Played On." From more recent times there was "Born Free," "Paloma Blanca," "On a Wonderful Day Like Today" and novelties such as "Itsy Bitsy Teeny Weenie Yellow Polka Dot Bikini" (guess how the chorus

The enormously popular *Black and White Minstrel Show* ran for 20 years on BBC television. Today the network all but denies its existence.

girls were dressed for that one!). From in between, the show offered 1930s–1940s hits like "Powder Your Face with Sunshine," "Brazil," and "Donkey Serenade."

Few songs were taken from the 19th-century minstrel songbook, aside from an occasional "Oh, Dem Golden Slippers" or "Camptown Races." As Michael Pickering writes, even in the rock era, "performers in the *Black and White Minstrel Show* continued to sing

The Black and White Minstrel Show spawned an equally popular touring troupe that lasted until 1987.

songs and dance dances that had virtually nothing to do with African-American music, though they still wore blackface."[36] He and others have referred to the show as "candy floss," the British equivalent of cotton candy. The music and dialogue were not offensive; it is just the blackface that looks bizarre and offensive today. The men reportedly used Max Factor "Negro #2" makeup.

There were comedy interludes between the dance numbers, with the most frequently seen comedians being Leslie Crowther (1960s), George Chisholm (1960s) and Keith Harris, a young ventriloquist with his dummies (1970s). The comedians sometimes served as hosts, not dominating the proceedings but helping to tie the show together. There were also guests, most notoriously a teenage Lenny Henry in 1975. Henry went on to become one of Britain's most famous black stand-up comedians, and he has spent years apologizing for his appearance on *Black and White Minstrel Show*.

The program's popularity went into overdrive in the early 1960s, after it won the top prize, the Golden Rose of Montreux, at the first world television contest at Montreux, Switzerland. It was now drawing 16 to 18 million viewers per telecast, a phenomenal total for British TV. In 1962, the cast performed at the annual Royal Variety Performances at the London Palladium, a highly prestigious charity event, before Queen Elizabeth and members of the royal family. In 1964, now in its sixth season, the program moved from Sunday to Saturday night, "a move which should please the many church groups who have written in the past two years complaining that the show clashed with evening service."[37]

With all this success, the minstrels' empire naturally began to expand into other media. In 1960, their first LP was released, "The George Mitchell Minstrels, from the Black and White Minstrel Show," consisting of the chorus singing medleys of vintage songs. It shot to number one and stayed on the British best-selling album chart for an incredible 142 weeks. Two follow-up LPs, "Another Black and White Minstrel Show" (1961) and "On Stage with the George Mitchell Minstrels" (1962), also reached number one and remained on the charts for several months. British chart expert Paul Gambaccini calls the minstrels "the most successful group in the British album charts before the Beatles." Many other LPs followed, and cumulative sales were in the millions, which was remarkable for the British market (much smaller than that in the United States).[38]

Also in 1960, the minstrels launched "a theatrical show which ran for 6,477 performances from 1960 to 1972 and established itself in the *Guinness Book of Records* as the stage show seen by the largest number of people." From 1962 to 1972, it played in the Victoria Palace Theatre, and after that it toured big-city and seaside resorts around the United Kingdom each summer until 1987, when a final tour of three resorts saw the last official show on stage. A second troupe toured Australia in 1962.[39]

There were parodies from the start. In 1963, the satirical series *That Was the Week That Was* mocked the minstrels' big dance routines, singing "We Love the Ku Klux Klan!" and "Mississippi, the Place I Want to Be" (in the wake of civil rights workers being killed there). In 1971, a first-season episode of *The Two Ronnies* (a comedy sketch series) presented "The Short and Fat Minstrel Show."

There were also protests. They were muted at first but grew louder as time went on. After *The Black and White Minstrel Show* won the Montreux prize in 1961, a black magazine called *Flamingo* dismissed the program as "a piece of outdated and degraded rubbish." Black professionals quoted in the article said the show made them feel "ashamed and disgusted." George Inns, the producer, responded, "I have never had a letter from a coloured person complaining about the show.... This is an innocent programme, providing entertainment ... as for finding a coloured choir to better our singers, I don't think I'd be able to do so."[40]

In May 1967, the BBC received a petition from the Campaign Against Racial Discrimination, signed by 200, calling *The Black and White Minstrel Show* "a hideous impersonation" and demanding its cancellation. Letters in the press, including some from black people, pushed back against this proposal. A BBC staff member reported complaining to Director General Hugh Carlton-Green, who replied, "For heaven sake, shut up. You're wasting valuable ammunition on a comparatively insignificant target." The issue was discussed at the highest levels of the BBC, but the ultimate decision was to keep the show on.

On November 18, 1968, the minstrels were scheduled for a second appearance at the Royal Variety Performances at the London Palladium. The queen was traveling, but the queen mother and other members of the royal family would be in attendance. One of the minstrels, Les Want, later described when it first occurred to him that black people might find the show offensive:

> It was during the dress rehearsal for our second Royal Variety Performance at the London Palladium. Diana Ross and the Supremes were topping the bill, and we were absolutely thrilled. When Diana Ross saw us she refused to carry on until we'd cleared the auditorium. As we left the stage she gave the Black Power salute. Then it all came home.... I didn't mind her objecting, but what annoyed me was the salute. I was going to have a word with her, but I was pulled back. I just wanted to know how it offended her. I didn't understand the great controversy. The thing was, she didn't object to sharing the stage with us at the end of the show when the Queen [sic] came along the line.[41]

In recent years, the minstrels have been deleted from listings of the performers at this event, as if they were not even there.

Feeling the heat, George Mitchell tried some variations on the successful formula. One was *Masquerade*, a November 1968 special in which the men appeared wearing masks instead of black makeup. Another, in 1969, was *Music Music Music*, a spin-off series in which the minstrels appeared without blackface. It failed and was canceled after 10 episodes, after which the original format was reinstated. Episodes were telecast less frequently during the 1970s, however.

By the late 1970s, the audience was down to six or seven million, less than half the levels from when the show was at its height. At this time, variety shows in general were becoming passé. Bill Cotton, the newly appointed controller of BBC1, wrote a memo saying that variety had had its day: "I think that [*The Black and White Minstrel Show*] had come to the end of its natural life on television. I also felt that there was this racist implication in it."[42]

The last regular telecast was on July 21, 1978. Some further specials were promised but did not materialize. The series was not officially cancelled; contracts simply didn't come through for a new season. The BBC did not formally admit that *The Black and White Minstrel Show* had been canceled until 1986, when it failed to acknowledge the series during the celebration of the fiftieth anniversary of television in Britain. There were protests about that omission, but by this time official policy was to ignore that the show had ever existed. As a 2004 documentary put it, "What had been a national institution suddenly disappeared ... airbrushed out of history."

It seems disingenuous to suggest that whites in Britain were simply unaware that *The Black and White Minstrel Show* might offend black Britons. The racial turmoil in the

United States was well publicized, and there had been race riots in Notting Hill (a district in West London) as early as 1958. An upsurge in immigration from Africa and the Caribbean inflamed nationalist elements. However, Britain was still an overwhelmingly white country. Less than 1 percent of its population was black (versus more than 10 percent in the United States at the time), and that community was far less militant and had fewer organizational or media vehicles with which to express its displeasure than were present in the United States. With hardly any blacks visible in society, blackface on television must have seemed a harmless bit of exotica for the bulk of the British population, especially when shown in such a happy, upbeat setting. Social attitudes toward race would begin to change dramatically in the 1970s and 1980s, however, along with unrest, making the minstrels very quickly a product of an earlier time.

George Mitchell handed the reins of the *Black and White Minstrel Show* empire to his son Rob, who kept the stage show going for another decade or so. The elder Mitchell retired to America. He died in 2002.

6

Epilogue and Conclusions

For many years during the 20th century, American media, as well as social and political leaders, validated blackface minstrelsy as an acceptable form of entertainment. It was seen and heard everywhere—on the radio, on movie screens, on early television, and on amateur stages in communities across the country, presented by respected organizations like the Elks Club, PTAs, churches, and schools. It was a people's form of entertainment. Leaders endorsed it. President Franklin D. Roosevelt was scheduled to attend a minstrel performance put on by schoolchildren in Warm Springs, Georgia, on the day he died, April 12, 1945.

Even the black community was divided on the subject. Until the mid-century point, complaints about minstrelsy were few and feeble. A well-publicized attempt in 1931 by the *Pittsburgh Courier* to circulate a national petition urging the cancellation of *Amos 'n' Andy* petered out when other major black newspapers, including the *Chicago Defender* and the *New York Age*, refused to support the effort.[1]

The continued popularity of minstrel shows did not mean that mainstream media was not also beginning to recognize advances by black Americans in other fields. Sometimes this recognition existed side-by-side in the same publication, with no apparent irony. For example, from the time of its founding in 1922, *Reader's Digest* published both serious articles about black leaders such as Booker T. Washington and George Washington Carver and jokes and witticisms, some of which reinforced black stereotypes, such as this one from World War II: "Learning the phrases incidental to sentry duty proved confusing for one Negro of the 76th. An officer of the day was surprised when this gentleman challenged him with 'Halt! Look who's here!'"[2]

In the 1950s, as we have seen, the situation changed rather suddenly. The minstrel show was banished from the national stage, and the term *minstrel* began to shift to a broader, less racial connotation, closer to its original definition of a wandering entertainer. Willie Nelson titled one of his popular albums *Minstrel Man* (1981). Today, if you perform a search for the term *minstrel* in eBay's records section, you'll mainly get listings for Jethro Tull's hard rock album *Minstrel in the Gallery* (1975). A highly popular 1960s folk group, the New Christy Minstrels, did pay tribute to one of the original minstrel show troupes with their name, but they did so while projecting a clean-cut, all-white image with no racial connotations at all.

The Minstrel Show and Blackface in the Late Twentieth Century

There were occasional attempts during the second half of the 20th century to revive the classic minstrel show or to use blackface to make a statement. Usually these efforts sought to avoid any overt racial disparagement, but they were attacked anyway, often angrily. The associations they represented were just too painful. The very term *minstrel show* and the use of blackface for any purpose were now forbidden.

In May 1964, producer Mike Todd, Jr., was commissioned to stage a "modern minstrel show" called "America, Be Seated!" at the Louisiana Pavilion of the World's Fair in Flushing Meadows, New York. It was billed as combining the "happy flavor of minstrel shows ... with original music and modern comedy skits." The cast was integrated, no one wore blackface, and the songs were relentlessly non-racial and apolitical.[3] The title song addressed the show's intent directly:

> Now, somebody said our minstrel show should not be done for sport,
> That we should have a message of significant import.
> And so we have a message, a most essential one,
> Please listen very carefully,
> Our message is ... have fun!

There were out-of-town tryouts for the show and, on May 3, 1964, a promotional appearance on *The Ed Sullivan Show*. Cast members Keith Charles, Bibi Osterwald, Lola Falana, Louis Gossett, Jr., and others appeared in an elaborate Mississippi showboat-style production. Todd, a promoter like his famous producer-father, predicted that the show would ride its World's Fair success to appearances across the country: "It could go anywhere." *Variety* said that it could be "the forerunner of a revival of minstrelsy."

Civil rights battles were raging at this time in the United States, and the NAACP initially blasted the very idea of such a show. But after seeing a preview in Boston, the organization changed its stance and praised the production as "an asset for integration." One official said, "I have no serious objections. There is nothing in this show detrimental to or ridiculing Negroes. In fact, it is a satire on the old-style minstrel show." But the intended audience felt differently. The show was widely ignored by the fair's patrons and was cancelled after two performances. Box-office receipts were only $300.

In 1978, Della Reese and Gregory Hines appeared in a socially conscious stage musical called *The Last Minstrel Show*, set in the world of a black minstrel show facing protests in 1926. Although promoting an anti-racist message, and generally assumed to be headed for Broadway, the play closed in Philadelphia before reaching New York.[4]

In a widely publicized incident, black actor Ben Vereen was heavily criticized for appearing in blackface at Ronald Reagan's inaugural in 1981. Vereen presented a tribute to the great black entertainer Bert Williams (who did, in fact, wear blackface), which was intended to be seen in two parts. Dressed as Williams in a shabby coat and tails, Vereen first sang the rollicking "Waiting for the Robert E. Lee." Then, after a pantomime with an imaginary bartender in which he was refused a drink because he was black, he eased into Williams' theme song, the doleful "Nobody," while slowly removing the black makeup from his face. Vereen had performed this routine before, and it was meant to serve as a message to the predominantly white audience about discrimination. But when his segment was broadcast on ABC-TV, the latter half of the act was deleted—destroying its

Mike Todd, Jr.'s, attempt to bring the "happy flavor of minstrel shows" to the New York World's Fair in 1964 fell flat despite having an integrated cast.

effect and bringing angry protests down on Vereen's head. He was forced to explain and apologize for years afterward.[5]

White actor Ted Danson faced even greater opprobrium when he appeared in exaggerated blackface at a 1993 Friar's Club comic roast of his then-girlfriend Whoopi Goldberg, who is African American. His routine included multiple uses of the "N-word," along with references to the couple's sex life. Black television host Montel Williams walked off the dais during the routine, and New York mayor David Dinkins (also black) said the jokes were "way, way over the line." This incident led to a loud and contentious discussion of political correctness and who is allowed to say (or wear) what. The *New York Times* later reported, "On computer networks, across telephone lines, under dryers at hair salons and on radio and television talk shows, 'Whoopi and Ted' have been the talk of the nation for almost a week." It turned out that Goldberg, a comic-provocateur if ever there was one, had written much of the material herself. "If [those complaining] knew me," she said, "they would know that Whoopi has never been about political correctness. I built my whole career destigmatizing words like 'nigger.'"[6]

As noted in chapter 4, recreations of minstrel shows were sometimes used in feature films attacking the genre, such as *Minstrel Man* (1977) starring Glynn Turman and *Bamboozled* (2000), produced by black filmmaker Spike Lee. There were also films that used blackface to explore blackness in America, including *Watermelon Man* (1970), the story of a bigoted white salesman who turns black, and *Soul Man* (1986), a comedy about a white kid who temporarily darkens his skin in order to qualify for a blacks-only scholarship to Harvard.

On television, a famous 1975 episode of the hit series *All in the Family* had lead character and "loveable bigot" Archie Bunker putting on blackface to take part in his lodge's annual minstrel show. Two lodge brothers even did a routine in his living room to convince him to go. However, before he could go on stage, he was abruptly called away to the hospital, where his daughter Gloria was about to give birth. He arrived still in blackface, leading to many misunderstandings and jokes.

Longer and less entertaining was *Black. White.*, a six-episode reality show that aired on the FX cable network in 2006. Billed as an "experiment in social understanding," it pitted two families, the white Wurgels and the black Sparks, against each other in a house in suburban Los Angeles. The gimmick was that when any of them went outside to interact with the community, the Wurgels had to be made up to appear black and the Sparks made up to appear white—to walk in each other's shoes, so to speak. Unfortunately, the Wurgel "dad" (actually a boyfriend) was strong willed and opinionated, while the Sparks' father was extremely touchy and saw racism everywhere. The wives tried to make peace, but only the kids seemed to have a "get over it" attitude. The show did not return for a second season.[7]

In another arena, blackface was integral to some long-established civic traditions, which presented further problems. Philadelphia's New Year's Day Mummers Parade, which originated in the 1800s and coalesced into a city-sanctioned event in 1901, is an all-day parade in which groups (or "clubs") of various national backgrounds march in outlandish, colorful costumes and ride on floats. The parade is televised. Nearly all the participants are white, but historically blackface, brownface, and redface caricatures were featured. During the 1960s, civil rights groups began to protest vociferously about the representation of African Americans, and blackface was officially banned in 1964, although it still sometimes appears.

Local Minstrelsy

Local amateur minstrelsy continued in the 1950s and beyond, albeit on reduced scale (see chapter 1). For example, on April 9, 1953, high school student Elvis Presley appeared in Humes High School's "Annual Minstrel Show" as a guitarist, reportedly singing "Til I Waltz Again with You." In 1961, a "Honey Boy Minstrels" show was advertised in Nashville, with tickets said to be available "from any policeman." Most of these performances were fundraisers by community groups.[8]

When was the *last* minstrel show? It probably hasn't been held yet. A search of U.S. newspapers for 1990 reveals at least seven minstrel shows in that year, long after the format was identified as the height of political incorrectness. The seven shows were held on a Mississippi riverboat in St. Louis; at the St. Cloud Senior Center in Orlando, Florida; by the Golden Age Club of St. Joseph's Roman Catholic Church in Pennsylvania; by the Springfield Lion's Club in Nashville, Tennessee; at the Senior Center Young Heart's Theatre in Louisville, Kentucky; at the Marion Harvest Moon Festival in Kansas; and by the St. George Street Players in St. Augustine, Florida. Most of these were billed as annual events. There was no indication of whether blackface was used.[9]

Musicologist Charles Hamm published an analysis of an event that took place in March 1991 that he called "the last minstrel show." The location was Tunbridge, a rural agricultural town in Vermont with a population of about one thousand. The annual show was produced

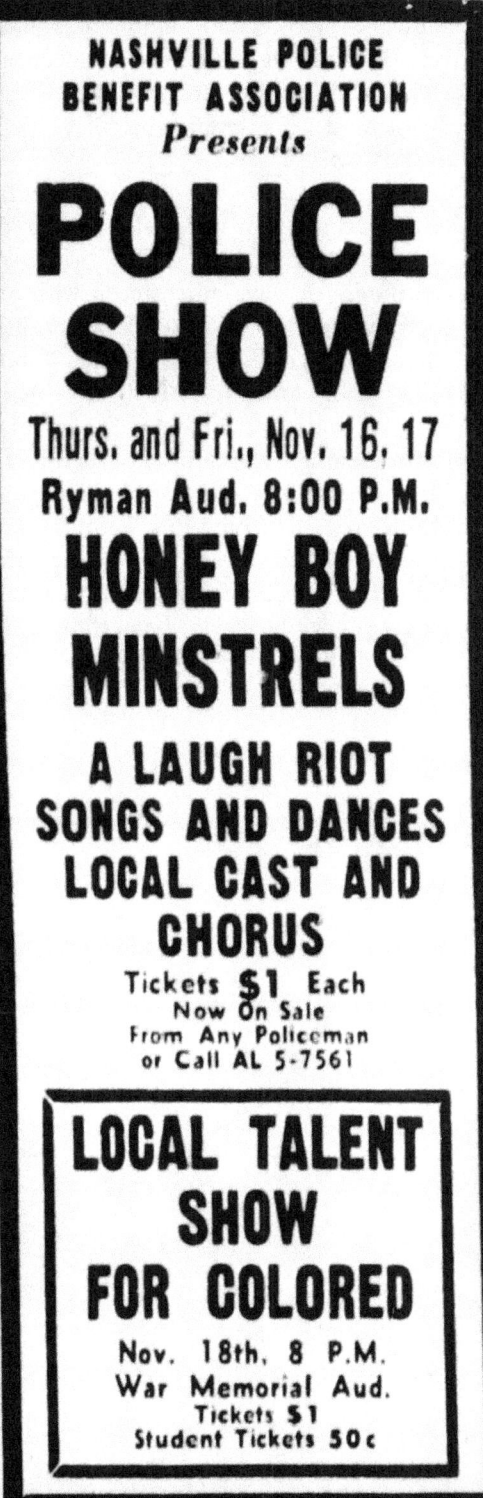

Ad for a "Honey Boy" benefit minstrel show in Nashville in 1961, at the famous Ryman Auditorium. Note that a "talent show for colored" was scheduled for the following day.

each fall in the town hall, which accommodated approximately 200 people, before an audience that was thoroughly mixed in age but all white. There were no African Americans in Tunbridge and never had been, as far as anyone knew. The performers, all locals, included an interlocutor in formal dress and top hat, flanked by two women in party dresses and six endmen in blackface. Behind them was a chorus in two ranks, accompanied by a pianist.[10]

Some of the jokes were directed at familiar local "characters" (who might have been in the audience) or were mildly off-color sex jokes, while others were about outsiders or current events, such as the "Eye-racky" war. None were directed at minorities. Nor did the music have much to do with black culture, although some of the songs were from the "coon song" era of the early 20th century, including "When the Midnight Choo Choo Leaves for Alabam," "Swanee," and "Are You from Dixie?" Others were pop songs or novelties of more recent vintage, including "Beep Beep" and "Rockin' Robin." Hamm reported that locals lamented the fact that their annual tradition would probably be shut down eventually (Vermont is a very liberal state). He then raised an interesting question. Ethnomusicologists, as he pointed out, actively encourage the use of music by "national, ethnic, regional, religious, economic, and other self-defining groups to assert and strengthen group identity in the face of attempted cultural domination by central governments or other institutions with a stake in controlling public thought." Shouldn't residents of a white enclave be permitted to do the same as a means of strengthening *their* group identity in the face of a national insistence on multiculturalism?

The Tunbridge minstrel show has since passed into history. Or has it? On its 2017

Unknown local minstrel show, probably in New Hampshire during the 1950s. Women were a major part of the cast, and the jokes and songs were presumably non-racial, but the endmen still wore blackface, reflecting minstrel tradition.

Facebook page, the text indicated that there was still an annual celebration, now called "The Tunbridge Civic Club Show," and claimed that blackface was no longer used. A photo showed about 20 people on stage in street clothes, seated in minstrel fashion, with an imposing "interlocutor" seated at the center wearing a tuxedo, with a top hat and cane. However, to his left was what appeared to be a white man in blackface. Old traditions die hard.[11]

Conclusions

Minstrelsy, the first truly American entertainment form, born as an expression of a unique national identity, did not "die out" in the 1880s–1890s. Nor did it linger on only in local productions, as is so often claimed. Instead, it maintained a strong presence in national culture until the early 1950s—more than a century after the Virginia Minstrels debuted in 1843. It was adapted by producers of recordings, radio, motion pictures and television as those new opportunities emerged. As with many other entertainment formats, as theaters closed and large national stage troupes ceased touring the country, it simply moved into the new media.

Nor did minstrelsy endure solely as an exercise in nostalgia for another era. While nostalgia was certainly an important component, the shows themselves were adapted—as much as they could be—to changing times and changing values. I would argue that Judy Garland and Mickey Rooney mugging and singing their way through endman-based jokes and big dance routines was what minstrelsy had become in the 1940s—at least on screen. The big radio minstrel shows were also adaptations, not literal recreations, of earlier versions of the genre.

Unless you take the viewpoint that an entertainment format can never adapt, that it is frozen in its first incarnation, it is apparent that the content of minstrelsy morphed dramatically throughout its history, incorporating contemporary elements and repertoire right into the mid–20th century. By then, most of the songs and jokes made no reference to race. What was left was singing, dancing, and corny, rapid-fire jokes—the "good, clean fun" that had always been the minstrel show's calling card. The two elements that eventually brought the minstrel show down were blackface and dialect. Those characteristics were core to what a minstrelsy was—you could scarcely have a minstrel show without them (though some tried)—and they were increasingly recognized as offensive in and of themselves.

Blackface—white men imitating blacks by putting on burnt cork—had a long tradition in the theater, dating at least back to the 1700s. Many scholars have reflected on the multiple uses of blackface, also known as "the minstrel mask." William Mahar enumerates four[12]:

    1. a racial marker, indicating that the wearer was presenting (arguably) aspects of African American culture;

    2. a disguise, enabling white performers to satirize majority values while still distancing themselves as the source;

    3. a vehicle for the creation of a distinctly American form of entertainment during the country's early years; and

    4. a masking device that allowed performers to "shield themselves from any direct personal and psychological identification with the material they were performing."

The second and fourth points raised by Mahar are particularly interesting. They suggest that blackface could be used as a clown's mask, a disguise, creating a figure who could do and say things that would be unnatural (and perhaps unfunny) coming from an ordinary person. This is the same function served by circus clown makeup or, for that matter, a cartoon. Likewise, for performers, blackface gave them permission to act in ways that might otherwise be uncomfortable. The great black entertainer Bert Williams, a reserved man, wore blackface, explaining that it freed him to be a character rather than himself.[13]

During the 20th century, there were at least four general types of blackface, and all are seen in the examples given in this book. With what I call "exaggerated" blackface, not only was the color used a very deep black, but both the mouth and the eyes were outlined, sometimes in red or bright white, producing an almost cartoonish appearance. Examples were *Minstrel Man*, *Bamboozled*, various cartoons, and much minstrel iconography. With "normal" blackface, usually only the mouth was outlined (and then in a normal skin tone). With "subdued" blackface, the object was to make the white subject look like a real African American, with no highlighting around the mouth or eyes (for example, endmen Popcorn and Peanuts on KTLA's *Dixie Showboat* in the 1950s). "Brownface" was lighter still and could suggest mixed race or even be mistaken for a tan. This format was often used for women (for example, Ethel Merman in *Kid Millions* and Joan Crawford in *Torch Song*). Subdued blackface and brownface were more commonly found in the later days of minstrelsy. Brownface has also been used in other contexts to represent Latinos, Indians, and other ethnic groups.

Dialect has a more complicated history. It, too, had been used for generations, sometimes in high art (e.g., the poetry of black author Paul Laurence Dunbar), to replicate the speech of ordinary people. Arguably the African American Vernacular English of hip hop is today's continuation of this theme. But when used by whites to make African Americans seem uneducated, or even unintelligent (unlike making white rubes seem the same), it became offensive. Ironically, blackface endmen, especially in later years, while portrayed as uneducated, were seldom presented as unintelligent. They were usually the stars of the show, and occasionally even *in charge* of the show (e.g., Lew Dockstader).

As the 20th century progressed, both blackface and dialect were increasingly seen as singling out African Americans for ridicule. Al Bernard, a highly successful minstrel on records and radio during the 1920s and 1930s, addressed this idea directly with historian Ulysses "Jim" Walsh in a remarkably frank conversation in 1949. Walsh later reported the conversation as follows:

> The last time I talked with [Bernard], in 1949, he asked me not to play on my radio program any of his records that latter-day black men and women might find offensive. "In the old days," Al said, "we didn't mean any harm by 'taking off' the lower class Negroes and using such words in records as 'nigger,' 'coon' and 'shine,' because that was what they called each other. But today it's different. Black people are better educated and things that used to be all right aren't right any more. Forty years ago the blacks laughed as much at my 'coon songs' as the whites. Today, though, I don't want to hurt their feelings, so please be careful which old records of mine you play."[14]

Not until the late 1940s, when it attempted to make the leap to television, was minstrelsy driven off the national stage due to dramatically changing social attitudes. Singling out African Americans as figures of fun—and blackface makeup in particular—was no longer acceptable.

What Killed Minstrelsy?

Alison Kibler's recent study of censorship in America during the first half of the 20th century, *Censoring Racial Ridicule*, reveals an interesting pattern. Irish and Jewish organizations were largely successful in reducing negative stereotypes of those groups in plays and films, through a combination of protests, lawsuits and direct political action. Anti-defamation laws were passed, and censorship boards were set up across the country (and endorsed by the Supreme Court in 1915). These efforts succeeded in modifying or outright banning hundreds of films that the Irish and Jews felt demeaned their respective groups. However, the NAACP and allied black groups were much less successful in lobbying on behalf of African Americans. This was true even in the notorious case of *Birth of a Nation*. Blacks were excluded from censorship boards, and censorship regulations largely ignored their concerns. Radio and movies continued to celebrate blackface minstrel shows and all manner of black stereotypes right up until World War II.

What seems to have finally turned the tide—at least in the major media—was the concentration of power over creative production in a small number of studios and networks, as well as the sensitivity of those entities to commercial pressure. Thus, while there were no laws or regulations restricting the presentation of a minstrel show, NBC, CBS and ABC "got the message." These networks were all regulated by the government, and they depended on nervous sponsors who shied away from controversy. Public opinion was changing in the liberal, postwar era, and they responded accordingly. So did the movie studios.

The formal government censorship apparatus was largely dismantled after the Supreme Court reversed its 1915 decision in 1950 and came down on the side of free speech. Ironically, at this same time, the minstrel show (which was never officially censored) was driven out of media by the forces noted above. It was free to continue on a local level, where community (not national) standards prevailed, but without endorsement by the major media, local minstrelsy also began to wither away.

As Kibler and others have pointed out, institutionalized censorship of speech in the United States began to re-emerge in the 1980s and 1990s, in the form of laws criminalizing "hate crimes" and forbidding a "hostile work environment." "Hate speech," while not criminal, has been increasingly and stridently suppressed by private entities such as universities and companies that punish speech of which they don't approve—sometimes severely. These, today, would probably effectively censor anything like a minstrel show. But by this time, public pressure—not institutional intervention—had caused the minstrel show to pass from the scene.[15]

What to make, then, of the longevity of this uniquely American phenomenon, the minstrel show, born of the raucous optimism of a new (and, in many ways, innocent) young nation, that was still going strong one hundred years later despite its obvious (at least to modern viewers) racial implications? What is the final verdict on this strange mixture, in Eric Lott's words, of the "love and theft," affection and appropriation, of a minority culture by the white majority? It lasted for a very long time, arguably even continuing in some forms to the present day. Perhaps Daniel Goldmark put it best: "Minstrelsy never really died—it simply changed media."[16]

Appendix 1 Prominent Minstrel Troupes Active After 1890

Evidence that stage minstrelsy was not dead or dying in the 1890s is found in the many prominent troupes still touring at that time. They provided a reference point (and inspiration) for the depictions of minstrelsy that emerged in the new media of records, movies, and later radio and television. Following are some of the troupes that continued to be active after the dawn of modern mass media in 1890.

This list is only a sample. There were literally thousands of minstrel troupes, large and small, crisscrossing the country in the late nineteenth and early twentieth centuries. They can be difficult to accurately trace, as many merged, spun off satellites, or periodically changed their names. It is particularly difficult to trace white troupes, which predominated, as there has been very little research done on white minstrelsy from this era. This listing focuses on major and/or historically significant troupes, both white and black.

Shown after each name is the *approximate* span of years during which that troupe was active. Other dates are often approximate as well. More research in this field is needed.

White or Mixed Troupes

"Big Troupes" of the 1870s–1880s Still Active in the 1890s

Haverly's Minstrels (active: 1864–1898). Theater owner J.H. "Colonel Jack" Haverly (1837–1901) formed his first troupe in 1864, followed by various combinations, including Haverly and Mallory and Haverly and Sands. He also managed other troupes and was the most famous promoter of the giant troupes of the 1870s and 1880s. In 1877, he merged four companies (Haverly, Emerson, New Orleans, Callender?) to form Haverly's United Mastodon Minstrels (slogan: "Forty—Count 'Em—Forty!"). Successive curtains would part, revealing additional rows of cast members. He also owned a black troupe from 1878 to 1882. At the height of his career in 1881, he owned six theaters, four minstrel troupes, and numerous other theatrical companies.[1] Known as "The Minstrel King."

Primrose and West (1877–1918). Also known as Primrose and West's Black and White Minstrels (1894). Big mixed-cast troupe ("40 whites and 30 blacks"). George Primrose (1852–1919) was a dancer in various troupes (including Haverly's) from 1867, with partner Billy West (1853–1902). They formed their first troupe as Barlow, Wilson, Primrose and West Minstrels (1877–1882), which was similar to Haverly's troupe. By 1882, they began downplaying blackface and plantation material in favor of high-class music, ballet, fancy European costumes, and spectacle. The show became Thatcher, Primrose and West (1882–1889), Primrose and West (1889–

1898), Primrose and Dockstader (1898–1903), and Primrose's own troupe after that. Primrose and Dockstader reformed from 1912 to 1914, and then it became Primrose and (George) Wilson from 1914 to 1915. From 1914 to 1918, Primrose also appeared with his own small "minstrel troupe" (seven men) in vaudeville. Clog dancer William H. "Billy" West teamed with Primrose starting in 1871 and, after they split, ran West's Big Jubilee Minstrels (1898–1901). West was briefly married to actress Fay Templeton.

Thatcher's Minstrels (1880–1897). Comedian/monologist George Thatcher (1846–1913) was with various troupes in the 1870s, including Haverly; he later headed his own troupes (Thatcher and Ryman, 1880–1881; Thatcher's Minstrels, 1881–1882; Thatcher, Primrose and West, 1882–1889; Thatcher's Minstrels, 1890–?; Thatcher and Johnson, 1895–1897). He then went into vaudeville.

Other Prominent Troupes Active after 1890

Carncross' Minstrels (1860–1896, Philadelphia). White tenor John L. Carncross (c. 1834–1911) was the dominant figure in minstrelsy in Philadelphia for almost 40 years, from 1858 to 1896. His troupes included Carncross and Sharpley (1860–1862), Carncross and Dixey (1862–1878), and Carncross' Minstrels (1878–1896).

Guy Brothers Greater Minstrels (1874–c. 1931). Founded by George Guy (1822–1895), originally comprising father, mother, daughter, and six sons, including Willie, George R., Charles, Albert, Edwin, and Arthur.

Barlow Brothers' Minstrels (1877–1907). Originally headed by song-and-dance team James (c. 1849–1900) and William "Billy" (d. 1914) Barlow. Around 1899, the troupe was taken over by manager J.A. Coburn, who in 1907 renamed it Coburn's Greater Minstrels.

McIntyre and Heath Minstrels (1878–c. 1890). James McIntyre (1857–1937) and Thomas Heath (1853–1938) were probably the biggest stars in minstrelsy during the 1880s and 1890s, as well as the highest-paid blackface stars ever. Described as "beyond all question the greatest duo of blackface delineators of the real Southern darky that the stage ever has or ever will know,"[2] they formed their partnership in 1874 and for the next fifty years alternated between fielding their own troupe, appearing in other major troupes, and headlining in vaudeville. McIntyre played the buffoon and Heath the sharpy.

Hi Henry's Minstrels (1879–c. 1922). Also known as Hi Henry's Premium Minstrels. Founded by Hiram Patrick Henry (1844–1920), a cornetist with the Wallace Sisters and Sam Price's Minstrels earlier in the 1870s. Toured annually for more than 30 years, remaining active until around 1910. Henry himself was not active in later years, but his troupe continued to make intermittent appearances in smaller towns as late as the early 1920s (after his death).

Al G. Field's Greater Minstrels (1886–1928). Alfred Griffin Hatfield (1850–1921) was a comedian in various troupes in the 1870s–1880s, including Haverly's and the minstrel show accompanying the Sells Bros. Circus. His own troupe was one of the most famous of the early 1900s, having the best day in its history in 1915 in Asheville, North Carolina, with 4,000 patrons and gross receipts of $2,500.[3] By 1926, the troupe was trying to stay up to date by advertising "bring on the jazz." An abortive revival in 1931 with a cast of 48 flopped. Also operated Al G. Field's Colored Minstrels (1898).

Dockstader's Minstrels (1886–1910s). Lew Dockstader (1856–1924) began as a song-and-dance man with Carncross, Thatcher, and Haverly in 1870s–1880s. After 1886, he alternated between his own troupes (Dockstader's Minstrels, 1886–1889 and 1891–1895; Primrose and Dockstader, 1898–1903; Dockstader's Minstrels, 1903–?; Primrose and Dockstader, 1912–1914) and performing in other troupes and vaudeville. He also made silent films and recorded for Columbia.

W.S. Cleveland's Minstrels (1888–1901). Cleveland (c. 1861–1923) was the manager of several troupes in the 1880s, including Haverly, Haverly-Cleveland Minstrels (1888), and Cleveland's Minstrels, and then others up to 1901. At one time he had four troupes on the road, as well as a black troupe (1890–1891, q.v.), and a mixed troupe (1895).

Al Reeves' Big Black and White Company (1890s). Reeves (1864–1940) was later known as "The King of Burlesque."

Martin and Selig's Mastodon Minstrels (1890s, mixed, five whites and four blacks). A minor troupe, although at one time it included future superstar Bert Williams.

John W. Vogel's Big City Minstrels (1896–1910s). Vogel (1863–1951) succeeded Haverly as "The Minstrel King." He fielded a fifty-person troupe and also ran Vogel's Afro-American Mastodon Minstrels and later the Honey Boy Minstrels.

De Rue Brothers Ideal Minstrels (1905–1920). Headed by Billy and Bobby De Rue.

Coburn's Greater Minstrels (1907–1929). Headed by cornetist J.A. Coburn (1868–1943), with Harry Frankel in the cast. Coburn's slogan: "Your money's worth or your money back." A continuation of the Barlow Brothers' Minstrels.

Cohan and Harris Minstrels (1908–1910). Formed by Broadway star George M. Cohan (1878–1942) and his business partner Sam Harris. Cohan had shot to fame with his hit musical *Little Johnny Jones* in 1904. Starring in the minstrel troupe was George "Honey Boy" Evans, who took over the troupe in 1910 and renamed it the Honey Boy Minstrels.

Honey Boy Minstrels (1910–mid-1930s). British-born George "Honey Boy" Evans (1870–1915) was a major star in minstrelsy in the 1890s, appearing with Haverly in 1892, Cleveland in 1893, followed by Primrose and West, and then Haverly again in 1894. After several years in vaudeville and musical comedy, he joined Cohan and Harris in 1908 and bought and renamed their troupe in 1910. The Honey Boy Minstrels continued after his death and toured until 1931, operated by John W. Vogel. That troupe closed in the spring of 1931, but in the mid-1930s both Vogel and John Van Arnam intermittently operated troupes called Honey Boy Minstrels. Evans' name continued to live on after that in the form of both amateur and small-time professional groups during the 1940s and 1950s. A late citation shows "Honey Boy Minstrels" being staged as a local police benefit show in Nashville in 1961. Evans was also an accomplished songwriter, with hits including "I'll Be True to My Honeyboy" (from which he took his nickname), "In the Good Old Summertime" and "Come Take a Trip in My Airship."

Neil O'Brien Great American Minstrels (1912–1920s). Founded by O'Brien (1868–1954), formerly a headliner with Lew Dockstader, and including such stars as Black Face Eddie Ross, Eddie Leonard, Will Oakland, and Manuel Romain.

John R. Van Arnam Minstrels (c. 1919–1930s). "The only remaining major minstrel troupe still touring in the summer of 1931."[4] In 1935, Van Arnam was operating the Honey Boy Minstrels.

Lasses White All Star Minstrels (1920–1928). Formed by rising star Lee Roy "Lasses" White (1888–1949), who had been with "Honey Boy" Evans, Neil O'Brien, and Al G. Field in the 1910s. White went on to a prominent career on radio and in films.

Major White or Mixed Troupes in Britain

Christy's was a generic name for "minstrels" in the United Kingdom.

Mohawk Minstrels (1867–1904). Founded on a small scale by brothers James and William Francis in 1867, this troupe grew into the large, major competitor to Moore and Burgess. Interlocutor and songwriter Harry Hunter (c. 1842–1906) was key to the group's success, as well as the foundation of its allied publishing empire Francis, Day & Hunter. In 1900, the troupe combined with Moore and Burgess to become the Mohawk, Moore and Burgess Minstrels for its last four years.

Moore and Burgess Minstrels (1870s–1904). American-born George "Pony" Moore (1820–1909) began in blackface in 1841 and was with U.S. minstrel companies in the 1850s. In 1859, he moved to the United Kingdom, appearing in various troupes, and in the late 1860s/early 1870s began his own troupe, originally called the Christy Minstrels. This later became Moore's, then Moore and Burgess Minstrels, eventually growing into a 70-person troupe. Moore's business partner was Fred Burgess (c. 1827–1893). Like the Mohawks, Moore and Burgess was based in London.

Sam Hague's British Minstrels (1870–1888, brief tours thereafter). Originally a black troupe, and then integrated. Refined, with little comedy. Englishman Hague (1828–1901) was a clog dancer who previously ran troupes in the United States in the 1850s–1860s, including Hague's Concert Co., Wagner and Hague's Minstrels, and Hague's Georgia Minstrels.

Important Post-1890 Black Minstrel Troupes

Georgia Minstrels was often used to designate black troupes in the 1800s.

Lew Johnson's Minstrels (1866–1897). Founded by pioneering black manager Johnson (c. 1840–1910), who was based in Chicago. His four main troupes were Lew Johnson's Minstrels (1866–1867), Lew Johnson's Plantation Minstrels (1871–1896), Lew Johnson's Refined Minstrels (1890–1897), and Johnson's Baby Boy Minstrels (1887–1888). Johnson's troupes generally played outside major cities and were smaller, averaging about twelve men, but they lasted for 30 years.

Callender's Original Georgia Minstrels (1872–mid-1890s). Charles Callender (c. 1827–1897) was a white tavern owner who made black minstrelsy big business with a 60-man troupe. Stars included Billy Kersands and Bob Height. Dominant in the 1870s, Callender sold out to Haverly in 1878, but then he started new troupes. In 1882, the Frohmans bought one of these troupes but continued to use the famous Callender name from 1882 to 1884.

McCabe and Young Minstrels (late 1870s–1907). Also known as McCabe, Young and Hun Brothers Refined Colored Minstrels (1886, Philadelphia, integrated?); McCabe, Young, and Gray's Pavilion Minstrels (1886, Pennsylvania, integrated?); McCabe and Young Minstrels (1880s); McCabe's Mastodon Minstrels (1890s). Producer/vocalist Dan W. McCabe (1860–1907) and comedian Billy Young (1860–1913), who were black, first teamed up in late 1870s and split in 1891, but their troupe remained very popular in the 1890s. Their stars included Billy Wisdom and old-timer Tom McIntosh. McCabe was on the road from 1894 to 1907 with a "20 white–20 black" mixed company. After his death, his son, William M. McCabe, took over briefly. Young stayed in minstrelsy until his death in 1913, with Mahara, Sam T. Jack, Haxpie, Billy Jackson, and others. Their other companies included McCabe and Young's Black Trilby Co. (1887–c. 1903), a minstrel and burlesque troupe, and McCabe's Georgia Troubadours (1900–1910), a variety company organized by William McCabe.

Richards and Pringle's Georgia Minstrels (1883–early 1910s). Another major black troupe from the 1890s, founded by white entrepreneurs O.E. Richards and C.W. Pringle (?–1893). The troupe was hugely popular in the South, advertising "45 people, two bands." Combined with Rusco and Holland's Minstrels in 1897–1899. Billy Kersands starred in the troupe from around 1885 to 1903, while S.H. Dudley joined in 1902.

Kersands' Colored Minstrels (1885–1907). Billy Kersands (c. 1842–1915), a major black star, apparently had his own troupe while appearing with Richards and Pringle. Kersands was famous for his huge mouth, into which he could place billiard balls and saucers.

Hicks and Sawyer's [Consolidated] Colored Minstrels (1886–1891). Formed by Charles B. Hicks and A.D. Sawyer. Hicks (c. 1840–1902) was a hard-driving African American manager who, despite many setbacks, achieved considerable success in the white-dominated field of minstrelsy with a series of troupes during the 1860s and 1870s. In 1886, he teamed with Sawyer, with whom he fought constantly, and their troupe toured Australia in 1889–1890. Hicks sold his interest in 1891 and thereafter managed a circus in Asia. Previously Sawyer ran A.D. Sawyer's Georgia Minstrels (1884–1886).

Mallory Brothers Minstrels (1890s). Headed by singer/dancers Ed and Frank (d. 1917) Mallory. Active since 1881, mostly with other troupes, but they occasionally had their own troupes, such as Crumbaugh and Mallory Brothers (1892) and Mallory Brothers Minstrels (late 1890s). They appeared in vaudeville during 1904–1906 with their wives as Mallory Brothers, Brooks and Halliday.

Sam T. Jack Creole (Burlesque) Co. (1890–c. 1899). Founded by Sam T. Jack (white, 1852–1899), who ran theater and burlesque companies in the 1870s–1880s. This troupe combined farce comedy and shapely black women; there was no plantation material, but performances included a traditional minstrel first part, with a female interlocutor and male endmen. It featured Sam Lucas and discovered Irving Jones, Bob Cole, Dora Dean; the troupe also introduced the hula at the 1893 World's Fair. Jack's advance man John Isham (a light-skinned black) split off and started his own company in 1895 (see transitional formats). Paved the way for black musicals.

W.S. Cleveland's Colored Minstrels (1890–1891). Cleveland, a white minstrel mogul, operated this 40-person black troupe in the early 1890s. Among the stars were James Bland and Billy McClain.

Rusco and Swift's Minstrels/Rusco and Holland's Georgia Minstrels/Rusco and Holland's Big Minstrel Festival/Rusco and Hockwald's Georgia Minstrels (1890–1927). Long-running white-owned troupe, headed by W.A. Rusco (1855–1931) in partnership first with Swift (1890) and then John J. Holland (1897). Joint tour with Richards and Pringle from 1897 to 1900, and then back on their own as Rusco and Holland's Big Minstrel Festival ("55 people, 3 bands"), starring S.H. Dudley and Billy Kersands. In 1920, Rusco partnered with the younger Arthur Hockwald, and by the fall of 1927 ("34th annual tour") the show was being promoted as "a composite of classic form of burnt cork entertainment and the 'jazz style.'"

Mahara's (Mammoth) Colored Minstrels (1892–1909). William A. Mahara (white, d. 1909) managed a number of troupes in the 1870s and 1880s and was McCabe and Young's advance man prior to launching his own black troupe with his brothers Jack and Frank in 1892. Its average roster was 40–60 men. W.C. Handy was the troupe's bandmaster from 1896 to 1903. Frank Mahara also had his own troupe on the road for a time in the 1900s.

Crumbaugh's Colored [Refined] Minstrels (1892–1894). Led by J.E. Crumbaugh.

Haxpie's Colored Georgia Minstrels/C.V. Moore's Colored Minstrels (1893–1895). Managed by C.N. Haxpie. Played 40 weeks at Worth's Museum in New York. Cast included the Unique Quartet, which recorded in the 1890s.

Howard McCarver's Operatic Minstrels (1894). In 1895, the McCarver Brothers were with Al G. Field.

Billy Jackson's Georgia Minstrels (1894). At Worth's Museum, with the cast including the Standard Quartet, which recorded. Jackson previously had two variety troupes from 1890 to 1892.

Denton's Genuine Colored Georgia Minstrels (1895). Based in Flushing, New York, but "toured the Northeast."

Al G. Field's Colored Minstrels (1895–1898). Also known as "Darkest America." This company launched by white minstrel mogul Field represented a substantial overhaul of the traditional minstrel format, substituting for the normal first part "scenes peculiar to the South," such as a camp meeting and a black military drill. In 1898, Field sold the company to John Vogel (white), who reincarnated it as Oliver Scott's Refined Negro Minstrels, with Scott as manager.

Dudley's Georgia Minstrels (1897–1898). Headlined by young black comedian Sherman H. Dudley (c. 1872–1940), early in his career. Dudley went on to become a major star of the black entertainment world, with the Nashville Students, McCabe and Young, and Richards and Pringle, and then with the Smart Set Company. He was known for his act with a live mule named Patrick. In the 1910s, he made history by turning to the business side and forming the first black-run vaudeville circuit, which evolved into the Theater Owners Booking Association (TOBA).

Black Diamond Minstrels (1898–c. 1902). Formed by the Cheatham Brothers, William and Lawrence.

Gideon's Minstrels/Mastodon Minstrels/Big Minstrel Carnival (1898–1902). Led by L.E. Gideon.

A.G. Allen's New Orleans Minstrels (1899–c. 1929). A tent show that toured southern states. It had a traditional format, with current "coon" and other songs, and a cast of approximately 60 people. A.G. Allen (1864–1926), who was white, claimed to have originated minstrel tent shows in 1899; his original partner was George Quine. After Allen's death, the show continued under manager E.S. Winstead, who then ran Winstead's Mighty Minstrels in the 1930s.

New Orleans Minstrels (1899–c. 1909). Run by Joseph M. Moore, manager of the Unique Quartette. Toured the Northeast.

Black Mixed Format and Tent Shows

During the early 1900s, a number of notable black touring shows began to move away from minstrelsy toward a more music-oriented format. Some of these performed exclusively in large circus-style tents, which allowed them to set up in almost any small community.

Isham's Octoroons (1895–1900). Founded by John W. Isham (1866–1902), a fair-skinned black who could pass for white, and who had been Sam T. Jack's advance man. Isham modified Jack's format, stole some of his stars, and launched a new type of show with 16 males and 17 females. There were three acts: (1) songs by chorus and soloists; (2) specialty acts built around a loose storyline; and (3) a finale—for example, a cakewalk, military drill, or jubilee. Isham also produced the musical extravaganza *Oriental America*. From 1901 to 1905, his brother Will reverted to a more traditional minstrel format.

Black Patti Troubadours (1896–c. 1916). Owned by Rudolph Voelckel and James Nolan (both white) and starring African American prima donna Madame Sissieretta Jones (c. 1868–1933), who was known as "The Black Patti" after one of the great white opera stars of the age. A curious mix of high and low art, with a cast of about 80. Act 1 was a farce comedy sketch, followed by songs and acrobatic performances; the show concluded with arias and operatic excerpts by Jones, who sang both opera and "Swanee River." Top stars were engaged for single seasons (e.g. Cole and Johnson, and Ernest Hogan).

Rabbit Foot Minstrels (1900–1959). An extraordinarily long-running tent show founded by Pat Chappelle (black, 1869–1911) and later bought by F.S. Wolcott (white). Included minstrels and other elements. Cast of about 60, including blues singers Ma Rainey, Bessie Smith, and Ida Cox.

Florida Blossoms Minstrels/Florida Blossoms Co. (1906–c. 1934). Tent show founded by R.S. Donaldson (black), Chappelle's early partner, who sold it in 1907 to Charles Douglass (black) and Peter Worthey (black). Cast of 36–40. "Minstrelsy, musical comedy, and high class vaudeville." By 1923, the minstrel first part was gone, and the show had become all "olio."

Silas Green from New Orleans (1907–1958). Another very long-running tent show, founded by circus owner Eph Williams, Salem Tutt Whitney and William A. Baynard, all of whom were black. Originally starred Sherman H. Dudley. The show originated as a sketch ("Silas Green") in other shows (including Williams and Baynard's Famous Troubadours in 1907–1908), moved to the Black Patti Troubadours in 1908–1909, and then returned to Williams and Baynard in 1909. In 1911, the entire troupe became known as "The Silas Green from New Orleans Company." The continuing story originally revolved around a philandering husband and his long-suffering wife; it later became the adventures of short, "coal-black" Silas Green and tall, "tannish" Lilas Bean. By the mid-1910s, the minstrel first part was being phased out. In the 1930s, the show featured contemporary songs like "Lovely to Look At" and "You're a Heavenly Thing," along with the Silas Green Swing and Jazz Band.

C.L. Erickson's Alabama Minstrels (1912).

Outside the United States

Corbyn's Georgia Minstrels (1876–1877). An American troupe founded by comedian-dancer Horace Copeland, which made its name in Australia.

McAdoo's Minstrel and Vaudeville Co./McAdoo's Georgia Minstrels (1895–1900). Owned by Orpheus M. McAdoo (black). A reworking of his 1890–1895 jubilee company, the troupe toured South Africa from 1897 to 1898, where they encountered considerable racial prejudice, and Australia from 1899 to 1900. McAdoo competed with M.B. Curtis in Australia and stress from this experience, as well as from battles within his own ranks, apparently led to his early death in July 1900.

M.B. Curtis Afro-American Minstrel Co. (1899–1900). Curtis (white) brought stars Billy McClain and Ernest Hogan to Australia, but then he abandoned the troupe. It was taken over by Hogan in New Zealand and continued as Hogan's Afro-American Minstrels in Australia and Hawaii.

Appendix 2
Discography of Minstrel Recordings

This discography lists recordings containing an audio recreation of a minstrel first part. Most begin with the familiar statement "Gentlemen, be seated!" Not included, for the most part, are individual songs that might be used in a minstrel show (as well as elsewhere) and standalone routines such as stump speeches and comic dialogues.

Section I covers recordings by the principal early multi-label recording troupes—the Imperial Minstrels, the Rambler Minstrels and the Peerless Minstrels. Section II lists other U.S. minstrel recordings, by label, including LPs. Section III covers British minstrel recordings, and Section IV is songs and sketches *about* minstrelsy.

The format is as follows, from left to right: the catalog number is on far left, followed by the release month/year in parentheses. Discs are 10-inch format, unless otherwise noted. Next is the artist credit, if not given in the header, and the principal songs performed, in the order they appear. Soloists are indicated by their initials. Where different artists appear on different takes, more than one name may be shown separated by a semi-colon. Other information, such as alternate issues, matrix numbers (mx) and recording dates (rec), may follow in square brackets. For full discographical detail, see the discographies listed in the bibliography.

Abbreviations for principal performers: Henry Burr (HB), Albert Campbell (ACa), Arthur Collins (ACo), Collins and Harlan (C&H), S.H. Dudley (SHD), George J. Gaskin (GJG), Billy Golden (BG), George Graham (GG), George W. Johnson (GWJ), Harry Macdonough (HM), Billy Murray (BM), J.W. Myers (JWM), Peerless Quartette (PQ), Steve C. Porter (SCP), quartet (qt), Dan W. Quinn (DWQ), Rambler Minstrels (RM), Harry Spencer (HS), Len Spencer (LS), Frank C. Stanley (FCS), Billy Williams (BW). For others, see header paragraphs.

Label abbreviations: Aretino (Are), Busy Bee (BsB), Columbia-Rena (UK) (C-R), Columbia (Col), Climax (Cx), Diamond (Dmd), Edison (Ed) (Blue Amberol cylinder—BA), Harmony (Har), Harvard (Hv), Kalamazoo (Kal), Manhattan (Man), Marconi (Marc), Oxford (Ox), Pathé (P), Perfect (Pe), Peerless (Peer), Rena Double Face (UK) (RDF), Regal (UK) (Re(UK)), Silvertone (Sil), Standard (Std), Victor (Vic), Velvet Tone (VT), Zonophone (Zon).

I. Principal Multi-Label Recording Groups

Imperial Minstrels (1894–1904)

Formed in 1894 by Len Spencer as the "Spencer, Williams and Quinn Minstrels," with "aged-Negro delineator" Billy Williams, Dan W. Quinn, and George W. Johnson. At first accompanied by piano, tambourine and bones, selections were remade with orchestra around early 1895. An 1897 catalog claimed more than 20 performers were by then involved. Len and Billy were the endmen. Columbia began issuing Imperial Minstrels cylinders around late 1895 (possibly made at first by New Jersey), and the troupe became exclusive to Columbia in June 1897. By 1901–1902, the endmen were Len and Harry Spencer, with solos sung by Len and various others (Stanley, Gaskin, Quinn, etc.). Although Spencer later produced minstrel recordings for numerous labels under various names, those that used the same core group of performers, including his brother Harry, are classified here as by the Imperial Minstrels. The last issues explicitly using the Imperial Minstrels name appear to be for Zonophone in 1903. Berliner also briefly used the name "Imperial Minstrels" for discs by Dudley and the Haydn Quartet.

New Jersey Cylinders (released 1894–1895).

No catalog numbers were assigned.

A High Old Time (LS)
Hear Dem Bells (LS)
Two Little Girls in Blue (DWQ)
Buckle on de Golden Sword (LS)
Old Log Cabin in the Dell (BW)
Laughing Song (GWJ)
Upon the Golden Shore (LS)
Dese Bones Shall Rise Again (LS)
Sweet Marie (DWQ)
Rock Dat Ship (LS)
Play on the Golden Harp (LS)

Columbia Cylinders (1895–1901)

Original numbers, briefly assigned in 1895, are shown in brackets.

13000 (1895) Dese Bones Shall Rise Again (LS) [2249]
13001 (1895) A High Old Time (LS) [2250]
13002 (1895) The Old Log Cabin (SCP) [2251]
13003 (1895) Two Little Girls in Blue (SCP) [2252]
13004 (1895) The Laughing Song (GWJ) [2253]
13005 (1896) Hear Dem Bells (LS)
13006 (1896) Upon the Golden Shore (LS)
13007 (1896) The Golden Harp (LS)
13008 (1898) Mamie Reilly (SCP)
13009 (1899) Hello Ma Baby (LS)
13010 (1899) Old Folks at Home (SCP; FCS)
31608 (1899) Goodbye Dolly Gray (FCS; DWQ)
31609 (1899) Coon, Coon, Coon
31610 (1901) Sadie Ray (Roger Harding)
31691 (1901) I'd Leave My Happy Home for You (LS)
31692 (1901) My Creole Sue (GJG)

(Imperial?) Minstrels: Consolidated Cylinders (1897)

Apparently late products of the U.S. Phonograph Co. of New Jersey, sold by them and by Walcutt & Leeds in New York in late 1897/early 1898. The name may have been a ruse to allow the New Jersey company to continue selling cylinders by the popular Imperial Minstrels after the group became exclusive Columbia artists in mid-1897. Same repertoire as Imperial Minstrels, although none have been heard and they would be difficult to identify since, according to the catalog, the label name was not mentioned in the opening announcement.

1501 Dese Bones Shall Rise Again
1502 Hear Dem Bells
1503 Play on the Golden Harp
1504 Old Log Cabin in the Dell
1505 High Old Time
1506 Two Little Girls in Blue
1507 Laughing Song
1508 Upon the Golden Shore

(IMPERIAL?) MINSTRELS: COLUMBIA 7-INCH AND 10-INCH DISCS (1901–1902)

Columbia did not identify minstrels by name on disc or in catalogs at this time. Even in the double face era, when most artist credits were reinstated, the reissues on A461 and A480 were labeled as by generic "minstrels." However, the Columbia releases prominently feature Len and Harry Spencer as endman and interlocutor, and the performers sound like the Imperial Minstrels. Disc repertoire matches the corresponding Imperial Minstrels Columbia cylinders, at least through the 600s—for example, Columbia 644 (Laughing Song) has identical text and performers as cylinder 13004. Nos. 33–646 have been reported on Columbia but not on Climax (except for no. 643); 798–805 were released on both labels. The few Climax discs heard feature "Mr. Fairchild" as the emcee, with the Spencer brothers not present, and thus do not appear to be by the Imperial Minstrels. Known client label reissues are shown in brackets, but there are undoubtedly more.

Late 1901
33 Dese Bones Shall Rise Again (LS & HS, solo: LS) [also Hv/Ox/Std 33, D&R 3565, Star 4000]

Early 1902
641 Coon, Coon, Coon (LS) [also Hv/Ox/Std 33, RDF 1242]
642 Hear Dem Bells (LS & HS, solo: LS) [also Har/Hv/Ox/Peer/Std 642, RDF 1241]
643 A High Old Time (LS) [also Cx/Ox 643]
644 The Laughing Song (LS & HS, solo: GWJ) [also A461, Hv/Ox/Std 644, Cort F366]
645 The Old Log Cabin in the Dell (LS & HS, solo: FCS; BM; Edward Metcalf) [also A480, Hv/Ox/Peer/Std 645, D&R 3565, Star 4008]
646 Sadie Ray (LS & HS, solo: LS; GJG; DWQ) [also Marc 0379]

Late summer/early fall 1902
798 I've a Longing in My Heart for You Louise (LS & HS, solo: HB; GJG) [also BsB/Cx/Hv/Ox 798]
799 My Heart Loves You Too (voc: G&C) [also Cx 799, Col (UK) D84]
800 Mandy Lee (solo: JWM; GJG) [also Cx 800]
801 My Wild Irish Rose (LS & HS, solo: GJG; ACa) [also Cx 801]
802 Tell Me (solo: HB) [also Cx/Ox 802]
803 When the Autumn Leaves Are Falling (LS & HS, v: GJG; G&C; JWM) [also Cx 803]
804 Old Folks at Home (LS & HS, solo: GJG; JWM; FCS; SCP) [also Cx/Hv/Ox/Peer 804, Marc 0378]
805 My Old Kentucky Home (LS & HS, v: FCS; HB) [also Cx/Hv/Ox/Peer 805, RDF 1241]

(IMPERIAL?) MINSTRELS: COLUMBIA "AN EVENING WITH THE MINSTRELS" SERIES (1903)

A–L played in sequence recreate a full half-hour minstrel show. Released around March 1903. All discs titled "An Evening with the Minstrels." Include Len and Harry Spencer, Collins, Myers, Gaskin, Billy Golden, George Graham, and others. These discs were remade numerous times, and in some cases different artists were used on later takes. I assume by the presence of Len and Harry Spencer that it's the Imperial Minstrels.

Cylinders
32045A Introductory Overture; Operatic Airs

32045B Our Land of Dreams (JWM)
32045C Endman Stories (LS & GJG)
32045D Endman Song: I'm a Nigger That's Living High (LS; BG)
32045E Jokes between Interlocutor and Endmen (HS & BG)
32045F I'm Wearing My Heart Away for You (GJG)
32045G Jokes Between Interlocutor and Endman (HS & BG; HS & Bob Roberts)
32045H My Friend from My Home (LS)
32045I Finale: The Black Hussar's March (JWM)
32045J Musical Specialty, Trumpet Solo, Original Air (Albert Bode)
32045K Monologue (GG; LS)
32045L Yankee Doodle (banjo solo by Vess Ossman)

7- and 10-inch discs
1109A Introductory Overture; Operatic Airs by the Entire Company
1109B Intro.: "Our Land of Dreams" (JWM)
1109C Endman Stories (LS & HS)
1109D Endman Song, "I'm a Nigger That's Living High" (LS; BG; ACo) [also Std 1109D, Star 4001]
1109E Jokes Between Interlocutor and Endmen (LS &HS, ACo, Bob Roberts) [also Silver-Tongued 263]
1109F "I'm Wearing My Heart Away for You" (GJG or HB) [also Cx K151, D&R 3566, Har/Star 4002, Kal 7475]
1109G Jokes Between Interlocutor and Endman (ACo & HS; LS & HS)
1109H Intro.: "My Friend from My Home" (LS) [also Cx K151, D&R 3566, Star 4007]
1109I Finale, "Black Hussar's March" (JWM)
1109J Olio: Musical Specialty, Trumpet Solo (Albert Bode) [also Silver Tongued 359]
1109K Olio: Monologue (GG)
1109L Olio: Yankee Doodle (banjo solo by Ossman)

1908 double sided reissues
A461 Reissue of Col 644
A480 Reissue of Col 645

ZONOPHONE DISCS (1903)

Identified in catalog, on label and in announcements as by "Imperial Minstrels." P = 7 inch, C = 9 inch. See also 1901 Zonophone Minstrels (without Len).

Early 1903 (etched label)
5072P Dese Bones Shall Rise Again
5073P Upon the Golden Shore
5074P Hear Dem Bells
5076P When the Autumn Leaves Are Falling
5077P Old Folks at Home
5078   (unknown title)
5080P My Old Kentucky Home
5081PC The Laughing Song (LS & HS, solo: GWJ)

Later 1903 (paper label)
5469C Dolly Gray (LS & HS, solo: FCS)
5470PC Dese Bones Shall Rise Again
5471PC Hear Dem Bells (LS & HS, solo: LS)
5472PC High Old Time (LS & HS, solo: LS)
5473C The Laughing Song
5474PC Dixie; My Old Kentucky Home (LS & HS, solo: ACa)
5475C Old Folks at Home
5476C Upon the Golden Shore (LS & HS, solo: LS)

Leeds Discs (c. 1904)

Identified as by "Spencer Minstrels" or "Len Spencer Quintet." Len dominates these recordings as the joking endman; the interlocutor is not addressed by name but may be Harry Spencer. Others in the troupe include Joseph Natus, Albert Campbell and Bob Roberts. Label on 4089 reads, "Ebony Empress," but it is announced as "Ebony Emperors." See also "Leeds & Catlin" (label)

4066 (1904) Mother's Watch by the Sea (LS & Natus, voc: Natus)
4075 (1904) Dese Bones Shall Rise Again
4077 (1904) My Heart Is Yours and Yours Alone (LS & Natus, voc: ACa)
4078 (1904) In the Valley of Kentucky
4081 (1904) An Evening with the Minstrels No. 3: Till Snow Flakes Come Again (Natus) [mx 5277. Also Concert 7081 as "Len Spencer and Quintet"]
4085 (1904) Take Me Back to Louisiana
4089 (1904) An Evening with the Minstrels No. 1: The Ebony Emperors of Melody (LS & HS?, sketch) [Also Concert 7089]
4090 (1904) An Evening with the Minstrels No. 4: Down in Mobile Long Ago (ACa) [Also Concert 7090]
4180 (1904) An Evening with the Minstrels No. 2: My Dinah (Roberts) [mx 5278. Also Concert 7180]
4203 (1904) An Evening with the Minstrels No. 6: Hear Dem Bells (LS) [Also Concert 7203]

Rambler Minstrels (1906–1909)

Billy Murray, Byron Harlan, Arthur Collins and Steve Porter. "Mr. Porter" is the interlocutor, with Murray, Collins and sometimes Harlan delivering the jokes. All are addressed by name. Columbia catalog labeled the Rambler Minstrels records as A, B, and so forth. The same group recorded songs as the Ramblers Quartet on minor labels around 1906.

Imperial Discs (Leeds & Catlin)

45000 (1906) First Minstrel Show: Sons of Aristocracy (chorus) I Kind of Like to Have You Fussin' Around (BM)   [mx 6907. Also Concert 71164, D&R 44959, Nassau 26000, Sun 45000]
45001 (1906) Third Minstrel Show: Stand Up and Fight (chorus), Dixie Dear (BM) [mx 6908. Also Are A-226, D&R 44960, Nassau 26001, Sun 45001]
45163 (1906) Second Minstrel Show: Goodbye, Mr. Greenback (ACo) [mx 6904. Also Century 1163, Concert 71163, Royal 153]
45181(10/06) Second Minstrel Show: Yankee Doodle Negroes (chorus); Goodbye, Mr. Greenback (ACo) [mx 6903. Also D&R 44846, Nassau 26181, Sun 45181]

Columbia Cylinders

32952 (7/06)   A: Goodbye Mr. Greenback (ACo) [also BsB 380]
32986 (9/06)   B: Dixie Dear (BM)
33031 (12/06) C: Moses Andrew Jackson, Goodbye (ACo) [also BsB 409]
33104 (4/07)   E: San Antonio (BM)
33161 (9/07)   D: I Know That I'll Be Happy Till I Die (ACo)
85065 (1906)   I Kind of Like to Have You Fussing 'Round
85110 (4/07)   My Kickapoo Queen
85144 (10/07) My Creole Saidee (BM)

Columbia Single-Faced Discs

3448 (9/06) A: Sons of Aristocracy; I Kind of Like to Have You Fussing 'Round (BM) [also A464, Ox/Sil/Std 3448, Marc 0380, Std K152, BsB/Har/Star 4003]

3449 (9/06) B: Yankee Doodle Negroes; Goodbye Mr. Greenback (ACo) [also A479, Std 3449, Std K152, BsB/Star 4004]
3478 (10/06) C: Stand Up and Fight; Dixie Dear (BM) [also A469, Cx K153, D&R 3567, BsB/Har/Star 4005]
3479 (10/06) D: Wait Til the Sun Shines, Nellie; Waltz Me Around Again, Willie (C&H) [also A466, Are D620, Cx K153, D&R 3567, Har/Star 4006]
3531 (1/07) E: Is Everybody Happy; Crocodile Isle (BM) [also A465, Clarion/Std 3531, Cx X605. BsB/Har/Star 5114]
3554 (2/07) F: Timbuctoo; Moses Andrew Jackson, Goodbye (ACo) [also A462, Std 3554, BsB/Star 5115]
3608 (5/07) H: In the Good Old United States; San Antonio (BM) [also A459, Are D546, BsB/Star 5414]

12-inch disc
30062 (5/07) College Life; My Kickapoo Queen (ACo) [also A5027, Are/BsB/Star 1223, RDF 145]

COLUMBIA DOUBLE-FACED DISCS:

A459 Reissue of Col 3608 (San Antonio)
A462 Reissue of Col 3554 (Moses Andrew Jackson, Goodbye)
A464 Reissue of Col 3448 (I Kind of Like to Have You Fussin' Around)
A465 Reissue of Col 3531 (Crocodile Isle)
A466 Reissue of Col 3479 (Waltz Me Around Again, Willie)
A469 Reissue of Col 3478 (Dixie Dear)
A479 Reissue of Col 3449 (Goodbye Mr. Greenback)
A658 (5/09) Smiling Star (BM) [mx 4017, also D&R 3605, Dmd A658, Ox 4017]
A667 (6/09) Down in Georgia on Camp Meeting Day; L-O-V-E Spells Trouble to Me (ACo) [mx 4016, also Ox/Sil 4016, Are D652, Dmd/Std A667, D&R 3615]

12-inch discs
A5027 (1908) Reissue of Col 30062 (My Kickapoo Queen)

Although labeled as by the Rambler Minstrels, A5123 and A5138 are actually by the Peerless Quartet, led by Frank C. Stanley. See under "Columbia" (label) for details.

VICTOR SINGLE- AND DOUBLE-FACED DISCS (1908–1909)

See under Victor, Christy Minstrels (5000s) and Victor Minstrels (16000s)

AMERICAN 10.5-INCH DISCS

Some shown simply as "male quartette." Same scripts as on Columbia, but different recordings per A/B comparison.

031359 (6/06) Minstrel Record A: Sons of Aristocracy; I Kind of Like to Have You Fussin' 'Round (BM) [mx X1130. Also BsB 1359, Peer 031359]
031360 (6/06) Minstrel Record B: Yankee Doodle Negroes; Goodbye Mr. Greenback (ACo) [mx X1110. Also BsB 1360, Peer 031360]
031361 (6/06) Minstrel Record C: Stand Up and Fight; Dixie Dear (BM) [mx unk. Also BsB 1361, Britannic (UK) 1361]
031423 (fall 1906) Minstrel Record D: Wait Til the Sun Shines, Nellie; Waltz Me Around Again, Willie (C&H) [mx X1434. Also BsB 1423]
031424 (fall 1906) Minstrel Record E: Is Everybody Happy; Crocodile Isle (BM) [mx unk. Also BsB 1424]
031425 (fall 1906) Minstrel Record F: In Timbuctoo; Moses Andrew Jackson, Goodbye (ACo) [mx X1350. Also BsB 1425]

ZONOPHONE 10-INCH DISCS

As Rambler Minstrels. See Zonophone (label) for 1909–1911 releases labeled as by Rambler Minstrels but actually by the Peerless Minstrels.

Single-faced
720 (4/07) No. 1: In the Good Old United States; San Antonio (BM) [also Ox 720]
741 (5/07) No. 2: Wait Till the Sun Shines, Nellie; You'll Have to Wait Till My Ship Comes In (BM) [also Ox 741]
789 (7/07) No. 3: Goodbye New York Town; My Creole Saidee (BM) [also Ox 789]
790 (7/07) No. 4: College Life; My Kickapoo Queen (ACo) [also Ox 790]
871 (10/07) No. 5: It's Always the Same in Dixie; I Know That I'll Be Happy Till I Die (ACo) [also Ox 871]
963 (2/08) No. 6: Bye Bye My Sailor Boy; Goodbye Honey Goodbye (ACo) [also Ox 963]
988 (3/08) No. 7: Bye Bye My Caroline; At the Meeting House Tonight (BM) [also Ox 988]
1056 (5/08) No. 8: Make a Lot of Noise; Every Day She Wanted Something Else (ACo) [also Ox 1056]
1078 (6/08) No. 9: Bronco Buster; I'm Happy When the Band Plays Dixie (BM) [also Ox 1078]
1146 (9/08) No. 10: In My Dream of the U.S.A.; Moonbeams (quartet) [also Ox 1146]
1184 (10/08) No. 11: I Wish I Was in Dixie; Some Day Melinda (quartet) [also Ox 1184]

Double-faced
5135 Reissue of No. 1/No. 2 [720/741]
5136 Reissue of No. 3/No. 4 [789/790]
5137 Reissue of No. 5/No. 6 [871/963]
5158 Reissue of No. 7/No. 8 [988/1056]
5139 Reissue of No. 9/No. 10 [1078/1146]
5190 (3/09) No. 12: When the Band Strikes Up Dixie; Smiling Star (BM)/No. 13: Down in Georgia on Camp Meeting Day; L-O-V-E Spells Trouble (ACo) (Murray, Harlan, Collins and Porter are listed by name on the label of this issue) [also Ox 5190]

INDESTRUCTIBLE CYLINDERS

As Dixie Minstrels (1907–1908). See under "Indestructible."

EDISON CYLINDERS (AS BY EDISON MINSTRELS)

9672 (10/07) Dixie Minstrels: Sons of the Aristocracy; My Creole Saidee (quartet) (Personnel: Meeker substitutes for Collins)
9953 (10/08) Jubilee Minstrels: College Life; I'm Happy When the Band Plays Dixie (quartet)
10135 (5/09) Model Minstrels: Bronco Buster; In the Good Old United States (quartet)

Peerless Quartet/Minstrels (1907–1917)

The Peerless Quartet was formed in 1906 by Frank C. Stanley as an offshoot of the Columbia Quartet, with which he had performed. It was very popular for the next 20 years, and in its early history it made numerous minstrel records on many labels, sometimes as the "Peerless Minstrels" but usually under other names. It largely replaced the Rambler Minstrels for new minstrel records. The original Peerless lineup was Henry Burr (lead tenor), Albert Campbell (tenor), Steve Porter (baritone), and Stanley (bass/manager). All four referred to each other by name in the spoken portions of their recordings, typically by first name except for "Mr. Stanley," who served as the pompous interlocutor. In 1909, Porter was replaced by Arthur Collins, who specialized in black delineations and was featured on many solos. Upon the sudden death of Stanley in December 1910, Burr took over management of the group, and bass/baritone John H. Meyer was hired to replace Stanley as interlocutor—although, unlike Stanley, he was seldom referred to by name (when he was, it was often as "Mr. Wilbur" since he sometimes used the pseudonym John Wilbur on recordings). The lineup for the rest of the Peerless Minstrel records is thus Burr, Campbell, Collins and Meyer.

See individual labels for Peerless Minstrel records.

II. Other Minstrel Records by Label

American (See Rambler Minstrels)

Aretino

Reissues of Columbia and Leeds discs by the Rambler Minstrels in the Aretino A200, D500 series

10-inch single-faced
A211 Minstrel Record G—?
A224 Minstrel Record D—?
A226 Minstrel Record C—Reissue of Imperial 45001
A228 Minstrel Record F—Reissue of Col 3554?

12-inch single-faced
A1223 My Kickapoo Queen—Reissue of Col 30062

10-inch double-faced
D546 Minstrel Record G—Reissue of Col 3608 (Minstrel Record H)
D620 Minstrel Record D—Reissue of Col 3479
D652 L-O-V-E Spells Trouble to Me—Reissue of Col A667 [mx 4016]

Banner

Henry Burr is the interlocutor on the following. Identities of the other participants, addressed as Tambo, Bones, Mose, and so on, are unknown.

6397 (1929) Carolina Minstrels: Minstrel Show Pt 1: Dixie; Ida Sweet as Apple Cider (Jubilee Four quartet); Rufus Rastus Johnson Brown (Tambo); Silver Threads Among the Gold (HB as "Col. Bob Lee")/Pt 2: Oh, Didn't He Ramble (Bones); My Gal Sal (quartet); Finale (Goodnight Ladies & Auld Lang Syne by entire co.). [mxs 8690–91. Also on Challenge 835 and Oriole 1590, and possibly Domino, Regal, and Romeo]

Berliner

Berliner released three groups of minstrel records during its short existence.

7-inch single-faced, released 1898
Berliner's first three minstrel discs were recorded around June 1898 and identified simply by the names of the principal performers, who traded jokes ("Parkham," John Terrell, and George Graham). On each, the interlocutor announces "introductory overture by the orchestra," but only a piano is heard. No. 6004 is announced as by "The Diamond Minstrels of Washington, D.C."
6004 (10/98) Parkham & Terrell: Minstrel Record—At a Georgia Camp Meeting; Up Dar in de Sky
6009 (10/98) Parkham & Terrell: Minstrel Show—Sally Warner (Terrell)
6010 (10/98) Graham & Terrell: Minstrel Show: Get Your Money's Worth (Terrell?)

7-inch single-faced, released 1899 (Imperial Minstrels)
The April 1899 catalog contained three new routines, all credited to "The Imperial Minstrels," a group consisting of S.H. Dudley and the Haydn Quartet and apparently not connected with the Len Spencer group of the same name. Dudley and W.F. Hooley traded jokes. The Haydn

lineup is uncertain. Dudley and Hooley were regular members of the quartet in 1898–1899, but there was turnover in the tenors. The original Haydn tenors, Roger Harding and "Leigh," were replaced during 1899 by Jere Mahoney, Fred Rycroft and John Bieling.

6021 (4/99) Minstrel 1st Part: My Coal Black Lady (SHD, Haydn Qt)
6022 (4/99) Minstrel 1st Part: A Hot Time in the Old Town (SHD, Haydn Qt)
6024 (4/99) Minstrel 1st Part: Sally in Our Alley (Mahoney, Haydn Qt)

7-inch single-faced, released 1900 (Gramophone Minstrels)
The final series of Berliner minstrel records was recorded on March 28, 1900, as by "The Gramophone Minstrels" and released later that year. The troupe was identified as Dudley, Hooley, Macdonough, and Banta.

01134 (1900) Minstrel 1st Part No. 1: The Old Log Cabin; How I Love My Lou (SHD)
01135 (1900) Minstrel 1st Part No. 2: Just One Girl (HM)
01136 (1900) Minstrel 1st Part No. 3: Massa's in de Cold, Cold Ground (WFH)
01137 (1900) Minstrel 1st Part No. 4: Darktown Is Out Tonight (SHD)
01138 (1900) Minstrel 1st Part No. 5: Old Black Joe; Old Folks at Home (WFH)

Brunswick

Br 2727 is a burlesque by old-time comedian Lewis, accompanied by Ernest Hare as interlocutor. With orchestra.

2727 (1924) Tom Lewis. Old Time Minstrel Scene: Sweet Antoinette (Lewis) [mx 13945, rec 10/14/24]

Busy Bee

Busy Bee (c. 1905–1906) drew masters from many sources, including American and Columbia. Following are minstrel records that have been identified. See also entries under Imperial and Rambler Minstrels.

Busy Bee Disc Records
1359 —from American 031359 [mx X1130]
1360 —from American 031360 [mx X1110; ctrl M4004]
1361 —from American 031361
1423 —from American 031423 [mx X1434; ctrl M4006]
1424 —from American 031424; later pressings use Col 3531 [ctrl M5114]
1425 —from American 031425 [mx X1350]; later pressings use Col 3554 [ctrl M5115]

Cameo

Cast includes James Stanley as interlocutor, Billy Murray, "Al" (Campbell?), Jack Kaufman, Walter Van Brunt. Presumably recorded in early 1929, just prior to the merger of Cameo/Pathé with Regal (Plaza) in July, to form the American Record Co.

9164 (1929) Dixie Minstrels. Minstrel Show Pt. 1: Make a Lot of Noise, Goodbye Eliza Jane (BM), Lindy (qt); Pt. 2: My Gal Is a High Born Lady (JK), Dear Old Girl (WVB), Massa's in the Cold, Cold Ground (company) [mxs 3826 27. Also Romeo 966]

Celebrity

"Al Bernard's Merry Minstrel Show," Al Bernard (endman) and the Home Town Minstrel Band, with Tom Shirley, interlocutor. Licensed by Beacon Record Co.; published by Joe Davis. Reissued on Jay-Dee LP No. 1.

2000-1-3 (1948) Pt 1: There's Nothing Like a Minstrel Show/Pt. 3: Trombone Jitters (band)

2000-2-4 Pt. 2: Truthfully (Henry Shope with Sunflower Qt)/Pt 4: Bill Bailey, Won't You Please Come Home (Al Bernard)

Chicago Talking Machine Company

The following are listed in catalogs under the heading "Minstrel First Part." The first series was renumbered in 1896, as indicated. It is uncertain whether these were made by CTMC or some other entity; CTMC resold cylinders from other makers, especially Columbia, giving them its own numbers, but it also made its own. The first five of the of the 1895 group were titles made by Len Spencer's Imperial Minstrels for New Jersey, although it is uncertain whether these are the Spencer cylinders. The last four are titles seen nowhere else, perhaps made exclusively for Chicago (possibly by the New Jersey company?). The 1899 list appears to be from a variety of sources, including Columbia, Edison, and the U.S. Phonograph Co.

c. 1895 cylinders (1896 numbers in parentheses)
1900 (2300) Playing on the Golden Harp
1901 (2301) Hear Dem Bells
1902 (2302) Laughing Song
1903 (2303) Two Little Girls in Blue
1904 (2304) High Old Times
1905 (2305) Standing on the Corner
1906 (2306) Pretty Mamie Casey
1907 (2307) Uncle Eph's Return
1908 (2308) Pussy Green

c. 1899 cylinders ("C" indicates available in Concert size)
850C Dese Bones Shall Rise Again
851 Hear Dem Bells
852C High Old Time
853C Old Log Cabin in the Dell
854 Play on the Golden Harp
855 Elsie from Chelsea (quartet chorus)
856 How I Love My Lou (with whistling chorus)
857 Laughing Song and Trombone Solo
858 Minstrel Scene (quartet chorus)
859 Remus Takes the Cake and Cornet Solo
860 Three Minutes with the Minstrels (quartet chorus)
861 Just One Girl

Columbia

From 1895 to 1903, most Columbia minstrel records featured Len Spencer's Imperial Minstrels, although a few early Climax discs issued in 1901–1902 were by a different group. After the Imperial Minstrels disbanded, Columbia replaced them in 1906 with Billy Murray's Rambler Minstrels. In November 1907, the supplement announced that, beginning with No. 3710, Columbia would feature a "new combination, known as 'The Peerless Minstrels.'" Researchers Guy Marco and Ulysses "Jim" Walsh say this is F.C. Stanley's Peerless Quartet—Henry Burr, Albert Campbell, S.C. Porter and Frank C. Stanley at the time. From that point through 1915, all new Columbia minstrel recordings (except A658 and A667) appear to be by the Peerless group, including two (A5123, A5138) that were labeled as by the "Rambler Minstrels." See the Imperial and Rambler Minstrels for Columbia recordings by those groups.

CLIMAX 7-INCH AND 10-INCH SINGLE-FACED DISCS

Only a few of the early Climax minstrel discs have been auditioned, but they are all by a different group than the later Columbia releases that used the same catalog numbers. The interlocutor is addressed as "Mr. Fairchild," an unfamiliar name on records at the time, whose voice and delivery are quite different from what is heard on other minstrel records. The featured numbers are duets by Gaskin and Campbell, which is also unusual. It is not known whether the rest of the Climaxes are by this group, but it seems likely. For later Columbia releases using the same numbers and titles, see "Imperial Minstrels."

Early 1902
643 A High Old Time [also Col/Ox 643]

Late summer/early fall 1902
798 I've a Longing in My Heart for You Louise [also Col/Hv/Ox 798]
799 My Heart Loves You Too [also Col 799, Col (UK) D84]
800 Mandy Lee [also Col 800]
801 My Wild Irish Rose (GJG & ACa) [also Col 801]
802 Tell Me [also Col/Ox 802]
803 When the Autumn Leaves Are Falling (GJG & ACa) [also Col 803]
804 Old Folks at Home (GJG & ACa); cornet solo by E. Keneke [also Col/Hv/Ox/Peer 804, Marc 0378]
805 My Old Kentucky Home (GJG & ACa) [also Col/Hv/Ox/Peer 805, RDF 1241]

COLUMBIA SINGLE-FACED DISCS
Porter rather than Stanley is the interlocutor on 3710.

3710 (11/07) Peerless Minstrels: Virginia; I Can't Find Another Girl Like You (FCS) [Also Man/Std 3710, Col/Har/Std A354, Star 5814, Col (UK) D186, RDF 1242]

COLUMBIA DOUBLE-FACED DISCS

10-inch discs
A354 (1908) Reissue of Col 3710 (Peerless Minstrels)
A461 (1908) Reissue of Col 644 (Imperial Minstrels)
A480 (1908) Reissue of Col 645 (Imperial Minstrels)
A3871 (7/23) Lasses White and Co. with Al Bernard: Lasses White Minstrels Levee Scene: Drag That Cotton; Camptown Races (qt)/Plantation Scene: Balm of Gilead (qt); The Blues Ain't Nothing But a Good Man Feeling Bad (White) (Personnel include White and Bernard cracking jokes, Wilfred Glenn as "boss" in the levee sketch, a prominent banjo player, and the Shannon Four—Lewis James, Charles Hart, Elliott Shaw and Glenn. The files also list Vernon Dalhart, but he is not aurally present.)
A3918 (9/23) Lasses White: Sweet Mama, Tree Top Tall ("minstrel song")
14004-D (1923) Gulf Coast Minstrels: I Ain't Skeered of Work/Darktown Camp Meeting (sketches by Cliff Ross and Perry Bradford, with music by the quartet from "Dinah")
1714-D (4/29) Dailey Paskman's Radio Minstrels, Pt 1: Oh! Susannah; My Old Kentucky Home (Diamond Studded Qt); Arkansas Traveler (Banjo Buddies)/Pt. 2: New Bully (Bones); Climbing Up the Golden Stairs (all)

12-inch discs (A5072 through A5614 are all by the Peerless Minstrels)
A5072 (11/08) Peerless Minstrels: We Won't Go Home Till Morning, Bill; Down in Jungle Town (qt) [also Std 1263] [SCP is interlocutor on this; FCS, called "Frank," is an endman]
A5123 (10/09) Rambler Minstrels [sic]: Kiss Your Minstrel Boy Goodbye; When a Pal of Mine Steals a Gal of Mine (ACo)/My Wild Deer; I Wish I Was in Heaven Sittin' Down (ACo)
A5138 (1/10) Rambler Minstrels [sic]: Virginia; The Humming Coon (ACo); Climb Up Ye Children Climb
A5173 (7/10) Minstrels: Linder Green; Fly Fly Fly (ACo); My Rosy Rambler
A5251 (3/11) Minstrels: Carrie from Caroline; Happy Days in Dixie (ACo); Balmoral [Also C-R 420]

A5309 (9/11)   Columbia Minstrels: Oh, Dem Golden Slippers; My Dusky Rose (ACo); I Ain't Gwine to Weep No More [Also C-R 334]
A5346 (2/12)   Columbia Minstrels: In the Morning by the Bright Light; Everybody Whistles Like Me (ACo); Melancholy Mose [Also C-R 334]
A5497 (11/13) Columbia Minstrels: De Golden Wedding; Angel Gabriel (ACo); Bye Bye Ma Eva
A5614 (1/15)   Columbia Minstrels: Push Dem Clouds Away; I Don't Care If You Never Come Back (ACo); Goodbye Manhattan Isle
A6231 (11/23) Lasses White Minstrel Co. with Al Bernard: Old Time Minstrels, Pt. 1: Oh, Dem Golden Slippers; Darling Nellie Gray (qt); Silver Threads Among the Gold (Hart); My Gal (Bernard)/Pt. 2: Asleep in the Deep (Glenn); Clap Your Hands (White); Finale—Polly Wally Doodle (entire co.) (Personnel include Wilfred Glenn as interlocutor, White, Bernard, and the Shannon Four—Lewis James, Charles Hart, Elliott Shaw and Glenn. The files also indicate Vernon Dalhart, but he is not aurally present.)

The following are obscure early 1930s U.S. reissues of British Regal releases; see under "British Minstrel Records."

55029-D Reissue of Re(UK) G1076 (1929)
55030-D Reissue of Re(UK) G1077 (1929)

Concert

See Len Spencer Minstrels, Leeds & Catlin masters (Concert 7000 series).

D&R

See Rambler Minstrels. Leeds & Catlin mxs (D&R 44000 series), Columbia mxs (D&R 3000 series).

Duplex

Reissues of Columbia masters.

Edison

Edison utilized a number of artists for its minstrel records over the years. The following are all cylinders, unless otherwise noted.

1. MANHANSETT QUARTETTE (?)

An early 1890s North American–style title slip has been found headed "Minstrel First Part: High Old Time." Although the slip does not identify the artists, the Manhansett Quartette recorded that title along with 19 others on September 27, 1891. A surviving Edison recording logbook does not specify whether the quartet's recording was done as a minstrel routine, so this identification is uncertain; the slip may refer to a later recording.

c. 1891 issue?
— Minstrel First Part: High Old Time

2. MINSTRELS, ACCOMPANIED BY BANTA'S ORCHESTRA

A North American catalog supplement for December 1, 1893, lists the following two titles as "Minstrel 1st parts, introducing middle and end men, gags and songs, accompanied by Banta's Parlor Orchestra." Artists and contents are unknown.

1893 issues
848	Minstrel, 1st Part, No. 1
883	Minstrel, 1st Part, No. 2

3. BILLY GOLDEN AND DICK CHALFANT

c. 1897–1898 issues
4016	Minstrel Scene
4018	Three Minutes with the Minstrels

4. BILLY HEINS AND THE ANCIENT CITY QUARTET, WITH ORCHESTRA (1898)

1898 issues
4700	How I Love My Lou
4701	Elsie from Chelsea
4702	Laughing Song (ACo); Rocked in Cradle of Deep (Joe Rockwell, tb)
4703	Remus Takes the Cake (with cornet solo)
4704	Minstrel Scene: Enjoy Yourselves (ACo)
4705	Three Minutes with the Minstrels

5. ARTHUR COLLINS, S.H. DUDLEY AND THE ANCIENT CITY QUARTET (1899–1901)

Copies heard feature Collins, Dudley and Billy Heins? (= CDH). "Sam" (Dudley) and "Billy" referred to in routines; the latter is probably Billy Heins, rather than Billy Williams, but I can't be certain. See also unidentified cylinder.

May 1899 issues
4700 How I Love My Lou (SHD, ACQ)
4701 Just One Girl (ACo, SHD, ACQ)
4702 Smoky Mokes; Laughing Song (ACo)
4703 My Ann Elizer (ACo, SHD, ACQ)
4704 Minstrel Scene: My Hannah Lady (ACo, ACQ)
4705 Three Minutes with the Minstrels: Break the News to Mother (SHD, ACQ)

Later issues
7164 (6/99) Minstrel Potpourri: Old Log Cabin in the Dell; Fly Fly Fly (ACo, ACQ)
7293 (11/99) Plantation Minstrels: Old-Time Songs—Old Black Joe; Massa's in the Cold, Cold Ground (SHD)
7376 (11/99) Echoes of Minstrelsy: In the Evening by the Moonlight; Darktown Is Out Tonight (ACo)
N4700 (4/01) California Minstrels (SHD, ACo)
N4701 (4/01) Alabama Troubadours: Goodbye Dolly Gray (SHD)
N4703 (4/01) Reminiscences of Blackface: My Rainbow Coon (ACo)

6. EDISON MINSTRELS

After a gap with no minstrels in the catalog, Edison introduced the Edison Modern Minstrels on black wax cylinders in 1903, succeeding Collins, Dudley and the Ancient City Quartet. There were also Edison Minstrels on 5-inch Concert cylinders (1898–1901), which may actually be by the Ancient City Quartet (note titles). Initially Dudley (cmcee) and endman Len Spencer traded jokes in the new combination. Len Spencer and Billy Murray were endmen beginning in 1905. Other participants included Arthur Clifford (pseudonym for George Alexander), Harry Macdonough, Will F. Denny, the Edison Quartet (EQ) and the Edison Male Quartet (EMQ). "Modern" was dropped from listings in 1904.

Edison 5-inch Concert cylinders (1899–1901)

These oversized Edison Concert cylinders duplicated titles in the regular catalog but provided extra volume. They were produced by a pantograph system from normal-sized molded masters. Concert-size cylinders were also produced before and after this special "B" series, using the regular catalog numbers.

B204 Minstrel Potpourri
B205 Echoes of Minstrelsy
B206 Three Minutes with the Minstrels
B237 Plantation Minstrelsy
B370 Christy Minstrel, 1st Part
B371 Minstrel Scene
B460 Minstrel 1st Part

Edison 2-minute cylinders

8325 (1/03) Reminiscences of Minstrelsy: Walk Along the Golden Shore
8326 (1/03) Echoes of Minstrelsy
8454 (8/03) Up to Date Minstrelsy No. 1: My Love I Dare Not Tell (Arthur Clifford)
8631 (3/04) Alabama Minstrels: The Tarrif Galop; Down in Mobile Long Ago (HM)
8672 (4/04) Georgia Minstrels: Uncle Billy's Dream (LS, EQ)
8690 (5/04) California Minstrels: Darling Clo (HM)
8920 (2/05) Louisiana Minstrels: Keep a Climbin' (LS & EMQ)
8951 (3/05) Tennessee Minstrels (LS & BM): My Love Remains the Same (HM & EMQ)
9024 (6/05) South Carolina Minstrels (LS & BM): Beneath the Starry Flag; It's Allus de Same in Dixie (BM & EQ)
9072 (8/05) Mississippi Minstrels (LS & BM): There's a Light in the Window (HM)

May 1906 release

According to the Edison cash books (February 23, 1906, entry), the following were paid for the "At the Minstrel Show" session: Arthur Collins, Byron G. Harlan, Billy Murray, Len Spencer, Harry Macdonough, George W. Johnson, Vess Ossman and the Edison Quartette. Will F. Denny also appears. Johnson is not audible, but he may have participated in the crowd laughter. There is no interlocutor; staff announcer Ed Meeker introduces the acts. Note that the routine on 9279 was recorded as "The Jokesmiths" on Ind cylinder 747 and Vic 31545.

9275 At the Minstrel Show No. 1: Around the World (entire co.)
9276 At the Minstrel Show No. 2: Jokes by ACo & BGH; When the Days Grow Longer (ACo)
9277 At the Minstrel Show No. 3: Jokes by LS & BM; The Lighthouse by the Sea (HM)
9278 At the Minstrel Show No. 4: A Matrimonial Chat (WFD monologue); It's All a Matter of Taste (WFD)
9279 At the Minstrel Show No. 5: Jokes by LS & BM; Everybody Jokes But Father (LS & BM)
9280 At the Minstrel Show No. 6: Plantation Sketch—A Darktown Serenade (all)
9672 (10/07) (See Rambler Minstrels)
9953 (10/08) (See Rambler Minstrels)
10135 (5/09) (See Rambler Minstrels)

Edison 4-minute wax Amberol

64 (1/09) Elks Minstrel Co. Elks' Minstrels: Anvil Chorus; My Own Wild Deer; Sweetheart (Harry Anthony); For the Old Red, White and Blue. (Personnel: Billy Murray, Steve Porter, Edw. Meeker, John Young [as Harry Anthony], Ada Jones. Eugene Jaudas, cond.)
Special K (4/10) Peerless Qtte & Co.: Peerless Minstrels: Virginia; Humming Coon (ACo); Climb Up, Ye Chillun, Climb (This was part of a special set [A–K] offered for $1 to customers who had their older two-minute Edison phonographs upgraded to play the new four-minute cylinders. See also 5378.)

Edison Blue Amberol cylinders

Special K (1913) Peerless Minstrels—reissue of Edison 4M Special K
2321 (6/14) Elks' Minstrels—reissue of Edison 4M 64
3755 (6/19) Premier Quartet Minstrels—dubbed from Diamond Disc 50750
5378 (9/27) Peerless Minstrels: "An Old Time Minstrel Show"—reissue of Edison 4M Special K

Edison Diamond discs

50750 (11/21) Premier Quartet Minstrels. Land of Minstrelsy: See Saw; Goodnight Dear (George Wilton Ballard) ("Premier Quartet" was generally used by Edison as an alternate name for the American Quartet, with Billy Murray as lead singer. The other members here seem to differ from those in the American Quartet, however. Besides Murray, those addressed by name are Steve Porter (interlocutor) and "Ed" (Meeker?). The American Quartet at this time consisted of Murray, Porter, John Young and Donald Chalmers.) [Recorded February 26–28, 1919]

51363 (8/24) Empire Vaudeville and Minstrel Co. Minstrelsy of Other Days, Pt. 1: Landstrum Galop, Down Where the Cotton Blossoms Grow (Jay Clay), Trans-Mag-Ni-Fi-Can-Bam-U-Al-I-Try (Harry Docken)/Pt. 2: When the Harvest Days Are Over Jessie Dear (James Doherty), My Castle on the Nile (Docken) (This group had no fixed membership. Docken and Doherty are endmen; the interlocutor is not identified.)

Emerson

PEERLESS QUARTET

7-inch disc
7210 (1917) Emerson Minstrels No. 1: Oh, Dem Golden Slippers, My Dusky Rose

Excelsior (1898 Cylinder)

One minstrel recording has been traced to the short-lived Excelsior Phonograph Co. of New York, which produced cylinders from 1898 to 1900. This recording probably dates from early or mid-1898. No titles or personnel given. May be either the Greater New York Quartet or the Excelsior Quartet, both of which included Porter and Harding(?).The unrelated Excelsior disc label of 1905–1906, a product of the International Record Co., does not appear to have issued any minstrel recordings, although it did release a number of non-minstrel recordings by "The Ramblers," a quartet with the same personnel as the Rambler Minstrels.

Excelsior Minstrel Co. (Steve Porter as interlocutor, Roger Harding, two others)
—(1898) Excelsior Minstrel Co.: A Hot Time in the Old Town Tonight (Roger Harding)

Imperial

This was the flagship label of Leeds & Catlin from 1905 to 1907, succeeding the foil-label Leeds label. See "Rambler Minstrels."

Indestructible Cylinders

Personnel are addressed by name in the skits.

Two-minute cylinders
Rambler Minstrels (Murray, Collins, Harlan, Porter as interlocutor):

654 (11/07) Dixie Minstrels #1: Bronco Buster; Two Little Baby Shoes (BGH)
655 (11/07) Dixie Minstrels #2: Bye Bye My Sailor Boy; Goodbye Honey, Goodbye (ACo)
807 (7/08) Dixie Minstrels #3: Bye Bye My Caroline; I'm Happy When the Band Plays Dixie (BM)
863 (10/08) Dixie Minstrels #4: My Dream of the U.S.A.; Moonbeams (quartet)
1013 (3/09) Dixie Minstrels #5: Down in Georgia on Campmeeting Day; L-O-V-E (ACo)

Peerless Minstrels (Campbell, Burr, Collins, Stanley as interlocutor):

1124 (8/09) Dixie Minstrels #6: Kiss Your Minstrel Boy Goodbye; My Pony Boy (FCS)
1231 (12/09) Dixie Minstrels #7: I Come from a Yankee Doodle Town; I Wish I Was in Heaven Sitting Down (ACo)

Four-minute cylinders
Peerless Minstrels (Campbell, Burr, Collins, Stanley as interlocutor):

3012 (1/10) Carolina Minstrels No. 1: Virginia I Love But You; The Humming Coon (ACo); Climb Up Ye Chillun Climb
3075 (6/10) Carolina Minstrels No. 2; Linder Green; Fly, Fly, Fly (ACo); My Rosy Rambler
3138 (10/10) Carolina Minstrels No. 3: Carrie from Caroline; Happy Days in Dixie (ACo); Balmoral

Keen-O-Phone

5032 (c. 1912) Peerless Quartet: Minstrel No. 1: My Rainbow Coon; All Coons Look Alike to Me

Leeds & Catlin

This company manufactured a group of budget labels from 1903 to 1909, in defiance of Victor and Columbia patents. From 1903 to 1906, its principal imprint was Leeds (originally distinguished by its embossed gold-foil label), which included original recordings by Len Spencer's Imperial Minstrels. By 1906, it had switched to the Imperial label and was using the Rambler Minstrels. Its last flagship label (1907–1908) was Sun, which does not appear to have originated any minstrel records.

Little Wonder

All of the following are believed to be by the Peerless Quartet: Burr, Campbell, Collins, and Meyer.

5.5-inch discs
53 (1914)   Minstrel First Part: Push Dem Clouds Away; Goodbye Manhattan Isle (qt)
340 (1916) Minstrels Pt. 1: My Rainbow Coon; All Coons Look Alike to Me (qt)
341 (1916) Minstrels Pt. 2: Oh, Dem Golden Slippers; Ma Dusky Rose (qt.)
342 (1916) Minstrels Pt. 3: You're a Grand Old Flag; Darktown Is Out Tonight (qt)
343 (1916) Minstrels Pt. 4: Way Down in Alabam'; Goodbye Eliza Jane (qt)
344 (1916) Minstrels Pt. 5 (Note: No copy has been found; may not have been issued)
345 (1916) Minstrels Pt. 6: I Guess I'll Have to Telegraph My Baby; I Want to Go Back to the Land of Cotton (qt)

Nassau (See Imperial)

Okeh

Members of this troupe (as named during the performance) are endman Al Bernard, interlocutor Lloyd Willing, Harry Docken (baritone), Harry Donaghy (bass), Dan DeSylva (tenor) and the National Male Quartet. Arranged by Justin Ring.

12-inch disc
7002 (5/24) Al Bernard's Minstrel Co.: Al Bernard Minstrels, Pt. 1: We Are Merry Minstrel Men; Sweet Genevieve (Willing); When You and I Were Young Maggie (DeSylva); Shine On Mr. Moon (Docken)/Pt. 2: When the Bell in the Lighthouse Goes Ding Dong (Donaghy); Jerusalem Morning (NMQ); Flip Them Jacks (Bernard); We Are Merry Minstrel Men [mx S-72329/30]

Par-O-Ket

Peerless Minstrel Co. (Side 1: CPL Burr, SGT Campbell, PVT Collins, LT Wilbur (Meyer))

7-inch disc

34 (1917) Military Minstrels: Yankee Doodle Dandy; Bunker Hill; I Love to Lead a Military Band/Minstrels No. 2: Bully Song; Black Jim; Just Kiss Yourself Goodbye

Regal (See Banner)

Rex

Peerless Quartet (Burr, Campbell, Collins, Meyer). Label of 5149 reads, "Arranged by Peerless Quartet."

5032 (1914) Peerless Quartet: Minstrel No. 1: My Rainbow Coon; All Coons Look Alike to Me (ACo); Take Plenty of Shoes [mx 541? From Keen-o-Phone 5032]

5149 (c. 1914) Peerless Quartet: Rex Minstrel No. 2: Push Dem Clouds Away; I Don't Care If You Never Come Back (ACo) [mx 0106]

Star

1907–1909 reissues of Columbia discs by the Imperial, Rambler, and Peerless Minstrels.

4000—from Columbia 33 (Imperial Minstrels)
4001—from Columbia 1109-D (Imperial Minstrels)
4002—from Columbia 1109-F (Imperial Minstrels)
4003—from Columbia 3448 (Rambler Minstrels)
4004—from Columbia 3449 (Rambler Minstrels)
4005—from Columbia 3478 (Rambler Minstrels)
4006—from Columbia 3479 (Rambler Minstrels)
4007—from Columbia 1109-H (Imperial Minstrels)
4008—from Columbia 645 (Imperial Minstrels)
5114—from Columbia 3531 (Rambler Minstrels)
5115—from Columbia 3554 (Rambler Minstrels)
5414—from Columbia 3608 (Rambler Minstrels)
5814—from Columbia 3710 (Peerless Minstrels)

12-inch single-faced discs

1223—from Columbia 30062 (Rambler Minstrels)
1263—from Columbia A5072 (Peerless Minstrels)

U.S. Everlasting Cylinders

All are by the Peerless Quartet. Stanley was the interlocutor until 1910, Meyer (aka John Wilbur) thereafter.

Two-minute cylinders

201 (1911) Peerless Minstrels No. 1: My Wild Deer; When a Pal of Mine Steals a Gal of Mine (ACo)

Four-minute cylinders

1017 (c. 1910) U.S. Minstrels No. 1: Virginia; The Humming Coon (ACo); Climb Up Ye Chillun
1258 (c. 1911) U.S. Minstrels No. 2: Oh, Dem Golden Slippers; My Dusky Rose (ACo); I Ain't Gonna Weep No More
1427 (c. 1912) U.S. Minstrels No. 3: In the Morning by the Bright Light; Everybody Has a Whistle Like Me (ACo); Melancholy Mose

U.S. Phonograph Company (New Jersey Cylinders)

U.S. Phonograph used Len Spencer's Imperial Minstrels from 1894 until 1897. In the company's last known catalog (c. 1900), a new group of minstrel cylinders was listed, credited to the Alabama Troubadours. The announcement suggests that this was an ad hoc group of recording studio regulars, which had made some earlier cylinders for the label. The announcement read as follows: "The records listed embrace the combined efforts of such well known phonograph artists as Messrs. Dan Quinn, S.H. Dudley, Jere Mahoney, William F. Hooley, John Bieling, assisted by the 'Old Homestead Quartette' and Mr. Edward Issler's incomparable orchestra." Billy Williams is also heard on some, and Williams, Dudley and Quinn all crack jokes and are addressed by name. Usually introduced "Be seated, gentlemen" rather than "Gentlemen, be seated."

ALABAMA TROUBADOURS

c. 1900 issues
Minstrel #1: Where the Sweet Magnolias Bloom
Minstrel #2: My Creole Sue
Minstrel #3: I'se Going Back to Dixie
Minstrel #4: Carry Me Back to Old Virginia
Minstrel #5: Tenting Tonight on the Old Camp Ground
Minstrel #6: Old Folks at Home
Minstrel #7: A Picture No Artist Can Paint
Minstrel #8: A Bird in a Gilded Cage
Minstrel #9: Blue and the Gray
Minstrel #10: My Lady Lu
Minstrel #11: Mandy Lee
Minstrel #12: Soldier's Farewell
Minstrel #_?: Because (SHD)
Minstrel #_?: All I Want Is My Chicken Back (DWQ)
Minstrel #_?: Old Black Joe (BW)
Minstrel #_?: Hear Dem Bells (BW)

Unidentified Cylinder

No announcement. May be Ancient City Quartet on Edison 4701 or possibly U.S. Phonograph. Jokes by "Sam" and "William" (Heins? Williams?). Performers and routines are identical on the two copies heard.
? Just One Girl (SHD)

Victor

THE GEORGIA MINSTRELS

These discs appear to be by the Haydn Quartet or a closely related group. The Haydn group had made some very similar minstrel records for Berliner just a few months earlier. Aural evidence confirms Macdonough, Dudley and Hooley of the quartet are present; the Victor files also list Arthur Collins as taking part, but his distinctive voice is not heard. (Collins was just beginning his career and might not have been featured.) There was some turnover in the Haydn group at this time. Most of the jokes are delivered by Dudley (often addressed as "Sam"), with Hooley as the interlocutor.

GEORGIA MINSTRELS—"FIRST PART" (7-INCH, RECORDED NOVEMBER 1900)
According to the files, 12-inch versions were made but not issued.

7-inch discs
506 (1901) No. 1: Just One Girl (SHD)
507 (1901) No. 2: Darktown Is Out Tonight (SHD)
508 (1901) No. 3: Old Black Joe: Old Folks at Home (WFH)
509 (1901) No. 4: Old Log Cabin: How I Love My Lou (SHD)
510 (1901) No. 5: Massa's in de Cold, Cold Ground (WFH)

GEORGIA MINSTRELS—"MONARCH MINSTREL FIRST PART" (10-INCH, ALL RECORDED JANUARY 1901)

Second title shown is "grand opening chorus." Canadian Berliner numbers are shown in parentheses. No. 3035 may have been issued in Canada on Imperial 044.

10-inch discs
3035 No. 1: Wake Up Hannah; I'se Gwine Back to Dixie (WFH)
3036 (5017) No. 2: Carry Me Back to Old Virginny; My Old Kentucky Home (SHD)
3037 (5021) No. 3: Hear Dem Bells; A Picture No Artist Can Paint (HM)
3038 (5025) No. 4: Old Home on the Hill (take 4 only); Mandy Lee (HM)
3039 (5026) No. 5: In the Evening by the Moonlight; The Blue & the Gray (HM)
3040 (5035) No. 6: The Old Log Cabin in the Dell; Fly, Fly, Fly (SHD)

"AN EVENING WITH THE MINSTRELS"

This elaborate production consisted of a series of discs that, when played in sequence, recreated a full half-hour minstrel show. The catalog boasted, "In the making of these records we have enlisted the largest company of comedians, singers and musicians which have ever been used for talking machine records, and no expense has been spared in their production." Personnel were not named, but Len Spencer dominated the proceedings, cracking jokes (often at the expense of stuffy interlocutor S.H. Dudley). Others who are aurally identifiable include tenor Harry Macdonough and baritone S.C. Porter. Although Spencer was involved, due to the large and varied cast, I have not considered these as recordings by his Imperial Minstrels. The records were quite popular, both as a set and individually, and were remade as late as 1909 with varying casts, including John Bieling, W.F. Hooley, Edward Meeker and Billy Murray. Canadian Berliner numbers are in parentheses.

(10-inch discs, most first recorded December 1902)
1824 No. 2: Minstrel Ballad: My Creole Sue (HM)
1825 (5288) No. 3: End Song: Chimes of the Golden Bells (SHD)
1826 (5289) No. 4: Musical Act: The Ebony Emperors of Melody (LS & SHD sketch)
1827 (5325) No. 5: Having Fun with the Orchestra (SCP & LS sketch)
1828 (5326) No. 6: The Cakewalk in Coontown (LS)
1829 (5327) No. 7: Sidewalk Conversation: Funny Things You See in the Papers (LS & SHD)
1830 (5328) No. 8: Grand After Piece, Scenes on the Levee: What You Gonna Do in the Winter; Roll on theGround (LS)
1834 No. 1: Ethiopian Carnival of Melody: Darktown Is Out Tonight; Old Folks at Home; Carry Me Back; Massa; Darktown Is Out Tonight; Dixie (all by qt)

(12-inch discs, first recorded c. 1903)
31076 No. 2: My Creole Sue (HM)
31129 (c. 1903) No. 1: Ethiopian Carnival of Melody: Old Folks at Home; Carry Me Back; Massa; Darktown Is Out Tonight; Dixie (all by qt)
31130 (c. 1903) No. 4: Ebony Emperors of Melody (LS & SHD sketch)
31131 (c. 1903) No. 5: Having Fun with the Orchestra (LS & orch. sketch)
31132 (c. 1903) No. 6: The Cakewalk in Coontown (sketch)
31193 (1904) No. 3: Chimes of de Golden Bells (SHD)

MINSTREL SHOW, NEW SERIES (10-INCH, RECORDED SEPTEMBER 1904)

Len Spencer once again took the lead in this series, appearing as the disruptive endman full of stories and jibes. His foil in the first three discs was either the interlocutor, S.H. Dudley, or endman Dan W. Quinn. In the last four, he was paired with Billy Murray ("the famous endmen, Spencer and Murray"). Also heard is tenor Harry Macdonough.

4081 (c. 12/04) Olden Time Minstrels A: End Song—Uncle Billy's Dream (LS)
4082 (c. 12/04) Olden Time Minstrels B: Military Song—Goodbye, Little Girl, Goodbye (HM)
4083 (2/05) Olden Time Minstrels C: Minstrel Ballard—Mother's Watch by the Sea (HM)
4244 (3/05) Olden Time Minstrels E: March Song—Good Bye Sis (BM)
4245 (3/05) Olden Time Minstrels D: Negro Shout—Keep on a Climbin' (LS)
4262 (4/05) Olden Time Minstrels F: Ballad—My Love Remains the Same (HM)
4599 (3/06) Olden Time Minstrels G: Darky Shout—Get Happy (BM) (aka Matinee Minstrels)

MATINEE MINSTRELS (RECORDED DECEMBER 1905)
    Len Spencer, Billy Murray, Harry Macdonough
31488 (3/06) Matinee Minstrels No. 1: Poets; Eileen Alanna (HM)

CHRISTY MINSTRELS (RECORDED MARCH 1907)
    Billy Murray and Arthur Collins are the endmen on these discs, with S.H. Dudley as the interlocutor. Harry Macdonough is heard in the quartet.

5097 (5/07) No. 1: College Life; My Kickapoo Queen (ACo)
5098 (5/07) No. 2: Yankee Doodle Negroes; San Antonio (BM)
5122 (6/07) No. 3: Good Bye New York Town; My Creole Saidee (BM)
5135 was scheduled to be "Christy Minstrels No. 4," but that master (B4392–1) was retitled No.
    3 and issued on 5122 instead. 5135 was apparently not issued.

VICTOR MINSTRELS (SOME AS BY CHRISTY MINSTRELS)
    Although labeled as by the Victor or Christy Minstrels, the next five are in fact by the Rambler Minstrels—Billy Murray, Arthur Collins, Byron G. Harlan and S.C. Porter (as interlocutor). All are addressed by name.

5363 (3/08) No. 9: Bronco Buster; Pride of the Prairie (BM)
5380 (4/08) No. 10: Bye Bye My Sailor Boy; Good Bye Honey Goodbye (ACo)
5449 (6/08) No. 11: Make a Lot of Noise; Every Day She Wanted Something Else (ACo)
5530 (9/08) No. 12: Dixie and the Girl I Love; H-A-S-H, Dat Am the Word I Love (ACo)
5544 (10/08) No. 13: My Dream of the U.S.A.; Moonbeams (qt)

VICTOR DOUBLE-FACED MINSTREL DISCS
    Many of the early double-faced issues were reissues of older single-faced recordings. New releases during 1908 and 1909 were generally by the Rambler Minstrels (RM: Murray, Harlan, Collins and Porter), while from 1910 onward it was usually the Peerless Minstrels (PM: Burr, Campbell, Collins and Stanley, with Meyer replacing Stanley in 1911). Exceptions as noted. Neither of these groups was named on the labels. Instead, most discs were credited to the "Victor Minstrels" (VM) or, after 1909, to the "Victor Minstrel Company" (VMC). (EM = "An Evening with the Minstrels.") In 1913, Victor began numbering its minstrel records, but the numbering was inconsistent, sometimes shown on the label and sometimes not. Sometimes sketches that appeared on the reverse side of these discs were called "minstrel specialty" or "minstrel scene," but these were not minstrel recreations within the definition of this discography and they are not included here.

10-inch discs
16042 (11/08) VM No. 14: Bye Bye Caroline; At the Meeting House Tonight (BM, with RM)
16149 Reissue of Vic 5380
16189 Reissue of Vic 5449
16258 Reissue of Vic 5122

16263 (4/09) VM No. 15: When the Band Strikes Up Dixieland; Smiling Star (BM, with RM)
16311 (5/09) VMC No. 16: Campmeeting Time; L-O-V-E Spells Trouble (ACo, with RM)
16415 Reissue of Vic 5530/5544
16553 Reissue of Vic 1834/26
16762 Reissue of Vic 1825/28
16763 Reissue of Vic 1830/5363
16914 Reissue of Vic 16042/16263
16925 Reissue of Vic 5449
17126 (9/12) Minstrels No. 21: Just Because She Made Dem Goo Goo Eyes; When Daddy Sings the Little Ones to Sleep (HB); Southern Girl (Personnel: PM)
17293 (5/13) Mobile Minstrels: Down Where the Band Is Playing; Honey You'se Ma Lady Love (BM) (Personnel: Murray, John Bieling, Porter, Hooley)

12-inch discs (35095 through 35321 are all by the Peerless Minstrels)

35072 Reissue of Vic 31129/31130
35073 (5/09) EM No. 8: Scenes on the Levee: What You Goin' to Do in the Winter; Hard Times Come Again No More; Roll on the Ground (Personnel: Macdonough, Bieling, Porter, Hooley, Ed Meeker)/Reissue of Vic 31132
35095 (2/10) Virginia Minstrels: Virginia; The Humming Coon (ACo); Climb Up Ye Little Chillun
35108 (7/10) Alabama Minstrels: Linda (aka Linder Green¹); Fly, Fly, Fly (ACo); My Rosie Rambler
35143 (3/11) Minstrels No. 18: A Hot Time in the Old Town; Goodbye My Lady Love (ACo); Dar's a Watermelon Spoilin' Down at Johnson's
35149 Reissue of Vic 31193
35183 (1/11) Minstrels No. 17: Carrie from Caroline; Happy Days in Dixie (ACo); That's How They Do in Balmoral
35197 (10/11) Georgia Minstrels No. 19: Golden Slippers; My Dusky Rose (ACo); I Ain't a-Gonna Weep No More
35202 (11/11) Carolina Minstrels No. 20: In the Morning by the Bright Light; Everybody Has a Whistle Like Mine (ACo); Melancholy Mose
35213 (3/12) Arkansas Minstrels: Alabama; Goodbye Eliza Jane (ACo); What the Brass Band Played/Louisiana Minstrels: Push Dem Clouds Away; I Don't Care if You Nebber Come Back (ACo); Goodbye Sweet Old Manhattan Isle
35226 (7/12) Texas Minstrels: Golden Wedding; Angel Gabriel (ACo); Bye Bye My Eva Bye Bye/South Carolina Minstrels: Bully Song; Black Jim (ACo); Just Kiss Yourself Goodbye
35233 (10/12) Mississippi Minstrels No. 22: I Guess I'll Have to Telegraph My Baby; I Want to Go Back to the Land of Cotton (ACo); Remus Takes the Cake
35260 (12/12) Kentucky Minstrels No. 23: My Gal Is a High Born Lady; My Dinah (ACo); When You Ain't Got No Money, Well You Needn't Come Around
35264 (1/13) Tennessee Minstrels No. 24: Nigger, Nigger, Never Die; Rufus Rastus Johnson Brown (ACo); I'm Going to Leave
35267 (2/13) Florida Minstrels No. 25: I'll Come Back Again to You; I'm a-Dreaming of You (ACo); Goodbye Susan Jane
35274 (3/13) Military Minstrels No. 26: Yankee Doodle Boy; Bunker Hill (HB); I'd Love to Lead a Military Band (Corporal Burr, Sergeant Campbell and Private Collins, with Meyer as the lieutenant and Collins as the colonel)
35280 (4/13) New Orleans Minstrels No. 27: At a Georgia Campmeeting; All I Want Is My Black Baby Back (ACo); On Emancipation Day
35294 (6/13) Rubetown Minstrels: All Hands Around; Old Bill Jones (ACo); Bingville Band (HB)
35307 (8/13) North Carolina Minstrels: My Rainbow Coon; All Coons Look Alike to Me (ACo); Take Plenty of Shoes
35321 (11/13) Missouri Minstrels: Grand Old Flag; Darktown Is Out Tonight (ACo); Ta! Ta! Au Revoir
35961 (5/29) Victor Minstrels: Minstrel Show of 1929 Pt. 1: Make a Lot of Noise; Down Where the

Watermelon Grows (BM); Lazy Moon (Cavaliers); Oh, Dem Golden Slippers/Pt. 2: Allus the Same in Dixie; By the Light of the Silvery Moon (HB); Abraham Lincoln Jones (Crumit); Under the Bamboo Tree and Carry Me Back to Old Virginny (Cavaliers); Climbing Up the Golden Stairs (Personnel: James Stanley as interlocutor, Billy Murray and Monroe Silver as the endmen, addressed as "Billy" and "Monty"; plus Henry Burr, Carl Matthieu, Stanley Baughman, Frank Crumit, and the National Cavaliers quartet. Rosario Bourdon, dir.)

Walcutt & Leeds

THE DIXIE MINSTREL TROUPE, "NEW YORK" CYLINDERS (C. 1896)
10516 Engagement of March 15, 1896
10517 Engagement of April 1, 1896
10518 Engagement of April 15, 1896
10519 Engagement of May 1, 1896

Zonophone

The label originally used its own group called the "Zonophone Minstrels," which included S.H. Dudley cracking jokes, William F. Hooley as interlocutor, and tenor Harry Macdonough. They were first listed in the October 15, 1901, catalog, but by the mid-1902 catalog only 583 and 589 remained. Zonophone then used the Imperial Minstrels in 1903, the Rambler Minstrels from 1907 to 1909, and the Peerless Quartet (billed as the Rambler Minstrels) for its last few issues in 1909–1911. (Peerless Minstrels: Burr, Campbell, Collins, and Stanley as interlocutor.)

THE ZONOPHONE MINSTRELS
7-inch etched label (1901)
1651 Good Bye Dolly Gray
1652 Old Folks at Home
1653 My Old Kentucky Home (SHD)
1654 Coon, Coon, Coon (SHD)

9-inch etched label (1901)
581 My Charcoal Charmer (HM)
582 My Rainbow Coon
583 Game of Eyes
584 Coon, Coon, Coon (SHD)
586 Sweet Annie Moore
587 Hear Dem Bells; Goo Goo Eyes (SHD)
588 Massa's in the Cold, Cold Ground (WFH)
589 In the Evening by the Moonlight; I'se Gwine Back to Dixie (WFH)

10-inch paper label (1909–1911); labeled Rambler Minstrels but actually Peerless Minstrels
5508 (7/09) No. 14: Kiss Your Minstrel Boy Goodbye; My Pony Boy (FCS)/No. 15: Yankee Doodle Girl; Liza (ACo) [also Ox 5508]
5571 (12/09) No. 16: My Wild Deer; When a Pal of Mine Steals a Gal of Mine (ACo)/No. 17: Climb Up Ye Chillun; The Humming Coon (ACo) [also Ox 5571]
5690 (3/11) No. 19: Carrie from Caroline; Happy Days in Dixie
5692 (3/11) No. 18: Hot Time in the Old Town; Goodbye My Lady Love (ACo)

LPs

A number of "minstrel" LPs were issued in the 1950s and early 1960s, but some of these were collections of songs rather than staged minstrel shows with interlocutor, endmen, and so forth.

"Merry Minstrel Show/Songs," Jay-Dee LP No. 1 (10-inch, c. 1954). A production of New York publisher Joe Davis. By Al Bernard and His Merry Minstrel Men, with Tom Shirley, interlocutor, and jokes by Al and Tom. Side 1 ("Merry Minstrel Show"): There's Nothing Like a Minstrel Show (chorus), jokes, Truthfully (Henry Shope), jokes, Trombone Jitters (band), jokes, Neptune (Harry Donaghy?), jokes, Bill Bailey Won't You Please Come Home (Al Bernard), There's Nothing Like a Minstrel Show (chorus). Side 2 ("Merry Minstrel Songs") is an organ medley of nineteenth-century songs: Oh! Susanna; My Old Kentucky Home; At a Georgia Campmeeting; You Tell Me Your Dream; Oh, Dem Golden Slippers; Old Black Joe; Camptown Races; Old Folks at Home; Old Gray Mare; Silver Threads Among the Gold; There'll Be a Hot Time in the Old Town Tonight. (*Songs and dialogue.* Side 1 is a reissue of 78-rpm album Celebrity 2000, plus one previously unissued title.)

"Gentlemen, Be Seated: A Complete Minstrel Show," Epic LN 3238 (1956) and Harmony HS-11339. With orchestra and chorus conducted by Allen Roth, the Merrill Staton Choir, Gordon Goodman, John Neher, Stanley Kimes, Osie Johnson, Uncle John Cole (bj), the Quartones. (The interlocutor was probably Kimes.) (*Songs and some dialogue*)

"Minstrel Show," Somerset P-1600 (1957) and Stereo Fidelity SF-1600 (stereo, 1959). Arranged and conducted by Joseph Kuhn, with Lee Gordon Singers; Bill Ornsby, interlocutor; Gilbert Smith, tenor; Warren Biggs, bass; Roland Ellis, bj. A Hot Time in the Old Town Tonight; Swanee River; Old Dan Tucker; Mandy Lee; Old Folks at Home; Camptown Races; Lassus Trombone; In the Evening by the Moonlight; Oh! Susannah; Shine On, Harvest Moon; Preacher and the Bear; Grand Old Flag; Asleep in the Deep; I Wonder Who's Kissing Her Now; Wait Til the Sun Shines, Nellie; Hello Ma Baby; Goodbye My Lady Love. Recorded at Capitol Studios, Hollywood. (*Songs and dialogue*)

"The Minstrel Men," aka "Benny Fields and His Minstrel Men," Colpix CP-501 (October 1958)/CP 434 (1962). 30 old-time songs by Benny Fields ("interlocutor"), Jack Benny, Milton Berle, George Burns, Phil Silvers, and a male chorus. Jacket claims they are "performing a full-length minstrel show," but in fact it is mostly music, with acts introduced by Fields. Applause dubbed in. No jokes or endmen. Arranged and conducted by Owen G. Masingill. (*Songs and dialogue*)

"Gentlemen, Be Seated Again," Epic LN 3596 (9/59 Schwann). Arranged and conducted by O.B. Masingill, with Gordon Goodman, J. Alden Edkins, Mac Perrin, Frank Raye, Uncle John Cole (bj), Mississippi Four, Stephen Collins Feldman (p). Mostly music. Interlocutor is Edkins. (*Songs and some dialogue*)

"Bill Cullen's Minstrel Spectacular," Bill Cullen (narr.) with the endmen (chorus) and band, ABC Paramount 264 (4/59 Schwann). The Glendy Burke; Oh, Didn't He Ramble; Rufus Rastus Johnson Brown; Shine On, Harvest Moon; Georgia Campmeeting; Shenandoah Erie Canal; Old Dan Tucker/Kingdom Coming; Beautiful Dreamer; Waiting for the Robert E. Lee; Asleep in the Deep; Old Folks at Home; Dixie; Camptown Races; Banjo on My Knee. (*Album of songs*)

"Minstrel Days," Eddie Foy, Jr. (interlocutor), with David Burns and Harold Adamson as endmen, Everest SDBR-1039 (11/59). Produced by Tutti Camarata and Harold Adamson. There's Nothing Like a Minstrel Show; Our Boys Will Shine Tonight; Mandy; Sleepy Time Gal; The World Is Waiting for the Sunrise; Kentucky Babe; I Want to Go Back to Oregon; Smiles; Shine On, Harvest Moon; There's a Long Long Trail; I'm Looking Over a Four Leaf Clover/There's Nothing Like a Minstrel Show; He Goes to Church on Sundays; Lassus Trombone; Tiger Rag; By the Light of the Silvery Moon; Flight of the Bumble Bee; Down by the Old Mill Stream; For Me and My Gal; My Gal Sal; Let Me Call You Sweetheart; Wait Till The Sun Shines, Nellie; Good Night Ladies; There's Nothing Like a Minstrel Show. (*Songs and dialogue*)

"Minstrel Show!" Frank Simms and His Minstrels, RCA Camden CAS-651 (1961). Unidentified cast. King Cotton and Washington Post March (orchestra); medley Dixie, Oh! Susanna, Our Boys Will Shine Tonight, Hand Me Down My Walking Cane (male chorus); jokes by interlocutor and "Mr. Roscoe"; I Love You Truly and Because (tenor); jokes with interlocutor and Bones; Teasin' and On the Banks of the Wabash (soft shoe dancer); jokes by interlocutor and Roscoe; In the Evening by the Moonlight and Old Folks at Home (quartet)/medley Little Liza Jane, Polly Wolly Doodle, Belle of Baltimore (orchestra); jokes by interlocutor and Bones; Beautiful Dreamer (whistling solo); jokes by interlocutor and Mr. Roscoe; medley Camptown Races, Ring Ring the Banjo, Little Brown Jug (banjo); jokes by interlocutor and Bones; Old Black Joe and Shortnin' Bread (bass solo); jokes by interlocutor and Roscoe; medley of Hello My Baby, Oh, Dem Golden Slippers, My Old Kentucky Home and Goodnight Ladies (male chorus). (*Songs and dialogue*)

"The Dixie Minstrels' Greatest Hits," Kapp Medallion ML7532/MS 7532 (3/62). Per *Billboard* review, 38 old-time songs "played and sung with the enthusiasm that befits a minstrel show." Dixie, Waiting for the Robert E. Lee, Aura Lee, Roll Dem Bones, etc. (*Album of songs?*)

"A Tribute to the Original Christy Minstrels," Dyna-Disc SCH-830 (c. 1963). No artists listed. Includes both songs and "comedy between Mr. Interlocutor and his end men." Applause and crowd noises dubbed in. Overture, Hot Time in the Old Town. "Gentlemen, be seated," followed by a long medley by male chorus (with solos): Old Dan Tucker, Mandy Lee, Jeanie with the Light Brown Hair, Old Folks at Home, Camptown Races, In the Evening by the Moonlight, When You Were Sweet Sixteen (Gilbert Smith, tenor w/chorus), Shine On, Harvest Moon (qt), Preacher and the Bear (Robert Lamb, baritone w/chorus)/Joke. My Gal Sal (Southland Chorus). Joke. Lassus Trombone (Sliphorn Four). Asleep in the Deep (bass), Grand Finale (chorus): Hello Ma Baby, Honeymoon, I Wonder Who's Kissing Her Now, Goodbye My Lady Love. (*Songs and dialogue.* This is a slightly edited reissue of Somerset P-1600 arranged and conducted by Joseph Kuhn, with the Lee Gordon Singers.)

III. British Minstrel Records

Many minstrel records sold in the United Kingdom were imports from the United States. Those recorded in the United Kingdom are listed here. Note that in the United Kingdom, the endman was known as the cornerman.

Label abbreviations (UK): Ber = Berliner; Gram = Gramophone; P = Pathé.

Ariel Grand

Ariel was produced for the John G. Graves mail-order company from 1911 to 1938, and it drew masters from many sources.

ARIEL MINSTRELS (RELEASED 1920S)

From 1913 "Zono Minstrels" sides. These are songs, not minstrel first parts.

271—reissue of Zon X49435/X49451 (Good Night/Far Far Away) [mxs Ak-16879/Ak-16908]

272—reissue of Zon X49436/X49448 (Dat's Berry Queer/De Ole Banjo)

273—reissue of Zon X44266/X49452 (Dis Ole Nigger/Way Down Dare in Tennessee) [mxs Ak-16909/Ak-16907]

888—reissue of Zon X49448/X49451 (De Old Banjo/Far Far Away) [mxs Ak-16876/Ak-16901]

889—reissue of Zon X44267/X49452 (Far Away Ober Dare/Way Down Dare in Tennessee) [mxs Ak-16882/Ak-16907]

ARIEL OLD TIME MINSTREL TROUPE (RELEASED 1920S; FROM FAVORITE, 1911–1914)

768—reissue of Favorite 448 (Minstrels Parts 1 and 2) [mxs 6569/6570]

827—reissue of Favorite 470 (Ariel Minstrels Parts 3 and 4, with the Great Little Thomas) [mxs 13288/89]

828—reissue of Favorite 581 (Ariel Minstrels Parts 9 and 10) [mxs 14252/53]

COONTOWN MINSTRELS (RELEASED IN C. 1912 CATALOG; FROM JUMBO)
1938–1939 are performances by Tom Birchmore
1940—reissue of Jumbo sides A28004/A28005
1941—reissue of Jumbo sides A28006/A28007
1942—reissue of Jumbo sides A28008/A28009
1943—reissue of Jumbo sides A28185/A28187
2062—reissue of Jumbo sides A28186/A28189

Beka Grand

Label founded in Germany in 1903 and launched in the United Kingdom in 1905. Originally issued as single-faced discs, later doubled (as shown). Its double-faced discs were given a different "face number" on each side, rather than a single catalog number.

Single-faced disc (released December 1905)
G9466 Tivoli Minstrels: Navajo
G9467 Tivoli Minstrels: Hello My Baby
G9468 Tivoli Minstrels: Strolling Home with Eugenie
G9469 Tivoli Minstrels: The Goldolier
G9470 Royal Cowes Minstrels: Ma Rainbow
G9471 Royal Cowes Minstrels: Go 'Way, Good Massa Bee
G9472 Royal Cowes Minstrels: Every Day Life
G9473 Royal Cowes Minstrels: Ain't I No Use, Mr. Jackson?
Note: These were later "doubled" as follows: G9466/67, G9468/69, G9470/71, G9472/73.

Bell Disc

Subsidiary of Edison Bell, active from 1908 until 1912, when it was replaced by Winner.

MANHATTAN MINSTRELS WITH TOM BIRCHMORE
On mx 2466, the interlocutor (Eric Farr) introduces Tom Birchmore as the cornerman. The ensemble sounds very much like Birchmore's Coontown Minstrels on Jumbo and Silvertone. "Mr. Chester" is presumably Ernie Chester from that ensemble.
219 (11/10) The Old Folks at Home (Chester) [mx 2466]
222 (12/10) Uncle Pete's Return [mx 2462]
225 (12/10) Massa's in the Cold, Cold Ground [mx 2465]
225 (12/10) I'm Going Back to Dixie [mx 2464]

Beltona

Independent label operated by J.G. Murdoch Co. from 1921 to 1960. Following were recorded for Beltona by Edison Bell. Number 1662 is described as a "coon sketch."
1662 (6/31) Rastus & Sambo (of the Kentucky Minstrels), A Dark Discussion, Parts 1 and 2 [mx M13438/39]
1663 (6/31) Kentucky Minstrels, Parts 1 and 2 [mxs M13436/37]

Berliner (UK) (See HMV)

Besttone

Produced for Leon Liebowich and Regent Record Co. around 1915, using Diploma masters.

1360 (7/15)—reissue of Diploma mxs 2105/2109 (as by the Pioneer Minstrels)
1361 (7/15)—reissue of Diploma mxs 2107/?? (as by the Pioneer Minstrels) (The selection on side 2 is "Comrades in Arms," which has not been traced to an original source.)

Burlington Record

Produced for an unknown store around 1913–1915, using Diploma masters.
128 (c. 1/14)—reissue of Diploma mxs 2107/2109 (as by the Oxford Minstrels)

Clarion (UK)

Minstrels conducted by George Ison. Researcher F. Andrews says descriptives are "possibly" minstrel in content.

Cylinders
26 (1907) Descriptive: Fun on the Plantation: Shine, Shine, Moon
129 (1908) Minstrels No. 1
130 (1908) Descriptive: A Cotton Fields Episode
629 (1913) Descriptive: Fun on the Plantation: Shine, Shine, Moon
790 Descriptive: A Cotton Fields Episode
791 Minstrels No. 1

Columbia (UK)

Columbia released numerous U.S.-made minstrel and minstrel-related cylinders between 1901 and 1907, including selections by the Imperial and Rambler Minstrels, as well as the "An Evening with the Minstrels" series. The following appear to be of British origin. The director of the minstrels is given as Celian Kottaun.

Cylinders
200274 (12/01) Mohawk, Moore and Burgess Minstrels No. 1: When the Children All Come Home (Ford Robinson)
200275 (12/01) Mohawk, Moore and Burgess Minstrels No. 2: They've Had 'Em Since Adam (Tom Birchmore)
200276 (12/01) Mohawk, Moore and Burgess Minstrels No. 3: The Girl Who Won't Have Me (Fred Melton)
200277 (12/01) Mohawk, Moore and Burgess Minstrels No. 4: A Sop in the Pan (Tom Birchmore)
200324 (12/01) Mohawk, Moore and Burgess Minstrels: Just Walk Along by the Side of Me (Fred Melton)

Discs
Marie Benson, Bryan Johnson, Teddy Johnson, and G.H. Elliott ("The Chocolate Coloured Coon"), with Norrie Paramor orchestra and chorus.

DX 1790 (1951) Way Down South (A Minstrel Show), Pt. 1: On the Mississippi (all); I Want to Be in Dixie (Benson); Beautiful Dreamer (B. Johnson); I Want a Girl Just Like the Girl That Married Dear Old Dad (B. Johnson); Waiting for the Robert E. Lee (T. Johnson)/Pt. 2: Camptown Races (Benson); I'm Just Wild about Harry (Benson); Carry Me Back to Old Virginny (T. Johnson); Sue, Sue, Sue (Elliott); Dixie's Land (all)

DX 1798 (1951 Way Down South No. 2 (A Minstrel Show), Pt. 1: Oh, Dem Golden Slippers (all); Swanee (Benson); Ma Curly-Headed Baby (T. Johnson); Josie (Elliott); Polly Wolly Doodle (B. Johnson)/Pt. 2: Are You from Dixie? (all); Old Kentucky Home (B. Johnson); On the Banks of the Wabash (Benson); By the Light of the Silvery Moon (T. Johnson); Oh! Susanna (all)

Curry's British Made Gramophone Record

Produced for Curry's bicycle shops, 1911–c. 1928.

50 (1912)—reissue of Bell Disc 219 (mx 2466) (as by the Munchausen Minstrels)

Decca (UK)

The following are by cast members from the popular BBC radio variety series *The Kentucky Minstrels*, which aired from 1933 to 1950. The conductor was Leslie Woodgate, with arrangements by Doris Arnold. The program featured racial humor by African Americans Ike Hatch, Harry Scott and Eddie Whaley, among others (referred to by names such as Tambo, Bones and "Mr. Pussyfoot"). See also "HMV."

12-inch discs

K719 (1934) Kentucky Minstrels. The Big Radio Minstrel Show, Pt. 1: Golden Slippers; bones solo (Rastus)/ Pt. 2: Camptown Races; banjo medley including Li'l Liza Jane, Massa's in de Cold, Cold Ground and Marching Through Georgia (Kentucky banjo team) (Personnel include Scott, Whaley, C. Denier Warren)

K733 (1934) Kentucky Minstrels. The Big Radio Minstrel Show No. 2, Pt. 1: Hear Dem Bells; So Early in the Morning/Pt. 2: Grand Finale, Plantation Medley (Dixie, Old Folks at Home, Polly Wolly Doodle) (Personnel: Scott and Whaley, C. Denier Warren, the Kentucky Banjo Team).

Diamond (See Pathé)

Diploma Record

Produced for J. Blum & Co., 1911–1915, from Bell Disc, Kalliope, and Disc Record Co. masters. Blum also recorded its own masters. See entries for Besttone, Burlington, Famous and Pelican for other issues of these mxs.

F.4 (1911) Kentucky Minstrels: My Old Kentucky Home (Note: Researcher F. Andrews says this is a reissue of Bell Disc mx 2466.)

G.1 (9/13) Oxford Minstrels: When Evening's Twilight/Lovely Night (mxs 2105/2106)

G.2 (9/13) Oxford Minstrels: The Piccaninni Lullaby/My Old Kentucky Home (mxs 2107/2109)

Edison (UK)

Thomas Edison assigned his UK rights to Edison Bell for the ten-year period 1893–1902 and was precluded from selling directly in Britain until that agreement expired in 1903. His company then began importing U.S.-made minstrel and minstrel-related cylinders but did not, as far as can be determined, record any locally.

Edison Bell

Although Edison Bell held exclusive rights to Edison's patents in the United Kingdom from 1893 to 1902, and did make small numbers of entertainment cylinders during the 1890s, it apparently did not record any minstrel cylinders until 1900, when it presented a group of studio regulars as the "Excelsior Minstrels." See also "Bell Disc."

The Excelsior Minstrels included Wilson Hallett, Harry Bluff, Eric Farr, Ernest Chester, Albert Pearce (tenor), Russell Hunting, William Doust, and Alma Jones. Hallett and Hunting were the cornermen. 6301–6308 are brown wax cylinders, issued in February 1900; the numbers shown in parentheses, 5554–5561, are molded remakes of the same titles issued in 1903; and 6500 upward are molded cylinders issued as shown. See also "Velvet Face."

Cylinders (see note for dates):
6301 (5554) Excelsior Minstrels No. 1: Daisy, etc. (Albert Pearce)
6302 (5555) Excelsior Minstrels No. 2: Three Women to Every Man, etc. (Harry Bluff)
6303 (5556) Excelsior Minstrels No. 3: Break the News to Mother, etc. (Eric Farr)
6304 (5557) Excelsior Minstrels No. 4: The Old Folks at Home, etc. (Ernest Chester)
6305 (5558) Excelsior Minstrels No. 5: Hello! Ma Baby, etc. (Russell Hunting)
6306 (5559) Excelsior Minstrels No. 6: My Coal Black Lady, etc. (Wilson Hallett)
6307 (5560) Excelsior Minstrels No. 7: My Love's the Same, etc. (William Doust)
6308 (5561) Excelsior Minstrels No. 8: The Honeysuckle and the Bee, etc. (Alma Jones)
6532 (4/05) Excelsior Minstrels No. 9: Old Black Joe (Pete Hampton)
6533 (4/05) Excelsior Minstrels No. 10: Dear Old Home Again (v. ?)
6890 (5/06) Excelsior Minstrels No. 4: Old Folks at Home (Pete Hampton)
10089 (12/06) Excelsior Minstrels No. 3: Break the News to Mother (Eric Farr)

Edison Bell Radio

Subsidiary of Edison Bell, specializing in small (8-inch) discs, marketed from 1928 to 1932. At first called simply "Radio" but quickly changed to "Edison Bell Radio." Number 1263 also issued on 8-inch Eclipse 256? (Crystalate, 1931–1935)

1263 (11/29) Darktown Minstrels: Parts 1 and 2 [mxs 89333/34]

Edison Bell Winner

The last incarnation of the Winner label, called Edison Bell Winner, operated from 1933 to 1935.

5625 (1933) The White Minstrels, Pts. 1 and 2

Exo

Produced for Moorhouse Ltd. by Edison Bell from 1911 to around 1914.

104 (1911)—reissue of Bell Disc mx 2462

Famous

Produced for J. Blum & Co., 1913–1915, from Bell Disc, Kalliope, and Disc Record Co. masters. Blum also recorded its own masters.

335 (8/13)—reissue of Diploma mxs 2105/2109 (as by the Kentucky Minstrels)
336 (8/13)—reissue of Diploma mxs 2106/?? (as by the Kentucky Minstrels) [The selection on side 2 is "Comrades in Arms," which has not been traced to an original source.]

Favorite

German label, active in the United Kingdom from 1906 to 1916. Artists include the Great Little Thomas (GLT), Billy Whitlock (BW), Wallace Scott (WS) and "other Palladium minstrels." First four were released in 1909 with only face numbers; double-faced catalog numbers were added in 1912–1913. Shown below are first the face numbers (e.g. I-60018 and I-60019) and then, in parentheses, the equivalent double-faced catalog numbers (e.g. 448). The second parentheses contain the issue date. Some of these were also released on Ariel Grand (400–900 series); 448 is on Ariel 768 as by "Ariel Old Time Minstrel Troupe."

Favorite Minstrels," double-faced discs:Face nos.
(D/F Catalog #.)(Original issue date)
I-60018/19 (448)(7/09) Pts 1 and 2: Laughing Song/Rocked in the Cradle of the Deep (GLT, BW) [mxs 6569/70]
I-60021/22 (470)(7/09) Pts 3 and 4: unknown titles (GLT, BW) [mxs 13288-o/89-o]
I-60023/24 (485)(7/09) Pts 5 and 6: unknown title/Camptown Races (GLT, others) [mxs 13290-o/91-o]
I-60025/26 (550)(7/09) Pts 7 and 8: Who'll Buy Pretty Flowers/Whistling Coon (GLT, BW) [mxs 13532-o/31-o]
I-60031/32 (581)(4/13) Pts 9 and 10: Blind Boy/I Carry My Sunshine with Me (GLT, WS) [mxs 14252-o/53-o]

HMV (UK)

Disc inventor Emile Berliner set up a company to market his records in the United Kingdom in 1898. Its principal labels were Berliner (1898–1901),[2] Gramophone (1902–1910, for a time manufactured by G&T Ltd.), and HMV (1910 onward). HMV stood for "His Master's Voice." The first issues were 7 inches, with 10-inch discs introduced in late 1901 and 12-inch discs in 1903. The 7-inch size was discontinued in 1906. Double-faced discs were introduced in 1912. Double-faced subsidiary the Twin was introduced in 1908 using Zonophone masters.

7-inch single-faced discs

Personnel on the first group of Christy Minstrels discs are unknown, but the cornerman is addressed as "Tom" (Birchmore?). Some researchers believe these are led by Chaudoir of Moore and Burgess.

Ber 9284-X (1899) Christy Minstrels: Elsie from Chelsea [mx 1095, recorded 1/27/99]
Ber 4058 (1899) Christy Minstrels: A Hot Time [mx 1236, recorded 2/9/99]
Ber 4074 (1900) Christy Minstrels 1st Part: My Coal Black Lady [mx 1684a]
Ber 4075 (1900) Christy Minstrels 1st Part: Hello My Baby [mx 1682a]
Ber 4076 (1900) Christy Minstrels 1st Part: My Hannah Lady [mx 1683a]
Ber 4077 (1900) Christy Minstrels 1st Part: Lads in Navy Blue [mx 1759a]
Ber 4080 (1900) Christy Minstrels 1st Part: Little Dolly Day Dream (Mr. Barrington) [mx 1761a]
Ber 4083 (1900) Christy Minstrels 1st Part: Laugh When'ere You Can [mx 1686a, 11/29/00]

7-inch (a) and 10-inch (b) single-faced discs

American artists the Haydn Quartet, including Harry Macdonough, S.H. Dudley and W.F. Hooley, traveled to the United Kingdom to record a series of Christy Minstrels discs in 1902. This appears to be the same group that made the Georgia Minstrels discs for Victor in the United States in 1900–1901. Hooley was the interlocutor and Dudley the joking endman. The identity of the fourth member of the quartet is uncertain.

Gram 4175 (1902) Christy Minstrels: Goodbye Dolly Gray [mx 2168a]
Gram 4176 (1902) Christy Minstrels No. 2: I'se Gwine Back to Dixie (WFH) [mx 2165b]
Gram 4207 (1902) Christy Minstrels: Carry Me Back to Old Virginny [mx 2166b]
Gram 4208 (1902) Christy Minstrels: Just Break the News to Mother [mx 2169b]
Gram 4223 (1902) Christy Minstrels: Massa's in de Cold, Cold Ground [mx 2164b]
Gram 4269 (1902) Christy Minstrels No. 5: Goodbye, Dolly Gray (HM) [mx 4900a]
Gram 4270 (1902) Christy Minstrels No. 7: Just Break the News to Mother (entire company) [mx 4902a]
Gram 4271 (1902) Christy Minstrels No. 2: I'se Gwine Back to Dixie (WFH) [mx 4897a]
Gram 4272 (1902) Christy Minstrels No. 4: Rosie, You Are My Posie (SHD) [mx 4899]

Note: Gram 4241, 42, 48, 49 and 4337–40 are Parts 1–8 of "An Evening with the Minstrels," recorded in the United States with matrix numbers B1824–34.

12-inch discs

HMV C1301 (12/26) Jack Hylton & His Orchestra: The Hylton Minstrels. "Being a Musical Burlesque on the Old Time Nigger Minstrels, Introducing Plantation Songs, Jokes, and Effects by Jack Hylton and His Orchestra." Arr: Major Williams. Pt 1: The Old Banjo; Oh, Dem Golden Slippers; Come Along, Sister Mary; My Old Kentucky Home; Old Folks at Home/Pt 2: Camptown Races; Jokes (Jones and Bones); instrumental imitations; By the Watermelon Vine; Razors in the Air. [mx CC-9401/2, recorded 11/4/26].

HMV C1739 (12/29) Minstrel Show of 1929 ("performed by Darktown melody makers") Note: This is a reissue of Victor 35961.
HMV C2305 (12/31) Minstrel Show of 1931: Camptown Races; My Moon; Speedwell (bj solo); Swanee River/De Old Banjo; Lily of Laguna; Tap Dance; Goodnight [mxs 32–2500/01]. (Artists: The English Minstrels with Alexander (James Carew) and Mose (Billy Bennett). Ray Noble Orchestra.)
HMV C2959 (12/37) Minstrel Show of 1937: O Dem Golden Slippers; Hear Dem Bells (bj solo); Oh, Lordy (bj solo)/I Wish I Was in Dixie; Massa's in de Cold, Cold Ground; Kemo, Kimo; Hear Dem Bells. (Artists: Kentucky Minstrels (12 voices) with Harry S. Pepper, C. Denier Warren, Doris Arnold, Ike Hatch, with 2 pianos and orchestra.)

The following are by cast members from the popular BBC radio variety series *The Kentucky Minstrels*, produced by Harry S. Pepper. However, these records consisted of vocalists and instrumentalists performing parlor ballads and songs reminiscent of the Old South, rather than a recreation of the show. See "Decca (UK)" for minstrel show recreations by the cast.

Kentucky Minstrels Series, 10-inch discs
HMV BD.535 (1938) Kentucky Minstrels: Abide with Me Pts 1 and 2 (v: Alexander Henderson)
HMV BD.546 (1938) Kentucky Minstrels: The Holy City 1 and 2 (v: John Duncan)
HMV BD.626 (1938) Kentucky Minstrels: Ora pro nobis (Pray for Us) 1 and 2 (v: John Duncan)
HMV BD.654 (1939) Kentucky Minstrels: Love Could I Only Tell Thee 1 and 2 (Herbert Dawson, organ)
HMV BD.681 (1939) Kentucky Minstrels: Banjo Song Medley 1 and 2: Ring de Banjo, Banjo Song, Mr. Punch, With a Banjo on My Knee (John Duncan and George James, with Kentucky Banjo Team)
HMV BD.707 (1939) Kentucky Minstrels: Plantation Medley No. 1, Pts 1 and 2 (G.S. Scott and J. Duncan, with Kentucky Minstrels Banjo Team)
HMV BD.761 (1939) Kentucky Minstrels: Bless This House/Passing By (v: John Duncan)
HMV BD.763 (1939) Kentucky Minstrels: The Star of Bethlehem 1 and 2 (v: John Duncan)
HMV BD.844 (1940) Kentucky Minstrels: The Song That Reached My Heart, 1 and 2 (Gwen Catley and John Duncan)
HMV BD.862 (1940) Kentucky Minstrels: She Wandered Down the Mountain Side 1 and 2 (Gwen Catley and John Duncan)
HMV BD.897 (1941) Kentucky Minstrels: A Hundred Years from Now; The Last Rose of Summer (Gwen Catley and John Duncan)
HMV BD.969 (1941) Kentucky Minstrels: I'll Walk Beside You/Rose of Tralee (v: John Duncan)
HMV BD.977 (1941) Kentucky Minstrels: Promise of Life 1 and 2 (v: John Duncan)

Kentucky Minstrels Series, 12-inch discs
HMV C3001 (5/38) Kentucky Minstrels: In the Gloaming (John Duncan)/The Lost Chord
HMV C3056 (12/38) Kentucky Minstrels: Love's Old Sweet Song (John Duncan)/Smilin' Through
HMV C3068 (1/39) Kentucky Minstrels: True Till Death (John Duncan)/Whisper, and I Shall Hear (Duncan)
HMV C3085 (4/39) Kentucky Minstrels: Carry Me Back to Green Pastures (George James)/Homing (Duncan)
HMV C3102 (6/39) Kentucky Minstrels: Flight of Ages (Duncan)/White Wings
HMV C3205 (1/41) Kentucky Minstrels: The Lord Is My Light/Arise, O Sun (Berkeley Mason, organ)
HMV C3298 (8/42) Kentucky Minstrels: The Church Bells of England (Duncan)/O Dry Those Tears (Duncan)

HMV C3313 (12/42) Kentucky Minstrels: Christopher Robin Is Saying His Prayers/The Better Land (Denis Wright)

International Indestructible (UK)

This company, formed in 1902 by a group of American entrepreneurs including Ademor Petit, Ellsworth Hawthorne, Horace Sheble and Frederick Prescott, marketed "unbreakable" celluloid cylinders, many of which were bootlegs of Edison and Edison Bell recordings. They also marketed under the Biophone label. It is not known whether the following listings were original recordings or bootlegs.

Cylinders
1801 (1902–1905) Minstrel: The Old Log Cabin in the Dell (from Columbia?)
1802 (1902–1905) Minstrel: Vaudeville Specialty, "Imitations"
1803 (1902–1905) Minstrel: Vaudeville Specialty, "Ma Lulu"
1804 (1902–1905) Minstrel: Echoes of Minstrelsy (from Edison?)

Jumbo

Jumbo was a low-price label produced by Fonotipia from 1908 to 1919. Catalog numbering was 1–1580 (occasionally preceded by an A or B); A28xxx were side numbers. Some discs were first issued with side numbers only (different on each side), with a single catalog number added later.

These recordings feature the Coontown Minstrels, with cornerman Tom Birchmore, late of Moore and Burgess Minstrels, and the Tally Ho! Trio (Ernie Chester, Eric Farr, William Doust). Interlocutor is addressed as "Mr. Johnson" in the first set and as "Mr. Farr" (a different voice) in the second. Members of the trio sometimes participate in telling jokes. Billy Whitlock was also in the cast. Remade in 1911. Reissued on Ariel Grand and Silvertone. Note: Different discographies have conflicting information on the numbering of some of these discs, though not on the contents.

1909 discs. Catalog no. (side nos.)
285 (A28004/05)(2/09) Old Folks at Home (Chester)/Hard Times (Farr) [mxs Lx0528/529]
293 (A28006/07)(3/09) Poor Old Joe/ My Old Kentucky Home [mxs Lx0530/531]
314 (A28008/09)(4/09) Massa's in de Cold, Cold Ground (Chester)/I'se Gwine Back to Dixie (Doust) [mxs Lx0532/533]

1911–1912 discs
659 (A28185/87)(11/11) No. 1: I Wonder If She's Waiting (Chester)/ No. 3: Good Old Jeff (Farr) [mxs Lxo 1389/1391]
660 (A28186/90)(1912) No. 2: I'm Waiting, Waiting in the Gloamin' Genevieve (v.?)/ No. 6: Down Where the Sugar Cane Grows (Birchmore?) [mxs Lxo 1390/1394]
661 (A28188/89)(1/12) No. 4: Sunny Tennessee (Doust)/No. 5: Nellie Gray(Doust) [mxs Lxo 1392/1393]

Note: 661 was first issued coupling A28186 and A28189.

Odeon

A major German label, founded in 1903 by the International Talking Machine Co. and active in Britain from 1906. Andrews says these were (also?) issued using only side numbers, X44389–X44394. Andrews also says Odeon reissued Tom Birchmore's Coontown Minstrels sides from Jumbo using only their side numbers, A28004–A28009 and A28185–A28190.

Black Diamond Minstrels: Russell Hunting, interlocutor; Johnnie Coles and Tom Hetherington, cornermen; and the Tally Ho! Trio (Ernie Chester, Eric Farr, William Doust).

December 1906 double-faced discs 10-inch no.
(10 3/4-inch no.)(side nos.)
589 (O351)(44389/90) No. 1: The Old Folks at Home/No. 3: Poor Old Joe
590 (O352)(44391/92) No. 2: I'se Gwine Back to Dixie/No. 4: Hard Times
591 (O353)(44393/94) No. 5: Massa's in de Cold, Cold Ground/No. 6: My Old Kentucky Home

Note: These were deleted from the catalog in 1915. The first four sides (44389–92) were reissued briefly in 1922 using only their side numbers and in slightly different couplings.

Pathé (UK)

The French Pathé Company began cylinder production in Britain as soon as the Edison patents expired there in March 1902, and it introduced discs in 1905. The discs numbered 1418/19 were 8.5-inch disc reissues of Sterling cylinders made in 1905–1906.

Cylinders
70050 (1902) Minstrel Record No. 1?
70051 (1902) Minstrel Record No. 2?
70052 (1902) Minstrel Record No. 3

Note: Details of cylinders 70053 and 70054 are unknown; they may also be minstrel records.

8.5-inch double-faced discs
1418 (9/08) Black Diamond Minstrels No. 1 & 2 (from Sterling 670 and 671)
1419 (9/08) Black Diamond Minstrels No. 3 (from Sterling 672)

10-inch discs
Black Diamond Minstrels. Personnel on these recordings are believed to be Tom Birchmore, Tom Hetherington, and Messrs. Farr, Cecil and Doust. Note sides reissued on Diamond in 1915, and possibly in the Pathé 1000 series in 1920. The "GR" numbers may refer to releases in another country, possibly Belgium.

8177 (3/10) No. 1: The Definition of a Kiss (Old Folks at Home)/No. 2: M-O-N-E-Y (Poor Old Joe) [mxs 78454/55] (Mx 78454 also on P 49042-GR; 78455 on P 49036-GR, and Diamond 0279)
8178 (12/10) No. 3: The Total Abstanuisance Man (My Old Kentucky Home)/ No. 4: The Absent Minded Preacher (Hard Times) [mxs 78456/57] (Mx 78456 also on P 49053-GR; 78457 on P 49039-GR and Diamond 0279)

10-inch disc
1222 (c. 6/20) Black Star Minstrels: Hard Times/Poor Old Joe (Note: Origin uncertain, although many in this numerical range are reissues from Diamond.)

Pelican

A J. Blum label, drawing sides from its Diploma label.

P.52 (11/13)—reissue of Diploma mxs 2106/2105 (as by the Cambridge Minstrels)
P.53 (11/13)—reissue of Diploma mxs 2109/2107 (as by the Cambridge Minstrels)

Phonograph Record Manufacturing Company (UK)

This shadowy entity, active from 1904 to 1906, appears to have been founded to sell off stock from the failed New Century Co. (1900–1904). The following titles from a 1904 PRMC catalog may have originally been recorded by New Century, although they have not been traced to that source. Content uncertain.

Cylinders
MR1 (1904) Minstrel Record: Break the News to Mother

MR2 (1904) Minstrel Record: My Coal Black Lady
MR3 (1904) Minstrel Record: The Old Folks at Home

Pioneer

Another J. Blum label, drawing sides from and possibly replacing the Diploma label.

G.1 (9/13)—reissue of Diploma mxs 2105/2106 (as by the Oxford Minstrels)
G.2 (9/13)—reissue of Diploma mxs 2107/2109 (as by the Oxford Minstrels)
127 (1914)—reissue of Diploma mxs 2105/2106 (as by the Oxford Minstrels)

Regal (UK)

The Mississippi Minstrels with Stan Greening (banjo); W.T. Best (piano); and Stan Greening band conducted by Charles Prentice. ("Columbia studio singers and musicians contracted by Greening.") "Poor Old Joe" is by Master Autry, but others are not named. G1076 and G1077 were reissued in the United States on Columbia 55029-D and 55030-D.

12-inch discs

G1076 (12/29) An Old Time Minstrel Show, Pt. 1: Camptown Races; Come Where My Love Lies Dreaming/Pt. 2: Stump Speech—Passing Events; There Was a Little Nigger; Massa's in the Cold, Cold Ground [mxs AX 5213/14]
G1077 (12/29) An Old Time Minstrel Show, Pt. 3: Poor Old Joe; Oh, Dem Golden Slippers/Pt. 4: Stump Speech—W.O.M.A.N.; My Old Kentucky Home; Marching Through Georgia [mxs AX 5215/5216]

10-inch disc (Regal-Zonophone)

This is an edited version of Regal G1076.

MR 2547 (1937) An Old Time Minstrel Show, Pt. 1: Camptown Races, Come Where My Love Lies Dreaming/Pt. 2: Stump Speech; There Was a Little Nigger; Massa's in de Cold, Cold Ground (mxs CAR 4362/63)

Scala

Active from 1911 to 1927, drawing masters from various sources. The following are from the "Dark-Town Series" featuring the Scala Minstrel Troupe and Harry Bluff and Billy Whitlock, comedians.

782 (11/15) Dark-Town Minstrel Show/The Dark-Town Police Court [mxs 36264/63]
783 (11/15) The Dark-Town Fire Brigade/The Dark-Town Races—minstrel sketch [mxs 36261/66]
784 (11/15) The Dark-Town Picnic/The Dark-Town Shaving Saloon—minstrel sketch [mxs 36265/62]

Silvertone (UK)

Obscure British label active around 1916 (Cooper Bros.) and again in the 1930s (8-inch discs pressed by Homophone for Selfridges). This acoustic recording is from the former and was pressed from Jumbo masters. Artists include cornerman Tom Birchmore and vocalists Ernie Chester, Eric Farr, and William Doust. The interlocutor is addressed as "Mr. Johnson."

410 (12/16)—reissue of Jumbo sides A28008 and A28190.

Star (UK)

Early cylinder label based in Norwich, United Kingdom, which recorded "minstrel performers from the nearby seaside resort of Great Yarmouth."

Cylinder:
1001 (1905?) Minstrel Troupe: Minstrel Series No. 1, "Always Jolly" (Note: There are conflicting reports on the content of this record; Andrews says it's "Hear Dem Bells.")

Sterling (UK)

Important independent cylinder label, founded in 1904 by American Louis Sterling (who later ran Columbia). It claimed to have shipped more than one million cylinders in its first year. Personnel on 670–72: Russell Hunting, Johnnie Coles, Tom Hetherington, Tally Ho! Trio. The Tally Ho! Trio (Ernie Chester, Eric Farr, and William Doust) recorded widely in the early days. Nos. 670–72 were reissued on Pathé discs.

Russell Hunting and the Tally Ho! Trio.

Cylinders:
3032 (1905) Black Diamond Minstrels No. 1: Old Folks at Home
3033 (1905) Black Diamond Minstrels No. 2: Gwine Back to Dixie (Doust)
3034 (1905) Black Diamond Minstrels No. 3: Old Black Joe (Farr)
670 (12/06) Black Diamond Minstrels No. 4: Hard Times (Farr)
671 (12/06) Black Diamond Minstrels No. 5: Massa's in de Cold, Cold Ground (Chester)
672 (12/06) Black Diamond Minstrels No. 6: My Old Kentucky Home (Doust)

Velvet Face

Subsidiary of Edison Bell, active from 1910 to 1914 and 1921 to 1927.

1019 (1910)—reissue of Bell Disc mx 2462 (Manhattan Minstrels)
1023 (1910)—reissue of Bell Disc mx 2466 (Manhattan Minstrels)

Winner

Winner was a moderately priced subsidiary of Edison Bell, launched in 1912.

2230 (1912)—reissue of Bell Disc mx 2466 (as by Christy Minstrels)

Zonophone (UK)

Christy Minstrels, conducted by Gustav Chaudoir of the Moore and Burgess Minstrels.

10-inch single-faced
X42696 (1908) No. 1: I'm Wearing My Heart Away for You; Shine, Shine Moon
X42697 (1908) No. 2: Somebody Loves Me; Meet Me at the Golden Gate
X42698 (1908) No. 3: Cheyenne; Waiting at the Church
X42699 (1908) No. 4: Waltz Me 'Round Again, Willie; It's a Different Girl Again

A quartet called "The Zono Minstrels," accompanied by piano, recorded ten plantation songs by British composer Alfred Scott Gatty on August 12 and 15, 1913, but these were individual songs not minstrel routines. See http://www.zonominstrels.co.uk/. Most were reissued on Ariel Grand as by the "Ariel Minstrels."

10-inch double-faced
Serial No./Face Nos.
1162 (X49435/ X49436) Good Night/Dat's Berry Queer
1184 (X44266/ X44267) Dis Ole Nigger/Far Away Ober Dare
1208 (X49447/ X49448) Click Clack/De Ole Banjo
1227 (X49451/ X49452) Far, Far Away/Way Down Dar in Tennessee
1251 (X49453/ X49454) Ding Dong Ding/Down by Dat Ribber

Zonophone Minstrels. Corner Man is addressed as "Norman" (Savage?).

5733 (1931) The White Blackbirds, Pt 1: Come Where My Love Lies Dreaming (co.); patter; I Want to Be Down Home in Dixie (co.); Pt 2: The Old Black Crow; Plantation Melodies, Old Folks at Home and Poor Old Joe (mxs 30–4601/02)

5734 (1931) The White Blackbirds, Pts 3 and 4

5963 (1931) The White Blackbirds, Pt 5: My Old Kentucky Home; patter; Belle of the Barber's Ball; Way Down in Dixie; Pt 2: patter (yodeling); Goodbye Liza Jane (mxs 30–7184/85).

5964 (1931) The White Blackbirds, Pts 7 and 8

LPs

The Black and White Minstrel Show was a very popular blackface variety show that ran on BBC television from 1958 to 1978. A big, lavish production, it was created by George Mitchell and featured music, production numbers, and comedy interludes. The main soloists were bass Dai Francis, tenor John Boulter and baritone Tony Mercer. These hit LPs (and others) consisted of the chorus and soloists singing medleys from the show.

HMV CLP 1399 (1960) George Mitchell Minstrels, from *The Black and White Minstrel Show*, featuring Tony Mercer, Dai Francis and John Boulter

HMV CLP 1460 (1961) George Mitchell Minstrels, from *Another Black and White Minstrel Show*, featuring Tony Mercer and Dai Francis

HMV CLP 1599 (1962) George Mitchell Minstrels, on stage with the George Mitchell Minstrels, from *The Black and White Minstrel Show*, featuring Tony Mercer, Dai Francis and John Boulter

IV: *Songs and Sketches About Minstrelsy*

Discs unless otherwise indicated. "Cyl" = cylinder.

An Amateur Minstrel Rehearsal (Comic sketch, including "Take Back the Heart That Thou Gaveth"). Edison Vaudeville Co., Ed cyl 9635 (9/07). (Cast includes Steve Porter as stage manager Birch Wood, Byron Harlan as tenor Wambold Merriman, and Billy Murray as endman Backus Black.)

Bring Back Those Minstrel Days (Broones-Macdonald) (from "Rufus LeMaire's Affairs").
Jack Kaufman and Al Campbell, Har 295H (1926), VT 1295V, Ed 51832, Pe 12293, P 32214.

Casey Interrupting a Minstrel Show (R. Hunting).
Leoni and Everett, Ed cyl 660 (11/1893).

Clancey's Minstrels (Comic burlesque on an Irish minstrel show).
Avon Comedy Four, Vic 35750 (1/25). (Personnel: Joe Smith, Charlie Dale, Frank Corbett, Eddie Miller. Interlocutor Clancy addresses McDuff, O'Brien, Kelly, Duffy, O'Toole, O'Connor Brothers. Originally recorded in 1917, remade in 1924 and issued in 1925.)

The Dusky Minstrel (Felix Burns)
Olly Oakley, banjo, Edison Bell cyl 10190, 20121 (1907)

Five Minutes with the Minstrels (Frank L. Collins)—instrumental.
F. Voss First Regiment Band, Edison cyl (recorded 10/2/1891).
23rd Regiment Band, Edison cyl 685 (11/1893)
23rd Regiment Band, Columbia cyl 2009 (11/1896)

Hippodrome Minstrel Medley (short excerpts from many songs, including Hot Time in the Old Town, Hear Dem Bells, Lazy Moon, Mammy's Little Pumpkin Colored Coons, Hello Ma Baby, Oh I Don't Know You Ain't So Warm, Golden Slippers, Under the Bamboo Tree, Oh Didn't He Ramble).
Manuel Romain, Emerson 7117 (1917).

I Got to See de Minstrel Show (Von Tilzer).
    Arthur Collins, Vic 5360 (3/08), Vic 16171, Zon 996 (3/08), Ed cyl 9812 (4/08), Indestructible cyl 719, Sun/Imperial/D&R 45591, Are A1191, BsB A143 (mx 92050)(4/08), Nassau B-51, Symphony 21591, Banner L5591.

I'd Rather Be a Minstrel Man Than a Multi-Millionaire (Mack-Orth).
    Eddie Morton, Vic 16697 (2/11).

I'm Crazy 'Bout a Ragtime Minstrel Band (Wm Tracey).
    Ed Meeker, Ed BA 2230 (4/14).

It's Got to Be a Minstrel Show Tonight (aka I Want to See a Minstrel Show Tonight) (Shields-Evans).
    Note: This is not the 1913 Leighton Bros.–Shields song "I Want to See a Minstrel Show."
    J.W. Myers, Col 75 (1901).
    Dan W. Quinn, Monarch 1414 (5/02).

The Jolly Minstrel.
    Duffy & Imgrund's Band, Ed cyl (recorded 8/29/1889).

Laughing Song—sketch. Porter and the boys want to organize a minstrel show but can't find anyone to sing Johnson's Laughing Song. Meeker finally obliges, accompanied by Vess Ossman, banjo.
    Ed Meeker & Empire Vaudeville Co. Ed BA 3427 (3/18), 50745 (8/21).

Me an' de Minstrel Ban' (Alex Rogers).
    Billy Murray, Ed cyl 9037 (2/05).

Merry Minstrel March.
    Edison Symphony Orchestra, Ed cyl 584 (1896–1897).
    Metropolitan Band, Norcross cyl S116 (8/1898).

The Minstrel Band (Gumble).
    Arthur Pryor's Band, Vic 16710 (4/11), Vic 16925 (10/11).

The Minstrel Parade (Hoffman).
    Victor Orchestra, Vic 4489 (1905).
    Hager's Orch., Zon 387.

The Minstrel Parade (Irving Berlin) (from "Watch Your Step").
    Collins & Harlan, Vic 17783 (7/15), Little Wonder 169 (1915)

Rap, Rap, Rap on Your Minstrel Bones (Brown-Von Tilzer).
    Edward Meeker, Ed BA 1576 (11/12).

Squashtown Amateur Minstrels (Spencer-Prince).
    Len Spencer, Col 1690 (1904), Col cyl 32392 (3/04), Leeds 4178.
    [Leeds as "Si Slocum's Squashtown Amateur Minstrels." LS's "Rehearsal of the Squashtown Orchestra" on Vic 4045 may be the same routine.]

The Stranded Minstrel Man
    Murry K. Hill, Ed 4M-16 (10/08)

That Minstrel Man of Mine (L. Spencer).
    Will F. Denney, Ed cyl 7536 (9/00), Col cyl 31331 (3/01).
    Len Spencer and Vess Ossman, Vic A818 (1901), Col cyl 31405 (3/01) (Collins?).
    Len Spencer and Parke Hunter, Leeds 4059, Concert 7059 (1904)

Whistling Minstrel—Caprice (Herman).
    Prince's Military Band, Col 3505 (12/06), Col A57, Star 2065

Appendix 3
Early Recording Artists with Minstrel Experience

Few major minstrel stars made recordings, so could the recorded minstrel recreations of the late nineteenth and early twentieth centuries be considered a true reflection of stage minstrelsy at the time? Is there any way to hear what actual stage performers sounded like? The answer to both questions, I think, is yes.

With the notable exception of Lew Dockstader, top minstrel stars such as George Primrose, McIntyre and Heath, and Billy Kersands did not record. However, a surprising number of professional recording artists, including many who took part in the recreations, did have minstrel experience. Many had been in major troupes, more had non-professional experience, and I would maintain that practically all of them had seen (and were familiar with) minstrel shows. They were thus intimately familiar with the type of entertainment they were recreating.

Following is a non-comprehensive list of recording artists of the 1890–1930 period who had significant minstrel experience on stage. "M" is followed by a brief summary of their minstrel careers, and "R" precedes a summary of their recording careers.

Al Bernard (1888–1949). M: Organized amateur minstrel troupes as a schoolboy and, while still a youth, reportedly joined an unnamed minstrel troupe. Later Bernard was a "coon song" singer in vaudeville. He also published minstrel folios in the 1930s and starred in network radio minstrel shows. R: Extensive recording career from 1919 to 1930, for many labels, specializing in "black" material and, on occasion, minstrel recreations.

Frederick Bowers (1874–1961). M: First appeared in vaudeville and then with the Cleveland, Cushman, Dockstader (1903) and West (1905) minstrels. Also a songwriter. R: Columbia (1910–1911).

Albert C. Campbell (1872–1947). M: A member of Len Spencer's stage troupe that performed in the Northeast in 1898–1899. Late in his career, in 1928–1929, he was a featured tenor with J.A. Coburn's Minstrels. R: Campbell recorded prolifically from 1897 to 1929, both solo and later in duets with Henry Burr and others. He was also a member of the much-recorded Peerless Quartet/Minstrels and the Sterling Trio.

George M. Cohan (1878–1942). M: Probably the biggest star on Broadway in the early 1900s, Cohan's background was primarily in vaudeville. He toured with his family as "The Four Cohans" from 1890 to 1901, and he was also a prolific writer, including writing sketches for minstrel shows. In 1908, he and partner Sam Harris produced the all-star Cohan and Harris Minstrels troupe, which played for two years. R: Several of his own songs for Victor, in 1911.

Frank Coombs (1871–1941), countertenor. M: With Dockstader in the 1890s (five years), and later with Weber and Fields, Primrose Minstrels, and vaudeville. R: Cylinders (1900), then Columbia, Victor, and U.S. Everlasting (1910–1915).

Lew Dockstader (1856–1924). M: A major star, Dockstader headed his own highly successful minstrel troupes from 1886 to the 1910s. Famous for impersonating U.S. presidents. R: Columbia (1905–1912); also made silent films.

Press Eldridge (1854–1925). M: A major star who alternated between vaudeville and minstrelsy. With Bloodgood's Minstrels (1878), Snellbaker and Benton (1880), Carncross' Minstrels (1886–1891), Moore and Burgess in the United Kingdom (1891), Haverly (1892–1893), and Al G. Field (1906–1907). Known as "The Commander-in-Chief of the Army of Fun." R: Edison (1899), Berliner (1900), Edison (1909).

Harry Ellis (1876–?). M: Primrose and Dockstader (1900–1903), Dockstader (1903–1907, 1910). R: Indestructible cylinders (1910), Gennett (1917), Okeh (1918).

Harry Frankel (Singin' Sam) (1888–1948). M: Coburn's Minstrels (1908), Al G. Field Minstrels (1924). R: 1916–1933 for Gennett, Columbia, and numerous smaller labels.

Arthur Fields (1888–1953). M: Guy Brothers Minstrels (c. 1905), then vaudeville. Also a songwriter. R: Victor (1914), Columbia (1915), and many others. One of the most prolific recording artists of the 1910s and 1920s; occasionally recorded thereafter.

Billy Golden (1858–1926). M: Golden made his name with a blackface vaudeville act during the 1870s and 1880s, but he also toured with Len Spencer's minstrel stage troupe in 1898–1899. His longtime partner Joe Hughes was an old-time minstrel man. R: 1891–1922 for many labels, specializing in "old-timey" songs and routines ("Turkey in the Straw," "Bye Bye Ma Honey") both solo and with partners including Hughes, Billy Heins, and Jim Marlowe.

George Graham (?–early 1900s). M: Monologist and stump speaker who appeared briefly with Primrose and West in 1895 and toured with Len Spencer's stage troupe in 1898–1899. R: c. 1895–1903 for Berliner, Victor, Columbia; then he disappeared.

Roger Harding (1858–1901). M: Sam Devere Company, Len Spencer stage troupe. R: 1897–1901 for Berliner, Edison, and Columbia (cylinders). He participated in several minstrel recreations, including at least one for his own Excelsior Phonograph Co.

Morton Harvey (1886–1961). M: Al G. Field Minstrels (c. 1913–1914). R: Victor (1914), Edison, Columbia, and Emerson, to 1917.

Lucille Hegamin (1894–1970). M: Leonard Harper Minstrel Stock Company (c. 1910). R: 1920–1932 for Arto, Paramount, Cameo, Columbia.

Billy Heins (1874–1971?). M: Gus Hill's Minstrels. R: Many labels from 1890s to early 1920s. Made minstrel records for Edison in 1890s. Partner of Billy Golden in 1917–1918.

Joe Hughes (1863–?). M: From 1887–1895 with Goodyear, Elitch and Schillings, Haverly, Carncross, and Dockstader minstrels. In 1907, he teamed with Billy Golden, who had been doing blackface acts in vaudeville since the 1870s, in a stage act. R: In 1908–1920, Golden and Hughes recorded much black dialect material for Victor, Columbia, Edison, and others (Golden had been recording since the 1890s).

Russell Hunting (1864–1943). M: Began as a stage actor and manager in Boston. Toured with Len Spencer's minstrel troupe in 1898–1899. R: 1891–c. 1925, known for his "Casey" stories beginning in the 1890s. Spent much of his career in Britain, where he was a recording executive.

George W. Johnson (1846–1914). M: According to one account, the popular black recording artist of the 1890s toured with the Georgia Minstrels in the 1870s and even traveled to Europe with them. R: 1890–1910 for New York, New Jersey, Columbia and other cylinder labels, as well as Berliner, Columbia, Victor and most other disc labels. Recorded with the Imperial Minstrels.

Al Jolson (1886–1950). M: First with Dockstader (1908–1909), then vaudeville, then became a superstar on Broadway in *La Belle Paree* (1911). R: Victor (1911–1913), Columbia (1913–1923), Brunswick (1924–1932), then Decca. One of the biggest stars of the twentieth century, his minstrel days are depicted in the film *The Jolson Story*.

Richard Jose (1862–1941). M: Active beginning in 1886, with Reed, Dockstader, Thatcher, and West Minstrels. R: Victor (1903–1909). According to Allen Debus, "one of the great countertenors of minstrelsy and truly a star of the 19th century."

Matt Keefe (1867–1920), yodeler. M: Al G. Field, Primrose and Dockstader, Dockstader, Cohan and Harris. R: Bacigalupi (1897), Edison (1908), Columbia (1914 and 1917), Pathé (1919).

Dan Kelly (1842–?). M: 1850s–1880s, with Bryant, Christy, and then on the stage. R: One of the earliest artists to become popular on cylinders, through his "Pat Brady" sketches for the Ohio Phonograph Co. (c. 1890–1895), and Columbia (1893).

Silas Leachman (1859–1936). M: According to his younger brother, "in his early adult years he was a minstrel, singing and playing the piano."[1] R: Chicago Talking Machine Co. (early 1890s–1900) and Victor (1901–1904), specializing in coon songs.

Harry Leighton (1866–1926), M: Haverly, Carncross, Cleveland, Dockstader, Thatcher and Johnson, and so on. R: New Jersey cylinders (1895) while with Dockstader troupe.

Tom Lewis (c. 1864–1927). M: George Wilson Minstrels (1890), Primrose and West (1891–1894), Cleveland, Haverly (1892–1893), Carncross, and West's Minstrels (1899–1900). Prominent minstrel in the 1890s, then went into vaudeville and theater. R: Brunswick (1924).

James McCool (1875–1935). M: Frank Dumont minstrels, Philadelphia. R: Edison, local companies (1890s), Victor (1900–1905 and 1919).

Edward Meeker (1874–1937). M: Miller's 20th Century Minstrels, Hoyt's Knickerbocker Minstrels (4 years). R: Edison from around 1905 to the late 1920s as staff announcer and singer, including minstrel recordings.

Elida Morris (1886–1977), "coon shouter." M: Unusual early career as a blackface "lady minstrel," generally as the endman. Began at age ten in a children's troupe in her native Philadelphia, then worked with Tim McMahon's Minstrel Maids (c. 1903–1904) and in the duo Lillian Mills (interlocutor) and Morris (endman). These were minstrel first part acts in vaudeville. After 14 years in blackface, she became a solo whiteface act in 1910. R: Victor, Columbia (1910–1921).

Billy Murray (1877–1954). M: Unknown (1896), Al G. Field (c. 1900–1904). R: Bacigalupi (1897), Edison (1903 onward), then Victor, Columbia. One of the most prolific studio artists in recording history, most active from 1903 to 1930, although he continued to record until the 1940s. Lead tenor of the Rambler Minstrels, who recorded widely from 1906 to 1909.

Joseph Natus (1860–1917). M: Primrose and West (1891–1892), Dockstader. R: Edison, Berliner, Victor (1891–1905). On some Imperial Minstrels records.

Will Oakland (1883?–1956). M: Primrose (1905), Dockstader (1907), Cohan and Harris (1909). R: Edison (1908), Victor (1909), and others up to 1926. Prolific. Succeeded Richard Jose as the leading minstrel countertenor.

George H. O'Connor (1874–1946). M: A successful Washington lawyer, O'Connor was much in demand for amateur minstrel shows staged there from the mid-1890s onward, often as endman, performing for presidents from McKinley to FDR. R: Columbia (1914–1918).

Geoffrey O'Hara (1882–1967), singer, songwriter, ethnomusicologist. M: According to ASCAP, his "early stage career included four years in minstrelsy and major vaudeville circuits as pianist, singer and accompanist." Appeared with Dockstader. R: Edison, Victor (1905–1928).

Chauncey Olcott (1858–1932), Irish tenor, actor, songwriter. M: His first ten years on stage (c. 1876–1886) were in minstrelsy, including the Alabama Serenaders, Lew Benedict's Minstrels, Simmons and Slocum, Hooley and Emerson's Megetharians, Haverly's Mastodons (1880), Emerson's Minstrels (1881), Carncross (two or three years), Thatcher, and Primrose and West (1884–1886). He then went on to achieve fame in stage plays. R: Columbia (1913, 1920). His minstrel days are depicted in the biographical film *My Wild Irish Rose* (1947).

Vess L. Ossman (1868–1923). M: Toured with Len Spencer troupe in 1898–1899. R: 1893–1917 for many companies. The leading banjo player on record during the 1890s and early 1900s, dubbed "The Banjo King."

Steve C. Porter (c. 1862–1936). M: Toured with the Len Spencer troupe in 1898–1899. R: Recorded widely from 1897 to 1928. Known for his quartet work and sketches portraying rural types and various ethnicities, especially Irish (e.g., Flanagan).

Charles A. Prince (1869–1937), orchestra leader. M: Walsh reports that as a young man, he "traveled with circuses, minstrel shows and legitimate companies for several years." R: Piano accompanist for the New York Phonograph Co. (1891), influential musical director and house band leader for Columbia (c. 1895-1922). As such, he presumably conducted the orchestra for most of Columbia's minstrel records. After 1922, he was briefly with Victor, and then he retired.

Gertrude "Ma" Rainey (1886-1939), blues singer. M: Rabbit's Foot Minstrels (1906-c. 1910s). R: Paramount (1923-1928).

William Redmond (1871-1945). M: Primrose and Dockstader (1900). R: Edison (1902-1904), Columbia (1908), Victor (1915-1916, as a member of the American Quartet). Perhaps best known for the 1902 hit "In the Good Old Summertime" on Edison.

Manuel Romain (1872-1926), tenor. M: Primrose and West (1893), Cleveland (1895), and Dockstader (total 15 seasons); then went into vaudeville. R: Edison (1907), Victor (1909), and others up to 1919, plus some late recordings in 1926.

Burt Shepard (1854-1913). M: Haverly's New Orleans Minstrels (1874-1877), Sweatnam's Minstrels (1878-1879), Billy Emerson and the Big Four Minstrels (1879), Carncross (1879-1881), Thatcher, Primrose and West (1882-1889), Burt Shepard and Billy Rice (1892-1893), Shepard's Modern Minstrels (1893), Cleveland (1895). Traveled to United Kingdom, Paris, South Africa and Australia in 1897. Monologues and parodies at the piano. R: Berliner (UK, 1898), Victor (1901-1906), and various UK labels to around 1908.

Six Brown Brothers, Tom Brown (1881-1950), leader. Saxophone band. M: Guy Brothers Minstrels (c. 1899), then with Ringling Brothers Circus and in vaudeville. A hit with Primrose and Dockstader Minstrels (1912-1914). R: Columbia (1911), Victor (1914-1920), Emerson (1920).

Bessie Smith (1894-1937), famous blues singer. M: First toured with the Moses Stokes Minstrel Troupe (1912-1913), then Rabbit's Foot Minstrels and vaudeville. R: Columbia (1923-1931), Okeh (1933).

Len Spencer (1867-1914). M: Produced and appeared in local minstrel shows in Washington and New York as early as 1891. By 1895-1896, he was playing gigs in the New York area in both vaudeville and minstrelsy, including the Cleveland and Haverly Minstrels. In 1898, he organized his own troupe called "Len Spencer's Greater New York Minstrels," which toured successfully in the New York region. R: Beginning in 1890 for Columbia, New Jersey Phonograph Co., Edison, Berliner, Victor and most other labels. Originated the recorded minstrel craze with his studio group the Imperial Minstrels (1894). Continued recording until around 1912.

Cal Stewart (1856-1919). Famous for his semi-serialized stories of Uncle Josh Weathersby of Pumpkin Center, New England. M: Toured with Len Spencer's troupe, 1898-1899. R: Around 1897-1919 for many labels.

William H. Thompson (1869-1945). M: Kelly and Leon Minstrels (1889), Cleveland (1890), Primrose and West (1890-1893 and 1897-1898), Primrose and Dockstader, Dockstader (to 1910). R: Edison (1902), Victor (1903), Columbia (1910-1913).

Francklyn Wallace (c.1869- ?). M: Dockstader (1904). R: Edison, Zonophone (1902).

Lee Roy "Lasses" White (1888-1949). M: Honey Boy Evans Minstrels (1914-1915), Neil O'Brien (1915-1917), Al G. Field (1917-1920), and then headlined his own troupe (1920-1928). A Dallas favorite, White wrote "Nigger Blues" (1912), one of the first published blues. Later starred with "Lasses White Minstrels" on WSM (1932) and *The Grand Ole Opry* (1934-1938); also in Hollywood westerns and B-flicks (1937-1950). Portrayed in 1944's *Minstrel Man* (also appeared in the film). R: Columbia (1923).

Bert Williams (1874-1922). The most famous African American performer of his era, and the best-selling black recording artist prior to 1920. M: Early in his career, he was with Lew Johnson's Minstrels (1893) and Martin and Selig's Mastodons (1893-c. 1895). Then went into vaudeville and Broadway with his partner George Walker. R: 1897-1922 for Victor, Columbia.

Billy Williams (1854-1910). M: Joined Billy Manning's Minstrels in Chicago in 1870, then the Original New Orleans Minstrels and Haverly. In minstrelsy for several years before moving into variety, where he had a blackface song-and-dance act as part of the duo Williams and Sully (1876-1887). In later years newspapers confused Williams with a Midwest evangelist/scam artist who adopted his name and persona. R: New Jersey Phonograph Co. (1892-1897), including as a key member of Len Spencer's original Imperial Minstrels.

Evan Williams (1867–1918). M: Although the eminent concert tenor seems an unlikely candidate for minstrelsy, he apparently sang popular songs such as "After the Ball" with the Primrose and West Minstrels in 1893, before his concert career began to take off in 1895. R: Nearly 200 recordings for Victor and HMV (1906–1917), also Pathé (1911).

Nat M. Wills (1873–1917), monologist. M: Ideal Minstrels in Washington (endman, in 1890s). R: Victor (1908), Columbia (1913), Emerson (1916).

Chapter Notes

Preface

1. See, for example, Murray Forman, "Employment and Blue Pencils: NBC, Race and Representation, 1926–55," in *NBC: America's Network*, edited by Michele Hilmes (Berkeley: University of California Press, 2007), 117–34.

2. Annemarie Bean, James V. Hatch and Brooks McNamara, eds., *Inside the Minstrel Mask: Readings in Nineteenth-Century Blackface Minstrelsy* (Hanover, NH: Wesleyan University Press, 1996), xi; Eric Lott, *Love & Theft: Blackface Minstrelsy and the American Working Class* (New York: Oxford University Press, 1993), 4; William J. Mahar, *Behind the Burnt Cork Mask* (Urbana: University of Illinois Press, 1999), 41; Greil Marcus in Lott, *Love & Theft*, ix; Nick Tosches, *Where Dead Voices Gather* (Boston: Back Bay Books, 2001), 12; John Strausbaugh, *Black Like You: Blackface, Whiteface, Insult & Imitation in American Popular Culture* (New York: Penguin Group, 2006), 62.

3. Merriam-Webster defines *minstrel* as initially "one of a class of medieval musical entertainers" and traces the origins of the term to medieval Latin *ministeriālis*: "servant, functionary in a lord's household, official." See https://www.merriam-webster.com/dictionary/minstrel.

4. *Amos 'n' Andy* is a favorite subject of researchers and has been extensively studied. It was for most of its history a comedic serial. See, for example, Melvin Patrick Ely, *The Adventures of Amos 'n' Andy: A Social History of an American Phenomenon* (New York: Free Press, 1991), and Elizabeth McLeod, *The Original Amos 'n' Andy: Freeman Gosden, Charles Correll and the 1928–1943 Radio Serial* (Jefferson, NC: McFarland, 2005). The program did present a traditional minstrel show in at least two episodes, which will be discussed in chapter 3.

Chapter 1

1. Robert C. Toll, *Blacking Up: The Minstrel Show in Nineteenth Century America* (New York: Oxford University Press, 1974), 26–27. The identification of "firsts" is always debatable. For example, William Mahar cites "Backside Albany," "the earliest known dialect song written by an American," as having been sung in a stage production in 1815. See William J. Mahar, "'Backside Albany' and Early Blackface Minstrelsy," *American Music* 6, no. 1 (Spring 1988), 1.

2. Virtually all histories of minstrelsy mention Rice and Dixon, but probably the most thorough profiles of these influential performers can be found in Dale Cockrell, *Demons of Disorder: Early Blackface Minstrels and Their World* (Cambridge: Cambridge University Press, 1997), 62–101.

3. Hans Nathan, *Dan Emmett and the Rise of Early Negro Minstrelsy* (Norman: University of Oklahoma Press, 1962), 116–18. As with most "firsts," there are various caveats in this declaration: Emmett and his friends appear to have practiced their act at the North American Hotel, across the street from the theater, in late January, and they held a benefit performance for Pelham at the Chatham Theatre on January 31. On February 6, they opened their regular run.

4. There is some debate about exactly who originated each of the elements of the minstrel show, and how long it took for the various pieces to come together; some sources say it was as late as the second half of the 1850s. Tom Fletcher claims that the black singing group known as the Luca Family originated the "minstrel first part" format, even though they were known primarily for serious music (Tom Fletcher, *100 Years of the Negro in Show Business* [New York: Burdge & Co., 1954 (reprint Da Capo Press, 1984)], 37–39).

5. Robert B. Winans, "Early Minstrel Show Music, 1843–1852," in Bean et al., *Inside the Minstrel Mask*, 143–44. Winans researched printed programs to determine the makeup and instrumentation of early troupes. See also Mahar, *Behind the Burnt Cork Mask*, 355–63.

6. Lew Dockstader, "The Search for the Oldest Minstrel Joke," clipping, December 25, 1916, Theatre Collection, New York Public Library, quoted in Toll, *Blacking Up*, 40.

7. Winans, "Early Minstrel Show Music," 147–48.

8. Winans tabulated the 22 songs most frequently found in minstrel playbills dated 1843–1852. Only three of them were by Foster ("Camptown Races," "Old Folks at Home," "Nelly Was a Lady"). None were near the top of the list. Mahar analyzed approximately 44 song books published between 1840 and 1860 and found only one Foster song ("Oh! Susanna") among the 80 or so most frequently included (Mahar, *Behind the Burnt Cork Mask*, 367–68). Foster experts offer several possible explanations for this anomaly.

Professor Deane Root has said that songbooks may not accurately reflect the performed repertory and that Foster was not always credited for his work at the time. Alternatively, his songs may have been added later, after they became a popular part of *Uncle Tom's Cabin* productions. In other words, they grew in popularity, rather than being immediate hits (correspondence with Root, February–March 2017).

9. Toll, *Blacking Up*, 92–93; Jennifer C.H.J. Wilson, "(Re)Establishing Southern Patriotism: Professional and Amateur Minstrelsy in Lynchburg, Virginia," in *Music, American Made: Essays in Honor of John Graziano*, edited by John Koegel (Sterling Heights, MI: Harmonie Park Press, 2011), 399–401.

10. Kit Clarke, "Some Cork and Sawdust 'Thinks' of the Past," *New York Clipper*, February 17, 1912, reprinted in William L. Slout, ed., *Burnt Cork and Tambourines: A Source Book for Negro Minstrelsy* (Rockville, MD: Borgo Press, 2007), 251.

11. *New York Clipper*, March 28, 1891, quoted in Wilson, "(Re)Establishing Southern Patriotism," 402.

12. Toll, *Blacking Up*, 195–229.

13. This summary is based on an analysis of advertisements and news stories in 1865–1866 newspapers, as accessed from www.fultonhistory.com (October 2016). Published summaries in various reference books are garbled and often incorrect, judging from these original sources. For a history of the later Georgia Minstrels and of Charles Hicks, see Eileen Southern, "The Georgia Minstrels: The Early Years," in Bean et al., *Inside the Minstrel Mask*, 163–75.

14. Toll, *Blacking Up*, 274.

15. The quotes are from Kenneth Padgett, http:///black-face.com/minstrel-shows.htm; Annemarie Bean, http://www.encyclopedia.com/literature-and-arts/performing-arts/theater/minstrel-shows; Yuval Taylor and Jake Austen, *Darkest America: Black Minstrelsy from Slavery to Hip-Hop* (New York: W.W. Norton, 2012), 202; and Dawn Amber Dennis, entry on "Minstrelsy," in *The Early Republic and Antebellum America: An Encyclopedia of Social, Political, Cultural, and Economic History*, edited by Christopher G. Bates (New York: Routledge, 2010), 665, respectively. Websites accessed October 26, 2016.

16. Most theater musicals of this period had very loose plots and frequently interpolated currently popular songs. The structured "book musical" did not become predominant until much later, with *Show Boat* (1927), *Oklahoma!* (1943) and similar shows.

17. See "Grand Minstrel Jubilee: Primrose and West, Madison Square Garden, Monday Eve., March 9th '96" (pamphlet), Harvard University Library.

18. Tosches, *Where Dead Voices Gather*, 241, plus my own research in period newspapers.

19. Primrose and Dockstader's Minstrels, New Westchester Theatre, Matinee and Night, Saturday, August 24, 1912, Harvard Theatre Collection.

20. Bobby Newcomb, "Bobby Newcomb's Hints to the Minstrel Stage," in Wehman Bros., *Wehman's Minstrel Sketches* (New York: Wehman Bros., 1879 & 1882). This combination of two resources remained in print for many years. The first section, "Bones: His Gags and Stump Speeches," is copyright 1879, while the second, "Tambo: His Jokes and Funny Sayings" by Newcomb, is copyright 1882. Newcomb was a major minstrel performer who was born in 1847 and died in 1888, and is described as "deceased," so the printing referenced must be later than that. The Newcomb quote is on page 3 of the second section.

21. Toll, *Blacking Up*, 226–28.

22. Nathan, *Dan Emmett*, 145.

23. Tosches, *Where Dead Voices Gather*, 16; Joseph Boskin, *Sambo: The Rise and Demise of an American Jester* (New York: Oxford University Press, 1986), 83–84.

24. Frederick Douglass, "Gavitt's Original Ethiopian Serenaders," *The North Star*, 29 June 1849. Douglass's earlier quote was in the context of a review of the abolitionist Hutchinson Family Singers.

25. James Monroe Trotter, *Music and Some Highly Musical People* (Boston: Lee and Shepard, 1878), 270–82.

26. Lynn Abbott and Doug Seroff, *Ragged But Right* (Jackson: University Press of Mississippi, 2007), 157–207.

27. Abbott and Seroff, *Ragged But Right*, 210–17.

28. *Billboard*, "Minstrelsy" column, December 8, 1928, 76; Tosches, *Where Dead Voices Gather*, 242; contemporary newspapers.

29. Paul Charosh, "Studying Nineteenth-Century Popular Song," *American Music* 15, no. 4 (Winter 1997): 459–92.

30. The Wehman book was actually a combination of two previously published pamphlets: "Bones: His Gags and Stump Speeches" (1879) and "Tambo: His Jokes and Funny Sayings" by minstrel veteran Bobby Newcomb (1882).

31. Joe Davis, ed., *Tip Top Entertainment and Minstrel Album* (New York: Tip Top Publishing, 1936), 4, 37.

32. Boskin, *Sambo*, 87–88.

33. Boskin, *Sambo*, 89.

34. This information comes from www.newspapers.com, a searchable database of more than 4,400 geographically dispersed, mostly U.S. newspapers of all eras (accessed October 2016). This data reflects trends rather than the actual number of shows, as some shows received multiple mentions while others were not reported at all or were mentioned in newspapers not included in the database. Also, the total number of newspapers for which data are available increased over time. It was relatively steady from 1920 to 1950 (at about 1.2 million pages per year), and then, after a jump in the 1950s, steady again from 1960 to 1990 (2.6 million per year). This is the opposite of the trend in *minstrel show* references so, if anything, the decline in references during the 1950s was even steeper than what is shown.

35. Nathan, *Dan Emmett*, 122.

36. Toll, *Blacking Up*, 31; Michael Pickering, *Blackface Minstrelsy in Britain* (Burlington, VT: Ashgate, 2008), 100.

37. Laura Vorachek, "Whitewashing Blackface Minstrelsy in Nineteenth-Century England: Female Banjo Players in 'Punch,'" *English Faculty Publications*, Paper 6 (2013), 31.

38. Pickering, *Blackface Minstrelsy in Britain*, 160–83.

39. Pickering, *Blackface Minstrelsy in Britain*, 59–63, 69–74.

40. Pickering, *Blackface Minstrelsy in Britain*, 82, 112, 159.
41. Boskin, *Sambo*, 76–77.

Chapter 2

1. The best analysis of recordings is in Patrick Feaster, "'The Following Record': Making Sense of Phonographic Performance, 1877–1908," (dissertation, Indiana University, 2007), chapter 6, "Complex Entertainments," 552–96. As stated in the title, this source deals with recordings up to 1908.
2. Columbia Phonograph Co. advertisement, *The Phonogram* 1, no. 5 (May 1891), unpaged at back.
3. Theo. E. Wangemann, "The First Book of Phonograph Records," reprinted in Allen Koenigsberg, *Edison Cylinder Records, 1889–1912*, Second Edition (Brooklyn, NY: APM Press, 1987), 133.
4. One minstrel show for which Banta wrote a sketch is described in "Larchmont Entertains," *New York Sun*, August 12, 1900, IV:5. Feaster believes that the aforementioned record slip refers to one of these 1893 recordings, not one made in 1891 (Feaster, "'The Following Record,'" 634, fn 7). This is certainly possible, although, considering the layout of the slip, the matter is open to debate.
5. "At Edison's Laboratory," *Orange Herald*, September 8, 1888, cited in Feaster, "'The Following Record,'" 634, fn 6.
6. This information comes from numerous newspaper reports, including *The Critic and Record* (Washington), April 27, 1891, 3; *New York Herald*, March 24, 1895, unpaged; *Eastern State Journal* (White Plains, NY), November 14, 1896, unpaged; *New York Clipper*, December 10, 1898, 701. See also Walsh, *Hobbies* (October 1958), 34.
7. Edward L. Rice, *Monarchs of Minstrelsy* (New York: Kenny Publishing Co., 1911), 256–58. Later (in the early 1900s), Williams seems to have been confused with a Midwest evangelist/scam artist who adopted his name and persona to raise money for his supposedly impoverished wife and child. There are numerous and often sensational press reports about the erratic behavior of this imposter during 1907–1910. See *Indianapolis Star*, March 16, 1909, 10; *Rochester Democrat*, July 26, 1910; *New York Dramatic Mirror*, August 6, 1910, 30 (obit.).
8. Quinn was not born in San Francisco in 1859, as is often reported. By far the most complete account of his life and career is contained in the notes to the CD *Dan W. Quinn Anthology: The King of Comic Singers 1894–1917*, written by Richard Martin (Archeophone ARCH 5505, 2015). This source expands on, and corrects errors in, Jim Walsh's pioneering profile of Quinn in *Hobbies* (March–May 1945).
9. Tim Brooks, *Lost Sounds: Blacks and the Birth of the Recording Industry, 1890–1919* (Urbana: University of Illinois Press, 2004), 15–71.
10. See, for example, Ed Marble, *The Minstrel Show, or Burnt Cork Comicalities* (unidentified publisher, 1893), 5; Frank Dumont, *The Witmark Amateur Minstrel Guide and Burnt Cork Encyclopedia* (Chicago: M. Witmark & Sons, 1899), 8–10; Harold Rossiter, *How to Put on a Minstrel Show* (Chicago: Max Stein Publishing, 1921), 3–15; Dailey Paskman and Sigmund Spaeth, *Gentlemen, Be Seated!* (New York: Doubleday, 1928 [revised 1976]), 25, 97–151.
11. United States Phonograph Co., *Catalogue of Standard New Jersey Records* (March 1, 1894), 17.
12. Surviving New Jersey literature is rare for this early period. The closest prior list seems to have been "Spring and Summer (1893) Announcement" printed in the final issue of the short-lived industry journal *The Phonogram*—namely, volume 3, nos. 3-4 (March–April 1893), 346.
13. Feaster, "'The Following Record,'" 556.
14. "A High Old Time," words and music by Harry C. Talbert (b. 1848), composed 1888. Spencer made some minor modifications to the words.
15. "New Songs, New Music, New Talks, New Artists, New Ideas, New Effects: Supplemental List of Records for the Phonograph from the United States Phonograph Co." (undated but c. January 1895), 9–10.
16. United States Phonograph Co., *Supplemental List of Standard New Jersey Records for the Phonograph, Revised to February 1st* [1895], 20–22.
17. United States Phonograph Co., *Sixth Supplemental Record Bulletin* (undated but early 1897), 18.
18. Columbia Phonograph Co., *List of the Famous Columbia Records* (June 1897), 11.
19. Dumont, *The Witmark Amateur Minstrel Guide*, 8, 18.
20. Imperial Minstrels, "The Laughing Song," Columbia cylinder 13004, c. 1902.
21. Imperial Minstrels, "Old Folks at Home," Columbia cylinder 13010, c. 1898.
22. The patent fights between Columbia, Berliner (succeeded by the Victor Talking Machine Co.), and Edison in the late 1890s and early 1900s were long and complicated. Each party asserted that it had a monopoly over key disc record-making patents. The legal warfare was resolved, more or less, in 1902–1903 when Columbia and Victor signed a cross-licensing agreement for lateral-cut recording (the most popular kind), allowing them both to proceed, while Edison restricted itself to vertical-cut cylinders (and later discs).
23. Jim Walsh, "Billy Golden," *Hobbies* (June 1944), 25–27; Tim Gracyk, *The Encyclopedia of Popular American Recording Pioneers, 1895–1925* (Granite Bay, CA: Self-published, n.d.), 134–36. There are numerous references to the Golden, Chalfant and Golden act in the *Clipper* and the *Dramatic Mirror* during the mid-1890s. The act is also referenced in Rice, *Monarchs of Minstrelsy*, 288, although Chalfant's name is misspelled. Feaster believes that Golden first toured with his wife, May Golden, and later with his stepdaughter Daisy Golden (Feaster, "'The Following Record,'" 561–62).
24. "New Jersey's Summer Retreats," *New York Herald*, 30 July 1893; "Fourteenth Street Theatre," *The Clipper*, 2 June 1894, 198; "At the Playhouse," *The Evening Review*, 4 March 1898, 2; "Best Ever Seen Here," *The Times Recorder* (Zanesville OH), 30 March 1898, 4; Berliner 4269.
25. Arthur Collins, S.H. Dudley and the Ancient City Quartet, "Laughing Song," Edison cylinder 4702, 1899.

26. Consolidated Phonograph Cos., Ltd., Newark, New Jersey, *Records for the Phonograph and Graphophone* (c. 1899), 24. More information on Consolidated and the death throes of the United States Phonograph Co. can be found in Ray Wile, "Duplicates of the Nineties and the National Phonograph Company's Bloc Numbered Series," *ARSC Journal* 32, no. 2 (Fall 2001), 195–97.

27. United States Phonograph Co., *High Grade Original Master Records for Phonographs and Graphophones* (c. 1900), 26. "Made at the laboratory of United States Phonograph Co., 87–91 Orange St., Newark, N.J."

28. *Temporary Catalog of the Columbia Phonograph Co.'s Musical Records* (January 1, 1895), 12.

29. United States Phonograph Co., *Supplemental List of Standard New Jersey Records for the Phonograph* (February 1, 1895), 11–12.

30. See Feaster, "'The Following Record,'" 570, which traces connections between Parkham and Berliner artists Fred Gaisberg and George Graham.

31. Jim Walsh, "More about S.H. Dudley," *Hobbies* (May 1946), 20.

32. Climax Minstrels, "My Wild Irish Rose," Climax 801, c. 1902.

33. "Coon! Coon! Coon!" is ranked by Edward Gardner, on page 254 of *Popular Songs of the Twentieth Century*, Vol. 1 (St. Paul, MN: Paragon House, 2000), as the fourth most popular song of 1901. It was widely recorded.

34. "Coon! Coon! Coon!" words by Gene Jefferson, music by Leo Friedman, composed 1900.

35. Zonophone Minstrels, "My Charcoal Charmer," Zonophone 581 (1901).

36. *Victor Talking Machine Records* (January 1903), fold-out supplement. According to the ledgers, the recordings were made on December 11–13, 1902, so, given normal processing time, the records may not have been available for sale until late January or early February 1903.

37. Dudley uses his frequent pseudonym "Frank Kernell" on this record. It should be noted that the routine was performed differently on certain takes. On some takes the endman badgers the tenor (Macdonough), who eventually sings the song anyway.

38. Dumont, *The Witmark Amateur Minstrel Guide*, 99–107. The copy of this popular guide held at Stanford University (and available online) is hand inscribed to Sam Sanford, "one of the oldest minstrels" (active from the 1840s), from Julius Witmark, "one of the youngest," with a date of June 1901.

39. "An Evening with the Minstrels No. 6: The Cakewalk in Coontown," Victor 1828, recorded several times beginning in December 1902.

40. Feaster, "'The Following Record,'" 576 (transcription of matrix B1024 3). The transcription here is from matrix C1024-5. Both were recorded on the same day in 1905.

41. Paskman and Spaeth, *Gentlemen, Be Seated!*, 97–151 ("A Working Model"). A movie example is *Yes Sir, Mr. Bones* (1951).

42. *New Columbia Disc Records* (February 1, 1903), 2 (Form 471-A, Supplement No. 4). This is a fold-out supplement. Release literature from this period is extremely rare, and cylinder supplements have not been located. The dealer card is reproduced in Timothy Fabrizio and George Paul, *Antique Phonograph Advertising* (Atglen, PA: Schiffer, 2001), 66, and explained in Feaster, "'The Following Record,'" 577.

43. Frank Hoffmann, Dick Carty and Quentin Riggs, *Billy Murray: The Phonograph Industry's First Great Recording Artist* (Lanham, MD: Scarecrow Press, 1997), 15–64. See also numerous newspaper reports accessible through www.newspapers.com and www.fultonhistory.com—notably *Indianapolis News*, August 22, 1902, 16, and *Harrisburg Telegraph*, February 8, 1904, 10.

44. *Rochester (NY) Democrat and Chronicle*, January 5, 1901, 9.

45. Rambler Minstrels, "My Kickapoo Queen," Columbia A5027 (30062), 1907.

46. Rambler Minstrels No. 9, "I'm Happy When the Band Plays Dixie," Zonophone 5139 (1078), 1908.

47. Rambler Minstrels No. 8, "Every Day She Wanted Something Else," Zonophone 1056, 1908. The song is from George M. Cohan's 1907 show *The Honeymooners*.

48. Columbia Phonograph Co., "November Additions to the List of Columbia Records" (November 1907), fold-out supplement.

49. Gracyk, *Encyclopedia of Popular American Recording Pioneers*, 347–50.

50. Peerless Minstrels, "Georgia Minstrels," Victor 35197, 1911.

51. Peerless Minstrels, "North Carolina Minstrels," Victor 35307, 1913.

52. Gracyk, *Encyclopedia of Popular American Recording Pioneers*, 275, quoting Campbell.

53. Peerless Minstrels, "Military Minstrels," Victor 35274, 1913.

54. Although Collins made personal appearances, and record companies occasionally printed his picture, in 1905 Edison found it necessary to issue the highly unusual disclaimer "Mr. Collins Is Not a Negro." This item, in Edison's trade paper, continued, "Possibly because of his great success in singing coon and ragtime songs for the Edison Phonograph some people seem to have gained the impression that Arthur Collins is a colored man. Such an impression is naturally amusing to Mr. Collins. It is complimentary, however, to imitate the colored race so closely as to be mistaken for the real article" (*Edison Phonograph Monthly* [July 1905], 10).

55. Tim Brooks with Merle Sprinzen, *Little Wonder Records and Bubble Books* (Denver, CO: Mainspring Press, 2011). The first release (Little Wonder 53) was followed by a series numbered "Minstrels Parts 1–6" (Little Wonder 340–45). However, part 5 was not listed and no copy has ever been located, so it may not have been issued.

56. Edison Modern Minstrels, "Georgia Minstrels," Edison cylinder 8672, 1904.

57. Edison Minstrels, "At the Minstrel Show No. 5: The Jokesmiths," Edison cylinder 9279, 1906.

58. Elks' Minstrel Co., "Elks Minstrels," Edison Amberol cylinder 64, 1909.

59. Dan W. Quinn, "It's Got to Be a Minstrel Show Tonight," Monarch 1414, 1902. The Columbia version by Myers is called "I Want to See a Minstrel Show Tonight." It should not be confused with the similarly

titled 1913 song by the Leighton Brothers and Ren Shields: "I Want to See a Minstrel Show."
60. Columbia Phonograph Co., *Columbia Disc Records Catalogue* (c. December 1904) (Form 711), 64.
61. Brian Rust and Allen G. Debus, *The Complete Entertainment Discography*, 2nd edition (New York: Da Capo Press, 1989), 256.
62. "Negro Melodies in Wax," *New York Evening World*, December 20, 1888, 2.
63. The Columbia "20th Century" (Model BC) cylinder phonograph, introduced in 1905, was equipped with an ingenious "Higham" reproducer that amplified the sound via a rotating amber wheel. It worked well but had to be kept in perfect alignment. The machine came with a large triple-spring motor and an extra-long mandrel capable of playing six-inch cylinders that lasted for three to four minutes. Dockstader presumably had a custom cylinder produced with gaps in the sound that allowed him to interact with the machine; thus, his timing had to be perfect. See Howard Hazelcorn, *Columbia Phonograph Companion*, Vol. 1 (Los Angeles: Mulholland Press, 1999), 134–35, for more information on this remarkable machine.
64. "Graphophone as Interlocutor," *Music Trade Review*, July 29, 1905 (reprinted in *Columbia Record* [September 1905], unpaged).
65. Allen Debus, notes to *Monarchs of Minstrelsy* (CD, Archeophone 1006, released in 2006), 18; Rice, *Monarchs of Minstrelsy*, 338.
66. Debus, notes to *Monarchs of Minstrelsy*, 21.
67. "George Wilson's Minstrels," *Vicksburg Evening Post*, September 12, 1890, unpaged.
68. Tom Lewis, "An Old-Time Minstrel Scene," Brunswick 2727, recorded 1924.
69. "Automatic Minstrels," *New York Dramatic Mirror*, October 27, 1906, 18, and April 13, 1907, 17; *Columbia Record* (August 1907).
70. "The June Record List," *Edison Amberola Monthly* (May 1919), 13. The recording was released on Edison cylinder 3755 in June 1919 and on Diamond Disc 50750 in November 1921.
71. Lasses White Minstrel Co., "Old Time Minstrels, Part 1," Columbia A6231, 1923.
72. The first reference I have found to a performance by Al Bernard's Southern Minstrels is in the *New Orleans Times-Democrat*, January 18, 1907. The troupe continued to appear (mostly in benefits) for the rest of the year.
73. Jack Kaufman and Al Campbell, "Bring Back Those Minstrel Days," Harmony 295-H. Sophie Tucker had been in the out-of-town tryouts for the show but was replaced by Greenwood before it reached New York.
74. Victor Minstrels, "Minstrel Show of 1929, Part 1," Victor 35961, 1929.
75. "Al Bernard's Merry Minstrel Show," Celebrity 2000-1 (c. 1948).
76. "The Minstrel Men," Colpix CP 434; *Billboard*, October 13, 1958, 21.
77. Nat Hentoff, notes to LP "Minstrel Days," Everest SDBR 1039, 1959; *Billboard*, August 24, 1959, 30.
78. *Billboard*, April 28, 1956, 32, and May 5, 1956, 45.
79. Berliner's original product in the United Kingdom was marked "E. Berliner's Gramophone," and these are commonly called Berliner records. However, over time the word *gramophone* became more prominent, and the "E. Berliner's" portion was dropped entirely at the end of 1901.
80. Rainer Lotz, *German Ragtime*, Vol. 1 (Chigwell, Essex, UK: Storyville Publications, 1985), 50.
81. Christy Minstrels, "Little Dolly Daydream," Berliner 4080, 1900.
82. Lotz, *German Ragtime*, 31, quoting Harry Reynolds, *Minstrel Memories: The Story of Burnt Cork Minstrelsy in Great Britain from 1836 to 1927* (London: A. Rivers, 1928).
83. Frank Andrews, "Minstrels, Minstrel Shows & Early Recordings," *Talking Machine Review*, no. 47 (1977): 1063–76.
84. Coontown Minstrels No. 5, "Nellie Gray," Jumbo 661 (A28189), 1912.
85. The Mississippi Minstrels, "An Old Time Minstrel Show," Regal G1076, 1929.
86. The English Minstrels, "Minstrel Show of 1931," HMV C2305, 1931.

Chapter 3

1. "Syria Chorus Will Give Minstrel Show Next Week," *Pittsburgh Post-Gazette*, November 19, 1921, 4; "Tonight's Radio Program," *Pittsburgh Gazette-Times*, November 22, 1921, 5. See also Noah Arceneaux, "Blackface Broadcasting in the Early Days of Radio," *Journal of Radio Studies* 12, no. 1 (2005), 63.
2. *Brooklyn Daily Eagle*, April 30, 1922, 38; *Schenectady Gazette*, May 3, 1922, 10. Six other Okeh shows aired on March 16 (on WJZ) and between April 12 and May 17 (on WVP). They featured a broad range of Okeh talent, including Vaughn DeLeath, Nathan Glantz, Byron G. Harlan ("Uncle Josh on the Radio"), Virginia Burt, and the Vincent Lopez Orchestra.
3. *Harrisburg Evening News*, February 5, 1923, 14; *Hudson Valley Times*, March 2, 1923.
4. *Schenectady Gazette*, July 5, 1923, 15.
5. Mel Watkins, *On the Real Side: A History of African American Comedy from Slavery to Chris Rock*, 2nd edition (Chicago: Lawrence Hill Books, 1999), 270–71.
6. "Gimbels' Radio Starts with Big Show," *Variety*, October 29, 1924, 32.
7. Charlotte Geer, *Theatre Magazine* (October 1925), 37.
8. "Minstrel Show to Head Vaudeville at Allyn Theater," *Hartford Daily Courant*, July 24, 1927 (clipping file, New York Public Library).
9. Dailey Paskman, "Paskman's Radio Minstrels Fill the New Place in Broadcasting," *Evening World*, December 29, 1927 (clipping file, New York Public Library).
10. "Black-Faced Fabricators of Fun and Music," *New York Times*, May 6, 1928, 60.
11. Although the record, Columbia 1714-D, was listed in the April 1929 Columbia supplement, a Landay store ad for it appears in the *Long Island Daily Press* as early as February 28, 1929. Copies are currently held by several archives, usually misidentified

as an actual radio broadcast (it is a studio recreation) and misdated as well. Excerpts were reissued on the circa 1966 Longines six-LP set "Jack Benny Presents Golden Memories of Radio," misidentified as a 1925 radio broadcast.

12. Louella Parsons, *Philadelphia Inquirer*, September 10, 1942.

13. "Lasses White, Famed Minstrel, to Join WSM October 1," *The Tennessean*, September 25, 1932, 40. Luther F. Sies, in *Encyclopedia of American Radio, 1920–1960* (Jefferson, NC: McFarland, 2000), Entry #14873, says that White's original partner was named Weil, an error that has propagated through the years. According to all original listings and other published material, White's partner on WSM was always Wilds.

14. "Lee 'Honey' Wilds, Comedian" (obituary), *Orlando Sentinel*, March 31, 1982, C-6.

15. Jim Walsh, "Al Bernard, Part XI," *Hobbies* (January 1975), 37–38.

16. *New York Herald Tribune*, undated, reprinted in *Hobbies* (January 1975), 37. A virtually identical story appears in the *Schenectady Gazette*, September 4, 1928, 14.

17. "Novelty Songs Will Be Given Over Network," *Rochester Democrat and Chronicle*, August 18, 1929, 12.

18. "A Typical Bit of Script from Dutch Masters Minstrels," *What's On the Air* (April 1930), 46.

19. "1929 Program Leaders," *1937–38 Variety Radio Directory*, 18.

20. Arthur Simon, ed., *Who Is Who in Radio* (New York: Who Is Who in Radio Inc., 1930), 20–21.

21. *Blue Coal Minstrels*, program no. 11.

22. WFBR ad, *Baltimore Sun*, November 5, 1931.

23. "New Minstrel Show," *Belvidere (IL) Daily Republican*, September 29, 1934, 7.

24. "Nothing New Is Wanted for Show," *Arizona Daily Star*, December 3, 1939, 11.

25. Pick and Pat ran briefly on Saturday at 6:45 on NBC before moving to Friday night.

26. Jim Ramsburg, *Network Radio Ratings, 1932–1953* (Jefferson, NC: McFarland, 2012); Harrison B. Summers, *A Thirty Year History of Programs Carried on National Radio Networks in the United States: 1926–1956* (Salem, NH: Ayer Co., 1958 [reprint edition 1993]). The first radio ratings were gathered by day-after recall and were considered inflated. More accurate measures (first same-day recall, and then coincidental) were introduced in 1935, and pre-1935 numbers have here been adjusted (see Ramsburg, *Network Radio Ratings*, 21, 48). A detailed explanation of the Cooperative Analysis of Broadcasting ratings can be found in Hugh Malcolm Beville, *Audience Ratings: Radio, Television, and Cable* (Hillsdale, NJ: Erlbaum Associates, 1988), 4–8.

27. "Sinclair Minstrels" (promotional brochure), c. 1932.

28. "Greater Sinclair Minstrels," undated (but c. 1936) episode, at Library of Congress, Washington, DC.

29. Jane Cooper, "Tracking Down Gene Arnold and His Sinclair Minstrel Men," *Radio Mirror* (March 1935), 74.

30. "Greater Sinclair Minstrels," c. 1936 episode at Library of Congress.

31. Cooper, "Tracking Down Gene Arnold," 44.

32. Ramsburg, *Network Radio Ratings*; Summers, *A Thirty Year History*.

33. Episodes dated July 28, 1937, and August 4, 1937, at Library of Congress, Washington, DC.

34. Henry T. Sampson, *Swingin' on the Ether Waves: A Chronological History of African Americans in Radio and Television Broadcasting, 1925–1955*, 2 vols. (Lanham, MD: Scarecrow Press, 2005), 8, 159.

35. Howard Wolf, "The Radio," *Akron Beacon Journal*, October 12, 1931, 4.

36. *Wilkes-Barre Record*, October 8, 1934, 10, and October 29, 1934, 14.

37. Beatrice Biggs, "Radio News," *Daily Clintonian* (Clinton, IN), November 18, 1935, 2.

38. The story of WLW being picked up on mattress springs may be an urban legend, but it is technically plausible and has been repeated in a great many places. See, for example, Dan Neil, "Why Nighttime Is the Right Time for the Great American Road Trip," *Wall Street Journal*, May 18, 2018; Allen J. Singer, *Stepping Out in Cincinnati: Queen City Entertainment 1900–1960* (Chicago: Arcadia, 2005), 111; John Price, "History of WLW, Cincinnati: The Nation's Station," 1979, http://jeff560.tripod.com/wlw.html.

39. Names are as spoken on the recording; therefore spellings are uncertain. The series often appeared in listings as "So-a-Tone," which was the trade name of the producer, National Radio Advertising, Inc. So-a-Tone transcriptions were marketed by radio pioneer Raymond Soat and were recorded in Chicago by Brunswick on 12-inch discs, with a separate series for each sponsor.

40. George Biggar, "Minstrels in the Hayloft," *WLS Weekly*, March 23, 1935, 5.

41. Most live network shows were performed twice, first for the East and Central time zones, and later for the West Coast. Parker appeared in the East Coast feed of the program. Reportedly, due to prior commitments, he was replaced by a different guest for the West Coast performance.

42. "Walter Winchell," *Minneapolis Sunday Tribune*, April 7, 1940, Theater Section, 1.

43. James was active on radio and stage from the early 1930s until about 1950; then she abruptly dropped out of sight. There is evidence that she had a nervous breakdown and later became active in religious pursuits (*New York Age*, April 7, 1956). She is believed to be the same Regina "Gee Gee" James who died in Philadelphia in 1971 (*Philadelphia Inquirer*, December 2, 1971, 42).

44. See Robert Cogswell, "Jokes in Blackface: A Discographic Folklore Study" (dissertation, Indiana University, 1984), for a detailed discussion of black buddy teams who recorded.

45. Review from *Chicago Defender*, July 31, 1931, quoted in Sampson, *Swingin' on the Ether Waves*, 61.

46. Cook, a veteran recording artist who had previously teamed with Van Fleming to portray the black duos Two Licorice Drops and Two Dark Knights, apparently originated Cotton and Morpheus. There is some confusion over the identity of his partner. Period newspaper listings identify Morpheus as John Mitchell. However, the 1929 Brunswick record cata-

log (page 118) identifies Cook's partner as Billy Hillpot, who was at that time appearing on radio with Harold "Scrappy" Lambert as the Smith Brothers. The Brunswick files also associate Hillpot with the recordings, although his exact role is not clear. Most likely Mitchell portrayed Morpheus on radio, while Hillpot (an experienced recording artist) took that role on records. The recorded routines, all built around songs, included "That's My Weakness Now" (Brunswick 3841), "Mississippi Mud" (4040), "'Tain't No Sin" (4667), and "Never Swat a Fly" (4951).

47. "Comedians Will Play in KSD Eveready Hour," *St. Louis Post-Dispatch*, April 17, 1927, 13.

48. Luther Sies, in *Encyclopedia of American Radio*, states that Fields' first partner was Bobbye Shreves, but if so, their partnership must have been brief, as I can find no documentation of that name.

49. "Days in Ol' Kaintuck Lead Way to Big Time," *Radio Digest* (March 1930), 71.

50. Jack Shafer, "Viewing Radio," *Long Island Daily Press*, September 29, 1937, 4.

51. "Lulu and Leander Make WXYZ Bow," *Detroit Free Press*, June 21, 1931, Part One, 12.

52. Roger Baudier, "Look Out fo' Mah Operation," *Radio Digest* (August 1930), 81–82.

53. "New Script Act on WDAE," *Tampa (FL) Times*, February 15, 1932, 13.

54. "Negro Characters on the Air," *New York Age*, February 13, 1932, 4.

55. Recordings by Snowball and Sunshine are found on Columbia 15722-D (two "hymns") and 15738-D (Snowball's mock sermon, "Moses and the Bull Rush"). The female vocalist on the former record is believed to be African American blues singer Clara Gholston (aka Georgia Peach). For the latter, see listing in Robert M.W. Dixon, John Godrich and Howard Rye, *Blues and Gospel Records, 1890–1943*, Fourth Edition (New York, Oxford University Press, 1997), 841, and the CD reissue "Church Choirs, Vocal Groups & Preachers," Document DOCD-5605.

56. "WGY Blackface Duo to Appear at Plaza," *Schenectady Gazette*, May 27, 1936, 12.

57. "Monologue and Dial Log," *Oakland Tribune*, May 30, 1932, 12.

58. "Ballad Writer on WGY Hour," *Schenectady Gazette*, August 10, 1938, 8.

59. "Mother's Protest to Bring Change in Radio Race Roles," *Pittsburgh Courier*, June 8, 1946, 18.

60. A thorough compilation of press reports from the *Age*, *Courier* and *Defender* can be found in Sampson, *Swingin' on the Ether Waves*, 702–20. The following quotes can all be found in that source, unless otherwise indicated.

61. "Swingtime at the Savoy" (review), *Variety*, August 4, 1948.

62. Sam Chase, "Swingtime at the Savoy" (review), *Billboard*, September 4, 1948, 12; Saul Carson, "Report to the Listeners," *Radio and Television Best* (November 1948), 43.

63. "Lucky Millinder Launches Show," *Pittsburgh Courier*, June 5, 1949, 25.

64. Pickering, *Blackface Minstrelsy in Britain*, 201. Unless otherwise specified, the following descriptions, including quotes, are from pages 186–212 in Pickering's book.

Chapter 4

1. The Black Maria studio was a small, moveable building covered in tar paper; it was so named by workers who thought it resembled a police van and used the popular slang term for the building (www.theclio.com/web/entry?id=54644).

2. Many of these early films can be found online. Others are in archives, and a good source for locating them is Jan-Christopher Horak, "Preserving Race Films," in *Early Race Filmmaking in America*, edited by Barbara Tepa Lupack (New York: Routledge, 2016), 215–24.

3. American Mutoscope and Biograph (AMB) Picture Catalogue, November 1902, 9.

4. Charles Musser, *The Emergence of Cinema: The American Screen to 1907* (Berkeley: University of California Press, 1990), 148; Paul Spehr, *The Man Who Made Movies: W.K.L. Dickson* (Bloomington: Indiana University Press, 2008), 428.

5. Horak, "Preserving Race Films," 207.

6. Horak, "Preserving Race Films," 215–24.

7. "Comments on Edison Gold Moulded Records for August 1905," *Edison Phonograph Monthly* (July 1905), 8. This rare wax cylinder, Edison 9052, can be heard at http://cylinders.library.ucsb.edu.

8. A fairly complete account of the incident can be found in "Disturbing Films Burned to Ashes," *Washington Times*, May 21, 1904, 2. There are many other accounts, which can be located through www.newspapers.com or similar sources.

9. Clarence Lusane, *The Black History of the White House* (San Francisco: City Lights Publishers, 2011), 254; "The South as It Might Be," *New York Times*, November 3, 1901, 10.

10. "Disturbing Films Burned to Ashes."

11. Charles Musser, *Before the Nickelodeon: Edwin S. Porter and the Edison Manufacturing Company* (Berkeley: University of California Press, 1991), 275.

12. "Kinetophone Is Success in New York," *Arizona Daily Star*, February 23, 1913, 10; "At the Varieties," *New York Tribune*, February 18, 1913, 9; and many other reports.

13. The "Little Pal" sung in *The Rainbow Man* was written by Eddie Dowling and James F. Hanley. The 1929 Jolson hit "Little Pal," from his tear-jerker man-with-cute-kid film *Say It with Songs*, was by Buddy G. De Sylva, Lew Brown, and Ray Henderson. Nine out of the ten reels of the Dowling film survive in the Library of Congress collection.

14. "New Type of Film Doubles Width of Pictures as Shown on Screen," *Decatur Herald*, March 2, 1930, 24.

15. *A Plantation Act* was praised at the time, but it was long thought lost until a mislabeled silent print of the film turned up in the Library of Congress collection. A few years later, after much detective work, the soundtrack (which was on a separate disc) was located by a group of volunteers called "The Vitaphone Project," but the disc was broken into four pieces. After some delicate restoration work, the film and sound were pieced together digitally and released to the public in the 1990s. It is now available online. See also www.picking.com/vitaphone22.html.

16. This film, or what survives of it, was viewed by the author at the Library of Congress.

17. Vere E. Johns, "In the Name of Art," *New York Age*, January 26, 1935, 4; Bernice Patton, "Eddie Cantor, Nicholas Brothers, Top Stage Bill. Noted Comedian Plays Tribute to Race Actors," *Pittsburgh Courier*, August 10, 1935, 16.

18. See "1936 in Film," Wikipedia, https://en.wikipedia.org/wiki/1936_in_film.

19. *Box Office Digest* (March 1940), 18.

20. *Box Office Digest* (March 1942).

21. Frederic Krahn, ed., *Educational Film Guide*, 11th edition (New York: H.W. Wilson, 1953), 790. The four songs excerpted were "Sunshine Special" with the minstrels, the "Remember Me to Carolina" duet by Dixie and his daughter from the film's conclusion, the "Cindy" solo, and the "My Bamboo Cane" solo. This film was viewed by the author at the Paley Center, New York.

22. Some sources say the joke originated with Joseph Weber and Lew Fields in the 1880s. See https://around.com/bartletts.html.

23. Ken Emerson, *Doo-dah!: Stephen Foster and the Rise of American Popular Culture*, 309; David Ewen, *American Popular Songs* (Random House, 1966), 82; Erskine Johnson, syndicated column (NEA), *Wilkes-Barre Times Leader*, Oct. 22, 1949, 7.

24. "Bing Crosby Coons in Paramount's *Dixie*," *New York Age*, September 25, 1943, 7; "Billy Rowe's Notebook," *Pittsburgh Courier*, September 4, 1943, 20; *Variety*, June 30, 1943; *Box Office Digest* (March 1944), 14.

25. Harold Heffernan, "Now It's Musical Films They're Making," *St. Louis Post-Dispatch*, June 20, 1943, 6H.

26. "New Personality Destined for Stardom," *New York Age*, December 14, 1946, 10; "'The Jolson Story' on Loew's Screens for Entire Week," *New York Age*, February 8, 1947, 11.

27. "Top Grossers of 1948," *Variety*, January 5, 1949, 6.

28. "Double Feature at Apollo Next Week," *New York Age*, February 5, 1938, 7; John Kinloch, review, *California Eagle*, December 16, 1937, 2-B.

29. Horak, in "Preserving Race Films," claims that *Harlem on the Prairie* is accessible through OV Guide.com, but it is not there, and Horak now says he is uncertain why (correspondence, April 18, 2017). Gregory Lukow of the Library of Congress advised that the film is not in any known archive but that, according to the *Video Source Book*, it was distributed on VHS in the mid-1990s by Nostalgia Family Video (correspondence, April 19, 2017). Stephanie Batiste, in *Darkening Mirrors: Imperial Representation in Depression-Era African American Performance* (Durham, NC: Duke University Press, 2012), claims that it is lost, as do Julia Leyda in "Black Audience Westerns and the Politics of Cultural Identification in the 1930s," *Cinema Journal* 42, no. 1 (Fall 2002), and numerous others on various websites.

30. Christopher Lehman, "The New Black Animated Images of 1946," *Journal of Popular Film and Television* (Summer 2001), cited in John Strausbaugh, *Black Like You: Blackface, Whiteface, Insult & Imitation in American Popular Culture* (New York: Penguin Group, 2006), 240.

31. "Censored Eleven," Wikipedia, https://en.wikipedia.org/wiki/Censored_Eleven, retrieved April 22, 2017. See also Daniel E. Slotnik, "Cartoons of a Racist Past Lurk on YouTube," *New York Times*, April 28, 2008, C4, and "NYCC2010: Warner Archive to Release the 'Censored Eleven,'" Toonzone.net, October 13, 2010.

32. For further discussion of black imagery on film during the Golden Age, see Strausbaugh, *Black Like You*, chapter 6, "Uncle Tom's Cinema," 201–46.

33. Jim Korkis, *Who's Afraid of the Song of the South? And Other Forbidden Disney Stories* (Orlando, FL: Theme Park Press, 2012); Jason Sperb, *Disney's Most Notorious Film: Race, Convergence, and the Hidden Histories of Song of the South* (Austin: University of Texas Press, 2012).

34. Bosley Crowther, "James Whitmore Stars in Book's Adaptation," *New York Times*, May 21, 1964.

35. Roger Ebert, "Soul Man," October 24, 1986, www.rogerebert.com.

36. *Bamboozled* at https://www.rottentomatoes.com/m/bamboozled.

37. Stephen Bourne, *Black in the British Frame: The Black Experience in British Film and Television*, 2nd edition (London: Continuum, 2001), 1–2.

38. The American Film Institute catalog dates *Swanee Showboat* as 1947 based on a review document, but other sources say 1940 or 1944. Besides McKinney, other talent listed as being in the film includes Dewey Pigmeat Markham and Mabel Lee. The film itself is apparently lost. The three numbers in *Minstrel Days* were "Camptown Races," "Louisiana Lou," and "I'm in Love with the Band" (all from *Kentucky Minstrels*). This film should not be confused with the 1941 Warner Brothers docudrama *Minstrel Days*. A copy is at the Smithsonian Institution.

Chapter 5

1. No photos of the production have been located, but a detailed list of supplies and props contains no mention of makeup, and neither do press reports.

2. Dorothy Shay (1921–1978) was a young singer who released several rural-themed comedy records in the late 1940s, the biggest of which was "Feudin' and Fightin'" (1947). She typically appeared in sophisticated evening dress while using a rural southern accent.

3. "Minstrels All," *Pittsburgh Post-Gazette*, May 10, 1948, 28.

4. "Ten Yanks Entertain," *Asbury Park Evening Press*, July 28, 1949, 23. Due to the poor reproduction of a picture accompanying this story, it is unclear whether any of the members wore blackface.

5. "Singing Video," *Broadcasting Magazine*, May 24, 1948, 94. The sponsor also used a hillbilly act and a Gay Nineties routine in other commercials.

6. Television listings, *Nassau Daily Review-Star*, February 27 and March 20, 1945; Jim Walsh, "Al Bernard," *Hobbies* (February 1975), 37.

7. John Caldwell, "Will Video Revive Vaudeville? Could Be, in View of Minstrel with 32 Years' Experience," *Cincinnati Enquirer*, November 21, 1948, 55.

8. "The Automotive Picture," *Sponsor*, March 2, 1949, 29.

9. "Old Time Minstrel Is Dead; Joseph Dunlevy

Got Start at Old Chester Park in '08," *Cincinnati Enquirer*, April 17, 1950, 18.

10. Free, "Mississippi Minstrels" (review), *Variety*, September 1, 1948, 37.

11. Walter Ames, "Mary Pickford Bans Video Offers for Story of Life; Stowe Recalls Early Radio," *Los Angeles Times*, March 30, 1951, 22.

12. "McMahan's Minstrels Delight Southland Video Audiences," *Van Nuys News*, April 27, 1950, Part 4, 2. Stowe was reported elsewhere to actually weigh 250 pounds.

13. Terry Vernon, "Tele-Vues," *Long Beach Independent*, March 22, 1950, 18.

14. Laura Risk, "Ginger Smock," http://www.laurarisk.com/research.html.

15. Joel Tator, *Los Angeles Television* (Charleston, SC: Arcadia Publishing, 2015), 45. *Teleforum* usually aired an hour or two later than *Dixie Showboat*, generally at 10:00 p.m., so there should have been time to correct a mistake like this one. However, shows were sometimes rescheduled at the last minute.

16. "Protest TV Show Minstrel Makeup," *Down Beat*, April 7, 1950, 8.

17. Mitchell Stephens, "History of Television," *Grolier Encyclopedia* (www.nyu.edu/classes/stephens/History%20of%20Television%20page.htm); www.earlytelevision.org; www.tvhistory.tv.

18. John Crosby, "Top Radio Stars Discuss Television," *St. Louis Post-Dispatch*, February 3, 1949, Part 4, 1.

19. Tim Brooks and Earle Marsh, *The Complete Directory to Prime Time Network and Cable TV Shows, 1946–Present*, 9th edition (New York: Ballantine Books, 2007), 184.

20. Brooks and Marsh, *Complete Directory*, 53–54; Tim Brooks, *The Complete Directory to Prime Time TV Stars* (New York: Ballantine Books, 1987), 159; https://www.imdb.com/.

21. *Variety*, January 19 and February 3, 1949 (quoted in Sampson, *Swingin' on the Ether Waves*, 735–36 and 740).

22. Bee Offineer, "Marriage for Millions Debuts," *Akron Beacon Journal*, January 31, 1949, 11.

23. "Raps Television Minstrel Act: Many Protest Pick and Pat Show on WJZ," *New York Age*, February 26, 1949, 2.

24. Bryant was a light-skinned African American known as "The Mayor of Harlem." See David Hinckley, "Willie Bryant Something Big," *New York Daily News*, June 23, 1999.

25. Walter Winchell, "Gossip of the Nation," *Philadelphia Inquirer*, March 11, 1949, 27.

26. Noble Sissle, "Show Business," *New York Age*, February 26, 1949, 7.

27. "High Budgets Oust 2 Video Sustainers: Is This an Omen?" *Billboard*, April 2, 1949, 4.

28. *Colgate Comedy Hour*, NBC-TV, April 26, 1953. Brewer had recorded the song in 1952.

29. The three *Fred Waring Show* episodes discussed here are available from the Fred Waring Collection, Special Collections Library, Pennsylvania State University, University Park, Pennsylvania.

30. "Fred Waring Show Here Monday," *Spencer (Iowa) Sunday Times*, April 8, 1956, 1.

31. Alice A. Dunnigan, "Theatre Jim Crow Vanished at Colorful Inaugural Fete," *Pittsburgh Courier*, January 31, 1953, 21.

32. "Blackface Minstrels on Sullivan TV Show Again," *Washington Afro-American*, June 20, 1953, 17. A CBS-TV press release and *TV Guide* listings have also been consulted.

33. Izzy Rowe, "Izzy Rowe's Notebook," *Pittsburgh Courier*, June 27, 1953; Pellis Davis, "An Open Letter Hits Izzy Rowe's 'Beefing,'" *Pittsburgh Courier*, July 18, 1953, 17.

34. "Ford Details Contents, Stars of 90-Minute 'Star Jubilee,'" *Broadcasting*, July 4, 1955, 35.

35. In the absence of detailed written analysis, perhaps the best study of *The Black and White Minstrel Show* and its history is contained in the excellent BBC4 documentary *The Black and White Minstrel Show Revisited*, which ran as part of the *Timeshift* series in 2004. This program has been available on YouTube and was accessed there by the author in 2016. Much of the following discussion is based on that documentary.

36. Pickering, *Blackface Minstrelsy in Britain*, 219.

37. "The Black and White Minstrels," unidentified clipping, c. 1964.

38. Email from Paul Gambaccini to the author, April 10, 2017; Don Wedge, "From the Music Capitals of the World," *Billboard*, July 2, 1966, 41 (cites more than two million in cumulative sales up to that date).

39. "Black and White Minstrel Show," Visit Nunney, www.visitnunney.com/black-white-minstrel-show/, accessed May 20, 2017.

40. "Bad Taste BBC!" *Flamingo* (September 1961), quoted in Bourne, *Black in the British Frame*, 5.

41. Les Want, in documentary *The Black and White Minstrel Show Revisited*.

42. Bill Cotton, in documentary *The Black and White Minstrel Show Revisited*.

Chapter 6

1. William Barlow, *Voice Over: The Making of Black Radio* (Philadelphia: Temple University Press, 1998), 41–44; Sampson, *Swingin' on the Ether Waves*, 57–64. The *Defender* actively supported *Amos 'n' Andy*, holding outdoor celebrations at which the white stars were feted (Sampson, *Swingin' on the Ether Waves*, 63). A *New York Age* columnist editorialized that "the Amos 'n' Andy program is nothing but clean, true-to-life comedy. Only fools would say that all Negroes are of the type these comedians depict.... Are we all intelligent, progressive, and free from stupidity? Every race has its 'Amos 'n' Andy' characters" (Cyril A. Wilson, "Over the Weekend," *New York Age*, May 30, 1931, 6).

2. Boskin, *Sambo*, 116.

3. Vicky Gan, "The Story Behind the Failed Minstrel Show at the 1964 World's Fair," Smithsonian.com, April 28, 2014 (accessed July 2016).

4. Bernard L. Petersen, *A Century of Musicals in Black and White* (Westport, CT: Greenwood Press, 1993), 214.

5. Pete L'Official, "When Ben Vereen Wore Blackface to Reagan's Inaugural Gala," *New Yorker*, January 6, 2017.

6. Lena Williams, "After the Roast, Fire and

Smoke," *New York Times*, October 14, 1993. A lengthy discussion of both nationally and locally publicized blackface "incidents" in recent years can be found in Strausbaugh, *Black Like You*, 13–23.

7. Brooks and Marsh, *Complete Directory*, 152.

8. Jerry Osborne, *Presleyana IV: The Elvis Presley Record, CD and Memorabilia Price Guide* (Osborne Enterprises, 2012), 316; advertisement, *The Tennessean*, October 16, 1961, 10.

9. See www.newspapers.com for detailed listings.

10. Charles Hamm, *Putting Popular Music in Its Place* (Cambridge: Cambridge University Press, 1995), 354–66.

11. www.facebook.com/pg/Tunbridge-Civic-Club-778407962240152/about/?ref=page_internal (accessed May 2017).

12. Mahar, *Behind the Burnt Cork Mask*, 1.

13. Bert Williams, "The Comic Side of Trouble," *American Magazine* (January 1918), 60; Mabel Rowland, *Bert Williams: Son of Laughter* (New York: English Crafters, 1923), 53 (both quoted in Eric Ledell Smith, *Bert Williams: A Biography of the Pioneer Black Comedian* [Jefferson, NC: McFarland, 1996], 18, 60).

14. Walsh, "Al Bernard," *Hobbies* (March 1974), 37.

15. Alison Kibler, *Censoring Racial Ridicule: Irish, Jewish, and African American Struggles over Race and Representation, 1890–1930* (Chapel Hill: University of North Carolina Press, 2015), 216; Nadine Strossen, *Hate: Why We Should Resist It with Free Speech, Not Censorship* (Oxford: Oxford University Press, 2018); Anthony Lewis, *Freedom for the Thought That We Hate: A Biography of the First Amendment* (New York: Basic Books, 2010). Strossen was the longtime president of the ACLU, and Lewis a Pulitzer Prize–winning columnist.

16. Eric Lott, *Love & Theft*; Daniel Goldmark, *Tunes for 'Toons: Music and the Hollywood Cartoon* (Berkeley: University of California Press, 2005), 84.

Appendix 1

1. Watkins, *On the Real Side*, 98.
2. Rice, *Monarchs of Minstrelsy*, 255.
3. Tosches, *Where Dead Voices Gather*, 49.
4. Tosches, *Where Dead Voices Gather*, 241.

Appendix 2

1. "Linda" on Victor 35108 is the same song as "Linder Green" on Columbia A5173. Both are by the Peerless Minstrels and are part of the same routine. The correct title is apparently "Linder Green," by black composer Nathan Bivins.

2. Berliner's original product in the United Kingdom was marked "E. Berliner's Gramophone," and these are commonly called Berliner records. However, over time the word *gramophone* became more prominent and the "E. Berliner's" portion was dropped entirely at the end of 1901.

Appendix 3

1. Walsh, *Hobbies* (August 1955).

Bibliography

Abbott, Lynn, and Doug Seroff. *Out of Sight: The Rise of African American Popular Music, 1889–1895.* Jackson: University Press of Mississippi, 2002.

———. *Ragged But Right.* Jackson: University Press of Mississippi, 2007.

Barlow, William. *Voice Over: The Making of Black Radio.* Philadelphia: Temple University Press, 1998.

Bates, Christopher G., ed. *The Early Republic and Antebellum America: An Encyclopedia of Social, Political, Cultural, and Economic History.* New York: Routledge, 2010.

Bean, Annemarie, James V. Hatch and Brooks McNamara, eds. *Inside the Minstrel Mask: Readings in Nineteenth-Century Blackface Minstrelsy.* Hanover, NH: Wesleyan University Press, 1996.

Beville, Hugh Malcolm. *Audience Ratings: Radio, Television, and Cable.* Hillsdale, NJ: Erlbaum Associates, 1988.

Boskin, Joseph. *Sambo: The Rise and Demise of an American Jester.* New York: Oxford University Press, 1986.

Bourne, Stephen. *Black in the British Frame: The Black Experience in British Film and Television.* 2nd edition. London: Continuum, 2001.

Brooks, Tim. *The Complete Directory to Prime Time TV Stars.* New York: Ballantine Books, 1987.

———. *Lost Sounds: Blacks and the Birth of the Recording Industry, 1890–1919.* Urbana: University of Illinois Press, 2004.

Brooks, Tim, and Earle Marsh. *The Complete Directory to Prime Time Network and Cable TV Shows, 1946–Present.* 9th edition. New York: Ballantine Books, 2007.

Brooks, Tim, with Merle Sprinzen. *Little Wonder Records and Bubble Books.* Denver, CO: Mainspring Press, 2011.

Carlin, Bob. *The Birth of the Banjo: Joel Walker Sweeney and Early Minstrelsy.* Jefferson, NC: McFarland, 2007.

Cockrell, Dale. *Demons of Disorder: Early Blackface Minstrels and Their World.* Cambridge: Cambridge University Press, 1997.

Cogswell, Robert. "Jokes in Blackface: A Discographic Folklore Study." Dissertation, Indiana University, 1984.

Davis, Joe, ed. *Tip Top Entertainment and Minstrel Album.* New York: Tip Top Publishing, 1936.

Dumont, Frank. *The Witmark Amateur Minstrel Guide and Burnt Cork Encyclopedia.* Chicago: M. Witmark & Sons, 1899.

Dunning, John. *On the Air: The Encyclopedia of Old-Time Radio.* New York: Oxford University Press, 1998.

Emerson, Ken. *Doo-dah! Stephen Foster and the Rise of American Popular Culture.* New York: Simon & Schuster, 1997.

Feaster, Patrick. "'The Following Record': Making Sense of Phonographic Performance, 1877–1908." Dissertation, Indiana University, 2007.

Fletcher, Tom. *100 Years of the Negro in Show Business.* New York: Burdge & Co., 1954 (reprint Da Capo Press, 1984).

Forman, Murray. "Employment and Blue Pencils: NBC, Race and Representation, 1926–55." In *NBC: America's Network*, edited by Michele Hilmes, 117–34. Berkeley: University of California Press, 2007.

———. *One Night on TV Is Worth Weeks at the Paramount: Popular Music on Early Television.* Durham, NC: Duke University Press, 2012.

Gardner, Edward Foote. *Popular Songs of the Twentieth Century.* Vol. 1. St. Paul, MN: Paragon House, 2000.

Goldmark, Daniel. *Tunes for 'Toons: Music and the Hollywood Cartoon.* Berkeley: University of California Press, 2005.

Gracyk, Tim. *The Encyclopedia of Popular American Recording Pioneers, 1895–1925.* Granite Bay, CA: Self-published, n.d.

Graham, Sandra Jean. *Spirituals and the Birth of a Black Entertainment Industry.* Urbana: University of Illinois Press, 2018.

Hamm, Charles. *Putting Popular Music in Its Place.* Cambridge: Cambridge University Press, 1995.

Harrison, Keith. *The Ultimate Cylinder Phonograph Handbook.* CLPGS Reference Series No. 6. City of London Phonograph and Gramophone Society, 2014.

Hazelcorn, Howard. *Columbia Phonograph Companion.* Vol. 1. Los Angeles: Mulholland Press, 1999.

Hickerson, Jay. *The 5th Revised Ultimate History of Network Radio Programming and Guide to All Circulating Shows*. Leesburg, FL: Self-published, c. 2015.

Hilmes, Michele, ed. *NBC: America's Network*. Berkeley: University of California Press, 2007.

Hoffmann, Frank, Dick Carty and Quentin Riggs. *Billy Murray: The Phonograph Industry's First Great Recording Artist*. Lanham, MD: Scarecrow Press, 1997.

Horak, Jan-Christopher. "Preserving Race Films." In *Early Race Filmmaking in America*, edited by Barbara Tepa Lupack. New York: Routledge, 2016.

Johnson, Stephen, ed. *Burnt Cork: Traditions and Legacies of Blackface Minstrelsy*. Amherst: University of Massachusetts Press, 2012.

Kibler, Alison. *Censoring Racial Ridicule: Irish, Jewish, and African American Struggles over Race and Representation, 1890–1930*. Chapel Hill: University of North Carolina Press, 2015.

Koegel, John, ed. *Music, American Made: Essays in Honor of John Graziano*. Sterling Heights, MI: Harmonie Park Press, 2011.

Lewis, Anthony. *Freedom for the Thought That We Hate: A Biography of the First Amendment*. New York: Basic Books, 2010.

Lhamon, W.T., Jr. *Raising Cain: Blackface Performance from Jim Crow to Hip Hop*. Cambridge, MA: Harvard University Press, 1998.

Lott, Eric. *Love & Theft: Blackface Minstrelsy and the American Working Class*. New York: Oxford University Press, 1993.

Lotz, Rainer. *German Ragtime*. Vol. 1. Chigwell, Essex, UK: Storyville Publications, 1985.

Lupack, Barbara Tepa, ed. *Early Race Filmmaking in America*. New York: Routledge, 2016.

Lusane, Clarence. *The Black History of the White House*. San Francisco: City Lights Publishers, 2011.

MacDonald, J. Fred. *Blacks and White TV: Afro-Americans in Television since 1948*. Chicago: Nelson-Hall, 1983.

Mahar, William J. *Behind the Burnt Cork Mask*. Urbana: University of Illinois Press, 1999.

Musser, Charles. *Before the Nickelodeon: Edwin S. Porter and the Edison Manufacturing Company*. Berkeley: University of California Press, 1991.

_____. *The Emergence of Cinema: The American Screen to 1907*. Berkeley: University of California Press, 1990.

Nathan, Hans. *Dan Emmett and the Rise of Early Negro Minstrelsy*. Norman: University of Oklahoma Press, 1962.

Osborne, Jerry. *Presleyana IV: The Elvis Presley Record, CD and Memorabilia Price Guide*. Osborne Enterprises, 2012.

Paskman, Dailey, and Sigmund Spaeth. *Gentlemen, Be Seated!* New York: Doubleday, 1928 (revised 1976).

Peterson, Bernard L. *The African-American Theatre Directory, 1816–1960*. Westport, CT: Greenwood Press, 1997.

_____. *A Century of Musicals in Black and White*. Westport, CT: Greenwood Press, 1993.

Pickering, Michael. *Blackface Minstrelsy in Britain*. Burlington, VT: Ashgate, 2008.

Ramsburg, Jim. *Network Radio Ratings, 1932–1953*. Jefferson, NC: McFarland, 2012.

Reynolds, Harry. *Minstrel Memories: The Story of Burnt Cork Minstrelsy in Great Britain from 1836 to 1927*. London: A. Rivers, 1928.

Rice, Edward L. *Monarchs of Minstrelsy*. New York: Kenny Publishing Co., 1911.

Rowland, Mabel. *Bert Williams: Son of Laughter*. New York: English Crafters, 1923.

Rust, Brian, and Allen G. Debus. *The Complete Entertainment Discography*. 2nd edition. New York: Da Capo Press, 1989.

Sampson, Henry T. *The Ghost Walks: A Chronological History of Blacks in Show Business, 1865–1910*. Metuchen, NJ: Scarecrow Press, 1988.

_____. *Swingin' on the Ether Waves: A Chronological History of African Americans in Radio and Television Broadcasting, 1925–1955*. 2 vols. Lanham, MD: Scarecrow Press, 2005.

Shapiro, Mitchell E. *Radio Network Prime Time Programming, 1926–1967*. 2 vols. Jefferson, NC: McFarland, 2002.

Sies, Luther F. *Encyclopedia of American Radio, 1920–1960*. Jefferson, NC: McFarland, 2000.

Simon, Arthur, ed. *Who Is Who in Radio*. New York: Who Is Who in Radio Inc., 1930.

Slout, William L., ed. *Burnt Cork and Tambourines: A Source Book for Negro Minstrelsy*. Rockville, MD: Borgo Press, 2007.

Smith, Christopher J. *The Creolization of American Culture: William Sidney Mount and the Roots of Blackface Minstrelsy*. Urbana: University of Illinois Press, 2014.

Smith, Eric Ledell. *Bert Williams: A Biography of the Pioneer Black Comedian*. Jefferson, NC: McFarland, 1996.

Spehr, Paul. *The Man Who Made Movies: W.K.L. Dickson*. Bloomington: Indiana University Press, 2008.

Strausbaugh, John. *Black Like You: Blackface, Whiteface, Insult & Imitation in American Popular Culture*. New York: Penguin Group, 2006.

Strossen, Nadine. *Hate: Why We Should Resist It with Free Speech, Not Censorship*. Oxford: Oxford University Press, 2018.

Summers, Harrison B. *A Thirty Year History of Programs Carried on National Radio Networks in the United States: 1926–1956*. Salem, NH: Ayer Co., 1958 (reprint edition 1993).

Sutton, Allan. *The American Stage Performers Discography*. Vol. 1. Denver, CO: Mainspring Press, 2007.

_____. *Edison Blue Amberol Records, A Discography*. Denver, CO: Mainspring Press, 2005.

_____. *Edison Two-Minute and Concert Cylinders: American Series, 1897–1912*. Denver, CO: Mainspring Press, 2015.

Tator, Joel. *Los Angeles Television*. Charleston, SC: Arcadia Publishing, 2015.

Taylor, Yuval, and Jake Austen. *Darkest America: Black Minstrelsy from Slavery to Hip-Hop*. New York: W.W. Norton, 2012.

Thompson, Katrina Dyonne. *Ring Shout, Wheel About: The Racial Politics of Music and Dance in North American Slavery.* Urbana: University of Illinois Press, 2014.

Toll, Robert C. *Blacking Up: The Minstrel Show in Nineteenth Century America.* New York: Oxford University Press, 1974.

Tosches, Nick. *Where Dead Voices Gather.* Boston: Back Bay Books, 2001.

Trotter, James Monroe. *Music and Some Highly Musical People.* Boston: Lee and Shepard, 1878.

Watkins, Mel. *On the Real Side: A History of African American Comedy from Slavery to Chris Rock.* 2nd edition. Chicago: Lawrence Hill Books, 1999.

Wilson, Jennifer C.H.J. "(Re)Establishing Southern Patriotism: Professional and Amateur Minstrelsy in Lynchburg, Virginia." In *Music, American Made: Essays in Honor of John Graziano,* edited by John Koegel. Sterling Heights, MI: Harmonie Park Press, 2011.

Wittke, Carl. *Tambo and Bones: A History of the American Minstrel Stage.* Durham, NC: Duke University Press, 1930 (reprint, Greenwood Press, 1968).

Articles/Pamphlets

Andrews, Frank. "Minstrels, Minstrel Shows & Early Recordings." *Talking Machine Review,* no. 47 (1977): 1063–76.

Arceneaux, Noah. "Blackface Broadcasting in the Early Days of Radio." *Journal of Radio Studies* 12, no. 1 (2005): 61–73.

Charosh, Paul. "Studying Nineteenth-Century Popular Song." *American Music* 15, no. 4 (Winter 1997): 459–92.

Cooper, Jane. "Tracking Down Gene Arnold and His Sinclair Minstrel Men." *Radio Mirror* (March 1935).

Mahar, William J. "'Backside Albany' and Early Blackface Minstrelsy." *American Music* 6, no. 1 (Spring 1988).

Vorachek, Laura. "Whitewashing Blackface Minstrelsy in Nineteenth-Century England: Female Banjo Players in 'Punch.'" *English Faculty Publications,* Paper 6 (2013).

Walsh, Ulysses "Jim." Numerous articles in "Favorite Pioneer Recording Artists" column. *Hobbies* (Chicago, 1942–1985).

Wile, Ray. "Duplicates of the Nineties and the National Phonograph Company's Bloc Numbered Series." *ARSC Journal* 32, no. 2 (Fall 2001).

Principal Websites

www.newspapers.com
www.newspaperarchive.com
www.fultonhistory.com

Note on discography: In compiling the discography, numerous discographies for individual U.S. and UK labels and artists were consulted, along with my own extensive collection of original cylinders, 78s and LPs, as well as catalogs and sales materials published by the record companies. What follows are some good starting points for major labels:

Victor, Columbia, Berliner, Zonophone: The Discography of American Historical Recordings (https://asp.library.ucsb.edu).

Edison: Alan Sutton books (see above).

British labels: The City of London Phonograph and Gramophone Society (www.clpgs.org.uk/) publishes a wide variety of British discographies, both standalone and in its magazine *For the Record.*

Others: www.78discography.com (U.S.), https://early78s.uk/ (listing of UK discographies).

Index

A&P Gypsies 108
Abbott, Lynn 26
ABC Paramount records 83
Abel, Neal 126
"Abide with Me" 136
"Abraham" 170, 171
"Abraham Lincoln Jones" 79
"Across the Breakfast Table Looking at You" 149
Adamson, Harold 81
Adlam, Buzz 125
"Ain't Dat a Shame" 108
Al Bernard's Merry Minstrel Men (radio) 110
"Al Bernard's Merry Minstrel Show" (LP) 79, 181
Al Bernard's Minstrel Men (TV show) 181
Al G. Field Minstrels 17, 18, 20, 22, 26, 56, 76, 90, 99, 128
Al Jolson's Minstrels 185
Al Jolson's Old-Time Minstrel Show 28
Al Reeves Minstrels 19
"Alabama Barbecue" 120
Alabama Troubadours 45
"Alabamy Bound" 122, 125, 155
"Alabamy Snow" 150
Albertson, Jack 186
Alda, Robert 171
Aldrich Family 123
Alexander, George 64
Alexander and Mose 92, 134
"All Coons Look Alike to Me" 21, 63
"All God's Children Got Rhythm" 136
All in the Family 200
All This and Rabbit Stew 172
"All You Want to Do Is Dance" 116
Allen, Fred 105, 120
Allen, Rex 160
"Allus the Same in Dixie" 78
"Always Jolly" 87
"Amateur Minstrel Rehearsal" 69
Ameche, Don 158, 159

"America" 175
America, Be Seated! 198, 199
American Council on Race Relations 131, 133
American Graphophone Co. 70
American Minstrels of 1949, 5, 186, 187
American Quartet 58, 60
American records 57
America's Advisors on the Home Front 113
Amos 'n' Andy 4, 5, 79, 108, 113, 115, 116, 118, 119, 126, 127, 129, 170, 187, 197
Anaesthetic and Cerebellum 130
Ancient City Quartet 44
Anderson, Eddie "Rochester" 119
Anderson, Judith 98
Anderson, Marian 187
Andrews, Frank 86
Andy Hardy 153
Angel Puss 172
"Angels Meet Me at the Crossroads" 188, 189
"Annie Laurie" 21
"Anniversary Waltz" 162
"Another Black and White Minstrel Show" 194
Anthony, Harry 65
"Anvil Chorus" 55
Any Bonds Today? 172
"April Showers" 121, 149
ARA records 102
"Are You from Dixie?" 94, 121, 202
Aretino records 65
Ariel Grand records 89, 90
"Arkansas Traveler" 101, 108
Armstrong, Louis 97, 124
Arno, Peter 123
Arnold, Doris 92, 134
Arnold, Gene 114, 115, 116
"Around the World" 64
Arpeako Minstrel Show 104
Arrow records 90
Arthur, Jack 124
Ashworth, Mary 120, 121

"Asleep in the Deep" 76, 96, 108, 118, 119
Association of National Advertisers 108
Astaire, Fred 170
Astaire, Marie 145
"At a Georgia Camp Meeting" 52, 53, 109, 172
"At the Minstrel Show" 64
Atherton, Sam 86
"Auld Lang Syne" 78, 170
"Aura Lee" 83
Autry, Gene 163, 164
Avery, Tex 173

Babbitt, Harry 125
Babes in Arms 153, 154
Babes on Broadway 154, 168
"Baby Face" 180
Bacigalupi Brothers 56
Baker, John 122
Baker, Kenny 119, 120
Ballard, George Wilton 76, 142
Bamboozled 175, 176, 200, 204
"Band Played On" 192
"Bandana Days" 169
Bandits of El Dorado 168
Banks, Sadie 122
Banner label 78
Banta, Frank P. 33, 47
Barlow and Primrose Minstrels 181
Barlow Brothers' Minstrels 19
Barlow, Wilson, Primrose and West Minstrels 17
Barnum and Bailey Circus 26
Barrie, Gracie 168
Barrymore, Lionel 102
Basie, Count 133
Baskette, James 173
Bates, Charles 140
Bauer, Hank 181
Baughman, Stanley 79
Baxter, Warner 147
Bean, Annemarie 3, 5
Beard, Billy 109, 126
"Beautiful Dreamer" 93, 161
Beavers, Louise 171

270 Index

"Because" 180
"Beep Beep" 202
Beka records 87
"Believe Me If All Those Endearing Young Charms" 142
Bell, Chichester (patents) 84
Bell records (UK) 89
"Belle of the Barber's Ball" 93
Belphor, Baker E. 86
Beltona records 93
Bennett, Billy 92, 134
Bennett, Jean 122
Benny, Jack 81, 105, 116, 119
Benson, Marie 93
Bently, Bob 181
Berkeley, Busby 154, 155
Berle, Milton 81, 82
Berlin, Irving 67, 68, 149, 151, 170, 192
Berliner, Emile 32, 43, 47
Berliner records 44, 46, 47, 48, 84, 85, 86
Bernache, Leo 188
Bernard, Al 76, 77, 79, 80, 106, 107, 108, 109, 110, 114, 117, 168, 181, 204
Bernard, Gertrude 77
Bernard, Rhoda 59
Bernie, Ben 98
Best, Willie 170
Best, W.T. 91
Besttone records 90
"Betsy, the Butterman's Daughter" 30
Better Half 123
Betty Boop 173
Bieling, John 45, 47, 54, 58
"Big Bass Viol" 117
"Big Bell" 44
Big Parade 102
"Big Radio Minstrel Show" 93
Big Show 73
Bigelow Show 185
Biggs, Bunny 105
"Bill Bailey Won't You Please Come Home" 56, 79
"Bill Cullen's Minstrel Spectacular" 83
Billy Manning Minstrels 35
Bing Crosby's Minstrel Song Folio 28
Biograph studio 139
Biophone records 87
Birchmore, Tom 84, 85, 86, 88, 89, 90, 93
"Bird in a Gilded Cage" 124
Birth of a Nation 205
Black America 16
Black and White Minstrel Show 94, 192, 193, 194, 195, 196
"Black Bottom" 77
The Black Crook 12
Black Diamond Minstrels 87, 88
"Black Jim" 63

Black Like Me 174
Black Star Minstrels 88
"Black Up for a Blackout Over Broadway" 155
Black. White (TV show) 200
Blackbirds of 1928 93
Blackface 2, 3, 4, 10, 14, 97, 161, 170, 174, 185, 203, 204
Blackface And Music: The Spirit of Minstrelsy 102
Blanc, Mel 105
Bloch, Ray 113, 124, 125
Block, Martin 120
Blondie 100
Blue, Ben 162, 163
"Blue Again" 109
"Blue and the Gray" 48
Blue Coal Minstrels 109, 110, 112
Bluff, Harry 85, 90
Bode, Albert 54
Bohee, James 30
Bolger, Ray 123
Bonime, Josef 113
"Born Free" 192
Boss of Rawhide 164, 165, 168
Boulden, Edward 143
Boulter, John 192
Bourne, Stephen 176
Boyce and Evans 157
Bradford, Perry 77
Bradley, Will 123
Brannum, Lumpy 188, 189
Brasselle, Keefe 170
Brauer, Stuart 128
"Brazil" 193
"Break the News to Mother" 44, 85, 87
Breckenridge, Paul 132, 133
Bren, Joe 28; see also Joe Bren Minstrels
Brewer, Teresa 187
Brewster, John 122
Brice, Carol 133
Brien, Vincent 67
"Brighten the Corner Where You Are" 129
Bring, Lou 121
"Bring Back Those Minstrel Days" 77, 83, 112, 113, 179
British Broadcasting Company 134
Broadway Brevities 168
Broadway Jamboree 186
Broadway Minstrels 186
Brooker & Clayton's Georgia Minstrels 14
Brooks, Mel 175
Brother Bones 157
Brother Jonathan 7
Brower, Frank 8
Brown, Bobby 181
Brown, Lew 68
Brown, Seymour 99
Browning, William 99
Brunswick records 74, 79, 127

Brusiloff, Nat 117
Bryan, William Jennings 141
Bryant, Willie 187
Buck and Wheat 128
"Buckle on de Golden Sword" 16, 39, 66
Buckley, Emerson 122
Buckley's Serenaders 30
"Buffalo Gals" 115, 161
Bugs Bunny 172
Bull, Frank 183
"Bully Song" 63, 101
Bumppo, Natty 7
Burch, Tex 128
Burgess, Fred 30
Burlington records 90
Burnett, Smiley 168
Burns, David 81
Burns, George 81
Burnt Cork Dandies 110
Burnt Cork Review 104
Burr, Henry 58, 59, 60, 61, 62, 63, 75, 78, 79
Burrell, Jimmy 186
Busby, Nate 99, 101
Busy Bee records 66
Butterworth, Wally 110
Button, Bob 179, 180
"By the Light of the Silvery Moon" 79, 81, 82, 94, 125, 155, 163
"By the Watermelon Vine" 91
"Bye Bye Ma Honey" 44

Cabin at the Crossroads 128, 129
Cabin in the Cotton 191
Cakewalk 24, 25, 52
Cakewalk (movie) 139
Cakewalk Parody (movie) 139
Cali, John 83, 112
Callender's Original Georgia Minstrels 44
"Calliope Medley" 46
Camarata, Tutti 82
Cambrian Minstrels 96
Camden records 82
Cameo records 78, 79
Campbell, Albert 35, 43, 48, 58, 60, 61, 75, 78
Campbell, Herbert 86
Campbell, Tom 86
"Camptown Races" 11, 89, 91, 92, 93, 124, 136, 153, 157, 160, 161, 163, 172, 177, 188, 189, 193
Canin, Stuart 120
"Can't You Heah Me Callin' Caroline" 179
Cantor, Eddie 98, 150, 151, 152, 169, 170, 190
Capitol Studios 80
Carew, James 92, 134
Carlson, Eric 188
Carlton-Green, Hugh 195
Carncross Minstrels 12, 19, 74
Carolina Minstrels 63, 78

"Carolina Rolling Stone" 96
Carpenter, Elliot 136, 157
Carpenter, Ken 121
Carroll, Jimmy 124
"Carry Me Back to Old Virginny" 51, 79, 85, 94, 170, 172
Carson, Shorty 116
Carter, Jack 186
Caruso, Enrico 50
Carver, George Washington 197
Casper, Emil 110
Cassi, Emil 35
Catlett, Walter 147
Catley, Gwen 92
Celebrity Minstrels 123
Celebrity records 79
Censored Eleven 172
Censoring Racial Ridicule 205
Chalfant, Dick 44
Chalmers, Donald 69
Chandler, Billy 118
Chaplin, Charlie 102
Charles, Keith 198
Charlie Chan 124
Charman, Jack 86
Chase, Chaz 105
Chaudoir, Gustave 84, 86, 88
Chauve Souris 97
Check and Double Check 170
Chester, Ernie 85, 87, 89
Chesterfield Supper Club 120
"Cheyenne" 88
Chicago Talking Machine Co. 41, 44
Childs, Bill 114, 115
Chilton, Charles 191
"Chimes of the Golden Bells" 51
"Chinatown, My Chinatown" 121, 179
Chisholm, George 194
Chordsmen Quartet 182
Christy, Edwin P. 8, 9, 11, 158, 160
Christy, George 8
Christy, Ken 116, 125
Christy Minstrels 8, 10, 12, 24, 30, 58, 84, 85, 88, 89
Chu Chin Chow 97
Churchill, Stuart 188, 189
Cinch records 90
"Cindy" 156
Claggett, Charles 132
Claire, Malcolm 114, 119, 130
"Clap Your Hands" 76
Clarion records 66
Clarion records (UK) 87
Clark, Fritz 114
Clark Sisters 122, 123
Clay, Jay 76
Clay, Stanley Bennett 174
Clean Pastures 172
Cleveland, Pres. Grover 141
Cleveland, W.S., Minstrels 19, 35, 74
Cliff, Laddie 86

Clifford, Arthur 64
Climax Minstrels 48
Climax records 43, 48
"Climbing Up the Golden Stairs" 16, 79, 101
Clooney, Rosemary 171
Cloutier, Norman 123
Coal Black and de Sebben Dwarfs 172
Cobb, Gene 130, 131
Cockrell, Dale 5
Cody, Harry 183, 184, 185
"Coffee Song" 122
Cohan, George M. 20, 58, 93, 96
Cohan and Harris Minstrels 19, 74
Coles, Johnnie 87
Colgate Comedy Hour 187
Coliseum records 90
College (movie) 170
Collier, Willie 147
Collins, Arthur 44, 45, 54, 55, 56, 57, 58, 59, 60, 61, 62, 64, 65, 68, 75, 107
Colonel Merriwether's Minstrels 118
Colpix records 81
Columbia Minstrels 60
Columbia records 34, 41, 42, 43, 44, 46, 47, 48, 50, 54, 55, 56, 57, 60, 62, 63, 64, 66, 67, 70, 76, 78, 82, 92, 101, 105, 109, 111, 128
Columbia records (UK) 85, 86, 87, 90, 91, 92, 93
"Come Along, Sister Mary" 91
"Come Where My Love Lies Dreaming" 91, 93, 160
Como, Perry 81, 120, 121
Concert records 66
"Congo Love Song" 108
Conjur and Caroline 129
Conn, Bob 99, 101
Consolidated records 45
"Constantly" 169
"Contradictions" 89
Coogan, Jackie 120
Cook, Phil 127
"Coon, Coon, Coon" 49, 50, 66, 174
"Coon! Coon! Git Out of This Saloon" 30
Coon songs 21, 66, 84, 90
Coontown Minstrels 88, 89
Cooper, Ralph 132
Corbett, James J. 147
Corbyn's Georgia Minstrels 31
Corn Cob Pipe Club 128
Correll, Charles 79, 119, 127
Cort records 66
Cotton, Bill 195
Cotton and Morpheus 79, 127
Cotton Blossom Minstrels 117, 182
"Cotton Fields Episode" 87

Cotton Queen Minstrels 105
"Cousin of Mine" 132
Covell, Walter 179
Cozzi, Mario 110
Craigen, Maida 98
Crawford, Joan 170, 204
Crockett, Davy 7
"Crocodile Isle" 57, 176
Crosby, Bing 3, 47, 116, 121, 161, 170, 171
Cross, Milton 123
Crossley, Archibald 108
Crothers, Scatman 157, 184
Crowther, Leslie 194
"Cruising Down the River" 180
Crumit, Frank 79
Cullen, Bill 83
Culley, Fred 188
Curry's records 89
"Curse of an Aching Heart" 73
Curtain Call at Cactus Creek 170
Curtis, M.B., Afro-American Minstrels 31
Curtiz, Michael 148
Cuthbert, Frank 108

D&R records 66
"The Dago's Grudge" 34
Dahl, Arlene 162
Dailey Paskman Radio Minstrels 99, 101
d'Albert, George 86
Dalhart, Vernon 131
Dalton, Sam 176
Daly, Lucy 138
Dan (movie) 72
Dancing Darkies 139
Dandy, Jim 117
Daniels, Bebe 123
Daniels, Mickey 170
Danson, Ted 200
Danvers, Johnny 86
Dark Town Quartet 125
Dark Town Swells 135
Darkest America 16
"Darktown Is Out Tonight" 21, 44, 47, 51
Darktown Melody Makers 91
Darktown Minstrels 92
"Darktown Poker Club" 117
"Darktown Strutters' Ball" 179
"Darling Clo" 64
"Darling Nellie Gray" 76
Darro, Frankie 145
"Dat's Berry Queer" 90
Dauscha, Billie 109
Davies, Edward 116
Davis, Ches 157
Davis, Frank 189
Davis, Freeman 157
Davis, Jimmie 165, 166
Davis, Joe 28, 79, 80, 82
Dean, Eddie 118
Dean, Jimmie 116

Dean Brothers (Eddie & Jimmie) 118, 119
"Dear Hearts and Gentle People" 158
"Dear Old Girl" 78
DeBaun, Steve 179
Debus, Allen 73, 74
Decca records (UK) 93
Deep River Boys 186
Delaney's Song Book 28
De Marco Sisters 120
Demarest, William 162
Dennis, Clark 113, 116
Dennis Day Show 132
Denny, Will F. 64, 65
"Dese Bones Shall Rise Again" 16, 40
DeSylva, Dan 77
Deutsch, Emery 117
Devere, Sam 31; see also Sam Devere Minstrels
De Wolfe, Billy 161
dialect 2, 4, 22, 126, 129, 204
Diamond, Neil 174, 175
Diamond records 66
Diamond records (UK) 88
Diamond Studded Quartet 99, 101
Dickens, Charles 24, 30
Dimples 152, 153
"Dinah" 119
Dinkins, Mayor David 200
Diplomat records 89
Disc records 89
"Dixie" 51, 78, 82, 83, 92, 94, 118, 136, 142, 161, 172, 189
Dixie (movie) 121, 161
"Dixie-Anna" 152
Dixie Memories 131
Dixie Minstrel Troupe 44
Dixie Minstrels 58, 63, 78
"Dixie Minstrels' Greatest Hits" 83
Dixie Showboat 183, 184, 185, 204
Dixiettes 183
Dixon, George 8
"Do Not Nurse Your Anger" 30
Docken, Harry 76, 77
Dockstader, Lew 21, 49, 70, 71, 72, 78, 121, 140, 141, 142, 162, 174, 204; see also Lew Dockstader Minstrels
Dodgen, James 130
Dodgen, Mary 130
Doherty, James 76
Dolly Sisters 98
Donaghy, Harry 77, 107, 117
"Donkey Serenade" 193
Donnelly, Andy 120
Donnelly, James 120
Dorsey, Tommy 123
Douglass, Frederick 24
Doust, William 85, 87
Dowling, Eddie 145

"Down in Mobile Long Ago" 43, 64
"Down South" 83
"Down Where the Cotton Blossoms Grow" 76
"Down Where the Sugar Cane Grows" 88
"Down Where the Watermelon Grows" 78
Drinard, Lawrence 128
Driscoll, Bobby 173
Dudley, Dick see Kuhn, Casper
Dudley, S.H. 44, 45, 47, 49, 50, 51, 52, 53, 60, 64, 85
Duffy and Imgrund's Band 70
Dumont, Paul 108, 110, 117
Dunbar, Paul Laurence 204
Duncan, Danny 118
Duncan, John 92, 137
Dunlevy, Joe 181, 182
Dunne, Irene 170
Duplex records 66
Durél, Rene 130
Dusky Four 150
"Dusky Stevedore" 112
Dutch Masters Minstrels 106, 107, 108, 116, 117
Dyna-Disc records 82

ear tubes, acoustic 40
Earl Carroll's Vanities 127
Easter Parade (movie) 180
Ebert, Roger 175
Ed Sullivan Show 5, 81, 187, 190, 198
Eddie Cantor Story 170
Edison, Thomas A. 32, 144
Edison Bell records 84, 85, 87, 89, 92, 93
Edison Minstrels 64, 142, 144
Edison Modern Minstrels 64
Edison Quartet 47, 64
Edison records 33, 43, 44, 56, 58, 63, 64, 68, 69, 70, 74, 76, 85, 86, 87, 140, 143
Edison studio 138, 139, 144
Edison Vaudeville Company 69
Edkins, J. Alden 83
Edwards, Cliff 98
Edwards, Ralph 126
Eisenhower, Pres. Dwight 189
"El Capitan March" 117
Elizabeth II, Queen 194
Elks' Minstrels 65
Ellington, Duke 97
Elliott, Billy 170
Elliott, G.H. 86, 93, 176, 191
Ellis, Harry 141
Elmo, Peenie 126, 166, 182, 183
"Elsie from Chelsea" 44
Emerson, Victor 42, 63
Emerson records 63
Emmaline and Easy 131
Emmett, Dan 8, 158, 161

Empire Vaudeville Company 69, 76
Epic records 82, 83
Errol, Bert 86
Ethiopian Serenaders 30
Evans, Charles E. 147
Evans, Frank 190
Evans, Honey Boy 20, 67, 72, 74, 76, 78, 90, 99, 102, 162, 169; see also Honey Boy Evans Minstrels
Evans, Maurice 120
"Evening with the Minstrels" 51, 54, 84, 85, 86
Eveready Hour 128
Eveready Minstrels 96
Everest records 81
"Every Day Life" 87
Everybody Sing 170
"Everybody Works But Father" 72
Excelsior Minstrel Company 44
Excelsior Minstrels 85
Excelsior records 44
Exo records 89

Fair Exchange 81
Fairchild, Mr. 48
Fairs, Edward 134
Falana, Lola 198
Famous records 89, 90
Farr, Eric 85, 87, 88, 89
Farrell, Charles 147
Farrington, Albert 99
Father Is a Bachelor 170
Favorite Minstrels 89
Favorite records 89, 90
Feaster, Patrick 38
Ferris, Ray 114, 115
Festival of British Popular Songs 191
Feudin' Rhythm 168
"Fiddle, Dee, Dee" 72
Fields, Benny 81, 82, 155, 156
Fields, George 128
Fields, Gracie 190
Finglass, Tom E. 86
Fink, Mike 7
Fintex Stores 111
Fisher, Ham 123
Fisk Jubilee Singers 16
Fitzgerald, Ella 132, 133
"Five Minutes with the Minstrels" 70
Five Rangers 118
Flagg, James Montgomery 123
Flamingo (magazine) 194
Fleming, Hugh 188
Fletcher, Dusty 168, 169
Fletcher, Tom 186
"Flip Them Jacks" 77
Flippen, Jay C. 123
"Floating Down to Cotton Town" 190
"Flying Saucer" 157

Flynn, Josie 122
Fontaine, Jacqueline 183
Ford, Sen. Ed 113
Ford Motor Company 190, 191
Ford Star Jubilee 191
Forepaugh-Sells Brothers Circus 26
Forepaugh Stock Company 97
Forrest, Ray 179, 180
Foster, Stephen 10, 11, 43, 66, 76, 80, 84, 87, 88, 90, 158, 160
Four Harmony Boys 150
Four Hobnobbers 157
Four Jacks 130
"Four Jolly Smiths" 34
Four Vagabonds 119
Fowler Varieties see Voice of Vaudeville
Fox, George H. 86
Fox studio 147
Foy, Eddie, Jr. 81
Francis, Dai 192
"Frankie and Johnnie" 105
"Franklin D. Roosevelt Jones" 103, 155
Frawley, William 158
Fred Waring Show 187, 189, 190
Freear, Louie 86
Freeman, Tony 124
Fresh Hare 172
Friml, Rudolf 97, 98
"Fun on the Plantation" 87
Funny Jokes for End Men 28

Gale, George 190
Gale, Lillian 190
Gale, Moe 132
Gambaccini, Paul 194
Gardella, Tess 128
Garden, William 179
Gardner, Stewart 90
Garfield, Pres. James A. 34
Garland, Judy 3, 152, 153, 154, 155, 160, 170, 203
Garner, John Nance 105
Garrett, Betty 162
Garry Moore Show 82
Gaskin, George J. 33, 42, 48, 54
Gatty, Alfred Scott 90
Gaynor, Janet 147
"Gentle Annie" 188
Gentlemen, Be Seated (book) 100, 102
"Gentlemen, Be Seated!" (LP) 82
Gentlemen, Be Seated (radio show) 191
"Gentlemen, Be Seated! (Again)" 83
George and Rufus 130
George Christy's Old Time Ethiopian Joker 28
George Mitchell Glee Club (radio show) 191
"George Mitchell Minstrels,

from the Black and White Minstrel Show" 194
Georgia Minstrels 16, 25, 36, 48, 85
"Georgia on My Mind" 109
Gershwin, George 98
Gerson, Betty Lou 131
Gest, Morris 97
"Get on Board" 152
"Get Your Money's Worth" 47
Gilbert and Sullivan 192
Gimbel Department Store 97, 98
Girard, Armand 117
"Girl Who Won't Have Me" 85
"Give My Love to Nellie" 46
Glen Alden Coal Co. 109
"Glendy Burke" 161
Glenn, Wilfred 76
"Go 'Way, Good Massa Bee" 87
"God Save the King" 144
"God's Country" 154
"Going to the Dogs" 179
Gold and Silver Minstrels 124
Gold Dust Twins 129
Gold Medal Minstrels 118
Gold Star Minstrels 124
Goldberg, Rube 98
Goldberg, Whoopi 200
Golden, Billy 35, 44, 54, 99
Golden, May 44
Golden Rose of Montreux 194
Goldilocks and the Jivin' Bears 172
Goldmark, Daniel 205
"Golondrina" 147
"Good Morning" 153
"Good Old Jeff" 88
"Goodbye Dolly Gray" 44, 49
"Goodbye Eliza Jane" 78, 93
"Goodbye, Good Luck My Darlin'" 165
"Goodbye, My Lady Love" 171
Goodman, Al 120
Goodman, Benny 109
Goodman, Gordon 82, 188, 189
"Goodnight Dear" 76
"Goodnight Ladies" 78
Gordon, Anita 183
Gosden, Freeman 79, 119, 127, 128
Gossett, Louis, Jr. 198
Graham, Charles 47
Graham, George 35, 46, 54, 55
Gramophone Minstrels 47
Gramophone records 84, 85
Grand Ole Opry 105
Grand Parade 145, 146
"Grandfather's Clock" 30
Grange, Red 114
Great Little Thomas (Jay Thomas) 86, 89
Green, Billy 157
Green, Eddie 125
Green, Col. Edward 98

Green, Hetty 98
Green, Johnny 123
"Green Eye of the Yellow God" 134
Green Pastures see Clean Pastures
Greening, Stan 91
Greenwich Village Follies 127
Greenwood, Charlotte 77
Greer, Bob 130
Gregory, Paul 191
Grenadiers Quartet 112
Grover, John Boyer 124
Guinness Book of Records 194
Gulf Coast Minstrels 77
Gulf Show 128
Gumps 127
Gus Hill Minstrels 44
Gypsy Joe 182

Hackett, James 7
Hager, Fred 95, 96
Hague, Sam 30
Hall, Cliff 125
Hall, Harry 181
Hall Johnson Choir 173
Hall Sisters 132
Hallett, Wilson 85, 86
Hamilton, Roy 81
Hamm, Charles 201, 202
Hampton, Pete 85
Handy, W.C. 20, 77, 133, 136
Happy Days (movie) 147
"Happy Days in Dixieland" 53
"Hard Times Come Again No More" 11, 87
Hard Wash 139
Harding, Roger 35, 42, 44, 47
Hare, Ernest 74, 75, 95
Harlan, Byron G. 56, 59, 64, 65, 68, 69, 75, 107
"Harlem on the Prairie" 164
Harlem on the Prairie (movie) 164
Harmony Lane 158
Harmony records 57, 66
Harrigan and Hart 16, 62
Harris, Connie 164
Harris, Joel Chandler 173
Harris, Keith 194
Harris, Phil 119
Harris, Sam 20
Harrison, Pres. Benjamin 32, 141
Harrison, Marvin 182, 183
Harry Reynolds Minstrels 93
Harvard records 66
Hatch, Ike 92, 134, 136, 191
Haverly, J.H. 13, 17
Haverly, Ned 157
Haverly Minstrels 13, 14, 17, 31, 35, 36, 99, 162
Haverly Negro Minstrels: Burnt Cork Specialties 28
Hay, Bill 119, 127
Haydn Quartet 47, 49, 85

274 Index

Hayes, Clarence 117, 124
Haymaker's Minstrels 104
Haynes, Chuck 114, 115
Haynes, Dick 182
"Head Over Heels" 160
Headin' South 26
"Hear Dem Bells" 16, 39, 42, 66, 73, 87, 92, 129, 136
Hearst, William Randolph 102
"Heartaches" 180
Heins, Billy 44, 45, 99, 105
"Hello Again" 175
"Hello Ma Baby" 42, 73, 82, 85, 87
Hemus, Percy 106, 107, 108
Henderson, Fletcher 97
Henrich, Tommy 181
Henry, Lenny 194
Henry De Marsan's Sentimental Singer and Singers' Journal 28
Herbert, Victor 125
Here Comes the Waves 121
Here's to Romance 124
Herman, Al 170
Herman Fowler studio 150
Hershfield, Harry 113
Hetherington, Tom 87, 88
Hi and Low banjo-piano team 99
"Hiawatha" 108
Hicks, Charles B. 14, 16
Hicks and Sawyer Minstrels 20, 31
"High Brown Blues" 122
"High Old Time" 33, 38, 41, 42, 43
"High Old Time in Dixie" 174
Hill, Murry K. 68
"Hills of Old Wyoming" 115
Hindermyer, Harvey 129
Hines, Gregory 198
Hines, Theodore 186
"Hippodrome Minstrel Medley" 73
Historicism 4
Hit Parade 113
Hitchcock, Raymond 98
Hittin' the Trail for Hallelujah Land 172
HMV records 84, 90, 91, 92, 137
Hodes, Art 185
Hoffa, Portland 120
Hogan, Ernest 31
Holden, William 170
Holiday, Billie 133
Holiday Inn 121, 170, 171
Hollywood Varieties 171
Holm, Eleanor 123
"Holy City" 92, 136
homophone 98
Honey Boy Evans Minstrels 19
Honey Boy Minstrels 201
Honeyboy and Sassafras 128

Honeyside Minstrels of Riverside 104
"Honeysuckle and the Bee" 85
Hood, Adelyne 131
Hood, Darla 170
Hooley, William F. 45, 47, 49, 50, 51, 58, 85
Hoosier Hot Shots 119
Hopkins, Barry 117
Horak, Jan-Christopher 139
Hornik, Joseph 117
"Horse That Knows the Way" 161
"Hot Time in the Old Town" 44, 47, 73, 82, 84, 121, 122, 125, 147, 172
Housman, Arthur 143
"How I Love My Lou" 44
Howard, Joe 180, 190
Howard, Tom 113
"Howdy Folks" 166
Howell, C. Thomas 175
Hughes, Langston 132
"Humming Coon" 60, 63, 65
Hunter, Harry 30, 89
Hunting, Russell 35, 85, 87
Hutton, Betty 169

"I Ain't Got a Gal to Come Home To" 164
"I Apologize" 109
"I Carry My Sunshine with Me" 89
"I Don't Care If You Never Come Back" 63
"I Don't Want to Walk Without You" 103
I Dream of Jeanie (with the Light Brown Hair) (movie) 160
"I Dreamt I Dwelt in Marble Halls" 30
"I Got to See de Minstrel Show" 67
"I See Her Still in My Dreams" 160
"I Want a Girl Just Like the Girl That Married Dear Old Dad" 93, 162
"I Want to Be a Minstrel Man" 151, 157
"I Want to Be Down Home in Dixie" 93
"I Want to Be in Dixie" 93
"I Want to See a Minstrel Show" 69
"I Wonder Who's Kissing Her Now" 180
"I'd Leave My Happy Home for You" 42
"I'd Rather Be a Minstrel Man Than a Multi-Millionaire" 68
"Ida Sweet as Apple Cider" 78, 103, 118, 153, 169, 179
If I Had the Chance 123

Ike and Jake 96
"I'll Be Dar" 188, 189
"I'm Gonna Quit on Saturday" 179
"I'm in Love with the Band" 177
"I'm Just Wild About Harry" 93, 153, 169
"I'm Looking Over a Four Leaf Clover" 180
Imperial Minstrels 35, 37, 39, 41, 42, 43, 45, 47, 48, 50, 55, 66, 67
Imperial records 57
Improved Gram-O-Phone records 47
"In the Evening by the Moonlight" 48, 124, 170
"In the Garden of My Heart" 21, 112
"In the Good Old Summertime" 20, 192
"In the Good Old United States" 66
"In the Morning by the Bright Light" 60
Indefinite talk 127, 157
Indestructible records 58, 63
Infernal Cakewalk 139
Ink Spots 133
Inki 172
Inns, George 191, 194
International Indestructible records 86
Ireland, George 119
Irwin, Dave 99, 101
"Is Your Rent Paid Up in Heaven" 157
"I'se Gwine Back to Dixie" 85, 89
Isle of Pingo Pongo 172
Ison, George 87
Issler, Edward 45
"It's Got to Be a Minstrel Show Tonight" 67, 68
"It's the Natural Thing to Do" 116
"Itsy Bitsy Teeny Weenie Yellow Polka Dot Bikini" 192
"I've a Longing in My Heart for You Louise" 43

Jack Benny Show 124
Jack Hylton and His Orchestra 91
Jackson, Pres. Andrew 7
James, Bob 115
James, Gee Gee 124
James, Jimmy 86
James, John "Dusty" 165
Jamison, Bud 170
Jamup and Honey 105
Jane Froman Show 128
Jasper 172
Jasper's Minstrels 172
Jaudas, Eugene 143

Index

Jay-Dee records 80
Jazz Singer 147, 149, 170, 174
Jazzmania 98
"Jeanie with the Light Brown Hair" 11, 157, 160
Jefferson, William 125
Jeffries, Herb 164
Jenkins, Harry 99
"Jerusalem Morning" 77
Jessel, George 98, 121, 123, 147
Jester Hairston Choir 157
Jethro Tull (band) 197
Joe Bren Minstrels 104
Joe Miller's Jests 169
Johnson, Bryan 93
Johnson, Eldridge R. 47
Johnson, George W. 36, 37, 38, 39, 40, 41, 42, 64, 69
Johnson, Osie 82
Johnson, Teddy 93
Johnson Family 182
Johnston Cracker Minstrels 105
"Jolly Minstrel" 70
Jolson, Al 3, 70, 121, 125, 147, 148, 149, 150, 158, 159, 160, 162, 169, 170, 172, 180, 185, 186, 190
Jolson Sings Again 162, 180, 185
Jolson Story 162, 180, 185
Jones, Ada 43, 65
Jones, Alma 85, 88
Jones, Chuck 172
Jones, Joseph Pope 168
Jose, Richard 73, 74
"Josie" 94
Jubilee Minstrels 58
Jumbo records 86, 88, 89, 90
"Jump Jim Crow" 7, 169
Jungle Jitters 172
Just Around the Corner 152
"Just Because She Made Dem Goo-Goo Eyes" 49, 67, 109
"Just Before the Battle, Mother" 30
"Just Hear That Slide Trombone" 109
"Just Kiss Yourself Goodbye" 63
"Just One Girl" 44
"Just Walk Along by the Side of Me" 86

Kalamazoo records 66
Kalliope records 89
Kamplain, Frank 109
Kapp records 83
Karns, Roscoe 156
Kaufman, Irving 124
Kaufman, Jack 78
Kaye, Danny 171
Kaye, Sammy 123
Keaton, Buster 144, 170
Keefe, Matt 56
Keeler, Ruby 162
Keen, Monroe 62
Keen-O-Phone records 62, 63
Keir, Donald 86

Keith-Albee 142
Kelly, Gene 102
"Kemo, Kimo" 92, 136
Kennedy, Edgar 100
"Kentucky Babe" 96, 118, 121, 188
Kentucky Minstrels 90, 92, 93, 134, 135, 136, 137, 177, 191
Kentucky Minstrels (movie) 31, 176
Kersands, Billy 20, 72
Kibler, Alison 205
The Kid 102
Kid Millions 150, 204
Kimes, Stanley 82
Kinetophone 142, 144
King, Andrea 162
"King for a Day" 109
King for a Day 168
King Odom Quartet 132
Kirby, Ward 99
"Kiss Me By Wireless" 96
Knickerbocker Quartet 117
Knickerbocker Quintet 140
Kogen, Harry 114, 116
Kottaun, Celian 86
Kraft Music Hall 121
Kramer and Stone 99
Kranendonk, Leonard 188, 189
Krazy Kat: The Minstrel Show 172
Krueger, Bennie 113
Kuhn, Casper 179, 180
Kuhn, Joseph 80

"Lads in Navy Blue" 85
"Lady Be Good" 132, 133
Lamare, Nappy 184, 185
Lamour, Dorothy 161
"Landstrum Galop" 76
Landt Trio 113
Lane, Dick 168, 183, 184
Lane, William Henry (Master Juba) 30
Lange, Judy 122
Langford, Frances 113, 115
Lashwood, George 85
Lasses and Honey *see* White, Lasses
Lasses White-Honey Wilds Minstrel Show 105
Lasses White Minstrels 118, 128, 182
Lasses White's Book of Humor and Song 28, 105
Last Minstrel Show 198
"Last Rose of Summer" 161
"Laughing Song" 36, 39, 40, 42, 45, 69, 89
Laughlin, Froggy 170
Lauriat Brothers 120
Lazy Dan, the Minstrel Man *see* Kaufman, Irving
"Lazy Moon" 73, 78, 170
Leavitt, John M. 75

Lee, Don 182
Lee, Johnnie 127, 132, 133
Lee, Spike 175, 176, 200
Lee Gordon Singers 80
Leeds records 43
Leeds, Andrea 159, 160
Leibowitz, Samuel 123
Leigh 47
Leighton, Harry 46
Len Spencer Greater New York Minstrels 35
Leno, Dan 86
Leonard, Eddie 118, 169, 187
LeRoy, Hal 186, 190
"Let Me Sing and I'm Happy" 149
"Let's Break the Ice" 167
"Let's Grow Old Together" 74
Levant, Oscar 121
Levin, Harry 105
Lew Dockstader Minstrels 17, 46, 73, 74, 90, 99
Lewis, Forrest 128, 131
Lewis, Mort 28, 123
Lewis, Ted 77
Lewis, Tom 74, 75
Lhamon, W.T., Jr. 5
Life Is Real 177
Lightfooted Darkey 176
"Lighthouse By the Sea" 65
"L'il Liza Jane" 136
Lilly, Carrie 122
"Lily of Laguna" 31, 92
Lincoln, Pres. Abraham 24
"Lindy" 78
Link, Goff 130, 131
Lippert studio 156
"Listen to the Mocking Bird" 157
"Little Annie Rooney" 192
"Little Brown Jug" 188
Little Colonel 152, 170
"Little Dolly Daydream" 31, 85
"Little Pal" 145
Little Wonder records 33, 63
Littlest Rebel 152, 170
Livingston, Mary 119
Lizzie Titus and Mrs. Emma Potts 130
Lonesome Trail 165, 166
Longfellow Tambourine Troubadours 190
Look for the Silver Lining (movie) 180
Looney Tunes 172
Lopez, Vincent 98, 113
"Lost Chord" 136
Lott, Eric 3, 5, 205
"Louisiana Belle" 163
"Love Is Magic" 167
"Love on the Rocks" 175
"Love Will Find a Way" 169
Lovello, Tony 183
"Lovin' Sam" 96
Lowe, Charles P. 35

Index

Lowe, Edmund 147
Lowell, Gene 122
Lowery, P.G. 26
Lubin, Lou 117, 118, 168
Luboff, Norman 124
Lulu and Leander 130
Lux Radio Theatre 161, 162
Lyceum records 90
Lyles, Aubrey 126, 127, 157

"Ma Curly-Headed Baby" 94
Mabley, Moms 132, 133
MacDonald, Jimmy 126
Macdonough, Harry 47, 49, 51, 59, 64, 85
MacFarlane, George 147
Mack, Charles 127
Mack, Keller 68
MacMichael, Florence 122, 123
Madame Rentz Female Minstrels 14
Madison's Budget 28
"Maggie Murphy's Home" 157
Magliozzi, Ron 139
Magnolia and Sunflower 130
Magnolia Minstrels 117
"Mah Lindy Lou" 189
Mahar, William J. 3, 5, 203, 204
Mahara Minstrels 20
Mahoney, Jere 45, 47
Majestic Theatre Hour 128
"Make a Lot of Noise" 58, 78
Making Stars 173
Mallory Brothers Minstrels 20
Malone, Pick 110, 113
"Mamie Reilly" 42
"Mammy" 121
Mammy (movie) 148, 149
"Mammy's Little Pumpkin Colored Coons" 73
"Mandy" 82, 119, 151, 152, 170, 171, 179
Manhansset Quartet 33
Manhattan Minstrels 89
Manhattan records 66
Maple City Four 119
"Marching Home to You" 109
"Marching Through Georgia" 91
Marconi, Guglielmo 95
Marconi records 66
Marcus, Greil 3
Mariani, Hugo 108
Marine, Joe 188, 189
Marks, Charles 99
Marlin, Ray 114
Marsh, Dixie 131
Marshal, Charles 117
Martin & Selig Minstrels 19
Masingill, Owen B. 81, 82, 83
Masquerade 195
"Massa's in de Cold, Cold Ground" 11, 45, 51, 78, 85, 87, 91, 92, 161
"Massa's Sent a Jellygram" 30
Massey, Raymond 189

Matthews, Chris 7
Matthieu, Carl 79
Maxwell House Show Boat 110, 119, 120
Mayo, Skeets 126
Mays and Hunter 86
Maytag Radioettes 118
McAdoo's Minstrels 31
McCabe & Young Minstrels 20
McClain, Billy 31
McClintock, Poley 188, 189
McCloud, Mac 114, 115
McCormack, John 149
McCormack, Owen J. 142
McCune, Vance 116, 128, 131
McFarland, Spanky 170
McGarity, Lou 79
McHargue, Rosy 184
McIntyre and Heath 26, 72, 169
McKinney, Nina Mae 177
McLaglen, Victor 147
McMahan's Minstrels 182, 183
McNamee, Graham 123
"Me an' da Minstrel Ban'" 67, 68
Mecca 97
Meeker, Edward 54, 64, 65, 68, 69
"Meet Me at the Golden Gate" 88
"Melancholy Baby" 156
Méliès, Georges 139
"Melinda May" 161
Melodeers 110
Melton, Fred 86
"Memphis Bill" 157
Mercer, Tony 192
Merman, Ethel 150, 152, 204
Merrie Melodies 172
Merrill Staton Choir 82
"Merry Minstrel Men" 160
Meyer, John H. 60, 61, 63
MGM studio 154
Middleton, Ray 160
"Mighty Lak' a Rose" 179
Miller, Emmett 157
Miller, Flournoy 126, 127, 132, 133, 157, 164
Miller, Joe 169
Millinder, Lucky 132, 133, 134, 187
Mills, Kerry 136
Milton Berle Show 124
"Mine All Mine" 165
"Minstrel Band" 70
"Minstrel Days" 81, 163, 170
Minstrel Days (movie) 169, 177
"Minstrel Man" 155
Minstrel Man (movie) 49, 155, 174, 200, 204
Minstrel Melodies (movie) 156
Minstrel Melodies (radio) 124
"Minstrel Memories" 147
"Minstrel Men" 81, 82
Minstrel Mishaps 72
"Minstrel Parade" 68, 70

"Minstrel Show" (LP) 80, 82
"Minstrel Show of 1929" 78, 91
"Minstrel Show of 1931" 92, 134
"Minstrel Show of 1937" 92
Minstrel Train 122, 125
Minstrels Battling in a Room 139
"Minstrelsy of Other Days" 76
The Miracle 97, 98
Mirth and Melody 125
"Miss Lucy Long" 11
"Miss Lucy Lou" 163
Mississippi Minstrels 91, 182
Mississippi Rhythm 165
"Mr. Bones" 171
Mr. Bones and Company 108, 117
Mitchell, George 191, 195, 196
Mitchell, John 127
Mitchell, Rob 196
Model Minstrels 58, 113
Modern Minstrels 117
Mohawk Minstrels 30, 86, 89, 91
Mohawk, Moore and Burgess Minstrels 85
Molasses and January 113; see also Malone, Pick; Padgett, Pat
Molle Minstrels 110
"Mona" 147
Monarch records 48
Monarchs of Harmony 122
Monarchs of Minstrelsy 101
Monogram studio 165, 166
Montesanto, Leroy 99
Montgomery, Douglas 158
"Moonlight Bay" 153
Moonshine and Sawdust 128
Moore, Carolyn 131
Moore, George "Pony" 30, 86
Moore, Sam P. 131
Moore and Burgess Minstrels 30, 31, 84, 86, 88, 89, 90, 91
Moran, George 118, 127, 184
Moran and Mack 110, 134, 170; see also Two Black Crows
Moran and Mack Show 128
Moreland, Mantan 127, 164
Morgan, Dennis 162
Morgan, Elizabeth 122, 123
Morgan, Frank 152
Moritt, Fred 123
Morning Bath 139
Morning Minstrels 105, 117
Morris, Frank 123
Morris, Wayne 166, 167
Morton, Eddie 68
Morton, John V. 86
"Mother, I've Called to See You" 30
"Mother Machree" 149, 163
Mother Wore Tights 180
"Mother's Watch By the Sea" 43
Mozart, George 86
Mulliner, Betty 124

Mummers Parade 200
Murphy, George 152, 170
Murphy Minstrels 105
Murray, Billy 54, 56, 57, 58, 59, 60, 64, 65, 67, 69, 75, 76, 78, 79
Music Hall (movie) 176
Music Music Music 195
Mustard and Gravy 168
"My Blushin' Rosie" 81
"My Castle on the Nile" 76
"My Coal Black Lady" 47, 85, 87
"My Country 'Tis of Thee" 144
"My Creole Sue" 51, 108
"My Daddy Was a Minstrel Man" 153
"My Dusky Rose" 60, 63
"My Gal" 76
"My Gal Is a High Born Lady" 78
"My Gal Sal" 78
"My Heart Is Bustin'" 125
"My Love Remains the Same" 64
"My Moon" 92
"My Old Kentucky Home" 11, 43, 49, 91, 93, 94, 96, 101, 160, 161, 172
"My Rainbow Coon" 49, 61, 63
"My Wife's Gone to the Country, Hurrah! Hurrah!" 67
"My Wild Irish Rose" 43, 48, 49
My Wild Irish Rose (movie) 162, 163
Myers, J.W. 54, 67, 75

NAACP 2, 132, 133, 174, 175, 185, 187, 198, 205
Nassau records 66
Nathan, Hans 5
Nation, Carrie 49, 53
National Association for the Advancement of Colored People *see* NAACP
National Barn Dance 113, 119
National Cavaliers quartet 79
National Male Quartet 77
National Minstrel Players and Fans Association 26
National Minstrel Show 132, 133, 185, 187
"Navajo" 87
Nazarro, Cliff 150
NBC Lady Minstrels 121
NBC Minstrels 116, 128
NBC Pages and Guides Minstrel Show 178, 180
Neale, Floyd 99
"Negro's Holiday" 46
Neher, John 82
Neil O'Brien Minstrels 76
"Nelly Bly" 161
"Nelly Was a Lady" 11
Nelson, Willie 197
"Neptune" 80

New Century records 87
New Christy Minstrels 10, 82, 197
New Jersey Phonograph Co. 34
New Jersey records 41, 44, 45, 46
New York records 44
New York Yankees 181
Newton, H. Chance 86
Nicholas, Harold 151
Nicholas Brothers 152
"Nigger Blues" 77
Nigger Courtship 176
1957 Television Minstrels, 191
"Nobody" 189, 198
Nogués, Ralph 130
Norworth, Jack 123
"Nothin' from Nothin' Leaves You" 117
Novak, Frank 123
"Now That You're Gone" 109

"O Dry Those Tears" 92
Oakland, Frederick 34
Oakland, Will 59, 74, 82, 190
O'Brien, Dave "Tex" 164
O'Brien, Jimmy 157
O'Brien, Neil 99; *see also* Neil O'Brien Minstrels
O'Connor, Donald 170
Odeon records 87, 88
"Oh Boys, Carry Me 'Long" 160
"Oh Brother What a Feeling" 96
"Oh Dem Golden Slippers" 60, 63, 73, 76, 78, 91, 92, 94, 122, 136, 179, 193
"Oh Didn't He Ramble" 73, 78
"Oh, I Don't Know, You're Not So Warm" 73
"Oh, Lordy" 92
"Oh! Sam" 188
"Oh! Susanna" 11, 82, 94, 101, 153, 160, 188, 189
"Oh You Coon" 96
O'Hara, Geoffrey 59, 140
Okeh records 77, 95, 127
Olcott, Chauncey 158, 162, 163
"Old Black Crow" 93
"Old Black Joe" 11, 45, 82, 85, 87, 91, 161, 167
"Old Dan Tucker" 8, 11, 83, 161
"Old Dog Tray" 11, 160, 188
"Old-Fashioned Valentine" 46
"Old Folks at Home" 11, 43, 47, 49, 51, 85, 87, 88, 89, 91, 92, 118, 149, 155, 158, 160, 163, 164, 166, 167, 172, 173, 189
"Old Irish Mother of Mine" 117
"Old Lamplighter" 180
"Old Log Cabin in the Dell" 39, 66, 87
"Old Man Mose" 169
"Old Man River" 122, 189
Old Oaken Quartet 124

"Old Time Minstrel Show" 91, 92
Old Virginia Minstrels 105
"Ole Banjo" 90, 91, 92
O'Leary's Irish Minstrels 105
Olsen, George 98, 147
Olympus Minstrels 181
"On a Wonderful Day Like Today" 192
"On Stage with the George Mitchell Minstrels" 194
"On the Banks of the Wabash" 94
"On the Mississippi" 93
"On the Old Fall River Line" 115
"On the Sunny Side of the Street" 125
One for the Book 169
"One Has My Name the Other Has My Heart" 166
One Night Stands with Pick and Pat 113
Oppenshaw, Violet 90
Original New Orleans Minstrels 35
Ornsby, Bill 80
Orth, Frank 68
Ossman, Vess L. 35, 55, 64, 69
Osterwald, Bibi 198
Our Gang 170
"Over the Waves" 167
Oxford Minstrels 90
Oxford records 57, 66

Padgett, Bob 128
Padgett, Pat 110, 128
Paige, Raymond 123
Pal, George 172
Palm Springs 115
"Paloma Blanca" 192
Par-O-Ket records 63
Paramor, Norrie 93
Paramount studio 145, 161, 171, 184
Parham, Meigs 46
Parker, Frank 119
Parkham *see* Parham, Meigs
Parks, Larry 162
Parmet, Leon 140, 143
Parsons, Chauncey 114
Parsons, Happy Jim *see* Kaufman, Irving
Parsons, Joe 114
Paskman, Dailey 3, 54, 78, 97, 98, 99, 100, 101, 102, 104, 145, 162
The Passing Show (1894) 138
Pastor, Tony 16
Pathe records 86, 87, 88
Pathé studio 145, 176
Pathétone Parade of 1936 176
Patricola, Tom 147
"Patrol Comique" 51
Paul, Elliot 123
Paulson, Arvid 98

Peabody, Eddie 181
Pearce, Albert 85
Peary, Harold 117
Peer Gynt 98
Peerless Minstrels 58, 60, 61, 62, 63, 65, 67
Peerless records 66
"Peg Leg Jack" 108
"Peg o' My Heart" 180
Pelham, Dick 8, 161
Pelican records 90
Pennington, Ann 147
Pepper, Dick 134
Pepper, Harry S. 92, 134, 135
Perkins, Ray 123
Perry, Commodore Matthew 31
Peters, Ralph 183
Peterson, James N. 83
Petrie, Howard 123
Phelps, Verne 126
Philco Radio Time 121
Phoenix records 90
Phonograph Record Manufacturing Co. records 87
Pick and Pat 112, 113, 114, 120, 121, 122, 123, 126, 168, 186, 187; *see also* Malone, Pick; Padgett, Pat
Pick and Pat and Their Minstrels 110, 111
Pickaninny Dance 138
Pickering, Michael 5, 31, 136, 137, 193
Pike, Ernest 90
Pious, Minerva 120
Pipe Smoking Time 113
Plantation Act 149
"Plantation Medley" 46, 92
"Play on the Golden Harp" 16, 40, 66
Playhouse 144
"Polly Wolly Doodle" 76, 94, 163, 172
Poor Old Joe *see* Old Black Joe
Porter, Edwin 142
Porter, Steve 35, 42, 43, 44, 51, 52, 54, 56, 57, 58, 65, 69, 75, 76, 107, 108
"Possum Up a Gum Tree" 7
"Powder Your Face with Sunshine" 193
Premier Quartet 69, 76
Prentice, Charles 91
Presby, G. Archibald 124
Preoentiom 4
Presley, Elvis 3, 201
"Pretty Mamie Casey" 41
Primrose, George 17, 169
Primrose and Dockstader Minstrels 15, 17
Primrose and West Minstrels 13, 15, 17, 21, 25, 44, 73, 74, 78, 93
Primrose Minstrels 74
Prince, Charles A. 57, 69

"Prisoner of Love" 180
The Producers 175
Producers Releasing Corp. studio 155
Pryor, Larry 109
Puppetoons 172
"Push Dem Clouds Away" 63
"Pussy Green" 41

Quinn, Dan W. 36, 38, 39, 40, 45, 51, 67

"Radiominstrelsy" 97
"Ragged But Right" 157
Raggety-Taggety Minstrels 96
"Railroad Overture" 11
"Rainbow Man" 145
Rainbow Man (movie) 145
Rambler Minstrels 56, 57, 58, 60, 62, 63, 65, 66, 86
Randolph, Jane 122
Rangers 119
"Rap, Rap, Rap on Your Minstrel Bones" 68
Rastus, Joe 138
"Rastus on Parade" 52, 136
Ray Brown Trio 132
Ray Noble Orchestra 92
Raybestos Twins 109
Raye, Frank 83
"Razors in the Air" 91
Rea, George P. 123
Read 'Em and Weep 101
Reagan, Pres. Ronald 198
Rebecca of Sunnybrook Farm 152
Record Boys 109
Red River 180
Reed, Alan 120
Rees, Annie 90
Reese, Della 81, 198
Reeves, Ernest 126
Regal records 91
"Remember Me to Carolina" 155, 156
"Remus Takes the Cake" 44, 53
Republic studio 158, 163
Reser, Harry 83
Rettenberg, Milton 110
Revelers 112
Rex records 63
Reynolds, Harry 86; *see also* Harry Reynolds Minstrels
Reynolds, Marjorie 170
Rhoads, George "Dusty" 118
"Ribbon in Your Hair" 160
Rice, Edward L. 4, 73, 101
Rice, Frank 168
Rice, Jack 99, 100, 101
Rice, Thomas "Daddy" 7, 169
"Rich Man, Beggar, Pauper, King" 112
Richards and Pringle's Georgia Minstrels 20, 163
Richardson, Billy 86

Rines, Joe 113
Ring, Justin 77, 96
"Ring, Ring de Banjo" 11, 155, 157, 160
Rizzuto, Phil 181
Roberts, Ken 125
Robinson, Bill 152, 168, 169, 170
Robinson, Ford 86
Robison, Carson 106, 107, 108
Rocco, Maurice 183
"Rock-a-Bye Your Baby with a Dixie Melody" 149
"Rock dat Ship" 40
"Rocked in the Cradle of the Deep" 68, 89
"Rockin' Chair" 122
"Rockin' Robin" 202
Roecker, Edward 113
Rogers, Alex 67
Rogers, Will 147
"Roll Dem Bones" 83, 150
"Roll On, Mississippi, Roll On" 109, 119
"Roll on the Ground" 44
Rollickers 168
"Roly Boly Eyes" 118, 187
Romain, Manuel 73
Roman Scandals 170
"Romance in the Rain" 164
Romeo label 78
Rooney, Mickey 3, 102, 152, 153, 154, 155, 160, 203
Rooney, Pat 190
Roosevelt, Pres. Franklin D. 2, 105, 154, 197
Roosevelt, Pres. Theodore 21, 70, 141
"Rosary" 140
Rosenfeld, Monroe 70
Ross, Cliff 77
Ross, Diana 195
Ross, Lanny 120
Roth, Allen 82
Rowe, Billy 132, 161
Rowe, Izzy 190
Roy, Cecil 122, 123
Royal Cowes Minstrels 87
Royal records 66
Royal Variety Performances 194, 195
Ruffner, Tiny 113, 122, 123
Rufus LeMaire's Affairs 26, 77
"Rufus Rastus Johnson Brown" 78, 83, 117
Rusco and Hockwald Minstrels 20, 26
Rusco and Holland Minstrels 20
Rusco and Swift Minstrels 20
Russell, Chuck 131
Russell, Lillian 162
Rutherford, Ann 163
Ryan, Ann 181
Ryan, Eddie 171
Rycroft, Fred 47

"St. Louis Blues" 77
"Sally in Our Alley" 47
"Sally Warner" 47
Sam Devere Minstrels 47
Sam 'n' Henry 79, 127
Sam T. Jack Minstrels 20
Sambo (movie) 176
Sambo and Mandy 131
"San Antonio" 57, 66
Sand dance 23
Sanders, Nat 96
Sanford, Harold 108, 117
Satisfiers 121
Saturday Night Live 4
Savage, Norman 93
Savannah Shufflers 99
Savoy Ballroom 132
Sax, Ray 188, 189
Say It with Songs 147, 148
Scala Minstrel Troupe 90
Scala records 90
"School Days" 96
Scott, Fred 145, 146
Scott, Harry 134, 135, 136, 137, 176, 177
Scott, Oliver, Big Minstrel Carnival 24
Scott, Wallace 89
Scribner, Jimmy 182
Scrub Me Mama with a Boogie Beat 173
Sealy Air Weavers 127
Sechler, Clyde 188, 189
"See-Saw, See-Saw" 76
Seeley, Blossom 155
Sentimentalists *see* The Clark Sisters
Seroff, Doug 26
Shannon Four 76, 95
Shay, Dorothy 180
Sheaff, Bernard 134
Sheehan, John 130
"Sheik of Araby" 179
Shelley, William 108, 117
Shelton, George 113
Sherman, Hal 169
"She's from Missouri" 161
"She's in the Jailhouse Now" 118
Shields, Ren 67
Shilkret, Nat 123
"Shine" 122
"Shine On Harvest Moon" 82, 103, 124
"Shine On Mr. Moon" 77
"Shine, Shine Moon" 92
Shirley, Bill 160
Shirley, Tom 79, 80
Shope, Henry 79, 80
Short, Al 116
Show Boat (movie) 170
Show Boat Minstrels 182
Shreve, Bob 181
Shubert, John 28
Shuffle Along 127, 169
Sierra Passage 166, 167, 168

Silver, Monroe 79
"Silver Threads Among the Gold" 74, 76, 78, 124, 142
Silver Tongued records 66
Silvers, Phil 81
Silvertone records 57, 66
Silvertone records (UK) 88
Simmons, Tom 86
Simms, Frank 82
Sinclair Wiener Minstrels 114, 115, 119
Singalong with Mitch 192
Singing Fool 145, 147
Singing Vagabond 163
Singleton, Zutty 185
Sissle, Noble 132, 133, 187
Sissle and Blake 127
Slavery Days 16
"Sleepiest Man in Town" 119
Sleepy Joe 182
"Sleepy Time Gal" 82
"Sleepy Valley" 145
Slick and Slim 130
Sloan, Estelle 186
Small, Mary 113, 120, 186
Smilin' Sam 117
Smith, Alfred E. 123
Smith, Charles 140
Smith, Jada Pinkett 175
Smith, Kate 113
Smith, Norwood 182
Smith, Whispering Jack 147
Smith and Dale 186, 190
Smock, Ginger 184
"Smoke Gets in Your Eyes" 180
Smokey Joe and Tee-Tain 130
"Smoky Mokes" 45
Snow White and the Seven Dwarfs (movie) see Coal Black and de Sebben Dwarfs
Snowball and Sunshine 130
Snowball and Willie 130
Sodja, Joe 190
"Some Folks" 160
"Somebody Else, Not Me" 119
"Somebody Lied" 108
"Somebody Loves Me" 88
Somers, Debroy 177
Somerset records 80
Song of the South 173, 180
"Sonny Boy" 145
"Sop in the Pan" 85
Sorey, Vincent 117
Sothern, Ann 152
Soubier, Cliff 114, 115, 116, 119
Soul Man 175, 200
South Before the War 16
Southern Fried Rabbit 172
Southern Harmony Four 117
"Southern Medley" 46
Spaeth, Sigmund 98, 99, 100, 101, 123
Spaeth, William 126
Sparks Circus 26
Speaking of Operations 168

Speed and Lightnin' 130
"Speedwell" 92
Spencer, Harry 42, 43, 54
Spencer, Leonard 3, 34, 35, 36, 38, 39, 40, 41, 42, 43, 51, 52, 53, 54, 55, 64, 65, 67, 69, 75; *see also* Len Spencer Greater New York Minstrels
Spencer, Sara Andrews 34
Spook Minstrels 140, 143
"Squashtown Minstrels" 69
Squibb Show 124
Stafford, Mr. 112, 113
"Standing on the Corner" 41
Standard records 57, 66
Stanley, Frank C. 42, 43, 58, 60, 62, 63, 65, 67, 75
Stanley, James 78, 79
Stanton, Harry 117, 182
Star records 66
Star records (UK) 87
"Star Spangled Banner" 7
"Stardust" 122
"Stardust Trail" 164
The Stargazers 93
Starrett, Charles 168
Stars records 90
Steel Pier Minstrels 104
Steele, Ted 120, 121
Steeplechase Park, Coney Island 75
Stennett, Stan 192
Stept, Sammy 109
Stereo Fidelity records 80
Sterling, Louis 87
Sterling records 87
Stern, Bill 123
Stevens, Bob 117
Stevens, Leith 110, 118
Stewart, Cal 35, 86
Stirnweiss, George "Snuffy" 181
Stokes, Ernest L. 168
Stone, Ezra 123
"Stop Dat Knocking" 11
Stowe, Harriet Beecher 11
Stowe, Tiny 118, 119, 182
"Stranded Minstrel Man" 68
Stratton, Eugene 31, 86
Strausbaugh, John 3
Streetcar Named Desire 124
Stuart, Leslie 31
Stump Speech 176
"Sue, Sue, Sue" 94
Sugarfoot and Sassafras 128
Sullivan, Ed 3, 190, 191
Sullivan, Maxine 186
Sully, Lew 67
Sun records 66
Sunday Go to Meetin' Time 172
"Sunday, Monday or Always" 161
Sunset Corners Minstrels 105
"Sunshine Will Come Again" 46
Sutton, Ellen 157
"Swanee" 94, 202

Index

Swanee River (movie) 158, 159
Swanee River Boys 181
Swanee Showboat 177
"Swanee Smiles" 96
Sweeney, William 99
"Sweet Antionette" 74
"Sweet Genevieve" 77
"Sweet Mama, Tree Top Tall" 77
"Sweet Marie" 36, 40, 66
"Sweet Rosie O'Grady" 190, 192
Swing Time 170
Swingtime at the Savoy 132, 133
Swor, Bert 117, 118, 128
Swor, John 126, 127, 183, 184, 185

Tainter, Charles S. (patents) 84
"Take Back the Engagement Ring" 46
"Take Back the Heart That Thou Gavest" 69
"Take Plenty of Shoes" 63
Talbert, Harry C. 38
Tally Ho! Trio 87, 88, 89
Taylor, Albert, Stock Company 126
"Teasing" 115
Ted Brown Minstrel Show 96
Teleforum 184
Television Toppers 192
Temple, Shirley 152, 153, 170
Terrell, John 46
Texaco Star Theatre 120
Thackeray, William 24
Thall, Bill 181
"Thanks, Mr. Roosevelt" 136
"That Minstrel Man of Mine" 67
"That Mysterious Rag" 124
That Was the Week That Was 194
Thatcher, George 17
Thatcher Minstrels 74
Thatcher, Primrose and West Minstrels 17, 23, 38
"That's What I Like About the South" 124
"That's Why Darkies Were Born" 112
"There Is a New Range in Heaven" 164
"There Was a Little Nigger" 91
"There's a Goldmine in the Sky" 113
"There's Danger in Delay" 30
"There's Nothing Like a Minstrel Show" 79, 82
"They've Had 'Em Since Adam" 85
This Is the Army 170
This Is the Army (movie) 186
This Is Your Life 126
Thomas, Buckwheat 170
Thomas, Danny 174
Thomas, Norman 123

Thompson, Bill 116
Thompson, Katrina Dyonne 5
Three Musketeers 102
Three Wiles 186
Three Winter Sisters 186
"Three Women to Every Man" 85
Three X Sisters 168
"Til I Waltz Again with You" 201
Tilden, Billy 96
"Till the Snow Flakes Come Again" 43
Tillman, Benjamin 141
Tilton, Martha 125
Tin Pan Alley Cats 172
Tiny Stowe's All Star Minstrels 183
Tip Top Entertainment and Minstrel Album 28
Tivoli Minstrels 87
"To Have, To Hold, To Love" 108
Toast of the Town see The Ed Sullivan Show
"Toast to the Girl I Love" 147
Todd, Mike, Jr. 198, 199
Toll, Robert C. 5, 16
Tolliver, Denny 138
Tom Mix Ralston Straight Shooters 131
"Too Bad, Little Girl, Too Bad" 165
"Too Much Mustard" 117
"Too Ra Loo Ra Loo Ral" 183
Torch Song 170, 204
"Toreador Song" 142
Tosches, Nick 3
"Trans-Mag-Ni-Fi-Can-Bam-U-Al-I-Try" 76
"Tribute to the Original Christy Minstrels" 82
"Trombone Jitters" 79
Trotter, James Monroe 25
Truman, Pres. Harry 2, 133
"Truthfully" 79
Tubb, Dick 86
Tuckerman, Earle 129
Tunbridge Civic Club Show 203
"Turkey in the Straw" 8, 44, 174
Turman, Glynn 49, 174, 200
Twain, Mark 20, 24
"Twelfth Street Rag" 180
Twelvetrees, Helen 145, 146
Twitchell, Archie 157
Two Black Crows 118, 127, 134
"Two Cigarettes in the Dark" 180
"Two Faced Woman" 170
"Two Little Girls in Blue" 36, 39, 66
"Two New Coons in Town" 174
Two Orphans 102

Two Ronnies 194
Tyler, Maurice 108

"Uncle Billy's Dream" 64
"Uncle Eph's Return" 41
Uncle Ezra 119
"Uncle Ned" 132
"Uncle Quit Work Too" 72
Uncle Remus 173
Uncle Tom's Bungalow 172, 173
Uncle Tom's Cabaña 173
Uncle Tom's Cabin (movie) 139
Uncle Tom's Cabin (novel) 11
Uncle Tom's Cabin (play) 152
Unconquered 180
"Under the Bamboo Tree" 73, 79, 81
"Under the Cotton Moon" 168
United Service Organizations (USO) 28
United States Marine Band 32
United States Phonograph Co. 37, 42, 44; see also New Jersey records
Universal studio 176, 177
"Up Dar in de Sky" 47
"Upon the Golden Shore" 16, 40
U.S. Everlasting records 63
Utopia Minstrels: A Complete Minstrel Show 28

Vallee, Rudy 105, 113
Van, Gus 116, 186
Van and Schenck 116
Van Brunt, Walter 78
Van Buren, Pres. Martin 7
Vaughan, James 67
Velvet Face records 89
"Venus, My Shining Star" 46
Venuti, Joe 109
Vereen, Ben 198, 200
Vernon, Glenn 171
Vettel, Fred 109, 112
Victor Book of the Opera 47
Victor Minstrels 58, 61, 78
Victor records 43, 47, 48, 50, 51, 52, 54, 56, 61, 62, 63, 64, 66, 85, 101, 128
Victoria, Queen 30
Victoria, Vesta 88
Village Barn 181
Vincent Lopez Show 113
Virginia Minstrels 8, 9, 11, 30, 161, 203
Virginia Serenaders 8
Vitaphone 149
Vogel, John W. 20
Voice of Vaudeville 150
Von Hallberg, Gene 112
von KleinSmid, Dr. Rufus 184
Von Tilzer, Albert 68, 99
Von Tilzer, Harry 67
Von Zell, Harry 118, 123

"Wait Til the Sun Shines Nellie" 163
"Waiting at the Church" 88
"Waiting for Nell" 46
"Waiting for the Robert E. Lee" 82, 83, 93, 121, 155, 179, 198
Wakely, Jimmy 165
Walcutt and Leeds 44
Walker, George 67, 68
Walking My Baby Back Home 170
Waller, Fats 97
Waller, Jack 86
Wallington, Jimmy 120
Walsh, Jim 204
Walt Disney studio 173
"Waltz Me Around Again Willie" 57, 66, 140
Wandering Negro Minstrels 176
Want, Les 195
Ward, Al 96
Waring, Fred 82, 188, 189, 190
Warner, Joe 114
Warner Brothers studio 148, 168, 169
Warren, C. Denier 92, 134, 135, 136, 137, 177
Washington, Booker T. 141, 197
Washington, Lew 96
Watch Your Step 68
Watermelon and Cantaloupe 130
Watermelon Contest 139
Watermelon Feast 139
Watermelon Man 200
Waters, Ethel 124
Watts, Cotton 157
"Way Down in Dixie" 93
"Way Down South (A Minstrel Show)" 93
"Way Down Yonder in New Orleans" 122, 125
"Way Down Yonder in the Cornfield" 170
Wayans, Damon 175
"We Are Merry Minstrel Men" 77
"We Just Couldn't Say Goodbye" 168
"We Love to See a Minstrel Show" 110
"We Must Have Some of Each" 89
Weener Mastodon Minstrel Show 104, 114
Wehman's Minstrel Sketches, Conundrums and Jokes 27, 28
Wellman, Charley 150
Welsh, Johnnie 128
West, Billy 17
Whaley, Eddie 134, 135, 136, 137, 176, 177
"What Is This Thing Called Love?" 184

Whelan, Albert 134
"When De Profundis Sang Low C" 170
"When I Marry Louisiana Lou" 177
"When Irish Eyes Are Smiling" 163
"When My Shoes Wear Out from Walkin', I'll Be on My Feet Again" 96
"When Other Lips" 89
"When the Autumn Leaves Are Falling" 43
"When the Bell in the Lighthouse Goes Ding Dong" 77
"When the Children All Come Home" 85
"When the Days Grow Longer" 65
"When the Harvest Days Are Over Jessie Dear" 76
"When the Midnight Choo Choo Leaves for Alabam'" 142, 202
"When the Red, Red Robin Comes Bob, Bob, Bobbin' Along" 149
"When This Cruel War Is Over" 12
"When You and I Were Young, Maggie" 77, 108, 149, 170
"When You See a Minstrel Show" 165
"When You Were Sweet Sixteen" 180
"Where Love Is King" 21
"Whispering Hope" 180
"Whistle While You Work" 113
"Whistling Coon" 31, 36, 89
"Whistling Minstrel Caprice" 70
"Whistling Rufus" 108
White, Betsy 131
White, Billy 114
White, Dan 164
White, Lasses 26, 76, 77, 103, 104, 105, 107, 126, 155, 156, 165, 166; *see also* Lasses White Minstrels
White, Marjorie 147
White, Wallace 140
White, Walter 132
White, Will 34
White Blackbirds 93
"White Christmas" 170, 171
White Christmas (movie) 171
White Coons Concert Party 134
White Minstrels 93
Whitlock, Billy 8, 86, 89, 90, 161
Whitman, Ernest 125, 168
Whitman, Walt 24
Whitmer, Kenneth 186

Whitmore, James 174
"Who Paid the Rent for Mrs. Rip Van Winkle" 149
"Why Do They All Take the Night Boat to Albany" 149
"Why Don't Someone Marry Mary Anne?" 166
Wilbur, John 61
Wilds, Honey 104, 105
Wilkins, Walter 138
"Will You Love Me in December as You Do in May" 140
William H. West Minstrels 21, 73, 74
"William Tell Overture" 147
Williams, Bert 103, 117, 119, 132, 169, 198, 204
Williams, Billy 35, 36, 38, 39, 40, 42, 45
Williams, Montel 200
Williams, Slim 157
Williams, Spencer, Jr. 164
Williams, Tudy 182
Willing, Lloyd 77
Wills, Chill 126
Wills, Walter 170
Wilson, Chester 126
Wilson, Derby 186
Wilson, Don 79, 119
Wilson, H.L. 143
Wilson Minstrels 74
Winchell, Paul 185
Winchell, Walter 123, 179, 187
Winner records 89, 90, 93
Winninger, Charles 119, 120
Winters, Roland 124, 125
"Without a Song" 179
Witmark Amateur Minstrel Guide 52
Witte, Parvin 140
Wizard of Oz 154
WJZ Minstrels 105
WLS Barn Dance 181
WLS Morning Minstrels 117
WLW Midwestern Hayride 181
WMBD Minstrels 105
WMCA Minstrels 105
Wood, Clement 123
Woodgate, Leslie 134
Woods, Tom 128
WOR Minstrels 105, 110
Works Progress Administration (WPA) 28
Wrightson, Earl 179
WTAM Morning Minstrels 117

Yankee Doodle Minstrels 113
Yes Sir, Mr. Bones 156, 157
"Yes! We Have No Bananas" 149
Yokeman, Milton 99
"You Can't Get Your Lodging Here" 109
Youmans, Vincent 97

Young, John 69, 143
Young, Victor 97
"Your Head on My Shoulder" 152

Ziegfeld Follies 74
Ziegfeld Follies of 1919 151
Ziegfeld Follies of 1920 127
"Zip-a-Dee-Doo-Dah" 173
"Zip Coon" 8
Zono Minstrels 90
Zonophone Minstrels 49, 93
Zonophone records 43, 49, 50, 57, 62
Zonophone records (UK) 87, 90, 93
Zorn, George 99, 101
Zouaves 144

www.ingramcontent.com/pod-product-compliance
Lightning Source LLC
Chambersburg PA
CBHW060337010526
44117CB00017B/2863